COMMON FOOD EQUIVALENTS

Unit	Approximate Measure
3 ounces Breadcrumbs	1 cup
1 lb. Butter or shortening	2 cups
1 lb. Cheese	4 cups, grated
1 oz. Chocolate	1 square
1 lb. Coconut — shredded	6 cups
1 lb. Cottage cheese	2 cups
1 lb. Cranberries	4 cups
1 lb. Currants	3 cups
1 lb. Dates, pitted	2½ cups
4-6 Eggs, whole	1 cup
8-10 Eggs, whites	1 cup
12-14 Eggs, yolks	1 cup
Flour:	
1 lb. All-purpose	4 cups, unsifted
1 lb. Cake	4½ cups, unsifted
1 lb. Marshmallows	4 cups (64)
1 lb. Molasses	1½ cups
1 lb. Nutmeats	4 cups
1 lb. Raisins	2 cups, packed
1 lb. Rice	2 cups, uncooked; about 6 cups, cooked
Sugar:	
1 lb. Brown	2 cups, firmly packed
1 lb. Confectioners'	4 cups, sifted
1 lb. Granulated	2 cups
½ pint Whipping cream	2 cups when whipped

TABLE OF STANDARD MEASUREMENTS

Dash	⅛ teaspoon
3 teaspoons	1 tablespoon
2 tablespoons	1 fluid ounce
2 tablespoons	⅛ cup
4 tablespoons	¼ cup
5-1/3 tablespoons	1/3 cup
8 tablespoons	½ cup
10-2/3 tablespoons	
12 tablespoons	
16 tablespoons	
1 cup	
2 cups	
2 pints or 4 cups	ices)
4 quarts (liquid)	1 gallon
8 quarts (solid)	1 peck
4 pecks	1 bushel
16 ounces	1 pound

Rochester
Hadassah
Cook Book

COVER DESIGN AND ILLUSTRATIONS
BY
MRS. HERBERT J. SCHWARTZ

First Edition 1972
Second Edition 1975

To order an additional copy, send name, address
and check for $6.00 plus $.60 postage and handling to:

Rochester Chapter of Hadassah
Mrs. Harold M. Hecker
150 Georgian Court Road
Rochester, New York 14610

HADASSAH

The first National Convention of Hadassah took place in Rochester, New York in 1914, two years after the organization was founded by Henrietta Szold. It was here that the name was officially adopted.

Attendance was so small that all the delegates were taken into the home of Miss Szold's friend, Mrs. Bernard (Tillie) Rose. Membership has grown to more than 300,000.

In the decades since, Hadassah has expanded its service to the people and the land which was Palestine and is now Israel.

From two nurses in 1912 has developed a complete medical program. The 700 bed Medical Center also treated 250,000 outpatients in 1971. Reopening Mt. Scopus Hospital will add another 300 beds for Jerusalem's growing population.

So it has been with all of Hadassah's projects. Youth Aliyah, founded in 1934 has rescued, educated and rehabilitated more than 135,000 youth. From all over the world, psychiatrists, and social workers, educators and government specialists come to Israel to observe how children so handicapped have become mature and stable members of society.

Hadassah Israel Education Services has evolved into a program which conducts a 900 pupil comprehensive high school, and Jerusalem's first Community College.

Since its founding, Hadassah has co-operated with Jewish National Fund in the great adventure of redeeming the land.

In the United States, Zionist activities, youth work, education and volunteer service in each community continues at a steady pace.

Hadassah helps its members realize their full potential as women who are Jews, Americans and Zionists, dedicated to "The Healing of the Daughter of My People".

Mrs. Lester Berlove

DEDICATION

The Rochester Chapter of Hadassah wishes to express its sincere appreciation to Mrs. A. Bernard Axelrod, editor: Mrs. Harold Hecker and Mrs. Harold Rosenbaum, co-editors for the tireless devoted effort they expended in the compilation of this outstanding book.

It is with a great deal of pride and heartfelt thanks, that we dedicate this book to them.

Mrs. Jack Tuchman

ACKNOWLEDGMENT

Too many cooks may spoil the broth, but not the Hadassah cookbook. Our sincere thanks to the many chairmen who, with the help of their committees, compiled the individual sections. Every aspect of assembling a book is represented here, from alphabetizing and arranging, to telephoning and typing.

Chairmen

Mrs. Sol Baker

Mrs. Leon Berman

Mrs. Alan Calderon

Mrs. Milton Drexler

Mrs. Ross Elkin

Mrs. Sam Feier

Mrs. Hyman Goldberg

Mrs. Joseph Goldsmith

Mrs. Milton Gross

Mrs. Leonard Horn

Mrs. David Jassin

Mrs. Arthur Kuh

Mrs. Richard LaBaer

Mrs. Harvey Levy

Mrs. Albert Lipman

Mrs. James Lippman

Mrs. Michael Mittleman

Mrs. Stewart Moscov

Mrs. Edgar Musicus

Mrs. Abraham Ouriel

Mrs. Louis Perlman

Mrs. Seymour Richman

Mrs. Daniel Rothman

Mrs. Jack Ruda

Mrs. Herman Salitan

Mrs. Harry Schiller

Mrs. Julius Simon

Mrs. Leonard Simon

Mrs. Jack Soloway

Mrs. Gary Wiseman

Mrs. Jack Wynar

Committee

Mrs. Lawrence Albert
Mrs. Manuel Apple
Mrs. Albert Barnett
Mrs. William Berk
Mrs. Oscar Block
Mrs. Emanuel Bracker
Mrs. Morton Brodsky
Mrs. Jack Cherry
Mrs. Lawrence Chesler
Mrs. William Cohen
Mrs. Peter DiMora
Mrs. Huon Donaldson
Mrs. Leonard Epstein
Miss June Fidelman
Mrs. Harvey Fine
Mrs. Harold Fishman
Mrs. Seymour Fogel
Mrs. Roger Freidlander
Mrs. Mac Gan
Mrs. Louis Gertzog
Mrs. Charles Gordon
Mrs. Irving Gordon
Mrs. Richard Green
Mrs. Joel Greenberg
Mrs. Warren Heilbronner

Mrs. Louis Herzog
Mrs. Jacob Joseph
Mrs. Marshall Levine
Mrs. Arthur Mendelson
Mrs. Mervyn Mink
Mrs. Seymour Morris
Mrs. Benjamin Oken
Mrs. Arnold Orlen
Mrs. Jack Parsky
Mrs. Beryl Present
Mrs. Benjamin Robfogel
Mrs. Herbert Roth
Mrs. Steven Rubens
Mrs. Robert Sadick
Mrs. Eugene Salesin
Mrs. Alfred Seppen
Mrs. Milton Shulman
Mrs. Marvin Spokane
Mrs. Stanley Steinberg
Mrs. Lee Stern
Mrs. Burton Tanenbaum
Mrs. Alvin Ureles
Mrs. Melvin Wheeler
Mrs. Charles Whitaker
Mrs. Seymour Zigman

We are most grateful to the following women who contributed their time and very special talents.

Mrs. Lester Berlove
Mrs. Sol Cohen
Mrs. Abraham Karp

Mrs. Herbert Schwartz
Mrs. Jack Tuchman

It has been a pleasure working with all of them.

Mrs. A. Bernard Axelrod
Editor

Mrs. Harold Hecker
Co-Editor

Mrs. Harold Rosenbaum
Co-Editor

TABLE OF CONTENTS

NOTE ON KASHRUT

The aim of this cookbook is to enhance the delights of daily and holiday meals and thus to deepen the pleasure of warm family living in the homes of our readers. Hadassah's policy has always been to love, to study, and to further Jewish custom and tradition, and to be suited for use in the observant home.

Our readers who keep the dietary laws will know that there are some foods that must be checked for "kashrut", some that may contain animal fat (when vegetable shortening is not specifically listed) or other non-kosher ingredients.

Gelatins, pudding mixes, cheeses, graham crackers, marshmallows, instant soups, cake mixes, breads, milk and cream substitutes — all can be found with the Ⓤ (label of the Union of Orthodox Jewish Congregations of America) or the K̄ symbol, or another rabbinic certification. The careful cook will examine these items and choose appropriately before bringing them into her home.

Mrs. Abraham Karp

Holidays and Traditions

The Jewish Home

How do we recognize a Jewish home?
We see the mezuzah on the door post as we go in or out.

The words of the Sh'ma written within remind us to remember our love for God and His commandments "when we sit in our home and when we walk by the way."

We see in the home the Sabbath candlesticks, the lighting of whose candles each Friday evening is, in the words of Henrietta Szold,

"symbolic of the Jewish woman's influence on her own home, and through it upon larger circles. She is the inspirer of a pure, chaste family life whose hallowing influences are incalculable; she is the center of all spiritual endeavors, the confidante and fosterer of every undertaking. To her the Talmudic sentence applies: "It is woman alone through whom God's blessings are vouchsafed to a house."

We will see a silver wine goblet, a Hanukkah Menorah, paintings and objects of art from Israel. We will see Jewish books: besides prayer book and Bible, there will be history, novel, picture book, poetry, for child and adult. There will be records that will play "Jerusalem of Gold" or melodies of the Passover Seder.

Eye and ear will tell us it is a Jewish home.

More pervasive, more insistent even than these appeals to mind and senses, however, are the aromas and sizzlings of the Jewish kitchen.

It used to be that Friday morning the child would awake to find the house filled with the warming fragrance of the baking Hallah. "Shabbos" was imminent and precious, an approaching guest of honor. Though this delight may be lost to many of our homes (need it be?), even now the soups and savors of Shabbat, and certainly the heady flavors of Passover preparation arouse the feeling of joy, of anticipation, of wonder, of holiness.

Through the year each "appointed season" has its special magic.

The greatest of the holidays is **Shabbat**, and the most familiar and welcome. All week long we look forward to its coming, and save the best meats, the newly arrived melons or grapes or cherries, to make it the day of feasting as well as of spiritual delight. When we prepare our food on Friday, when we bake Hallot, when we concoct tzimmes and cholent whose flavors mix and deepen as they warm overnight, we can then enjoy a Shabbat free of work and rich in rewards.

When the year begins, we dip our hallah in honey, so that we may say not only the traditional "Hamotzi" but also the **Rosh Hashanah** wish: "May it be Thy will, O Lord our God and God of our fathers, to renew for us a good and sweet year."

The Hallah itself may be round, symbolizing the never-ending continuity of life. It may be raisin-studded as is fitting for a festive occasion, and may be topped with the forms of birds and ladders — both promising ascent to heights. Besides dipping apple slices also in the honey, we begin the dinner with new fruit that we have not eaten yet this season, in order that there may be true meaning to our blessing for new and good happenings, the "Shehehiyanu." "Blessed art Thou O Lord our God and God of our fathers, who has kept us in life and preserved us and enabled us to reach this season."

Taiglach boiled in honey, tzimmes glazed with sugar — these add sweet hopes for a sweet year. And of course, honey cake, in any of its golden varieties.

A time for feasting, and a time for fasting. The meal before **Yom Kippur** must be a good one, just as the day must be one of austerity.

The holiday of **Sukkot** is graced with many festive family meals, with the extra flavor of picnic excitement if you serve them in your own self-decorated Sukkah. While all favorite foods are suitable, kreplach are essential. Do have fun making them!

Perhaps since filled foods suggest the plenty of harvest at this time of thanksgiving, stuffed cabbage leaves (Do you call them holishkes? prakes?) are also in season. Strudel is in tune for dessert.

Why potato latkes on **Hanukkah**? Don't believe that the Maccabees ate them; potatoes were not known to us until Columbus discovered America. But pancakes of some sort, fried in oil, are fine for a festival of light, reminding us of the little cruse of holy oil that burned so long. Did you know that your grandmother may have roasted a goose for Hanukkah?

On **Tu Bish'vat**, our Jewish Arbor Day, we eat "bokser" (or carob or St. John's bread) as Israeli fruit. Raisins and almonds also signify. We hope you know these "rozhinkes mit mandeln" were the greatest treat for shtetl children.

Purim afternoon is proper time for the Purim Seudah, one of the family holiday feasts. We all have already eaten hamentaschen, and have sent some of our baked goodies to friends for Shalach Manot. Is it possible that mon-taschen — poppyseed pockets — became hamentaschen?

The never-forgotten enchantment of the **Passover** holiday is invoked by mother's work and ingenuity. The home is polished, the table different, the atmosphere magic. The Seder is a king's banquet, spiced with song and ceremony.

The first sip of wine, the first bite of matza renew the ancient spell. The parsley dipped in salt water, the ruddy grainy "haroset," the eye-watering bitter horseradish, all are new adventures each year. Those whose custom it is to eat a hard-cooked egg in the salt water (for eggs are symbols of spring and new life) think it a treat — but never during the year do they try it again.

Every dish evokes nostalgia and praise, for the favorite dishes of generations are served: the gefilte fish, the chicken soup with matza balls, the roast or fowl, the matza or potato kugel, the tzimmes, even the dozen-egg sponge cake served proudly at the end. During the week mother does more baking than ever, and thinks up school lunches. Did you know you could take farfel pancakes to school?

Two blintzes together on a plate may look like the Ten Commandments — or is it because the Torah is compared to milk and honey that we eat dairy foods on **Shavuot**? It is no hardship when we can have delicious cheesecake for dessert.

The menu for a Shabbat or holiday meal is not hard and fast. It depends on the traditions of your own family, and the likes and dislikes of your children. Gefilte fish and chicken soup and kneidlach may be essential to your idea of a Jewish meal. In this book you may find other traditions. You may decide to attempt long-ago favorites that once your grandmother served. Perhaps you will try a Sephardi recipe or one from Israel. Other cultures can teach us.

What is a Jewish home?

It is one where through the work and love of the woman of the house, "God's blessings are vouchsafed," made manifest.

We hope this book will help you to build up heart-warming experiences and fragrant memories for your family.

Mrs. Abraham Karp

SUGGESTED FESTIVE MENUS

Sabbath Meal
Wine   for   Kiddush   Challah
Gelfilte Fish   or   Chopped Liver
Chicken Soup   and   Noodles
Roast Chicken   with   Tzimmes   or   Potato Kugel   or   Kishka
or
Veal Breast   with   Potato Stuffing
Savory Green Bean Casserole   Tossed Salad
Pumpkin   Cake   or   Apple   Cake   Fresh
Fruit
Tea

Rosh Hashanah
Wine   Apple Slices dipped in Honey   Round Challah
Gelfilte Fish   or   Chopped Liver
Chicken Soup   with   Farfel   or   Kreplach
Roast Turkey   or   Chicken   with   Rice-pecan Stuffing
Carrot Tzimmes   with   Potato Kneidel
Rhubarb   or   Cranberry Gelatin Mold
Honey Cake   Taiglach   Fresh Fruit in Season
Tea

Rosh Hashonah Mid-day Meal
Wine   Apple Slices dipped in Honey   Round Challah
Chopped Liver   or   Fruit Cup   or   Melon
Roast Brisket   or   Roast Tongue in Raisin Sauce
Baked Limas   or   Scalloped Potatoes   Relishes
Hot Fruit Brulee   Mandel Bread
Tea

Rosh Hashonah (Alternate)
Cold Cherry Soup
Gelfilte Fish   or   Sweet and Sour Fish
Upside-down Noodle Kugel
Carrots in Savory Sauce   Cucumber Salad
Sour Cream Coffee Cake
Coffee

Yom Kippur Eve
It is customary to serve no highly seasoned foods before the fast begins.
Apples dipped in Honey   New Year Challah
Chicken Soup   with   Kreplach or   Noodles
Boiled Chicken   or   lightly seasoned Broiler
or
Chicken Fricassee
Mashed Potatoes   Green Salad   Fresh Apple Sauce
Golden Almond Cake
Tea

Yom Kippur — to Break Fast
Assorted Juices
Gelilte Fish   or   Smoked Fish   Pickled   or   Chopped Herring
Lox   Cream Cheese   and   Bagels
Scrambled Eggs   Fresh Vegetable Platter   Sweet Noodle Kugel
Puterkuchen   or   Schnecken   Coffee

Succoth
Vegetable Soup
Sweet and Sour Rolled Cabbage   with   Kasha Varnishkes
or
Roast Duck   with   Fried Kreplach
Harvest Baked Squash   Peach Mold
Esrog Cookies   Tea   Strudel

Chanukah
Beef and Barley Vegetable Soup
Roast Veal   or   Roast Goose
Potato Latkes or Kugel   Sesame Broccoli
Apple Sauce   Tea   Chanukah Cookies

Purim
Triflach Soup
Glazed Chicken   Flomen Tzimmes
Spinach   with   Walnuts   Relishes
Hamantaschen   Tea   Poppy Seed Piroshkes

Passover Seder
Wine for Kiddush   Matzo
Hard Boiled Eggs   in   Salt Water
Gefilte Fish   with   Horseradish
Chicken Soup   with   Matzo Balls
Roast Turkey   or   Cornish Hens   with   Matzo Stuffing
Glazed Carrots   Tomato and Cucumber Platter
Sponge Cake   with   Rhubarb-strawberry Sauce   Tea

Passover Lunch
Borscht Bisque
Matzo Meal Pancakes   or   Baked Matzos and Cheese
or
Matzo Spinach Pie
Passover Ice Cream   or   Buenueloes (Fritters)   Coffee

Shavuoth
Cheese Bourekas
Beet   or   Spinach Borscht
Poached Salmon   with   Sauce   or
Sweet   and   Sour Fish   or   Pickled Fish
Cheese Blintzes   Dill Green Beans
Strawberry Ambrosia Squares   Coffee

Passover

Gefilte Fish

3 pounds yellow pike, filleted
¾ pound whitefish, filleted
3 onions
2 eggs
2 tablespoons matzo meal

¾ cup cold water
2 teaspoons white pepper
⅛ cup coarse salt
2 carrots, sliced
3 onions, sliced

Wash fish, clean all fish from bones. Wash and clean skin and bones. Grind fish and onions. Add all other ingredients except carrots and sliced onions and chop mixture in large wooden mixing bowl. Mixture should become tacky. Place sliced onions, skin and bones of fish on bottom of large pan. Sprinkle with salt and pepper to taste and half fill pan with cold water. Add sliced carrots. Roll chopped fish into balls, dipping hands in cold water, and drop balls into pan. Cover and bring to boil on high heat. Reduce heat immediately and continue to cook for 2½ hours or more. Remove cover after 1 hour. Serves 12-16.

Sylvia Gertzog

Crunchy Chicken Spread

1 cup chopped cooked chicken
3 tablespoons minced celery

3 tablespoons chopped walnuts
Mayonnaise

Mix all ingredients, using enough mayonnaise to hold the mixture. Chill. Spread on pieces of matzos or use to fill bagels or puffs.

Walnut-and-Egg Spread

4 hard-cooked eggs
¼ cup chopped walnuts
Mayonnaise

Pinch salt
Dash pepper

Push eggs through coarse sieve or chop finely. Add remaining ingredients. Use enough mayonnaise to hold ingredients together. Season to taste. Mixture may be spread on pieces of matzos or used to fill bagels or puffs.

Pickled Herring and Cream Cheese Spread

1 8-ounce jar pickled herring
or herring in wine sauce

8 ounces cream cheese

Drain and bone herring. Chop herring and onions from the jar. Mix with cream cheese, blending well. Chill before serving. Spread on pieces of matzos or use to fill bagels or puffs.

Borscht Bisque

2 cups (4 large) mashed
potatoes
¼ teaspoon onion powder

¾ teaspoon salt
¾ cup sour cream
1 quart jar borscht, strained

Mix potatoes, onion powder, salt and sour cream. Gradually stir in borscht. Chill and serve. If a blender is used, do not strain borscht. Blend all ingredients at high speed for ½ minute, using only half the ingredients at a time if the blender jar is not large enough. Serves 4-6.

Potato Spinach Soup

1½ tablespoons pareve margarine
1 large onion, chopped
4 large potatoes, peeled and quartered

2 10½-ounce cans condensed clear chicken soup
5 cups water
1½ teaspoons salt
1 pound spinach

Saute onion in margarine until tender. Set aside. Cook potatoes in condensed soup, water and salt until tender. Rice the potatoes by working through a sieve and return them to the soup. Add washed and chopped spinach and sauteed onions. Cook over high heat for 3 minutes, stirring constantly. Do not overcook. Serves 6.

Easy Vegetable Soup

2 medium potatoes, peeled
1 small zucchini squash, unpeeled
2 large carrots, scraped
1 small onion
3 scallions
2 celery stalks
3 tablespoons margarine or

chicken fat
2 10½-ounce cans condensed clear chicken soup
2 soup cans water
1 teaspoon sugar
Pinch salt
Dash pepper

Cut all vegetables and saute in fat for a few minutes in a 3-quart saucepan. Add condensed soup, water and sugar. Cover and simmer for 20 minutes or until vegetables are tender. Season to taste with salt and pepper. Serves 6.

Kneidlach

3 eggs, separated
1 teaspoon salt
3 tablespoons chicken fat

¼ teaspoon white pepper
¾ cup matzo meal

Beat egg whites and salt until stiff. Beat egg yolks with fat and pepper. Pour yolk mixture over whites, sprinkle matzo meal over lightly, a little at a time folding gently after each addition. Keep folding until well blended. Let stand a few minutes. Make balls and drop into rapidly boiling salted water and cover. Cook on medium heat for one hour. Test with fork, and if not soft enough cover and continue cooking about 10-15 minutes longer. Transfer to hot chicken soup. These matzo balls can be reheated several times.

Sarah Derman

Kneidlach Cubes

4 eggs, beaten
½ cup water
¼ cup melted shortening
1 teaspoon salt

Dash of pepper
Dash of garlic powder
1 cup matzo meal

Combine eggs with water, melted shortening, salt, pepper and garlic powder. Mix well. Add matzo meal. Pour the batter into plastic ice cube tray of the pop-out variety. Fill each section with a spoon and scrape off excess with knife. Freeze. When ready to use, remove from the tray and pop into boiling, salted water. Boil gently for 25 minutes. Do not thaw before cooking. Note: If kneidlah do not pop out, use a knife point to ease out. Also, oiling the molds would be helpful.

Gertrude Greenberg

Concord Hotel's Famous Matzo Balls

2 cups eggs (about 8 large)
3 cups matzo meal
Salt and pepper to taste
Accent

1 cup water
½ cup chicken fat
½ cup oil

Beat eggs, add matzo meal and combine with remaining ingredients. Refrigerate overnight. Wet hands and form into small balls, size of a large walnut. Cook in boiling salted water in large covered pot for 1 hour. Note: may be cooked in advance and frozen. Makes 28.

Frances Eichen

Fat Free Matzo Balls

2 eggs
½ cup matzo meal

Salt

Beat yolks and salt. Beat whites separately until very stiff. Fold together and add matzo meal. Shape into balls. Drop immediately into vigorously boiling salted water in a large pot. Boil 45 minutes with pot covered. Matzo balls may be warmed in chicken soup before serving to gain flavor.

Mrs. Aaron Karp

Fluffy Potato Kneidlach

1 egg
1 cup cold water
1 3-ounce package potato

pancake mix
¼ cup matzo meal
2 tablespoons oil or melted fat

Beat egg with a fork and stir in water. Add remaining ingredients. Allow to thicken for 10 minutes. Form into walnut-sized balls. Drop into large pot of rapidly boiling salted water. Cover tightly, reduce heat and simmer for 30 minutes. Drain and serve in soup, stew or as a side dish. Makes 15-18.

Toasted Farfel

1 cup matzo farfel
2 egg yolks

½ teaspoon salt
2 tablespoons oil or chicken fat

Mix together all ingredients. Spread in flat baking pan. Separate the particles and brown in 350° oven. Serve in hot soup.

Noodles

6 eggs
6 water-filled half egg shells
9 heaping tablespoons potato

starch
Pinch salt
1 teaspoon oil

Beat eggs and water, add potato starch slowly and beat well. Coat 8-inch frying pan very lightly with fat. Ladle thin coat of mixture into frying pan and make sure it is completely covered. Fry until golden brown. Turn out on a clean cloth, cooked side up and immediately roll. Leave rolls to dry for 1 hour. Take short knife and cut on cutting board in very thin slices.

Bea Hoschander

Beef in Wine

2 pounds lean boneless chuck, cubed
1 cup medium-dry Concord wine
½ cup matzo meal or cake meal
½ teaspoon salt
⅛ teaspoon pepper
¼ cup oil or vegetable shortening
1½ cups boiling water
1 pound carrots, sliced
1 pound small white onions
1 teaspoon salt

Marinate meat in wine; cover and refrigerate several hours or overnight. Drain and reserve wine. Roll meat in mixture of meal, salt and pepper and brown in hot fat. Add boiling water and half the wine. Cover and simmer 2 hours or until almost tender. Add balance of wine, carrots, onions and salt. Cover and simmer 45 minutes or until tender. Serves 6.

Meat with Potatoes and Prunes

1 pound prunes
3 pounds beef
Salt and pepper to taste
6 medium potatoes
¾ cup brown sugar
Juice of 1 lemon

Wash prunes and soak in water overnight. Sprinkle meat with salt and pepper. Lightly brown on both sides and place in a dutch oven. Add prunes, plus water, to meat. Cover pan and simmer until meat is tender. Remove meat and prunes from pan and arrange potatoes in bottom. Arrange meat and prunes over potatoes and top with brown sugar and lemon juice. Cover pan and simmer until potatoes are tender.

Millie Rosenbaum

Hidden Treasure Meat Loaf

2 pounds ground meat
2 eggs, beaten
¾ cup matzo meal
½ teaspoon salt
⅛ teaspoon pepper
1 11-ounce can tomato and mushroom sauce
6 hot dogs

Combine meat with eggs, matzo meal, salt, pepper and ½ cup of tomato and mushroom sauce. Pack half this mixture into a greased 9 x 5 loaf pan or shape in a greased shallow pan. Arrange 4 hot dogs lenthwise on the meat, cut the remaining two in half and arrange lengthwise also, so that the hot dogs cover the entire loaf. Top with balance of meat mixture. Pour remaining tomato and mushroom sauce over the top. Bake at 350° for 1 hour. Serves 8.

Frosted Meat Loaf

2 pounds ground beef
¾ cup matzo meal
½ cup tomato and mushroom sauce
2 eggs, beaten
½ cup minced onion
1 teaspoon salt
¼ teaspoon pepper
9 medium potatoes, cooked
5 tablespoons chicken fat
1/3 cup condensed chicken soup, heated
½ teaspoon salt
⅛ teaspoon pepper

Mix ground beef with next 6 ingredients. Pack into well-greased loaf pan and bake at 350° for 1 hour. Unmold onto baking sheet or heat-proof platter. Mash potatoes and whip with fat, soup and seasonings. Spread top and sides of beef loaf with this mixture. Brush lightly with chicken fat and place in moderate oven for 15-20 minutes or until lightly browned. Serves 6-8.

Sweet and Sour Meatballs

2 pounds ground beef
½ cup matzo meal
½ cup water
2 eggs slightly beaten
½ cup minced onion
1 teaspoon salt
¼ teaspoon pepper

1 large onion diced
½ cup lemon juice
1 cup sugar
1 11-ounce can tomato-mush-
room sauce
½ cup water

Combine beef, matzo meal, water, eggs, minced onion, salt and pepper. Shape into meat balls. In a large pot, combine sliced onion, lemon juice, sugar, tomato and mushroom sauce, and water. Add meat balls. Bring to a boil, reduce heat and simmer for about 1 hour. Serves 6.

Sylvia Wynar

Swiss Steak

2 pounds lean boneless chuck or
beef shoulder about 1½-inches
thick
1/3 cup matzo meal

1 large onion diced
1 11-ounce can tomato and
mushroom sauce
½ cup water

Pound matzo meal into meat with a wooden potato masher or the edge of a heavy plate. Brown meat on all sides in a little fat in a heavy skillet or Dutch oven. Add onion, tomato and mushroom sauce and water. Cover and simmer 1½ hours or until meat is very tender. Serves 5-6.

Shish Kebabs

2 pounds shoulder lamb, cubed
½ cup medium-dry Concord
wine
¼ teaspoon pepper
1 large onion, finely chopped
¼ cup oil
2 tablespoons vinegar

Firm tomatoes, cut into thick
wedges
Small white onions, parboiled
Whole mushroom caps
Green pepper, cut into 1¼-inch
squares

Blend wine, pepper, minced onion, oil and vinegar and pour over lamb cubes. Cover and marinate in refrigerator for at least 3 hours or overnight. Using 10- or 12-inch skewers, arrange meat and vegetables alternately. Broil slowly until meat and vegetables are tender. Turn when necessary. Baste occasionally with the leftover wine mixture. Serves 5-6.

Almond-Raisin Sauce for Tongue

½ cup white raisins
10½-ounce can condensed chick-
en soup
¼ cup sugar
1 tablespoon margarine
1½ tablespoons grated orange

rind
1 tablespoon potato starch
mixed with ½ cup water
¾ cup blanched, slivered almonds

Cook raisins in chicken soup until soft. Add remaining ingredients, except almonds. Stir for 1 minute over low heat or until thickened. Add almonds; heat. Serve hot on sliced tongue. Serves 6.

Chicken Giblet Fricassee

Giblets from 2 chickens (hearts, gizzards and necks)
3 medium onions, diced
2 matzos, finely broken
2/3 cup cold water

2 pounds ground beef
2 eggs, slightly beaten
2 teaspoons salt
¼ teaspoon pepper
2 teaspoons paprika

Cut giblets into small pieces. Add diced onion and cover with water. Simmer, covered, until tender, about 1½-2 hours. Soak broken matzos in cold water. Combine with ground beef and beaten eggs. Shape into small meatballs and drop into hot giblet mixture. Add seasonings, cover and simmer for at least ½ hour. Longer cooking gives a better flavor. Serves 4-6.

Honeyed Chicken

½ cup peanut oil
2 eggs
2 tablespoons water
½ cup matzo meal
1 teaspoon salt

⅛ teaspoon pepper
2 cut-up fryers
1 cup hot water
¼ cup honey
1 cup orange juice

Heat oil in skillet or frying pan. Beat eggs and the 2 tablespoons water together. Mix matzo meal, salt and pepper. Dip chicken in egg mixture and then roll in matzo meal mixture. Brown in hot oil. Remove to a Dutch oven or covered roaster. Mix hot water, honey, and orange juice. Pour over chicken and cover. Simmer slowly on top of stove or place in a moderate oven, 325°, for about 45 minutes or until tender. Baste occasionally. Serves 6-8.

Chicken Casserole

½ cup chopped onions
½ cup chopped green pepper
½ cup chopped celery
Vegetable oil
3 cups cut-up cooked chicken

3 cups matzo farfel
3 cups chicken soup
2 eggs, beaten
Salt and pepper to taste

Saute vegetables in oil. Mix with remaining ingredients. Bake in greased 2½-quart casserole, covered, at 350° for 1 hour. Serves 6-8.

T'Mahry Axelrod

Stuffed Cornish Hens

¾ cup chopped onion
1 cup chopped celery
½ cup oil
2 tablespoons chicken fat
10 matzos or ½ large box matzo farfel
1 teaspoon salt
¼ teaspoon pepper

1 tablespoon paprika
1 egg, beaten
1 10-ounce can chicken soup, undiluted
6 Cornish hens, split
Nyafat
Salt, pepper, paprika

Saute onion and celery in shortenings. Crush matzos, wet and squeeze dry. Combine with sauteed vegetables, seasonings, egg and chicken soup. On large aluminum foil lined pan, scoop 12 mounds of dressing. Place each half of Cornish hen, skin side up, over a scoop of dressing. Place each half Nyafat, sprinkle with seasonings and bake at 350° for 1½ hours or until browned. Serves 12.

Arlene Stolnitz

Chicken Blintzes with Hot Cranberry Sauce

Batter

3 eggs
¼ cup water
½ teaspoon salt

1 can condensed clear chicken
soup, undiluted
2/3 cup cake meal

Chicken Filling

2½ cups diced cooked chicken
2 eggs
1 medium onion diced and
sauted in 1 tablespoon chicken

fat
½ teaspoon salt
Dash white pepper

Hot Cranberry Sauce

1 can cranberry sauce

2 tablespoons water

Break up cranberry sauce with a fork. Add water. Cook over low heat stirring occasionally until blended and smoth. Combine eggs, salt, water and condensed chicken soup. Add gradually to cake meal, stirring constantly to avoid lumps. Pour about 3 tablespoons of batter on a hot lightly greased skillet and rotate pan so batter forms a 6-inch circle. Fry over moderate heat until edges pull away from pan. Turn out on a clean cloth, cooked side up. Repeat until all batter is used. Place a heaping tablespoon of filling in the center of each leaf. Fold in side edges and roll tightly. Fry until golden brown in a small amount of chicken fat. Serve with Hot Cranberry Sauce. Makes 16.

Tipsy Chicken Salad

1½ cups diced apples
3 tablespoons Concord grape
wine
3 cups cooked, diced chicken

1½ cups diced celery
1 teaspoon salt
½ cup mayonnaise
Slivered almonds or walnuts

Marinate apples in wine. Combine all ingredients and toss gently. Serve on lettuce and sprinkle with nuts. Serves 5-6.

Crisp 'N' Tart Turkey Salad

Dressing

¾ cup condensed clear chicken
soup, undiluted
1/3 cup cider vinegar

2 tablespoons sugar
1 tablespoon potato starch
2 egg yolks, beaten

Cook soup, vinegar, sugar and potato starch over low heat, stirring frequently, until mixture is clear and slightly thickened. Beat this mixture gradually into the beaten egg yolks. Return to pot and cook until thickened (2 to 3 minutes). Cool thoroughly.

Salad

4 cups diced, cooked turkey
2 cups diced celery
1 cup small white seedless

grapes
½ cup toasted slivered almonds
(optional)

Combine above ingredients with dressing. Serves 6-8.

Basic Matzo Stuffing

¾ cup vegetable shortening or
   chicken fat
¾ cup minced onion
10 matzos, finely broken
1 teaspoon salt

¼ teaspoon pepper
1 tablespoon paprika
1 egg
1½ cans (2 cups) condensed
   clear chicken soup undiluted*

Saute onion in fat until tender but not browned. Add broken matzos and toast lightly. Combine seasonings, egg, and soup. Add to matzo mixture. Enough for a 10-12 pound bird.

Variations

Celery Stuffing
Saute 1 cup diced cleery with the onion.

Mushroom Stuffing
Saute 1 cup diced, fresh mushrooms with the onion.

Nut Stuffing
Toast 1½ cups coarsely chopped nuts with the onion before adding matzo crumbs.

Giblet Stuffing
Cook giblets in water until tender (2-3 hours.) Mince and add to dressing.

*Note — This makes a dry dressing. If you prefer the moist type stuffing increase the condensed soup to 2 cans.

Stuffing

4 onions, diced
4 stalks celery, diced
8 matzos

6 eggs
Dash pepper
Salt to taste

Fry diced onions with diced celery until golden brown. Soak matzos and then drain. Combine with fried onions and celery. Beat eggs, pepper and salt and add to mixture.

Anna Greenberg

Baked Fish

6 pieces fish
2 large onions, sliced thin
6 tablespoons butter
Salt and pepper to taste
1 can tomato and mushroom

sauce
1 cup diced celery
2 cups sliced carrots
4 cups diced potatoes

Wash fish. Arrange onions on bottom of greased 9 x 13 pan. Place fish on top of onions. Dot with 2 tablespoons of butter and sprinkle with salt and pepper. Pour sauce over all. Bake at 400° for 15 minutes. Cook celery, carrots and potatoes in rapidly boiling, salted water for 15 minutes. Drain vegetables and add to fish. Add remaining butter. Bake 20 minutes longer, basting occasionally.

Helen Hecker

Honey Glazed Carrots

1 pound carrots	fat
1½ tablespoons melted chicken	¼ cup honey

Cook small whole carrots, or quartered large ones in boiling salted water until tender. Drain thoroughly and then allow to stand a few minutes to dry. In a skillet, blend 1½ tablespoons melted chicken fat with honey. Add carrots and simmer slowly until browned and glazed, turning frequently. Ginger-Honey Glazed Carrots: add ½ teaspoon ginger to fat honey mixture.

Carrot Mold

4 eggs, separated	ening
6 carrots, cooked and mashed	¾ cups sugar
1 onion, grated	2 cups matzo meal
6 stems parsley, chopped	1½ cups water
6 tablespoons vegetable short-	Salt and paprika to taste

Beat egg whites until they form stiff peaks. Beat carrots, onion, parsley, shortening and sugar. Add egg yolks and blend thoroughly. Add matzoh meal, water, and seasonings. Fold in egg whites. Bake in greased 3-quart ring mold at 350° for 1 hour. Serves 12.

Esther Parsky

Passover Carrot Pudding

½ cup shortening	¾ cup cake meal
½ cup sugar	2 tablespoons potato starch
2 eggs, separated	½ teaspoon cinnamon
1½ cups grated carrots	2 tablespoons lemon juice
1 teaspoon salt	1 tablespoon water

Cream shortening and sugar until light and fluffy. Add egg yolks and beat well. Stir in grated carrots, salt, meal, starch, cinnamon, lemon juice and water. Beat egg whites until stiff and fold into batter. Spread in a greased 9 x 9 or 7 x 11 pan and bake at 350° for 1 hour.

Anne Gottfried

Prune Tzimmes

2 cups matzo meal	1 pound prunes
1 tablespoon salt	1 cup sugar
½ cup fat or pareve margarine	¼ cup lemon juice
2 cups boiling water	Sufficient water to cover prunes
3 eggs	

Put matzo meal, salt, fat in bowl and pour boiling water over all. Mix well, let cool. Add eggs, one at a time, and mix well until blended. Put prunes in a large pot, cover with water, add sugar, lemon juice and bring to boil. Simmer gently for about ½ hour. Form balls of matzo meal mixture the size of small walnuts. Drop into cooking prunes. Cover and simmer slowly for about 3 hours, or until most of the juice is absorbed. Taste for right sweetness and tartness.

Sarah Derman

French Dressing

½ teaspoon salt	1 teaspoon paprika
¼ teaspoon pepper	½ cup vinegar
1 tablespoon sugar	½ cup peanut oil

Put ingredients into a jar with a tight cover, shake until thoroughly blended.

Bagels or Rolls

1 cup water
½ cup oil
1½ cups matzo meal
½ cup cake meal

1 tablespoon sugar
½ teaspoon salt
5 eggs

Bring water and oil to a boil and let stand 10 minutes. Add dry ingredients. Stir in eggs, one at a time, beating well after each addition. Drop from tablespoon on greased cookie sheet. For bagels, wet forefinger with water and make hole in center; for rolls, leave without hole. Bake at 350° 50 minutes. Makes about 2 dozen.

Elaine Simon

Matzo Meal Muffins

2 eggs
½ teaspoon salt
1 cup water

1½ cups matzo meal
4 tablespoons chicken fat

Beat eggs with salt and water. Stir in matzo meal to make a smooth batter. Heat fat and grease muffin pans, and stir remaining hot fat into the batter. Fill muffin pans 2/3 full and bake at 350° for 30 minutes or until brown. Serve with clear soup, roast chicken or meat. Makes 8 large or 16 small muffins. **Variation 1:** For sweet muffins, use butter in place of fat, and milk instead of water. Add sugar and cinnamon, grated rind of lemon. Bake in the same manner. **Variation 2:** For a more delicate muffin, omit water and use matzo cake flour. Add ½ cup applesauce, or drained and chopped canned peaches. A dash of nutmeg or cinnamon gives added flavoring. Bake in buttered muffin tins. Serve with sliced canned peaches or with applesauce. **Variation 3:** Use 1 cup soaked and pitted prunes, sliced or cut fine. **Variation 4:** Finely cut dates, raisins, chopped nuts or a mixture of all three make delicious fruit muffins. Sprinkle with powdered sugar or top with frosting.

Inez Lipman

Matzo Meal Pancakes

½ cup matzo meal
½ cup cold water
4 eggs

1 teaspoon sugar
⅛ teaspoon salt
Dash cinnamon

Mix matzo meal, water, egg yolks. Combine thoroughly and let stand for 5 minutes. Add remaining ingredients, and fold in stiffly beaten egg whites. Drop from tablespoon into hot fat and fry until golden brown. Serve with cinnamon and sugar.

Estelle Fisher

Orange Matzo Meal Pancakes

3 eggs, separated
½ teaspoon salt
½ cup orange juice

¾ cup matzo meal
Fat for frying

Beat egg yolks well. Add salt and cold orange juice and beat thoroughly. Stir in matzo meal. Let stand ½ hour. Beat egg whites until stiff and fold into mixture. Drop by tablespoon into very hot fat. Brown on both sides. Serve warm with cinnamon and sugar or jelly.

Anne Gottfried

Chremsel

3 matzos
2 tablespoons raisins, cut fine
2 tablespoons chopped nuts
Yolks of 3 eggs
¾ cup sugar

Grated rind of 1 lemon, plus 1
 tablespoon juice
1 heaping tablespoon matzo meal
3 beaten egg whites

Soak matzo in warm water and squeeze dry. Mix ingredients in order given. Drop from tablespoon in deep, hot fat. Drain on brown paper. Sprinkle with sugar.

Martha Prenner

Filled Matzo Meal Pancakes

5 potatoes, cooked in skins
1 cup matzo meal
3 eggs
2 teaspoons salt
¼ teaspoon pepper

½ pound cooked beef, chopped
 fine
½ pound broiled beef liver,
 chopped fine

Peel and mash hot potatoes. Add matzo meal, eggs and seasoning. Mix well and make a soft dough. Divide into 10 small sections. Mix chopped beef and liver. Season to taste. Roll out the pieces of dough and cover half of each piece with a spoonful of the meat and liver mixture. Fold dough over filling. Press the edges together firmly, but carefully. Fry in hot fat until golden brown on both sides. Serves 6-8.

Kneidlach

6 eggs, separated, reserve 2
 yolks
1 teaspoon salt
2 cups water

2 tablespoons chicken fat
3 cups matzo meal (approximately)
½ onion

Stuffing

2 yolks from above
1 cup matzo meal
1 teaspoon sugar

1 teaspoon cinnamon
Grieben

Beat together eggs, salt, chicken fat and mix with water. Grate in onion. Add matzo meal gradually until mixture is cake batter consistency. Refrigerate at least 1 hour or overnight. As mixture sits it will thicken and puff up. Mix stuffing ingredients together by hand. From batter make a patty ½-inch thick in palm of hand. (Moistened hands prevent sticking). Put tiny scoop of stuffing in center of patty. Enfold stuffing with patty making a ball. Drop ball into 6 quarts of salted boiling water, one at a time. Cook for 10 minutes. They will increase in size about 3 times. Delicious brushed with chicken fat and browned in 350° oven for 1 hour.

Mrs. P. Vick

Potato Knishes

4½ cups mashed potatoes
3 eggs
½ cup matzo meal
¼ teaspoon pepper

3 teaspoons salt
3 large onions
4 tablespoons cooking fat

Combine potatoes, beaten eggs, matzo meal, pepper and 2 teaspoons salt. Mix well. Brown onions in hot fat and then add 1 teaspoon salt. Flatten small pancakes out of the potato mixture in your hand. Cover with brown onions. Press another pancake on top. Roll pancakes in matzo meal and bake them in hot oven at 400° or fry in hot fat. Serves 6-8. (Meat or liver mixture can be used instead of onions.)

Baked Matzos and Cheese

1 pound dry cottage cheese
½ teaspoon salt
5 eggs
6 matzos (whole)

½ teaspoon cinnamon
1 teaspoon sugar
2 tablespoons butter

Combine cheese with salt and 3 eggs. Mix well. Dip whole matzos in remaining 2 eggs, beaten lightly. Place layer of matzos in an 8-inch square buttered pan. Cover with a layer of cheese. Sprinkle with mixture of cinnamon and sugar. Alternate layers of matzos and cheese until all is used. Bake in moderate oven at 350° for 30 minutes. Serves 6.

T'Mahry Axelrod

Fried Matzo or Matzo Brei

3 large matzos
2 eggs

1 teaspoon salt
2 tablespoons fat or butter

Break matzos in small pieces and soak in cold water. Beat eggs with salt. Squeeze water from matzos, but not quite dry. Add eggs, and mix thoroughly. Drop mixture by spoonfuls into melted fat in frying pan, and fry until golden brown, turning once. Serve with cottage cheese or jelly.

Esther Solomon

Matzo Polenta (Milchig)

3 eggs, separated
½ cup water
1 cup matzo meal
1 teaspoon salt
Dash of pepper

1 onion, finely diced
3 tablespoons butter
½ pound mushrooms, sliced
3 cups fresh tomatoes, diced
½ cup cheese

Beat egg yolks, add water and half the matzo meal. Fold in the stiffly beaten egg whites, salt, pepper and remaining matzo meal. Saute onion in butter until golden brown and remove from pan. Drop the egg mixture by spoonfuls in the butter and fry until light brown. Arrange in baking dish. Put the onions, mushrooms, tomatoes and cheese over the fried dumplings and bake at 325° for 45 minutes. Serves 4-6.

Matzo Kugel

3 egg matzos	Juice of one lemon
3 eggs, separated	Juice of one orange
½ cup sugar	3 apples, sliced and peeled
¼ teaspoon salt	½ cup walnuts
Dash cinnamon	¼ cup butter

Soak matzo in cold water for a few minutes, and squeeze thoroughly. Beat yolks with sugar, salt and cinnamon. Stir in juices, matzos, apples, walnuts and melted butter. Beat whites until stiff and fold into egg mixture. Bake in greased casserole at 350° for 45 minutes.

Mrs. Robert Friedman

Passover Fruit Nut Kugel

2 large tart apples	2 tablespoons sugar
1 cup chopped walnuts	1 tablespoon lemon juice
¼ cup honey	1 tablespoon grated lemon rind
½ teaspoon salt	5 eggs, separated

Pare, core and slice apples. Line bottom of a greased 9-inch square pan with apple slices. Beat egg yolks until light and frothy. Add nuts, honey, salt, sugar, juice and rind. Blend well. Beat egg whites until stiff, but not dry. Fold into mixture. Pour carefully over apple slices. Bake for 30 minutes in a 350° oven or until set. Serves 8-10.

Rachel Hyman

Matzo Kugel with Grieben

6 matzos	3 eggs, beaten
1 onion, diced	3 tablespoons sugar
¼ cup schmaltz (chicken fat)	1 teaspoon salt
¼ cup chopped grieben	Pepper to taste

Break up matzos and soak in cold water until soft. Drain off water. Brown onion in schmaltz and add these onions with grieben to the matzos. To beaten eggs, add sugar, salt and pepper. Combine this mixture with matzos and bake in well-greased 1½-quart casserole in a 350° oven for 1 hour or until brown. Serves 6-8.

Lillian Gordon

Passover Cheese Blintzes

Batter	**Cheese Filling**
3 eggs	1 pound cottage cheese
¾ cup matzo cake flour	1 egg
1½ cups water	½ teaspoon salt
½ teaspoon salt	½ teaspoon sugar
Butter for frying	1 tablespoon sour cream

Beat eggs; add flour and water alternately to make a thin batter. Add salt. Pour about 3 tablespoons of batter on a well-greased frying pan, spreading it as thin as possible. Fry until brown and turn out on a towel, browned side up. Mix filling ingredients and spread evenly over each leaf, tuck in ends and roll up. Brown in butter. Sprinkle with sugar and cinnamon and serve hot. Makes 12 blintzes. **Variation 1:** Spread a thin layer of perserves over each pancake and fold over in the same manner. Brown lightly under broiler flame. Serve with stewed fruit or plain. **Variation 2:** Sprinkle with sugar, cinnamon and chopped nuts. Tuck in sides and roll. Brown. Serve plain or with sugar.

Inez Lipman

Cheese Pancakes

½ pound dry cottage cheese
4 eggs, beaten
1 tablespoon sugar
1 teaspoon melted butter

½ cup matzo meal
½ teaspoon salt
Powdered sugar, cinnamon or
syrup

Mix dry cottage cheese and eggs. Stir in sugar, melted butter, matzo meal and salt; mix well. Drop by tablespoonsful into hot fat and fry until brown on both sides. Serve with sprinkling of powdered sugar, cinnamon or syrup. Serves 6.

Apple Cake

Cake
9 eggs, separated
1½ cups sugar
9 tablespoons matzo meal
9 tablespoons potato starch
1 lemon, juice and zest

Filling
6 green apples
½ cup sugar
1 tablespoon lemon juice
1½ teaspoons cinnamon

Beat egg yolks with sugar until mixture is light and lemon colored. Add matzo meal and potato starch gradually, both sifted. Add lemon juice and zest. Fold in stiffly beaten, but not dry egg whites. Pour half the batter in ungreased 13 x 8 pan and bake at 325° for 20-30 minutes or until lightly brown. Peel and coarsely grate apples and drain in a colander. Combine remaining ingredients. Spread apple mixture over baked cake, spread the rest of the batter over the filling and bake for another 50-60 minutes.

Rachelle Strickman

Apple Cake

8 eggs, separated
½ teaspoon salt
¾ cup sugar
8 apples, grated

1 cup matzo meal
¼ cup ground almonds
1 teaspoon cinnamon
1 tablespoon orange juice

Add salt to egg whites and beat until stiff. Add sugar gradually; beat in egg yolks. Add apples, matzo meal, almonds, cinnamon and orange juice. Bake at 325° for 1 hour and 15 minutes in tube pan.

Anne Gottfried

Chocolate Cake

7 eggs, separated
¼ teaspoon salt
1 cup sugar
½ cup cake meal

3 tablespoons cocoa
2 tablespoons water
½ cup nuts, chopped

Beat the egg whites with salt until stiff but not dry and gradually beat in sugar. Beat egg yolks about 5 minutes and then gently mix in beaten egg whites, folding carefully. Mix and sift cake meal and cocoa and fold in a little at a time. Gradually add water and fold in nuts. Pour into an ungreased tube pan. Bake at 325° for 45 minutes. Invert cake in pan to cool.

Helen Hecker

Chocolate Cake

6 eggs, separated
1 cup sugar
2 tablespoons water
1 tablespoon lemon juice

½ cup cake meal
3 tablespoons cocoa
½ teaspoon salt

Beat egg whites until stiff and set aside. Mix together yolks, sugar, water, and lemon juice. Sift together flour and cocoa into yolk mixture and beat. Fold in egg whites. Pour into tube pan and bake at 350° for 35 minutes. Invert pan until cool.

Claire Levison

Chocolate Roll

¼ cup cake meal
¼ cup potato starch
2 tablespoons cocoa
6 eggs, separated

½ teaspoon salt
¾ cup sugar
½ tablespoon lemon juice

Sift cake meal with potato starch and cocoa. More cocoa may be added for color. Beat whites until frothy. Add salt and sugar. Beat until stiff. Beat yolks, add juice and beat until lemon colored. Fold yolks and flour mixture alternately into egg whites. Bake in greased 13 x 15 pan, covered with greased waxed paper, at 325° for 35-40 minutes. Invert and remove paper immediately. Roll in towel. When cool, unroll and fill with whipped cream. Roll and freeze.

Esther Parsky

Chiffon Wine Cake

9 eggs, separated
¾ cup cake meal
Juice of 1 orange

1½ cups sugar
2 tablespoons cocoa
¼ cup wine

Beat egg yolks with sugar; add cake meal, cocoa, juice of orange, and wine. Beat whites until stiff and fold into yolk mixture. Pour into tube pan and bake at 325° for 50 minutes.

Eleanor Chiger

Jelly Roll

4 eggs, separated
½ lemon or orange rind
½ cup sugar

½ cup cake meal
¼ teaspoon salt
Jelly or boiled frosting

Beat together yolks and sugar until creamy and light. Add rind. Sift meal 3 times and add to mixture. Add salt to whites, beat until stiff and fold into batter. Line an 8 x 12 pan with waxed paper. Spread batter evenly in pan and bake at 350° for 12 minutes. When done, lift out cake with paper and place on a damp cloth for a few minutes then turn over on to waxed paper. Sprinkle with superfine sugar. Remove paper in which cake was baked and spread cake with jelly or boiled frosting and roll up. Wrap in waxed paper, then in damp cloth, let stand 15 minutes. Remove wrapping and dust cake with superfine sugar.

Gertrude Wynar

Nut Cake

6 eggs, separated
1 cup sugar
½ teaspoon salt
¾ cup matzo meal

¼ cup potato starch
1 teaspoon cinnamon
1 cup chopped nuts

Beat egg whites until stiff, adding sugar a little at a time. Beat yolks and add to whites. Add nuts to sifted matzo meal, starch and cinnamon. Fold into egg mixture and bake in round or 9-inch square pan at 325° for 1 hour.

Sarah Derman

Raspberry Cake

8 eggs
1½ cups sugar
1 lemon, juice and grated rind
2 tablespoons raspberry jelly

2 tablespoons crushed walnuts
½ cup potato starch
½ cup cake flour
¼ teaspoon salt

Beat yolks with sugar until very light. Add lemon rind, juice, jelly, nuts and flour and mix. Add salt to egg whites and beat until stiff. Fold whites into first mixture. Bake in a 9 x 13 pan that has been lined with wax paper. Bake at 325° for 1 hour.

Becky Byer

Spice Cake

¾ cup matzo meal
8 eggs, separated
1½ cups powdered sugar
Grated rind of 1 lemon
2 squares chocolate, grated
1 teaspoon allspice

2 teaspoons cinnamon
Juice of 1 orange
3 tablespoons wine
1 cup blanched almonds, chopped
¼ teaspoon salt

Sift matzo meal 4 times. Beat egg yolks until light; slowly sift in sugar; beat together until creamy. Add grated lemon rind, chocolate, spices, orange juice, wine and nuts. Blend well after each addition. Add sifted meal. Beat egg whites with salt until stiff and fold carefully into batter. Pour into 9 x 13 waxed paper lined pan. Bake at 325° for approximately 1 hour.

Never-Fail Sponge Cake

9 eggs, separated
1½ cups sugar
½ cup cake meal

¼ cup potato starch
Juice and rind of 1 lemon or orange

Beat egg whites until they hold their shape, add sugar slowly. Fold in cake meal and potato starch which have been sifted together. Fold in beaten yolks to which have been added the lemon juice and rind. Pour into large size ungreased tube pan. Bake in 325° or 350° oven for 50-60 minutes. Invert on cake rack and let cool in pan.

Esther Robfogel

Sponge Cake

9 large eggs, separated
1 cup sugar
2/3 cup potato starch

1/3 cup cake flour
½ large orange or lemon, juice and rind

Beat whites and add sugar. Beat yolks and add juice. Fold yolks into whites and fold in well-sifted flour and starch. Bake in tube pan at 325° for 1 hour and 15 minutes; invert until cool.

Alice Paul

Sponge Cake

9 eggs, separated
1½ cups sugar
½ cup oil
½ cup potato starch

½ cup cake flour
Juice of ½ lemon
Juice of ½ orange

Beat egg whites well, adding sugar gradually. Mix together and add yolks, oil, and juices. Mix together sifted potato starch and cake flour. Sprinkle over mixture and fold in. Pour into tube pan. Bake at 350° for 1 hour; invert until cool.

Ruth Alva

Passover Dessert Elegant

1 8-inch or 9-inch sponge cake, baked
1 pound Passover bitter chocolate

6 tablespoons sugar
6 tablespoons water, cold
8 eggs, separated

Melt chocolate in double boiler. Add sugar and water and remove from heat. Blend in well-beaten egg yolks. Cool. Beat egg whites until stiff. Fold into chocolate mixture. Line sides and bottom of a 10-inch spring form pan with slices of sponge cake. Pour half of chocolate mixture into pan. Add a layer of sponge cake slices and then remaining chocolate mixture. Refrigerate overnight. May be topped with whipped cream.

Sora Lee Goldberg

Refrigerator Loaf Cake

½ of a 6-egg sponge cake
1 1-pound can cranberry sauce
1 egg white

½ cup sliced almonds
1 cup heavy cream, chilled
2 tablespoons sugar

Cut cake into very thin slices. Mash cranberry sauce until smooth. Beat egg white until stiff. Fold in cranberry sauce and nuts. Place alternate layers of cake and sauce, starting and ending with cake, in a loaf pan. Cover with waxed paper and place a weight on top. Chill for several hours or overnight. Loosen around edges with a knife and unmold onto a serving plate. Frost with whipped cream, which has been sweetened with sugar.

Walnut Cake

9 eggs, separated
1-1/3 cups confectioners sugar
½ cup cake meal

1½ cups walnuts, ground
¼ teaspoon salt

Beat egg yolks until light; sift in sugar; beat until creamy and light. Sift meal 3 times and blend into creamed mixture. Add walnuts. Mix well. Beat egg whites with salt until stiff and fold lightly into creamed mixture. Pour into spring form or waxed paper lined pan. Bake at 325° for 50 minutes. Remove from oven. Invert and cool in pan.

Lemon Sauce

1 cup sugar
2 tablespoons butter

1½ lemons, juice and rind
3 eggs, well beaten

Cream together sugar and butter, add juice and grated rind. Heat. Pour ½ cup of hot liquid very slowly into beaten eggs. Return egg mixture to remainder of hot liquid and stir very quickly for 5 minutes. Serve warm over fruit, such as sliced pineapple and bananas or over sponge cake.

Rose Nevid

Rhubarb and Strawberry Sauce

1 1-pound package frozen rhu-
    barb, thawed
1 10-ounce package frozen
    sliced strawberries, thawed

½ cup granulated sugar
¼ cup potato starch
¼ cup water

Drain rhubarb and cut into small pieces, reserving juice. In a saucepan, stir sugar and potato starch together, mixing well. Add rhubarb and juice, strawberries and juice, and water. Bring to a boil over medium heat, stirring constantly. Reduce heat, simmer about 5 minutes, stirring occasionally. Remove from heat. Pour into bowl, cover with wax paper. Refrigerate for at least 2 hours. Serve over sponge cake.

Sylvia Gertzog

Wine Sauce for Sponge Cake

1 cup sugar
1 teaspoon potato starch
1 cup white wine

¼ cup water
¼ cup lemon juice
3 eggs

Mix sugar and potato starch together in large pan. Add wine, water, lemon juice and eggs. Beat over medium heat until mixture comes to a full boil and is thick. Remove from heat, beat a few minutes longer. Cool in refrigerator.

June Lovenheim

Cheese Pie

6 matzos
6 tablespoons butter
1 pound cottage cheese
3 eggs, beaten

¼ teaspoon salt
½ cup sugar
Juice of ½ lemon

Dip matzos in water and drain. Grease 9-inch square baking dish with 4 tablespoons melted butter. Fit bottom and sides of dish with the matzos. Beat cheese, eggs, salt, sugar and lemon juice. Spread half of mixture over layer of moist matzos. Repeat with cheese filling and then another layer of matzos. Brush top with 2 tablespoons of melted butter. Bake at 350° until golden brown, about 1 hour. Sprinkle with powdered sugar and cut into squares. Serve hot or cold.

Passover Blender Cheesecake

Crust

1 egg, beaten
3 matzos

¼ teaspoon cinnamon
1 teaspoon sugar

Filling

1 cup sour cream
3 egg yolks
1 teaspoon vanilla
1 tablespoon lemon juice
2 tablespoons sugar

¼ teaspoon salt
¼ cup cake meal
1 pound creamed cottage cheese
3 egg whites
¼ cup sugar

Wet matzos with hot water, dip into beaten egg and line bottom and sides of a buttered 9-inch square pan. Sprinkle matzo with a mixture of cinnamon and sugar. Blend first 8 ingredients for filling in blender for 1 minute. In a large bowl, beat egg whites until stiff. Add sugar gradually. Gently fold in cheese mixture. Pour into prepared pan. Bake at 325° about 1¼ hours or until center is firm.

Helen Hecker

Passover Lemon Chiffon Pie

Crust

1 cup matzo meal
¼ cup oil
Pinch of salt

Pinch of cinnamon
1 teaspoon sugar

Filling

Juice of 2 lemons
Grated rind of 1 lemon
½ cup sugar
1½ cups water
3 egg yolks creamed with
½ cup sugar

3 tablespoons potato flour
  moistened with
½ cup cold water
3 egg whites
Pinch of salt

Mix ingredients for crust in order given and pat evenly over bottom and sides of a 9-inch pie pan. Bake 10 minutes at 375° or until lightly browned. To make filling, bring to a boil in top of a double boiler and first 4 filling ingredients. Stir in creamed yolks and sugar as water continues to boil. Blend in moistened potato flour by mixing until smooth. Cook 10 minutes or until well blended and creamy. Remove from heat. When filling is cool, stir in egg whites which have been stiffly beaten with salt and turn mixture into pre-baked pie crust. Serves 6-8.

Lemon Meringue Pie

Crust

1 cup matzo meal
¼ cup peanut oil
2 tablespoons sugar

⅛ teaspoon salt
¼ teaspoon cinnamon

Blend ingredients together. Press into a 9-inch pie pan and bake at 375° for 15-20 minutes or until golden brown. Cool.

Filling

5 tablespoons potato starch
¼ teaspoon salt
1 cup sugar
2 cups water
3 eggs, separated
2 tablespoons vegetable short-

ening (or butter)
5 tablespoons lemon juice
1 tablespoon grated lemon rind
Dash salt
6 tablespoons sugar

Combine potato starch, salt and ½ cup of sugar in top of double boiler; add water. Cook over boiling water until thick, stirring constantly. Cover and cook 10 minutes, stirring occasionally. Combine egg yolks with ½ cup sugar. Spoon in a little of the hot, cooked mixture. Stir rapidly until smooth and pour back. Cook 2 minutes, stirring constantly. Remove from heat. Stir in fat, lemon juice and rind. Cool to room temperature without stirring (not in the refrigerator). Pour into baked shell. Cover with meringue made by beating 6 tablespoons sugar into stiffly beaten egg whites until smooth and glossy. Bake in a moderate oven at 325° for 15 minutes or until lightly browned. Chill and serve.

Passover Brownies

1 cup sugar
¼ cup shortening or peanut oil
2 eggs
6 tablespoons cocoa
¼ cup liquid black coffee

Dash salt
¼ cup cake meal
¼ cup potato starch
1 cup chopped nuts

Cream sugar and shortening, add eggs. Make a paste of cocoa and coffee and add to first mixture. Blend in rest of ingredients. Bake in greased 9 x 12 pan at 325° for 25-30 minutes. Cut into bars.

Betty Tuchman

Fudgies

4 eggs
2 cups sugar
1 cup melted butter
½ teaspoon salt

6 tablespoons cake flour
1 cup cocoa
1 cup nuts

Beat eggs and add sugar gradually, add butter and beat well. Sift dry ingredients and add to mixture. Stir in nuts. Pour into 9 x 13 greased pan. Bake at 375° for 20-25 minutes.

Sylvia Wynar

Jam Knish Bread

3 eggs
1 cup sugar
1½ cups cake meal
½ teaspoon salt

1 cup oil
1 cup chopped nuts
Jam
Cinnamon and sugar

Beat eggs and sugar until fluffy. Add cake meal, salt and oil and stir well. Add nuts and refrigerate 20 minutes. Grease cookie sheet. Divide dough into 4 rolls. Wet hands and shape in long strips, making a ridge down center of each. Bake for 10 minutes at 350°. Remove from oven and put a different flavored jam in ridge down center. Sprinkle with cinnamon and sugar. Bake 25 minutes longer. Cut when cool.

Marge Gold

Lemon Cookies

¾ cup cake flour
½ teaspoon salt
¼ cup potato flour
1 cup sugar

3 eggs, separated
1 lemon
1 cup nuts, chopped fine

Beat yolks and add sugar. Add juice and rind of lemon. Add the nuts after adding sifted dry ingredients. Beat egg whites stiff and fold in. Let mixture stand ½ hour until it thickens. Drop by teaspoonfuls on greased cookie sheet. Bake at 350° for 20-25 minutes. Place ½ nut on each cookie. Makes 36.

Eve Gold

Mandel Bread

3 eggs
¾ cup sugar
Grated rind of lemon and orange
5 tablespoons oil

1¼ cups cake meal
½ cup nuts
¼ cup coconut

Beat eggs and sugar, add oil and rinds. Add flour and fold in nuts. Let stand 10 minutes in refrigerator. Divide into 4 parts and roll into strips. Bake at 350° for 20 minutes. Cut while warm.

Millie Rosenbaum

Nut Cookies

1 cup peanut oil
1 cup sugar
1¾ cups cake meal
½ cup matzo meal

2 eggs
½ cup ground nuts
Jelly, for filling

Beat oil and sugar, add eggs and other ingredients. Roll into 1-inch balls. Put on cookie sheet and make thumb print. Add jelly. Bake at 350° for 20-30 minutes.

Helene Wynar

Walnut Patties

3 cups powdered sugar
3 eggs
3 cups finely ground walnuts

½ teaspoon salt
¾ cup cake meal

Mix sugar and eggs and cream until light. Add walnuts, salt and cake meal. Mix thoroughly. Drop by teaspoonfuls on a greased cookie sheet. Allow plenty of room for spreading. Bake at 325° for 20 minutes. Yields 48 cookies.

Apple Sponge Pudding

4 apples
⅛ cup raisins
½ teaspoon cinnamon
⅛ cup blanched almonds,
  chopped
1 tablespoon white wine

1 cup sugar
4 eggs, separated
Grated rind of ½ lemon
½ cup sifted cake meal
⅛ teaspoon salt

Peel apples. Cut off tops and reserve as covers. Hollow out insides. Chop and mix scooped out apple with raisins, cinammon, almonds, wine and 1 tablespoon sugar. Fill apples with mixture. Cover with tops and place in a greased casserole. Add a few spoons of water and simmer 10 minutes. Beat egg yolks and remaining sugar until light and fluffy. Blend in lemon peel and cake meal. Beat egg whites with salt until stiff and then fold into batter. Pour over apples. Bake in a 350° oven for 45 minutes. Serves 4.

Passover Ice Cream

1 10-ounce package frozen
  strawberries or raspberries
½ cup sugar

1 egg white
1 banana

Partially thaw berries. Put all together in large mixing bowl. Beat on highest reading on mixer until thickened. Freeze in plastic container or ice cube tray. Serves 6.

Esther Silverstein

Carrot Candy

3 pounds carrots
3 pounds sugar
1 orange, grated
1 lemon, grated

½ cup chopped walnuts
2 teaspoons cinnamon (level)
1 heaping teaspoon ginger

Grate carrots fine and squeeze juice. Mix with sugar and place over very low heat, stirring almost constantly. Increase heat to moderate, and stir for 40 minutes or until mixture becomes thick and syrupy. Add orange and lemon and continue cooking 20 minutes more. Add chopped nuts, cinnamon, and ginger. Cook and stir for 10 minutes. Spread hot mixture on a moistened cookie sheet or wet board to cool. Cut into diamond shaped pieces. These may be rolled in powdered sugar if desired.

Esther Silverstein

Ingberlach

1 cup sugar
½ cup honey
2 eggs

1 cup matzo meal
2 tablespoons ginger
½ cup ground almonds

Bring sugar and honey to a boil in deep saucepan. Cook until it turns a reddish golden color (10 minutes). Remove from fire, combine other ingredients, and add to sugar-honey mixture. Cook on low heat until thick, stirring constantly (10 minutes). Turn out on wet board and pat out to ½-inch thickness, with palm of hand, dipped in cold water. Sprinkle with sugar and a little ginger. Cut into squares.

Matzo Farfel Taiglach

1 pound honey
1 cup sugar
1 cup nuts, cut up

2 eggs
3 cups matzo farfel
½ teaspoon ginger

In bowl put beaten eggs over farfel and mix. Bring honey and sugar to rolling boil in heavy soup pot, add farfel, nuts, and cover pot. Boil until golden brown, stirring frequently. Put on wet board to cool, spread to about ½-inch thickness. Cut when cool.

Ruth Drexler

Honey Taiglach

4 eggs, separated
1 teaspoon peanut oil
Pinch of salt
¾ cup cake meal
½ cup potato flour

1 pound honey
¾ cup sugar
1 teaspoon ginger
½ cup water
Finely chopped nuts

Beat egg whites to a peak. Beat yolks until creamy, add oil and salt and keep beating until thick. Fold in whites. Sift cake meal, potato flour and salt 4 times. Fold into batter. Roll this dough into a long narrow piece, cut in 1-inch squares. Bring honey, sugar, ginger and water to a boil in a large deep pan. Drop dough squares into this syrup. Boil on a medium flame for 45 minutes. Place on a wet board and sprinkle with finely chopped nuts.

Passover Praline

2 tablespoons sugar
¾ cup honey
1 pound walnuts

1 pound almonds
1 tablespoon lemon juice

Over very slow flame, melt sugar into honey. Add nuts and lemon juice. Cook mixture until brown. Rinse cutting board with cold water. Moisten hands with cold water. Pour mixture on cutting board and flatten with moistened hands. Allow to cool. Cut into serving pieces.

Arlene Bush

Glazed Prunes

1 pound sour prunes
1 cup cold water
1½ cup sugar

Juice of 1 lemon
1 cup walnuts

Bring prunes and water to boil. Add sugar and lemon juice. Boil for 20 minutes. Cool slightly. Remove pits from prunes. Stuff prunes with walnuts then dip in syrup and roll in chopped nuts.

Carolyn Miller

Passover "Sugar Pops"

Butter (enough to grease pan)
½ cup honey

2 cups matzo farfel

Lightly butter jelly roll pan. Sprinkle single layer of matzo farfel into pan. Lightly drizzle honey over farfel. Bake at 325° for 1 hour. Turn over once. Should be like honey coated cereals. Good for breakfast with milk for children.

Helen Hecker

Beet Preserve (Eingemachts)

3 pounds winter beets
Sugar
1 or 2 lemons
½ teaspoon dry ginger or more

to taste
1 cup blanched walnuts or almonds

Peel lemons so that all white membrane is removed. Cut lemon in half lengthwise and cut in thin slices. Grate or cut beets in match-stick strips. Soak overnight in cold water. Drain beets, reserving water. Weigh and place in heavy kettle, adding enough reserved water to barely cover beets. Bring to a boil. Sugar used should be in equal proportion to weight of prepared beets. Bring to a slow rolling boil until jells. Stir so that it doesn't stick to bottom of kettle. During last 5 minutes of cooking, add thinly sliced lemon and nuts. Remove from stove, add ginger. Pour into hot sterile fruit jars.

Charoses

1 apple
6 walnuts

⅛ teaspoon cinnamon
3 tablespoons wine

Peel and grate or mash apple. Crush nuts with mallet or grate very fine. Add cinnamon and wine.

Esther Silverstein

Appetizers

Garlic Cheese Ball

1 package (8 ounces) cream
  cheese
1/3 cup grated Parmesan
  cheese

1 package garlic cheese roll
½ teaspoon Worcestershire
  sauce
½ teaspoon salt

Mix all ingredients thoroughly and shape into a ball. Serve as a spread with crackers.

Linda Rock

Nut Cheese Ball

8 ounces softened cream cheese
8 ounces blue cheese, crumbled
¼ cup softened butter

2/3 cup well-drained, chopped
  green olives
1/3 cup chopped walnuts

Blend cheeses and butter, stir in olives. Chill slightly for easier shaping. Shape into ball, roll in nuts (coating the ball completely), wrap in foil and chill overnight or freeze until ready for use. Serve with crackers.

Renee Serling

Sharp Cheese Ball

12 ounces cream cheese
5-ounce jar Old English sharp
  cheddar cheese
1 ounce blue cheese
¾ teaspoon A-1 sauce
2 teaspoons grated onion

1 teaspoon Worcestershire
  sauce
1-2 tablespoons sherry
Chopped pecans
Parsley

Place all ingredients (except pecans and parsley) in large bowl and let sit at room temperature until they can be mixed well with electric mixer. Shape into ball; refrigerate, wrapped in wax paper, until ball holds shape. Roll in chopped pecans and parsley. This cheese ball can be frozen.

Judy Kaplan

Cheese Beignets

3 tablespoons butter
½ cup water
½ cup all-purpose flour
2 eggs
1 teaspoon salt

4 tablespoons grated, sharp
  cheddar cheese
⅛ teaspoon white pepper
1 egg white, stiffly beaten
Shortening for deep frying

Combine water and butter in saucepan and bring to a boil. Remove from heat. Add flour all at once. Beat until glossy and dough clears sides of pan. Beat in eggs one at a time, beating well after each addition; add cheese, salt and white pepper. Fold in the beaten egg whites; drop from teaspoon into hot, deep fat at 365°. Brown on all sides. Remove from fat and drain on paper towel. Serve very hot. These can be frozen.

Ruth Baker

Cheese Balls

1 egg white
2 cups Parmesan cheese, grated

Fat for frying

Beat white until stiff. To 1/3 of beaten egg white, add 1 cup cheese and beat well. Add remaining egg white and cheese alternately; beating constantly until thoroughly mixed. Shape into balls the size of small marbles and fry in deep hot fat 365° until golden brown; drain and serve as a cocktail canape.

Dora Levy

Cheese Fondue

½ pound Swiss cheese
1½ teaspoons flour
½ cup Chablis or Sauterne
  wine
¼ teaspoon salt

Pinch pepper
Dash nutmeg
French bread
1 clove garlic

Grate cheese and toss with flour. Cut French bread into bite size pieces. Assemble all ingredients on tray. At the tables: Rub fondue pot with garlic. Pour in wine and heat almost to boiling. Then add cheese tossed with flour and stir until melted. Add salt, pepper and nutmeg. When mixture is bubbly, it's ready. Guest spears bread with fork and then dunks bread into fondue, stirring. Fondue should bubble gently. (If it becomes too thick, a little heated wine may be added.) Serves 3-4.

Maxine Peters

Cottage Cheese Mousse

2 teaspoons unflavored
  gelatin
¼ cup cold water
2 cups sour cream
2 teaspoons dry Italian salad
  dressing mix

¼ cup blue cheese, crumbled
8 ounces cottage cheese, small
  curd, creamed
Crackers, melba toast, cocktail
  rye bread

Soften gelatin in water, place over hot water (double boiler) and stir. Stir in sour cream; add Italian salad dressing and mix. Add crumbled blue cheese and cottage cheese. Beat until well blended and pour into a 4 cup mold. Serve with crackers, melba toast or cocktail rye bread.

Flo Lurie

Quick Hors D'Oeuvres

½ cup grated American cheese
½ cup India relish
½ teaspoon prepared mustard

Paprika
Long wafers or finger toast

Mix together all ingredients and spread on long wafers or finger toast. Sprinkle with paprika and broil until cheese melts.

Julia Berlove

Hot Cheese and Onion Appetizer

1/3 cup Parmesan cheese,
  grated
¾ cup mayonnaise

½ cup chopped onion
Dash of Worcestershire sauce
Salt and pepper to taste

Combine all ingredients. Spread on party rye or bread squares. Bake at 450° until golden brown. (Mixture can be made several days ahead).

Maxine Strauss

Crisp Parmesan Strips

12 slices white bread
1 cup melted margarine or
  butter

1½ cups grated Parmesan
  cheese
Paprika

Trim crusts and cut each slice into 4 strips. Dip strips into melted butter or margarine; then into cheese. Place strips ½ inch apart on cookie sheet. Bake at 400° 8-10 minutes, until golden brown. Remove from oven and place strips on wire rack. Sprinkle lightly with paprika. Makes 48 strips.

Louise Vigdor

Little Pizzas

1 pound sharp cheese
3 hard boiled eggs
1 onion

½ bottle chili sauce
½ bottle green olives, small
Party rye

Put cheese, eggs, onion and olives through food chopper. Add Chili Sauce and mix well. Refrigerate for a few hours. Place some mixture on party-rye rounds. Heat on cookie sheet in 400° oven, until bubbling. These can be made in advance and frozen.

Arlene Stolnitz

Miniature Quiche

Pie pastry (enough for 2 shells)
2 cups Swiss cheese, grated
1 cup Half and Half
2 eggs beaten

¼ teaspoon salt
Dash of dry mustard, cayenne
Dash of Worcestershire sauce

Roll out half of dough at time. Cut out rounds 2½ inch in diameter and press down in tiny cupcake tins (makes 4 dozen). Combine remaining ingredients. Fill about 2/3 full with mixture. Bake at 425° for 15 minutes. Cool slightly; remove from tins. Cool and place in container next to each other; freeze. To serve, put on cookie sheet, bake at 400° for 15 minutes until they puff up and get nicely brown.

Edith Perlman

Cheese Savories

1 8-ounce package processed
  sharp Cheddar cheese
½ cup margarine

1 cup flour, sifted
¼ teaspoon salt
Paprika

Cream together softened cheese and margarine. Blend in flour and salt. Shape into ¾-inch balls. Sprinkle with paprika. Chill 2 hours or freeze. Place on ungreased baking sheet. Bake at 450° for 15 minutes. Yield 30.

Carolyn Steklof

Greek Cheese Spinach Rolls

1 onion chopped
10 scallions, sliced
¼ cup butter, melted
3 cups cooked, chopped drained
  spinach
1 teaspoon salt
¼ teaspoon pepper

1½ teaspoons dill
3 eggs
½ pound Greek feta cheese
½ cup grated Parmesan cheese
3 tablespoons chopped parsley
1 package Filo pastry leaves
1 cup melted butter

Saute onions and scallions in melted butter. Add spinach, salt, pepper and dill. Cool for 10 minutes. Beat eggs in bowl and add feta and Parmesan cheeses and parsley; add spinach mixture to above until well blended. Test for correct seasoning. Carefully separate leaves. Spread leaf flat, brush with melted butter. Make 4 layers of Filo brushing each layer with melted butter. Spread spinach mixture over 2/3 of the leaf. Roll up like jelly roll. Place in baking pan; prick top in several places. Pour remaining butter over it. Bake at 400° for 30 minutes or until brown and crisp on top. Makes 4 rolls. Slice and serve hot.

Judy Kaplan

Curried Cantaloupe Dip

½ pint sour cream
2 tablespoons mayonnaise
¼ teaspoon curry powder
1 teaspoon catsup

1 teaspoon onion, minced
½ teaspoon salt
Pepper to taste
Cantaloupe

Combine all ingredients except cantaloupe. Make balls from the cantaloupe. Serve dip in cleaned melon half surrounded by the cantaloupe balls.

Terri Ross

Dill Dip

1 cup mayonnaise
1 cup sour cream
3 tablespoons shredded green
onion

3 tablespoons shredded parsley
3 tablespoons dill weed
1 teaspoon Beau Monde
seasoning

Blend or mix all ingredients together. Makes 2 cups. This dip is especially good for dipping raw vegetables, but chips, etc. may also be used. It is best when made a day ahead so spices have time to blend.

Ruth Salesin

Green Goddess Dip

1 clove garlic, minced
½ of a 2-ounce can anchovy
fillets, mashed
3 tablespoons chives, finely
chopped

1 tablespoon tarragon vinegar
½ cup sour cream
1 cup mayonnaise
1/3 cup parsley, finely chopped
Salt and pepper to taste

Blend ingredients thoroughly. Add green food coloring for more appetizing appearance. Best if made the day before. Serve with assorted raw vegetables (cherry tomatoes, cauliflowerets, carrot sticks, celery fans, green pepper sticks).

Judy Kaplan

Guacamole Dip

1 large ripe avocado, cut in
half (save shell, rinse with
lemon juice)
1 tablespoon lemon juice
1 teaspoon Worcestershire
sauce

½ teaspoon salt
½ teaspoon grated onion
1 clove garlic, minced
Pinch cayenne pepper
1 tablespoon mayonnaise

Thoroughly scoop out pulp of avocado, mixing in blender with other ingredients. Fill the avocado shell with the dip, cover and refrigerate. Serve with tortilla chips or with crisp raw vegetables.

Judy Kaplan

Vegetable Dip

8 ounces cream cheese
2 teaspoons grated onion

3 tablespoons ketchup
¼ cup French dressing

Mix all ingredients in electric mixer. Serve with cut up fresh vegetables.

Linda Ruda

Yogurt Dip

1 clove garlic, mashed
¼ cup walnuts, finely chopped
1 teaspoon oil
1 cup yogurt

Salt and pepper to taste
Dash of vinegar
½ cucumber, finely diced

Mix mashed garlic and chopped walnuts with oil, add to the yogurt with the salt, pepper, vinegar and cucumbers. Chill; serve as a dip.

Dora Levy

Caviar Mousse

1 envelope unflavored gelatin
¼ cup cold water
2 ounces black caviar
3 hard cooked eggs, sieved
½ cup mayonnaise

1 teaspoon Worcestershire
sauce
1 teaspoon onion, minced
Salt and freshly ground pepper
to taste

Dissolve gelatin in cold water. Mix thoroughly with remaining ingredients and pour into mold rinsed with cold water. Chill at least 4 hours. Unmold and serve on crackers.

Margie Wiseman

Chopped Herring

1 pound jar of pickled herring
filets in wine sauce
2 dry small pieces of challah
2 hard boiled eggs

1 apple, peeled and cored
1 small onion
Sugar to taste

Drain liquid off herring. Soak bread in liquid. Chop herring, eggs, apple and onion together (or put through grinder). Add soaked bread and mix well. Sugar may be added to taste.

Jennie Levinson

Herring Cacciatore

1 12-ounce jar herring in wine
sauce
2 fresh tomatoes, cut in eighths
2 green peppers, cut in rings
1 Spanish onion
1 can (7 ounces) ripe olives

Chili sauce
1 firm apple, peeled, cored, and
cut into slices
1 carrot, peeled and cut into slices
A few black peppercorns

Remove herring from jar. Fill jar with chili sauce. Mix herring juice and chili sauce well. Place all ingredients in a bowl, pour liquid over other ingredients. Toss a couple of times to marinate well. Chill and serve. Serves 8 as an hors d'oeuvre.

Julia Berlove

Salmon Ball

1 1-pound can red salmon
8-ounce package cream cheese
1 tablespoon lemon juice
2 teaspoons grated onion
1 teaspoon horseradish

¼ teaspoon garlic salt
¾ teaspoon liquid smoke
½ cup chopped walnuts
Parsley

Mix all ingredients together with exception of nuts and parsley. Chill for several hours. Shape into ball. Roll in nuts and parsley.

Sue Kiner

Mim's Salmon Mousse

1 1-pound can red salmon
½ cup celery
¼ cup onion flakes
2 packages gelatin
½ cup cold water
½ cup catsup
¼ cup white vinegar
1 cup mayonnaise

Drain salmon; reserve liquid. Flake salmon, mix with celery and onion. Soften gelatin in water. Combine salmon liquid, catsup and vinegar; bring to boil. Add softened gelatin; stir until dissolved. Blend hot liquid with salmon mixture. When cool add mayonnaise. Pour into 1-quart mold which has been coated with mayonnaise.

Mim Braverman

Salmon Mousse

1 envelope plain gelatin
2 tablespoons lemon juice
1 small sliced onion
½ cup boiling water
½ cup mayonnaise
¼ teaspoon paprika
¼ cup chili sauce
1 teaspoon dill
1 16-ounce can salmon
1 cup heavy cream or whipped topping

Empty gelatin into blender, add lemon juice, onion slices and water. Cover blender and blend at high speed. Add mayonnaise, paprika, dill, chili sauce and salmon. Blend at high speed. Add cream which has been whipped (or whipped topping). Pour into mold and chill overnight. Unmold on bed of salad greens and serve with party rye bread.

Arline Wiseman

Salmon Snappers (Japanese)

½ pound can of salmon, drained
3 tablespoons grated onion
½ teaspoon salt
¼ teaspoon pepper
1 egg yolk
10 slices day old bread

Decrust bread, cut each slice into 6 parts, then cut each piece as though slicing again, but not all the way through. Mix all ingredients together and place 1 teaspoon of mix in each slit and press together firmly. Fry in oil until browned. May be prefried and reheated. May be frozen before or after frying. Makes about 60.

Ruth Baker

Sardine Appetizer

1 can sardines, drained
1 small onion
1 hard boiled egg
1 small apple, peeled
Salt and pepper to taste
White vinegar to taste
Sugar to taste

Put all ingredients together in blender. Chill. Serve as dip with crackers or rye rounds. Tastes like mock herring salad.

Bunny Skirboll

Tuna Puffs

⅛ cup parsley, chopped
1 cup dry bread crumbs
¼ cup onion, chopped
1 7-ounce can tuna, flaked
½ cup pareve consomme
1 egg

¼ cup mayonnaise
1 tablespoon mustard
1 teaspoon salt
1 teaspoon pepper
Crushed corn flakes

Combine all ingredients except corn flakes, and form into 1-inch balls. Roll in crushed cornflakes. Bake at 450° for 10 minutes. May be prepared in advance and refrigerated on a foil-lined cookie sheet; then baked before serving. Yield: about 60.

Eleanor Goldsmith

Tuna Spread

1 7-ounce can tuna fish
1 package dried onion soup mix
1 pint sour cream

1 teaspoon lemon juice
Dill seed

Mix above ingredients except dill seed, chop fairly fine. When in serving bowl, sprinkle with dill seed.

Bea Horn

Whitefish Appetizers

1 egg
3 tablespoons sour cream
1½ tablespoons mayonnaise
2 teaspoons prepared mustard
1 tablespoon parsley, minced

1 tablespoon chives, minced
Salt to taste
1½ pounds ocean whitefish,
cooked (sole may be substituted)

Beat the egg lightly and stir in the sour cream, mayonnaise, mustard, parsley and chives. Add salt to taste. Pour over the fish, toss lightly and spoon into 6 individual shell-shaped baking dishes. Bake in a pre-heated, 400° oven for 12 to 15 minutes.

Alyne Phillips

Chinese Barbecued Chicken Wings

2-3 pound chicken wings

Salt, pepper, Accent

Clean and dry wings. Season with salt, pepper and Accent. Bake covered at 375° for ¾ hour; pour off juice.

Sauce

½ cup honey
¼ cup soy sauce
¼ cup ketchup

4 tablespoons brown sugar
1 crushed garlic clove

Mix together above ingredients and pour over wings. Bake uncovered at 400° basting every 15 minutes for 1 hour or until tender. Prepare day before and reheat before serving.

Ruth Baker

Chinese Egg Roll

Egg Roll Dough

1-1/3 cups sifted all-purpose
   flour
2/3 cup cornstarch
½ teaspoon salt

2 unbeaten eggs
1½ cups water
Fat for frying

Sift dry ingredients. Blend the eggs and ½ cup of water with a fork. Add gradually to dry ingredients blending thoroughly in electric mixer. Save 1/3 cup batter to seal edges of egg rolls. Grease lightly heavy skillet and place over medium heat. Pour about 3 tablespoons batter all at once into skillet, tip quickely in all directions to make a thin 7 inch pancake. Remove from heat when edges begin to dry and curl. Turn over on toweling or tablecloth. Repeat procedure until all pancakes are done on one side. Place ¼ cup filling in center of cooked side of each egg roll and fold two sides over filling. Brush edges with reserved batter, roll up egg roll pressing edges to seal. Fry in hot fat at 360° until crisp and golden turning only once. Serve hot with apricot sauce or hot mustard sauce or both. Makes about 20 egg rolls.

Filling

¼ cup raw carrot, shredded
¼ cup shredded celery
1½ cups cooked diced chicken breasts
2 tablespoons oil
Salt and pepper

1 teaspoon brown sugar
Few dashes of soy sauce
2 water chestnuts, finely
   chopped
½ can bean sprouts, drained

Saute all ingredients except chestnuts & bean sprouts in oil until tender. Add seasonings; add chestnuts and bean sprouts.

Apricot Sauce

2 cups apricot jam   2 tablespoons vinegar

Combine jam and vinegar in saucepan. Bring to a boil and simmer for 2 minutes, stirring occasionally.

Hot Mustard Sauce

Blend dry mustard and hot water to make a paste.

Ruth Drexler

Curried Baked Chicken Appetizer

3 whole chicken breasts

Bake whole seasoned chicken breasts at 325° for 1½ hours. When cool, cut in large pieces and refrigerate. Serve on lettuce bed with mayonnaise curry sauce. This is served as an appetizer on a buffet table with toothpicks and will serve 8.

Curry Sauce

½ cup mayonnaise   1 tablespoon curry powder

Combine above ingredients and chill.

Louise Vigdor

Chopped Liver

1 pound liver
2 eggs, hard boiled
1 onion, medium
2 tablespoons chicken fat

1 stalk celery
Salt and pepper to taste
1 tablespoon dry chicken soup mix

Broil liver until it is thoroughly cooked, but do not over cook. Brown the onions in chicken fat. Put the liver through food chopper with eggs, browned onion and the stalk of celery. Mix well. If the mixture appears dry, add one tablespoon fat, and two or three tablespoons of warm water to which the dry chicken soup mix had been added. Mix and refrigerate.

Sarah Derman

Chopped Baked Liver

1 pound chicken livers
2 cups tomato juice
1 onion, large, diced
1 green pepper, diced
4 stalks celery, diced

6 eggs, hard boiled
Lawry salt, to taste
Dash ginger
Dash nutmeg

Combine liver, juice, onion, green pepper and celery. Bake in a 350° oven for one hour, turning once. Mash liver with a fork, add eggs and seasonings; chop. Place in a mold or serve from a bowl.

Arline Wiseman

Grandma's Great Chopped Liver

2 pounds beef liver
2 onions, large, sliced
1 McIntosh apple, peeled

2 eggs, hard boiled
1 cup oil
Salt, to taste

Fry liver in ¼ cup oil until well done. Saute onions in ¼ cup oil until brown. Alternately grind the liver, onions, apple and eggs. After above ingredients are ground, chop in chopping bowl. Add about ½ cup oil and season with salt, according to taste.

Beverly Leopold

Chopped Liver and Mushroom Spread

½ pound chicken livers
1 4-ounce can mushrooms
3 tablespoons chopped chives
¼ cup parsley flakes

½ teaspoon salt
¼ teaspoon pepper
1 cup mayonnaise

Saute chicken livers and then chop with rest of ingredients. Add mayonnaise. Heat and serve hot. Spread on party rye or crackers.

Elaine Simon

Vegetarian Chopped Liver

1 cup diced onions
1 cup diced celery
¼ cup diced green pepper
Nye fat or margarine
1 4-ounce can mushrooms, drained

1 4-ounce can yellow string beans, drained
6 walnuts
4 hard boiled egg yolks

Saute diced vegetables in nye fat or margarine until golden brown. Add mushrooms, string beans and walnuts, mix thoroughly, then grind. Grated yolks of eggs may be mixed in or used as garnish on top.

Sora Lee Goldberg

Dipsy Doodle Liverwurst Pate

½ pound liverwurst
3 tablespoons chopped sweet or
   dill pickle
¼ cup chopped onion
¼ cup salad dressing

2 teaspoons prepared mustard
¾ teaspoon Worcestershire sauce
¼ teaspoon Tabasco sauce
Salt to taste

Mash liverwurst well with remaining ingredients; chill thoroughly. Remove from refrigerator ½ hour before serving. Makes about one cup.

Elaine Simon

Cocktail Hots

1 pound hot dogs, cocktail size
½ bottle ketchup

2 cups corn flake crumbs

Coat the hot dogs in the ketchup. Roll in the corn flake crumbs. Place on a greased cookie sheet. Bake at 425° until nicely brown, about 20 minutes. These may be prepared ahead and frozen.

Eve Berk

Hot Dogs in Wine Appetizer

1 dozen hot dogs
1½ cups sweet wine (Man-
   ischewitz Concord Grape)

2/3 cup light brown sugar
½ cup water
¾ cup ketchup

Cut hot dogs in bite size pieces. Combine all ingredients in pot and simmer together for about 3 hours.

Ruth Salesin

Cocktail Meatballs

2 pounds ground beef
1 envelope onion soup mix
1 egg
2 teaspoons Accent
¼ cup bread crumbs

14 ounces pizza flavored
   ketchup or regular ketchup
1 jar (10 ounces) apple jelly
Pineapple chunks

Mix beef, soup mix, egg, Accent and bread crumbs. Form into bite-size meatballs. Refrigerate 30 minutes. Before serving, heat electric fry pan to 215°. Stir together ketchup and jelly, add meatballs and simmer about 25 minutes. Thread meatballs and pineapple chunks on skewers.

Maxine Peters

Meat Balls

2 pounds ground beef
1 slice bread, soaked

Garlic salt to taste
Salt and pepper to taste

Combine and form into balls.

Sauce

1 bottle chili sauce
1 jar currant jelly

Juice of 1 lemon
1 bay leaf

Combine above sauce ingredients and cook over slow flame for 30 minutes. Add meat balls and cook until done.

Marge Gold

Swedish Meatballs

1½-2 pounds ground chuck
1 large egg
2 slices dry bread, crumbled
½ teaspoon salt
½ teaspoon pepper
¼ cup catsup
Ginger ale or water, enough to make workable
2 teaspoons salad oil
1 onion, diced
1 large clove garlic, crushed
¼ teaspoon oregano
½ teaspoon dry mustard
2 tablespoons flour
Water
Dash of bitters
1½ ounce sweet vermouth
2-3 ounces rye whiskey

Combine chuck, egg, bread, salt, pepper, catsup, ginger ale or water and form into small balls. Brown in oil. Remove meatballs from pan. In same pan, cook onion and garlic until tender. In cup, mix oregano, dry mustard, flour and enough water to make 1 cup. Add this mixture to onion and garlic. Stir and cook until smooth. Then add bitters, vermouth and whiskey. Add meatballs. Store in refrigerator 24-48 hours. Heat slowly before serving.

Mr. and Mrs. Robert Buonomo

Sweet and Sour Meatballs

1½ pounds hamburger
1 small grated onion
1 egg
Salt and pepper to taste

Mix together all ingredients and shape into very small meatballs for appetizers; larger ones for main meal. Put into casserole and brown slightly in 350° oven. Meanwhile prepare sauce.

Sauce

1 can of tomato juice (medium size)
Juice of one lemon
3 tablespoons sugar
¾ jar grape jelly (small size)
Salt to taste

Blend together; simmer for a few minutes. Pour sauce over slightly browned meatballs in casserole. Bake uncovered at 350° for 2 hours. Serves 8 to 10.

Helene Kroll

Rare Roast Beef Slices with Horseradish Sauce

Rare roast beef slices
1½ cups mayonnaise
3 tablespoons horseradish
3 tablespoons snipped chives
½ teaspoon salt
1 tablespoon lemon juice

Place roast beef slices on large tray on bed of greens (lettuce, raw spinach, romaine, etc.) with sauce in center, (May pass French bread slices along with this appetizer).

Louise Vigdor

Brussels Sprouts Appetizer

1 10-ounce package frozen Brussels sprouts
½ cup Italian dressing
½ teaspoon dill weed
2 tablespoons sliced green onion

Cook Brussels sprouts, drain. Mix Italian dressing, dill weed and green onion. Pour over sprouts. Chill several hours.

Rachel Hyman

Eggplant Hors D'Oeuvre

1 eggplant	Salt
1 onion	Few drops bland salad oil
¼ fresh green pepper, sliced	2 tablespoons vinegar
1 tomato	Crackers
Freshly ground pepper	

Bake eggplant until soft. Peel and remove seeds. In wooden chopping bowl, add onion, green pepper and tomato. Chop all these ingredients and add pepper, salt, salad oil and vinegar. Mix well, refrigerate and serve with crackers or firm garlic bread. It is best when made a day before and left to marinate.

Fritzie Levine

Mushroom Canapes

Dough

1 cup flour	½ cup creamed cottage cheese
½ teaspoon salt	½ tablespoon caraway seeds
½ cup butter or margarine	

Filling

1 pint mushrooms	Salt and pepper to taste
3 tablespoons margarine or butter	1 egg, well beaten
	Onion salt to taste

Make dough of flour, cutting in butter and salt, until crumbly. Add cottage cheese and caraway seeds; mix. Form into a ball and refrigerate in wax paper a few hours. Chop mushrooms and saute in butter. Add salt and pepper to taste. Roll out chilled dough on a floured board into a piece, approximately 9 x 14. Coat each piece with additional melted butter. On each piece, arrange one half of mushrooms in a line just inside the lengthwise edge. Roll dough around mushrooms and pinch gently together to enclose mushrooms securely. Return to refrigerator to chill. To serve, spread each roll with a mixture of beaten egg and onion salt to taste. Slice rolls into 1-inch pieces. Place cut side down on greased cookie sheet. Bake at 400° for 12-15 minutes. Serves 8.

Norma Erdle

Mushroom Caviar

1 cup green onions with tops, chopped	Salt and pepper to taste
4 tablespoons butter	¼ teaspoon cayenne pepper
2 cups chopped mushrooms	4 tablespoons dill seed
2 tablespoons lemon juice	2/3 cup sour cream
	Black bread

Saute onions in butter for one minute. Add the mushrooms, lemon juice, salt, pepper and cayenne pepper. Saute 4 minutes, stirring occasionally. Remove from heat, stir in dill and sour cream. Serve with black bread.

Brenda Babitz

Curried Mushroom Puffs

Pastry for shells (double pie
  crust recipe)
½ pound mushrooms
¼ cup minced onion
¼ cup butter or margarine
2 tablespoons flour
½ teaspoon salt

⅛ teaspoon white pepper
1 teaspoon curry powder
½ cup light cream or Half and
  Half
1 tablespoon minced parsley
Pimento

Shells: Make pastry according to recipe. Cut into small rounds and fit in tiny cup-cake size tins. Prick pastry very well. Bake 10 minutes in pre-heated 375° oven. Take out of pans and cool. Filling: Cook mushrooms, finely chopped, and onion in butter over medium heat. Stir constantly until most moisture has evaporated and vegetables are soft. Combine flour, salt, pepper and curry. Sprinkle over vegetables and cook 1 minute. Add cream slowly, stirring constantly until mixture is thick and bubbly. Cool. Add parsley. Fill shells and bake about 10 minutes in 350° oven. Serve hot. Shells may be made ahead of time and frozen, but do not fill until second baking period. Makes about 5 dozen.

Beula Sonders

Marinated Mushrooms and Artichoke Hearts

1 bottle (8 ounces) Italian
  salad dressing
½ cup sherry wine
1 tablespoon lemon juice

1 pound mushroom caps, washed
1 can (6 ounces) artichoke
  hearts, drained

Mix salad dressing, sherry and lemon juice in a large bowl. Marinate mushrooms and artichoke hearts in mixture for at least 24 hours. Stir carefully many times so all surfaces are covered with marinade. Serve with toothpicks.

Shirley Axelrod

Stuffed Mushrooms

24 large mushrooms
¼ cup minced onions
2 tablespoons minced scallions
2 tablespoons minced green
  pepper (optional)
¼ cup butter or margarine
¾ cup Italian bread crumbs

¼ cup chopped parsley
¼ cup milk or pareve George
Washington broth (enough to
  moisten)
1 teaspoon salt
Freshly ground pepper

Wash mushrooms and remove stems. Chop stems and also 6 of the mushrooms caps, reserving 18. Saute chopped mushrooms, green peppers, onions and scallions in butter or margarine for 5 minutes. Remove from heat and cool slightly. Add bread crumbs, parsley, salt, pepper and milk, (or broth) mixing well. Stuff mushrooms caps with mixture, arrange mushrooms, stuffed sides up in baking dish. Add ¼-½ inch boiling water and bake in preheated 425° oven for 20-25 minutes.

Sheila Markin

Stuffed Mushrooms

24 mushroom caps (reserve
   stems)

3 tablespoons butter
Salt and pepper to taste

Brush caps with melted butter; salt and pepper to taste. Place hollow side up in greased pan.

Filling

3 tablespoons onion, minced
2 tablespoons butter
3 tablespoons scallions, minced
Mushroom stems, minced and
   squeezed dry in a towel
¼ cup Madeira wine
3 tablespoons bread crumbs
¼ cup Swiss cheese, grated

¼ cup Parmesan cheese, grated
4 teaspoons parsley, minced
½ teaspoon tarragon vinegar
Salt and pepper
Enough cream to moisten
3 tablespoons Swiss cheese,
   grated
2 tablespoons butter, melted

Saute the onion for 3-4 minutes. Add the scallions, mushroom stems and wine. Boil down rapidly. Remove from heat and add the next 6 ingredients. Stuff the mushroom caps with the above mixture. Mix together 3 tablespoons grated Swiss cheese and 2 tablespoons melted butter and brush tops of mushrooms. Refrigerate until serving time. (Do not freeze; mushrooms tend to get rubbery). Bake at 375° for 15-20 minutes.

Judy Kaplan

Toasted Mushroom Roll-ups

½ pound mushrooms
¼ cup butter or margarine
3 tablespoons flour
¾ teaspoon salt
¼ teaspoon M.S.G.

1 cup light cream
2 teaspoons minced chives
1 teaspoon lemon juice
25 slices bread

Chop mushrooms and saute in butter about 5 minutes. Blend in flour, salt and M.S.G. Stir in cream and cook until thickened, stirring constantly. Add chives and lemon juice; cool. Cut unsliced sandwich bread into 25 thin slices and remove crusts. Spread with mushroom mixture and roll up each slice, jelly-roll fashion. Pack in boxes, cover with foil or saran and freeze. Before serving, cut each roll in half. Place under the broiler, toasting each sandwich on all sides. Serve very hot. This makes 50 sandwiches.

Elaine Simon

Mushroom Toasties

1 package (3 ounces) chive
   cream cheese
1 can (4 ounces) mushrooms,

drained and chopped
30 onion or garlic bread rounds

Combine above ingredients and spread on bread rounds. Place on ungreased cookie sheet. Place under broiler until hot and bubbly.

Terri Ross

Hot Garlic Olives

1 7½-ounce can ripe olives with liquid

2 cloves garlic, minced
2 tablespoons salad oil

Mix olives with liquid and minced garlic. Chill for 2 hours. In saucepan, heat 2 tablespoons salad oil and 2 tablespoons of olive liquid. Add drained olives and heat.

Rachel Hyman

Potato Knish Hors D'Oeuvres

Liver Mixture

2 medium onions, minced
3 tablespoons chicken fat
   or margarine

1 pound chicken livers
Salt and pepper to taste

Potato Mixture

2 pounds peeled, boiled mashed potatoes
Salt and pepper to taste

3 tablespoons chicken fat
1/3 cup matzo meal

Saute onion in chicken fat until transparent. Remove from pan. Cook chicken livers quickly until they begin to brown. Cool slightly. Chop livers, mix with onion, salt and pepper to taste. Combine potatoes with rest of ingredients of potato mixture. Cool this mixture before using. Use large tablespoon of potato mixture to form balls. Make a depression in center of each ball with finger. Put 1 tablespoon chopped liver in depression. Cover, patting potato mixture over the liver. Place knishes on well-greased baking sheet. Bake in preheated 370° oven until lightly browned. Serve hot.

Arlene Stolnitz

California Dip Deviled Eggs

8 hard cooked eggs
1 envelope onion soup mix
1 pint dairy sour cream

¼ cup finely chopped celery
½ teaspoon lemon juice

Cut eggs in half lengthwise. Remove yolks and mash, blend in onion soup mix, sour cream, celery and lemon juice. Generously fill egg white halves; then chill. Makes 16 appetizers.

Edith Parker

Rum and Grapefruit Halves

½ grapefruit per person
1 tablespoon butter

1 tablespoon brown sugar
Dash of rum

Cut grapefruit into halves and section. Melt sugar and butter together and spread mixture over fruit. Add dash of rum. Broil 7 minutes or until slightly browned. Great for breakfast or an appetizer for dinner.

Susan Horwitz

Beverages

Hot Chocolate

2 squares unsweetened chocolate
1 cup water
3 tablespoons sugar
Dash salt

3 cups milk
Whipped topping
Marshmallows

Over very low heat, melt chocolate in 1 cup water, stirring constantly until thoroughly blended. Stir in sugar and salt; bring to a boil, stirring constantly. Reduce heat and simmer for 3 minutes. Add milk slowly until thoroughly heated. Before serving, beat with rotary beater. Whipped topping or marshmallows are optional.

Nancy Moscov

Chocolate Eggnog

3 quarts eggnog, chilled
1¼ cups chocolate syrup
¾ cup rum, optional
1½ cups whipping cream

3 tablespoons granulated sugar
1 tablespoon cocoa
About ½ 1-ounce square semi-
   sweet chocolate, grated

About 20 minutes before serving, in large punch bowl, combine eggnog, chocolate syrup and rum. In small bowl with electric mixer at high speed, whip cream, sugar and cocoa until stiff. Spoon cream onto eggnog. Sprinkle with chocolate. Makes 24 half cup servings.

Margie Wiseman

Cafe Brulot Diabolique

1 1-inch cinnamon stick
8 whole cloves
Peel of 1 lemon, cut thin
Peel of 1 orange, cut thin

3 lumps sugar
3 jiggers brandy
3 cups strong hot coffee

Place in chafing dish or silver Brulot bowl, the cinnamon, cloves, lemon and orange peel and sugar cubes. Place brandy in large ladle, ignite brandy and pour over ingredients in bowl Keep stirring brandy and spices until sugar is dissolved. Gradually add coffee, ladling until flames fade. Serve immediately in demi-tasse cups. Serves 6.

Ruth Baker

Coffee Eggnog

6 eggs, separated
¼ cup instant coffee
1 cup sugar

1 quart milk
1 pint rum, brandy or whiskey
1 quart vanilla ice cream

Beat egg whites to form soft peaks, add egg yolks and beat well. Combine instant coffee with sugar and add, beating well. Add milk and beat slowly. Add rum and ice cream, beat slowly for 1-2 minutes. Pour into punch bowl and serve. Serves 12.

Margie Wiseman

Coffee Punch

6 tablespoons instant coffee
2/3 cup sugar
2 tablespoons sherry

3 quarts cold milk
Whipped cream
Nutmeg

Combine instant coffee, sugar, sherry, and 3 cups of milk. Beat with rotary beater or at high speed of mixer for 30 seconds. Pour into punch bowl along with remaining milk and mix well. Top with a float of whipped cream and sprinkle with nutmeg. Makes 24 four-ounce servings.

Nancy Moscov

Hot Coffee Punch

½ cup instant coffee
½ cup water plus 1½ quarts boiling water

1½ cups white corn syrup
2 cups sherry or sauterne wine
1 cup whipping cream, whipped

Bring to a boil, coffee, water and syrup. Add 1½ quarts boiling water. Add wine. Put into warmed punch bowl with spoon in bowl to prevent cracking; keep bowl on towel. Fold in whipped cream, mix slightly and serve hot. Makes 22 5-ounce cups.

Ruth Baker

Turkish Coffee

4 teaspoons Yemen-style coffee
4 teaspoons sugar

4 demitasse cups of cold water

Add coffee, sugar, and water to pot. Do not stir. Bring just to full boil. When coffee turns over, coffee is done. Serve immediately.

Carole Berlove

Viennese Coffee

12 cups hot extra-strength coffee
Granulated sugar to taste

1 cup heavy cream,
whipped stiffly

At serving time, pour coffee into warmed punch bowl. Sweeten with sugar to taste. Top with cream. Makes 12 cups.

Margie Wiseman

Tangy Apple Punch

4 6-ounce cans frozen concentrated
apple-red Hawaiian punch
2 6-ounce cans frozen grapefruit
juice concentrate, prepared as

labels direct
2 28-ounce bottles ginger ale,
chilled
Thin apple slices

Combine first 3 ingredients in a large bowl, add ginger ale just before serving. Garnish with apple slices. Serve over ice. Makes 58 4-ounce servings.

Nancy Moscov

Rudi's Champagne Punch

1 ounce cognac
½ cup sugar
1 bottle Reisling wine
2 bottles champagne
2 large bottles Seven-Up
Curl of lemon peel
Block of ice

Combine cognac, sugar and wine. Let stand for at least 2 hours. Add champagne and Seven-up just before serving. Place curl of lemon peel in punch, add block of ice. Remove lemon peel after 15 minutes; do not fail to do this, as it will spoil the flavor if left too long.

Ruth Baker

Hot Cranberry Punch

2 32-ounce bottles cranberry
    juice cocktail
20 cups water
4 cups granulated sugar
½ cup lemon juice
8 whole cinnamon sticks
2 tablespoons whole cloves
2 cups orange juice

About 20 minutes before serving, heat in large kettle over medium heat, first 6 ingredients. Simmer 10 minutes. Add orange juice. Remove spices, if you like. Serve hot. Makes 36 ¾-cup servings.

Millie Rosenbaum

Pineapple-Cranberry Punch

1 large can pineapple juice,
    less 1 cup
½ gallon cranberry juice
1/5th of Vodka
1½ quarts ginger ale

Mix together; chill. Serve from punch bowl.

Stella Gelman

Gin and Fruit Punch

2 46-ounce cans pineapple juice
3 6-ounce cans frozen orange
    juice
2 6-ounce cans frozen lemonade
1 12-ounce box strawberries
2 large bottles ginger ale
1 bottle gin
Ice

Mix above ingredients and serve

Maddy Rubens

Graduation Punch

1 quart lemon sherbet
1 6-ounce can frozen orange
    juice
1 quart cranberry juice
1½ cups pineapple juice
¼ cup lemon juice
1 quart chilled ginger ale
Fresh whole strawberries
Mint leaves

Pack sherbet into a 1-quart ring mold and freeze. Reconstitute orange juice and combine with cranberry, pineapple, and lemon juice. Chill. Just before serving add ginger ale. Unmold sherbet, garnish with strawberries or mint leaves and float on top of punch.

Alyne Phillips

Lawrenceburg, Kentucky Punch

2 quarts strong tea
2-3 cups superfine sugar, or
  granulated
1 quart lemon juice

1 quart orange juice
1 quart grapefruit juice
1 quart ginger ale
2 quarts good Kentucky Bourbon

Make strong tea: 5 tablespoon tea steeped 5 minutes in 2 quarts boiling water. Strain tea, add sugar. Stir until dissolved. Cool and add fruit juices and bourbon. Add ginger ale at time of serving, and place on ice ring in bowl. Makes 2 gallons.

Ruth Baker

Easy Pitcher Punch

1 12-ounce can pineapple juice
1 12-ounce can pear nectar
1 cup orange juice

3 7-ounce bottles lemon-lime
  carbonated beverage

Chill above ingredients and combine in large pitcher; stir well; serve at once. Makes 12 6-ounce servings.

Nancy Moscov

Sherbet Tea Punch

4 cups hot tea
2 cups granulated sugar
2 cups orange juice, chilled
1 cup lemon juice, chilled

2 16-ounce bottles ginger ale,
  chilled
1 pint orange sherbet

Pour tea over sugar early in day and stir until dissolved. Chill. Into a large chilled punch bowl, stir tea, orange juice, lemon juice and ginger ale. Spoon in orange sherbet. Makes 24 4-ounce servings.

Margie Wiseman

Rhine Wine Punch

3 quarts Rhine wine
1 quart soda water, chilled
2½ jiggers brandy

3 jiggers creme de menthe
1 cup strong tea
½ pound powdered sugar

Combine all ingredients in punch bowl filled with crushed ice. Decorate with fruit, as desired. Serve chilled. Makes 25-30 cups.

Margie Wiseman

Wine Punch

½ gallon Thunderbird wine
½ gallon club soda
½ gallon ginger ale

2 small packages frozen
  raspberries

Place ice mold in punch bowl and pour in wine, soda and ginger ale; add raspberries. Serves 40.

Linda Ruda

Hot Spiced Apple Cider

2 quarts sweet apple cider	1/3 cup lightly packed brown
1 teaspoon whole cloves	sugar
1 teaspoon whole allspice	Few grains of salt
2 3-inch cinnamon sticks	

Bring ingredients to a boil in a large kettle. Simmer 30-60 minutes. Remove spices. Serve hot in mugs. Thread raisins and orange sections on skewers and use as stirrers.

Carole Berlove

Mock Champagne

1 cup sugar	½ cup orange juice
1 cup water	1 quart ginger ale, chilled
1 cup grapefruit juice	

Boil sugar with water 5 minutes. Cool. Add fruit juices and chill. At serving time, lightly stir in ginger ale. Serve in champagne glasses. Serves 8.

Eulah Feier

Strawberry Daiquiris

1 6-ounce can frozen limeade	½ of a 10-ounce package frozen
concentrate, thawed	strawberries, slightly thawed
6 - 12 ounces light rum	Crushed ice

Place the first 3 ingredients in blender. Fill almost to top with crushed ice. Blend until all ingredients are mixed and frothy.

Debby Goldman

Spiked Tomato Juice

For every quart of juice:

¼ teaspoon salt	sauce
1 tablespoon lemon juice	½ teaspoon sugar
1½ teaspoons Worcestershire	1 lime, sliced

Selma Kay

Mulled Wine

1 6-ounce can frozen lemonade	2 dozen whole cloves
1 12-ounce can frozen orange	1 cup water
juice	1 bottle Burgundy
2 sticks cinnamon	1½ cups water

Partially defrost lemonade and orange juice. Combine lemonade, cinnamon, cloves, 1 cup water in large pan. Boil for 15 minutes. Add orange juice, 1½ cups water and Burgundy. Heat gently, do not boil. Pour through strainer and serve warm.

Maxine Peters

Breads and Coffee Cakes

Apricot Bread

2 cups dried apricots	4 cups flour
2 cups sugar	4 teaspoons baking powder
4 teaspoons soft butter	½ teaspoon baking soda
2 eggs	2 teaspoons salt
1 cup orange juice	1 cup nuts

Add water to cover apricots. Soak 30 minutes. Then drain. Reserve liquid. Chop apricots. Mix sugar, butter, and eggs. Add ½ cup of reserved drained water and orange juice. Add flour, baking powder, soda, salt, and nuts. Pour into greased 13-inch loaf pan. Let stand 20 minutes. Bake at 350° for 1 hour.

Esther Parsky

Banana Bran Nut Bread

¼ cup shortening	1½ cups flour
½ cup sugar	2 teaspoons baking powder
1 egg	½ teaspoon salt
1 cup all bran	½ teaspoon baking soda
1½ cups mashed banana	½ cup chopped nuts
1 teaspoon vanilla	

Combine first six ingredients. Sift and add the next four ingredients. Add ½ cup chopped nuts. Bake in greased 5 x 9 loaf pan with wax paper on bottom Bake at 375° for about 1 hour. Cool before cutting.

Ethel Winters

Banana Tea Bread

1¾ cups sifted enriched flour	1/3 cup shortening
•2 teaspoons baking powder	2/3 cup sugar
¼ teaspoon baking soda	2 eggs, beaten
½ teaspoon salt	1 cup mashed, ripe bananas

Sift together first four ingredients. Work shortening with a spoon until fluffy and creamy; add sugar gradually; continue to work until light; add eggs and beat well. Slowly add flour mixture, alternating with banana, beating smooth after each addition. Turn into greased 9 x 5 loaf pan. Bake at 350° for 60-70 minutes until done. For banana nut or date bread, add ½ cup chopped walnuts or 1 cup chopped pitted dates.

Renee Rosenbaum

Buttermilk Caraway Raisin Bread

5 cups sifted flour	2½ cups white seedless raisins,
1 cup sugar	washed and dried
1 tablespoon baking powder	3 tablespoons caraway seeds
1½ teaspoons salt	2½ cups buttermilk
1 teaspoon baking soda	1 egg, slightly beaten
½ cup butter	

Sift flour, sugar, baking powder, salt and soda. Cut in butter with pastry blender until mixture resembles coarse cornmeal. Stir in raisins and caraway seeds. Add buttermilk and egg to dry mixture, blending only until flour is moistened. Mixture will appear lumpy. Butter generously an 11-inch heavy cast iron skillet. Turn batter into skillet. Bake at 350° until firm and brown, about 1 hour.

Millie Rosenbaum

Caraway Tea Cake

3½ cups sifted cake flour
1 tablespoon baking powder
½ cup shortening
½ cup butter or margarine
1½ cups sugar

3 medium eggs
1 large can evaporated milk
½ cup finely chopped candied
orange peel
1 tablespoon caraway seeds

Sift flour and baking powder together and set aside. Cream shortening and butter (or margarine) together until light and fluffy, add sugar gradually, creaming well after each addition. Add eggs, one at a time, beating thoroughly after each addition. Add flour in fourths and evaporated milk in thirds, mixing until blended after each addition. Blend in orange peel and caraway seeds at end of mixing. Turn batter into two 9 x 5 loaf pans, greasing bottoms only. Bake at 350° for 55 minutes or until cake tests done. Cool for 10 minutes on wire rack before removing from pans. When completely cool, sift confectioners sugar over tops.

Hetty Jacobson

Carrot Bread

2 cups flour
2 teaspoons baking soda
2 teaspoons cinnamon
½ teaspoon salt
1½ cups sugar
½ cup raisins
½ cup coconut

½ cup chopped nuts
1 cup vegetable oil
2 teaspoons vanilla
3 eggs
2 cups grated raw carrots or
2 jars junior size baby food
carrots, including juice

Mix dry ingredients, add liquids and then add rest of ingredients. Pour into two greased 1-pound loaf pans. Bake at 350°, 50 to 60 minutes.

Ruth Bloom

Carrot Fig Loaf

1½ cups all-purpose flour
1 cup sugar
1 teaspoon baking powder
1 teaspoon baking soda
¼ teaspoon cinnamon
¼ teaspoon salt
2/3 cup oil

2 eggs
1 teaspoon vanilla extract
1 cup finely shredded raw
carrot
½ cup flaked coconut
¾ cup snipped dried figs

Lemon Glaze

1 teaspoon grated lemon rind
1 cup confectioners sugar

Hot water

Put dry ingredients in large bowl of electric mixer. Add oil, eggs and vanilla. Mix for 2 minutes. Stir in carrots, figs and coconut. Bake in greased and lightly floured 9 x 5 loaf pan. Bake in 350° oven for 1 hour or until done. Cool for 5 minutes. Remove from pan. Combine lemon rind and confectioners sugar. Add enough hot water to make a stiff frosting. Glaze and cool.

Rachel Hyman

Carrot Nut Bread

2 cups sugar
1 cup cooking oil
4 eggs
3 cups flour
½ teaspoon salt

2 teaspoons baking powder
2 teaspoons baking soda
2 teaspoons cinnamon
2 cups raw grated carrots
1 cup chopped pecans

Cream sugar and oil. Add eggs, one at a time. Sift dry ingredients together and add to creamed mixture. Add carrots and pecans. Bake 55 minutes in 350° oven in greased large loaf pan, or 2 small loaf pans.

Dolly Brenner

Challah

2 packages yeast
2 cups warm water
7 tablespoons sugar
4 teaspoons salt
¼ cup salad oil

3 slightly beaten eggs, at
room temperature
6-7 cups flour
1 egg, set aside for glaze

Soften yeast in water. Add rest of ingredients, except flour. Mix. Add 4 cups of flour and mix well. Add more flour to make workable dough. Knead until smooth and elastic. Turn into oiled bowl and cover. Let rise until doubled. Punch down. Divide dough in half. Cut each half into 3 equal pieces. Roll each piece into a strip about 15 inches long. Place 3 strips on greased baking sheet. Braid, fastening strips securely at both ends. Repeat with second half of dough. Cover, let rise again until doubled. Brush top and sides with slightly beaten egg. Sprinkle with sesame seeds. Bake in 325° -350° oven for 30-40 minutes. Makes 2 loaves.

Mrs. Robert Temkin

Lil's Shabbos Challah

1 envelope dry yeast
¼ cup lukewarm water
1 cup hot water
4 tablespoons vegetable
shortening
3 tablespoons sugar
2 teaspoons salt

1 pinch saffron (or 4 drops
yellow food coloring)
6 cups flour
1 tablespoon salad oil
2 eggs, slightly beaten
1 egg yolk
1 tablespoon water

Dissolve yeast in lukewarm water. Turn hot water and shortening into large bowl; stir until shortening melts. Blend in sugar, salt and saffron. Stir in beaten eggs (the 2 eggs). Add yeast and blend well. Gradually stir in flour to make a soft dough. Knead dough in bowl until smooth. Top with oil, turning to coat soft dough. Cover and set in warm place until doubled, about 2 hours. Punch down, turn on lightly floured board. Knead until smooth and elastic, then cut into 3 portions, rolling each into a 24-inch long roll. Pinch one end together, braid, and then pinch ends to close. Lift carefully onto lightly greased baking pan, about 8 x 15. Blend egg yolk with a little water and brush braid with the egg yolk mixture. Repeat rising as before (about 2 hours). Brush top again with egg mixture and bake in 350° oven 50-55 minutes. Put on rack to cool.

Lillian Cohen

Braided Bread

1 cup lukewarm milk
½ cup sugar
½ teaspoon salt
½ teaspoon almond extract
Grated rind of 1 lemon
1 cake yeast or 1 package
  dry yeast
¼ cup warm milk or water

2 eggs, beaten
¼ cup soft butter
3½-4 cups sifted flour
1 egg yolk
1 teaspoon melted butter
½ cup sugar
1 teaspoon cinnamon

Mix together first 5 ingredients. Crumble yeast in ¼ cup water or milk. Stir until yeast is dissolved. Add to milk mixture. Stir in eggs. Add ¼ cup soft butter. Mix in, with spoon or by hand, flour adding in 2 additions. Beat and knead until smooth and elastic. Set aside until double in bulk. Punch down and refrigerate over night. Divide dough into 3 parts. Round up each part. Cover and let rest 15 minutes.

Roll each part into ropes, 2 inches in diameter by 15 inches long. Place 1 inch apart on greased baking pan. Braid, beginning in middle and working toward either end. Seal ends well. Cover and let rise until light. Brush top of braid with egg yolk mixed with 1 teaspoon melted butter. Sprinkle with cinnamon and sugar mixture. Bake 30 minutes in 350° oven.

Jennie Komesar

Jewish New Year Bread

1 cake compressed yeast or
  1 package active dry yeast
¼ cup warm water
¾ cup lukewarm milk
¼ cup sugar
1 teaspoon salt
1 large egg
¼ cup soft shortening
3½-3¾ cups sifted flour

¼ cup soft butter
½ cup brown sugar, packed
1 egg
¼ cup milk
½ teaspoon vanilla
½ teaspoon lemon extract
1½ teaspoons almond extract
2 cups walnuts, finely ground

Dissolve yeast in water. Stir together lukewarm milk, butter, sugar, salt and egg. Add to yeast. Mix in flour until dough is easy to handle. Turn out on lightly floured board; let stand 10 minutes; knead until smooth and elastic. Round up in greased bowl; bring greased side up. Cover with damp cloth, let rest at 85° until hole remains when finger is pressed deeply into dough, (double in bulk) about 2 hours. Punch down; round up on board; cover, let rest 15 minutes. While dough is resting, prepare filling.

Mix thoroughly the butter, brown sugar, egg. Stir in milk, add flavoring and ground nuts. Place dough on large floured cloth and roll out thin, spread with filling; roll like jelly roll or strudel. Place on greased cookie sheet in snail shape. Let rise. Brush with egg yolk diluted with a little milk or cream. Sprinkle with cinnamon sugar. Bake in 325° oven for 40-45 minutes.

Jennie Komesar

Cherry Nut Loaf

2 cups sifted all-purpose flour
1 cup sugar
3 teaspoons baking powder
½ teaspoon salt
2 eggs
¼ cup Marashino cherry juice

¾ cup milk
3 tablespoons salad (cooking) oil
¼ teaspoon almond extract
1 cup Marashino cherries, cut
in halves
½ cup chopped walnuts

Sift flour, sugar, baking powder and salt together in mixing bowl. Beat eggs, cherry juice, milk, oil and almond extract together with a fork. Stir into dry ingredients and beat hard until smooth, about 30 seconds. Stir in cherries and nuts. Spoon and bake about one hour in a lined 9 x 5 loaf pan at 350° or until toothpick inserted in center comes out clean.

Reva Zeesman

Cranberry-Orange Bread

2 cups sifted flour
¾ cup sugar
1½ teaspoons baking powder
1 teaspoon salt
½ teaspoon soda
1 cup coarsely cut cranberries

½ cup chopped walnuts
1 teaspoon grated orange peel
1 beaten egg
¾ cup orange juice
2 tablespoons salad oil

Sift together dry ingredients. Stir in cranberries, nuts and orange peel. Combine egg, orange juice and salad oil. Add to dry ingredients, stirring just until moistened. Bake in greased 9½ x 5 loaf pan at 350° for 50 minutes or until done.

Marlene Raustler

Date and Nut Bread

1 cup boiling water
1 cup chopped dates
2 eggs
1 cup sugar

2 cups flour
1½ teaspoons baking soda
1 cup chopped walnuts

Pour boiling water over chopped dates. Mix eggs and sugar. Mix flour and soda. Alternate date and flour mixture. Add chopped nuts. Grease pan. Round soup cans are best to bake in. Fill half full. Bake at 325° for 30-45 minutes, depending on pan used.

Celia Mittleman

Date-Pumpkin Loaf

4 eggs
1½ cups oil
2 cups sugar
2 cups canned pumpkin
3 cups flour
1 teaspoon baking powder

2 teaspoons pumpkin pie spice
2 teaspoons baking soda
1 teaspoon salt
1 cup chopped pitted dates
½ cup walnuts
1 teaspoon vanilla

Beat eggs and add oil. Add sugar and pumpkin and beat for 2 minutes. Add sifted dry ingredients and beat for 2 minutes. Add dates, nuts and vanilla, beating until well mixed. Bake 1 hour at 350° in lightly greased loaf pans. Makes 3 one-quart loaves.

Maxine Peters

Old-Fashioned Herb Bread

1 cup warm water
1 package active dry yeast
1½ teaspoons salt
2 teaspoons sugar
1 tablespoon soft shortening
1 teaspoon marjoram leaves

¾ teaspoon dill weed
¾ teaspoon thyme leaves
½ teaspoon rosemary leaves
2-3 cups flour, or enough to be
  able to handle
Poppy seeds

Pour water into bowl. Sprinkle yeast on top and stir until dissolved. Add salt, sugar, shortening and herbs. Stir. Add flour to make a soft dough. Turn out on lightly floured board and knead until smooth and elastic, 5 to 7 minutes. Put dough in greased bowl, turn to bring greased side up. Cover. Set in warm place and allow to double in bulk, about 1½ hours. Shape dough into a roll 18 inches long. Place on greased baking sheet. With a sharp, floured knife, make ¼-inch-deep slashes in top of loaf about 1½ inches apart. Brush with water. Set in warm place and allow to rise until double in bulk, about 1 hour. Brush again with water. Bake in 425° oven 15 minutes. Brush a third time with water and sprinkle poppy seeds on top. Bake 15 minutes longer. Makes 1 loaf.

Beatrice DiMora

Orange Bread

3 cups flour
4 teaspoons baking powder
¾ teaspoon salt
1 cup sugar
1 egg, slightly beaten

¼ cup grated orange rind
1 cup orange juice
1/3 cup salad oil or melted
  shortening

Sift flour, measure; adding baking powder, salt, sugar. Sift again. Combine egg, orange rind, juice and salad oil. Pour into flour mixture and stir just enough to moisten dry ingredients. Do not beat. Turn into greased 9 x 5 loaf pan. Bake in moderate oven, 350°, about 1 hour.

Ethel Simon

Pumpkin Bread

3½ cups flour
3 cups sugar
2 teaspoons baking soda
1½ teaspoons salt
1 teaspoon cinnamon
1 teaspoon nutmeg

1 cup cooking oil
4 eggs
2/3 cup water
2 cups pumpkin
1 cup nuts
1 cup raisins

Sift all dry ingredients. Make a well in them and add the rest of the ingredients. Mix until smooth. Grease and flour 3 small loaf pans. Bake at 350° for 1 hour.

Edythe Fien

Pecan Muffins

2 eggs
1 cup brown sugar
½ cup flour

¼ teaspoon baking powder
1/3 teaspoon salt
1 cup pecans

Combine all ingredients. Fill 12 greased cup cake tins ¾ full and bake at 400° for 10 minutes.

Eve Mendelson

Swedish Rye Bread

2 cakes compressed yeast or
  2 envelopes dry yeast
1½ cups 85° water
¼ cup dark corn syrup
1/3 cup sugar
1 tablespoon salt
3 tablespoons grated orange rind

3 tablespoons caraway seeds
2½ cups rye flour
2 tablespoons softened butter
2½ to 3 cups sifted all-purpose
  flour
Corn meal

In a large bowl, crumble yeast into water. Let rest 10 minutes. Stir until dissolved. Add next 5 ingredients. Stir in rye flour and butter. Beat together with wooden spoon until smooth. Add all-purpose flour. If the dough is soft to handle use larger amount of flour. Knead dough on floured board by folding dough in half toward you. Press with heel of hand. Turn ¼ turn and fold and press again. If dough seems sticky, add flour to board and hands. Repeat this process until dough is smooth, elastic and satiny.

Grease large bowl. Put dough in it and turn bread dough once, so entire surface will be lightly greased. Cover bowl with damp cloth. Let rise until doubled, about 2 hours. Punch bread down. Knead once or twice. Form into slightly flattened ovals on a greased baking sheet dusted with corn meal. Cover with damp cloth and let rise until almost double in bulk, about one hour. Make four ¼ inch deep diagonal slashes in the top of the loaves.

Bake in a preheated 375° oven for 30 to 35 minutes. When done place on wire rack to cool. Bread is done when it has a hollow sound when tapped on bottom.

Lois Kuh

Apple Kuchen

3 pounds of apples, peeled
1 teaspoon cinnamon
¾ cup sugar or more, depending
  on tartness of apples
1 cup shortening

3 eggs
½ cup orange juice
Orange rind
3½ cups flour
3 teaspoons baking powder

Slice apples thin, mix with sugar and cinnamon, and cover bowl while making the dough. Cream shortening and eggs, and orange juice and rind. Add dry ingredients. Spoon ½ dough into greased baking pan, place apples over batter, and cover with remaining dough. Sprinkle with additional sugar and cinnamon. Bake in a greased 9 x 12 pan at 350° for about 50 minutes.

Ruth Halperyn

Fruit Kuchen

2 cups flour
2 tablespoons sugar
½ teaspoon salt
¼ teaspoon baking powder
½ cup margarine

6 apples
¾ cup sugar
1 teaspoon ground cinnamon
1 cup sour cream
2 egg yolks

Sift together flour, 2 tablespoons sugar, salt and baking powder. Cut in margarine until dry ingredients are mealy. Pat mixture firm on the bottom of the greased 12 x 8 pan. Pare, core and slice apples. Arrange over pastry. Mix ¾ cup sugar and cinnamon together. Sprinkle over fruit. Bake the kuchen 15 minutes in 400° oven. Beat together sour cream and egg yolks. Pour the mixture over the fruit. Continue baking the kuchen for 30 minutes longer. Serve warm or at room temperature.

Hetty Jacobson

Coconut Butter Coffee Cake

¼ cup butter
½ cup flour
½ cup brown sugar
2 cups sifted flour
½ teaspoon soda
½ teaspoon salt
2 teaspoons baking powder

½ cup butter
8-ounce package cream cheese
1¼ cups sugar
2 eggs
1 teaspoon vanilla
½ cup milk
2 ounces Angel Flake coconut

Cut ¼ cup butter into ½ cup flour and brown sugar until mixture resembles coarse crumbs. Reserve. Sift together rest of flour, soda, salt and baking powder. Cream ½ cup butter with cream cheese and 1¼ cups sugar. Blend in eggs and vanilla. Alternately blend in milk and dry ingredients, beginning with dry ingredients. Pour batter into greased 13 x 9 pan. Sprinkle batter with crumb mixture, then with coconut. Bake 40 minutes at 350° .

Edith Perlman

Orange Butter Coffee Cake

1 packet dry yeast
¼ cup warm water
1 cup sugar
1 teaspoon salt
2 eggs

½ cup sour cream
½ cup melted butter
2¾-3 cups flour
1 cup coconut, toasted
2 teaspoons grated orange rind

Soften yeast in warm water in mixing bowl. Stir in ¼ cup sugar, salt, eggs, sour cream and 6 tablespoons melted butter. Gradually add flour to form a stiff dough, beating well. Cover. Let rise in warm place until doubled. Combine ¾ cup sugar, ¾ cup toasted coconut and orange rind. Knead dough on well-floured board about 15 times. Roll half of dough into a 12-inch circle. Brush with 1 tablespoon melted butter. Sprinkle with ½ coconut mixture. Cut into 12 wedges. Roll up, starting at wide end. Place rolls, point side down in 2 greased 10 x 6 pans. Repeat with other half of dough. Cover and let rise in warm place about 1 hour. Bake at 350° for 30 minutes. Leave in pans. Top with glaze. Sprinkle with ¼ cup coconut.

Orange Glaze

½ cup sugar
½ cup sour cream

¼ cup butter
2 tablespoons orange juice

Combine in sauce pan. Boil 3 minutes, stirring occasionally. Pour over cake and remove from pan as soon as glaze is absorbed.

Mickey Liftshutz

Golden Plum Coffee Cake

2 cups sifted flour
¼ teaspoon salt
½ teaspoon baking powder
¾ cup sugar
¼ pound butter

1 teaspoon ginger
2 egg yolks, beaten
2 tablespoons heavy cream
18 ripe yellow plums, pitted
and halved

Sift flour, salt, baking powder and half cup sugar into a bowl. Add butter and work in by hand. Mix the egg yolks and cream together and add, mixing until a ball of dough is formed. Chill for one hour. Roll out the dough to fit a 10 x 16 baking pan. Form a ridge around the edges. Arrange plums in even rows on the dough. Mix remaining sugar and ginger together and sprinkle over the plums. Bake in 375° oven for 15 minutes, then reduce heat to 350° and bake for 30 minutes longer. Serve hot or cold.

Nancy Hoffman

Peach or Apricot Flip

2 packets of active dry yeast
½ cup warm water
½ cup sugar
½ cup margarine or butter

½ cup hot water or scalded milk
2 teaspoons salt
3 unbeaten eggs
5-5½ cups all-purpose flour

Filling

2/3 cup sugar
2 teaspoons cinnamon
1 cup walnuts, chopped

2 tablespoons margarine
1 10-ounce jar apricot or
    peach preserves

Vanilla Glaze

1 cup sifted confectioners sugar
1 teaspoon pure vanilla

2-3 teaspoons water or milk

Soften yeast in warm water. Combine sugar, margarine or butter, water or milk and salt. Stir until butter or margarine is melted. Cool to lukewarm. Blend in unbeaten eggs and the softened yeast. Gradually add flour to form a stiff dough. Knead on floured surface 3 to 5 minutes until smooth. Place in greased bowl and cover. Let rise in warm place for 1-1½ hours.

Combine sugar, cinnamon and walnuts. Set aside. Roll out half of dough on floured surface to form a 20 x 10 rectangle. Spread with margarine and ¼ of preserves. Sprinkle with ½ of filling mixture. Roll up, starting with 20-inch side. Seal edge and ends. Place seam side down on greased cookie sheet, curving ends to make U shape. With knife, cut down center 1/3 of the way through roll to within 2 inches of ends. Repeat with remaining dough. Let rise in warm place 30 minutes. Place a spoon of preserves in center of each cut. Bake at 325° for 25 minutes or until golden brown. Combine confectioners sugar, vanilla and milk. Glaze with this mixture.

Rachel Hyman

Prune Apricot Coffee Cake

¾ cup dried prunes
¾ cup dried apricots
2 cups sifted all-purpose flour
2 teaspoons baking powder
½ teaspoon salt
2/3 cup light brown sugar, packed
1 tablespoon flour
1 tablespoon cinnamon

¾ cup soft shortening
¾ cup granulated sugar
2 eggs
¾ cup milk
1 teaspoon vanilla
6 tablespoons butter or margar-
    ine, melted
1/3 cup chopped walnuts

Let prunes and apricots soak in hot water 5 minutes. Drain fruit, chop fine, and set aside. In medium bowl sift flour with baking powder and salt; set aside. In small bowl combine brown sugar, 1 tablespoon flour, and cinnamon, mix well. In large electric mixer bowl, at medium speed, beat shortening with sugar until light and fluffy. Beat in eggs, one at a time, beating well after each addition. At low speed beat in flour mixture alternately with milk and vanilla, beating just until combined. With rubber scraper gently fold in prunes and apricots.

Turn 1/3 of batter into lightly greased and floured 9-inch tube pan, spreading evenly. Sprinkle with 1/3 brown sugar mixture, then with 2 tablespoons melted butter. Repeat layering twice. Sprinkle top with chopped nuts. Preheat oven to 350° and bake 55 minutes — or until tester comes out clean. Let cool in pan on wire rack about 25 minutes.

Marion Gottfried

Sour Cream Coffee Cake

1 cup butter
2 cups sugar
2 eggs
1 cup sour cream
½ teaspoon vanilla
2 cups flour

1 teaspoon baking powder
¼ teaspoon salt
1 cup chopped pecans or walnuts
3 tablespoons sugar
1 teaspoon cinnamon

Cream butter, add 2 cups sugar gradually, beating until very light and fluffy. Beat in eggs, one at a time, very well. Mix in cream and vanilla. Fold in flour sifted with baking powder and salt. Combine nuts, sugar and cinnamon. Place 1/3 batter in well-greased and floured bundt or 9-inch tube pan. Sprinkle with ¾ of nut mixture. Spoon remaining batter in and sprinkle with remaining nut mixture. Bake about 60 minutes at 350°. Remove from pan after 10 minutes and cool on rack.

Brenda Babitz

Streusel Layered Coffee Cake

Topping

½ cup brown sugar
2 tablespoons butter or margarine
2 tablespoons all-purpose flour

1 teaspoon cinnamon
½ cup chopped walnuts

Mix all five ingredients and put aside.

Batter

¾ cup sugar
½ teaspoon salt
1 egg
1/3 cup melted butter or
    margarine

½ cup milk
1½ cups all-purpose flour
2½ teaspoons baking powder
1 teaspoon vanilla

Mix together first five ingredients. Sift together flour and baking powder and add to mixture. Add vanilla. Turn half of the batter into an 8 x 8 pan, evenly. Sprinkle half of the topping over the batter. Pour remaining batter over top, then add balance of topping. Bake at 375° for 25-30 minutes. (350° for glass pan.)

Mrs. Morris Cohen

Tarty Coffee Cake

¼ pound butter or margarine
¾ cup sugar
2 large eggs
1 cup flour, sifted
1 teaspoon baking soda
½ teaspoon salt

1 large lemon, juice and rind
¾ cup chopped walnuts
¾ cup coconut
2 tablespoons sugar
¼ teaspoon cinnamon

Cream butter and sugar, add eggs and beat together. Add sifted dry ingredients. Add remaining ingredients, except cinnamon and sugar, and blend well. Pour into a greased 8 x 8 pan, and sprinkle batter with sugar and cinnamon mixture. Bake in 350° oven until cake tester comes out clean, about 45 minutes. Cut in squares, serve warm, but also good cold.

Beatrice Di Mora

Yogurt Coffeecake

½ cup butter
2 cups sugar
2 eggs
2½ cups cake flour

1 teaspoon baking soda
Pinch of salt
1 cup plain yogurt
½ cup nut meats

Cream butter and sugar; add eggs and beat well. Add alternately sifted dry ingredients and yogurt, beginning and ending with dry ingredients. Fold in nuts. Bake at 350° for 1 hour in greased Bundt pan.

Syrup

1 cup water
1 cup sugar

¼ cup orange juice
¼ cup brandy or rum

Combine water and sugar and boil for 5 minutes. Add juice and rum or brandy. Spoon over warm cake.

Ruth Goldberg

Sweet Roll Dough

½ cup warm water
2 packages active dry yeast
1½ cups lukewarm water
½ cup sugar

2 teaspoons salt
2 eggs
½ cup soft shortening
7 cups flour

Filling

Cinnamon
Sugar
Melted margarine

Raisins
Nuts, chopped, optional

Dissolve yeast in ½ cup water, add 1½ cups water, sugar, salt, egg, shortening and half of flour to yeast. Mix until smooth. Add enough remaining flour to handle easily (usually a total of 5¾ cups). Knead until smooth. Round up in large greased bowl with greased side up. Cover with cloth and let rise until double in size, about 1½ hours. Punch down and let rise again until double, about ½ hour. Divide dough into thirds. Roll each third on floured board. Spread with margarine. Fold dough in half, margarined sides together, and roll into rectangle. Spread with margarine and generously sprinkle with cinnamon, sugar (add raisins and nuts, if desired). Roll lengthwise and cut into 2 inch pieces. Put pieces into greased pan, or cupcake pan, with a dab of margarine and cinnamon on top and let rise 10 minutes. Bake in 400° oven for 10-15 minutes.

Ruth E. Gordon

Boller (Norwegian Sweet Buns)

2 cups milk, warm
½ cup butter
¾ cup sugar
1 teaspoon salt
½-1 teaspoon cardamon

1 egg
1 cake yeast
6 cups flour, approximately
½ cup raisins

To warm milk, add butter, sugar, salt and cardamon. Beat egg, add to mixture and crumble yeast into mixture. Add enough flour until elastic and smooth; knead. Return to bowl and cover bowl. Let rise to double in bulk. Knead again. Roll into 2 long strips. Cut into 12 pieces. Roll each piece into a ball, kneading in raisins. Let rise double in bulk. Brush with water or eggs. Bake at 375°, 10 minutes.

Nancy Berger Hauger

Mixer Made Danish Rolls

4½ to 5 cups all-purpose flour
2 packages active dry yeast
1/3 cup sugar
2 teaspoons salt
1 teaspoon mace

1 cup milk (or water for pareve)
1-1/3 cups shortening
¾ teaspoon lemon extract
½ teaspoon vanilla extract
3 eggs

Glaze

2 cups sifted confectioners
  sugar

3-4 tablespoons milk or water
1 teaspoon vanilla

In a large mixer bowl combine 2 cups flour, dry yeast, sugar, salt and mace. In a small pan heat milk and 1/3 cup shortening until slightly melted. Add warm milk, lemon extract, vanilla and eggs to dry ingredients. Beat for 2 minutes at medium speed. By hand, stir in the remaining flour to form a stiff dough. Toss on floured surface until it is no longer sticky.

Roll out dough on floured surface to a 15 x 10 inch rectangle. Spread 2/3 of dough with 1/3 cup shortening. Fold ungreased 1/3 of dough over 1/3 greased dough and the remaining 1/3 over all. Repeat rolling, spreading and folding process twice more using 1/3 cup shortening each time. Roll out again to a 20 x 10 inch rectangle. Starting with 20-inch side, roll up jelly roll fashion. Seal edges. Cut in 24 ¾-inch slices. Place cut side down on greased cookie sheet. Cover, let rise in warm place for 50-60 minutes or until light.

Bake at 400° for 12 to 15 minutes, until golden brown. Remove from cookie sheets. While warm, drizzle with glaze. You may garnish with cut Maraschino cherries.

Rachel Hyman

Puter Kuchen

1 cup milk
1 cup sugar
3 teaspoons salt
½ pound butter
1 cup warm water
4 cakes yeast

4 eggs, beaten
6 cups flour
4 cups flour
2 cups sugar
3 teaspoons cinnamon
Raisins

Scald milk. Stir in sugar, salt and butter. Cool to lukewarm. Put warm water in bowl and crumble yeast into it. Stir until dissolved. Stir in milk mixture. Add beaten eggs and 6 cups flour. Beat until smooth. Stir in 4 cups flour. Turn dough out on lightly floured board. Knead until smooth and elastic. Place in greased bowl, brush top with butter. Cover. Let rise in warm place. When dough rises, punch down and let rise again. Repeat this a few times. When dough is doubled in bulk, divide into many parts. Roll each part out to long narrow sheet ¼-inch thick. Brush with melted butter. Mix sugar and cinnamon. Sprinkle some over each strip. Sprinkle with raisins (white). Roll jelly roll fashion and cut 1-inch slices. Place in pan so each roll is touching the next. Brush top with milk and sprinkle with cinnamon and sugar mixture. Let rise until doubled in bulk. Bake at 375° for 25 minutes. Makes quite a bit, at least two 8 x 13 pans.

Phyllis Kasdin

Puter Kuchen

1 cup sugar
4 cups flour
½ tablespoon salt
1 cake yeast
½ cup warm water
2 eggs

¼ pound butter
½ cup sour cream
Sugar
Cinnamon
Raisins, white

Sift sugar, flour, and salt into bowl, making a well in the center. Dissolve yeast in warm water, letting stand for a few minutes until it makes a "sponge." Add yeast sponge, beaten eggs, melted butter, and sour cream to dry ingredients. Mix together to make a soft dough. Cover with a cloth and let stand several hours until it rises or doubles in bulk. Divide dough in thirds. Roll out each piece ½ inch thick. Sprinkle with sugar, cinnamon, and white raisins. Roll as for jelly roll. Set into 3 greased loaf tins. Let rise again. Bake in 350° oven 30-40 minutes.

Anna Spring

Schnecken

Dough
1 package yeast
¼ cup warm water
4 cups all-purpose flour, unsifted
1 teaspoon salt
1 cup milk
¼ pound butter
½ cup sugar
2 eggs

Filling
1 cup brown sugar
1 teaspoon cinnamon
1/3 cup butter, melted
Caramel Topping
2/3 cup butter, melted
1 cup brown sugar, packed
2 tablespoons corn syrup
30 pecan halves

Night before baking, dissolve yeast in warm water. Measure flour and salt into a large bowl. Scald milk and butter; add sugar. Cool. Beat eggs and pour into well of flour, add milk and yeast mixtures. Beat until smooth and well mixed. Cover bowl with cloth and refrigerate overnight. Next morning, punch down dough and let rest for approximately 1 hour. Remove from bowl onto floured board and knead for 3-4 minutes.

For topping, combine butter, sugar and corn syrup. Place teaspoon of this mixture in bottom of greased muffin tins. Place 1 pecan half on top of mixture. Set aside pan. Divide dough in half. Roll out first half on floured pastry cloth (approximately 9 x 5). Brush with melted butter. Sprinkle with cinnamon and sugar. Roll up jellyroll style. Slice ½ inch thick with sharp floured knife. Place rounds in muffin tins. Repeat with other half of dough. Let rise until double in volume (approximately 45-60 minutes). Bake in 350° oven for 20-25 minutes until nicely browned. Turn out of pan immediately onto foil. Makes 30.

Marjorie Relin

Cakes and Frostings

Golden Almond Cake

¾ cup sliced almonds
1 tablespoon sugar
¾ cup margarine
1½ cups sugar
1½ teaspoons vanilla extract
¼ teaspoon almond extract
1 teaspoon grated lemon peel

3 egg yolks
2½ cups sifted cake flour
3 teaspoons baking powder
1 teaspoon salt
3 egg whites
1 cup pareve milk

Generously grease bottom and sides of 10-inch tube pan with margarine. Press the sliced almonds into the margarine on both bottom and sides; sprinkle with 1 tablespoon sugar. Thoroughly cream ¾ cup margarine with 1½ cups sugar. Add vanilla, almond extract and lemon peel. Beat in egg yolks until light and fluffy. Sift together flour, baking powder and salt. Add to creamed mixture, alternately with milk, beating after each addition. Beat egg whites until stiff but not dry. Gently fold into batter. Carefully turn into prepared pan. Bake in slow oven 325° about 1 hour and 10 minutes. Let cake stand in pan about 10 minutes, then invert onto wire rack to cool.

Rachel Hyman

Apple Cake

4 cups peeled, diced apples
2 cups sugar
1 cup chopped black walnuts
3 cups flour
½ teaspoon nutmeg or cinnamon
½ teaspoon salt

½ teaspoon soda
1 cup vegetable oil
1 teaspoon vanilla
2 well beaten eggs
½ cup apple jelly, melted

Mix apples, sugar and nuts and let stand for 1 hour. In a large bowl, mix together remaining ingredients, except apple jelly. When blended, add apple mixture and stir. Bake in greased tube pan for 1¼ hours at 325°. Cake should be dark brown when done. When cake has cooled brush with apple jelly.

Jeanette Presberg

Easy Apple Cake

4 large apples, pared and sliced
2 teaspoons cinnamon
2½ cups sugar
3 cups unsifted flour
3 teaspoons baking powder

1 teaspoon salt
4 eggs
1 cup cooking oil
¼ cup orange-pineapple juice
2½ teaspoons vanilla

Combine apples, cinnamon and ½ cup of the sugar; blend and set aside. Combine all remaining ingredients in a large bowl and beat until smooth (3 or 4 minutes with electric mixer). Pour half of batter into a greased and floured 10-inch tube pan. Spread half apple-cinnamon mixture over the batter. Add remaining batter and top with the rest of the apple-cinnamon mixture. Bake at 350° for 1¼ hours, or until toothpick comes away clean when inserted. Cool and remove from pan.

Belle Lovenheim

Apple Scotch Cake

½ cup butter
1¼ cups sugar
2 eggs
1 teaspoon vanilla
1 cup applesauce
2 cups flour

1 teaspoon baking soda
1 teaspoon salt
1 teaspoon cinnamon
½ teaspoon cloves
2/3 cup butterscotch pieces

Cream butter, add sugar gradually, beat well. Blend in eggs and vanilla flavoring, beat well. Add applesauce, dry ingredients and butterscotch pieces. Pour into greased 9 x 13 pan and bake at 350° for 30 minutes.

Topping

2 tablespoons butter
1 cup coconut
½ cup brown sugar

¼ cup cream
¾ cup nuts
1/3 cup butterscotch pieces

Mix butter, coconut, brown sugar, cream and nuts and heat until well blended. Add butterscotch pieces and spread on cake. Place under broiler for 2 minutes, watching carefully to prevent burning. Yield: 20 servings.

Millie Rosenbaum

Apple Pan Walnut Cake

1 can apple pie filling
2 cups flour
1 cup sugar
1½ teaspoons soda
1 teaspoon salt

2 eggs, beaten
1 teaspoon vanilla extract
2/3 cup cooking oil
¾ cup chopped walnuts

Spread apple pie filling in bottom of 13 x 9 pan. Combine flour, sugar, soda and salt. Sprinkle over pie filling. In mixing bowl, combine eggs, vanilla, oil and ½ cup walnuts. Mix well. Pour over ingredients in pan. Stir only until blended. Smooth batter in pan. Bake 40 to 50 minutes at 350°.

Topping

1 cup sugar
½ cup sour cream

½ teaspoon baking soda

Combine three ingredients in saucepan over medium heat, stirring constantly until mixture comes to a boil. Remove from heat. Prick warm cake with fork. Pour topping over cake — sprinkle with remaining walnuts. Cut in squares. A can of cherry, apricot, peach, pineapple or poppy seed filling may be substituted for apple pie filling.

Bea Horn

Applesauce Cake

1 cup vegetable shortening
2 cups sugar
2 eggs
3 cups sifted flour
½ teaspoon salt
2 teaspoons baking soda
1 tablespoon cinnamon

½ teaspoon nutmeg
1 teaspoon cloves
2½ cups applesauce
2 tablespoons corn syrup
1 cup raisins
1 cup nuts

Blend sugar and shortening. Add eggs, one at a time. Combine flour, salt, baking soda and spices. Alternately add the applesauce and dry ingredients. Add corn syrup, nuts and raisins. Bake at 325° for 1¼ hours in a greased 13 x 9 pan.

Betty Tuchman

Banana Cake

1½ cups sifted regular flour
1 teaspoon baking soda
¼ teaspoon salt
1 stick of margarine
1 cup sugar

1 teaspoon vanilla
2 large eggs
1 cup finely mashed bananas
¼ cup commercial sour cream

Butter the bottom of a 8 x 8 cake pan, line bottom with wax paper, butter paper. Sift together flour, soda and salt. In a medium mixing bowl, cream margarine, sugar and vanilla; thoroughly beat in eggs, 1 at a time, then bananas. Stir in sifted ingredients in 3 additions alternately with sour cream. Turn into prepared pan. Bake at 350° about 35 minutes, until cake tester inserted in center comes out clean. Turn out on wire rack. Remove paper.

Merle Markus

Blueberry Cake

Batter

2 cups flour, sifted
2 teaspoons baking powder
½ teaspoon salt
¼ cup butter or margarine

¾ cup sugar
1 egg, unbeaten
½ cup milk
2 cups blueberries, fresh

Sift together flour, baking powder, and salt. Cream butter and gradually beat in sugar. Add egg and milk and beat until smooth. Add dry ingredients and fold in berries. Spread batter in greased and floured 8-inch or 9-inch square pan. Sprinkle with crumb mixture.

Topping

½ cup sugar
¼ cup flour

½ teaspoon cinnamon
¼ cup butter or margarine

Mix together sugar, flour and cinnamon and cut in butter to form coarse crumbs. Bake at 375° for 40-45 minutes.

Sylvia Wynar

Bundt Cake

1½ cups pecan halves
3 cups cake flour
2 teaspoons baking powder
½ teaspoon salt
1 cup butter
2 cups sugar

4 eggs, separated
1 cup milk
Juice and grated peel of 1 lemon
1 teaspoon vanilla
2 teaspoons whiskey

Grease well a large fluted tube pan; place pecan halves in grooves, bottom and sides of pan (must be done carefully and slowly). Sift flour, measure, and sift with baking powder and salt. Cream butter and gradually add sugar; cream well. Beat in egg yolks, one at a time, beating until smooth. Add dry ingredients alternately with milk. Stir in lemon juice and peel, whiskey and vanilla. Beat egg whites stiff, but not dry, fold into batter. Carefully spoon batter into nut-lined pan. Bake in 400° oven for 15 minutes. Reduce heat to 350° ; bake 1 hour longer. Cool slightly and turn out of pan. (Cake may bake sooner, test 10 minutes before hour.)

Edith Perlman

Carrot Cake

3 cups flour	¼ teaspoon salt
2 cups sugar	1½ cups cooking oil
2 teaspoons baking soda	3 cups grated carrots
2 teaspoons baking powder	4 well beaten eggs
2 teaspoons cinnamon	½ cup chopped nuts

Sift dry ingredients together into large mixing bowl. Make a well in the center and add the oil. Beat well and then add carrots and eggs. Add nuts and mix thoroughly. Pour into greased 9-inch tube pan and bake at 350° for 1 hour and 15 minutes.

Ruth Kravetz

Cheese Cake

Crust

1 box zweibak	½ cup butter
1 cup sugar	

Crush zweibak and mix well with sugar and butter. Press mixture into spring pan.

Filling

1½ pounds dry cottage cheese	½ pint sour cream
3 8-ounce packages cream cheese	1 cup sugar
5 eggs	1 teaspoon vanilla

Beat all ingredients until smooth. Pour over crust and bake for 1 hour at 300°. Do not open oven while it is baking. Turn off oven and let cake cool in oven. When cool put in refrigerator overnight. Serves 10-12.

Julia Berlove

Regal Cheese Cake

Crust

1½ cups graham cracker crumbs	2 tablespoons sugar
2 tablespoons butter	

Blend crumbs with butter and sugar; press into bottom of greased 9-inch spring form pan.

Filling

2 8-ounce packages cream cheese	1 teaspoon vanilla
1 cup sugar	1 teaspoon lemon juice
5 egg yolks	5 stiffly beaten egg whites
1 pint sour cream	

Stir cheese to soften, add sugar and cream well. Add unbeaten egg yolks, one at a time, beating thoroughly after each addition. Add sour cream, vanilla and lemon juice. Fold in egg whites. Pour mixture into crumb lined pan. Bake in slow oven (300°-325°) for 1 hour. Turn off oven and let cake remain in oven 1 hour more with door closed and ½ hour with door open. Refrigerate overnight.

Topping

Whole strawberries, fresh or frozen	Currant jelly

Cut whole berries in half lenghwise; arrange on cake. Soften jelly over hot water; spoon over berries to glaze. Refrigerate to set glaze. (If you prefer, a stawberry glaze may be used instead.)

Bertha Cravets

Cottage Cheese Cake

Crumb Crust

8-10 double graham crackers, crushed

5 tablespoons melted butter
Sugar, if desired

Combine crumb mixture and press into bottom and sides of 8 x 8 x 2 pan.

Filling

1½ pounds cottage cheese, any curd
¾ cup sugar
2 eggs

1 teaspoon vanilla
2 tablespoons corn starch
4 heaping tablespoons sour cream

Strain cottage cheese (easiest method is with a Foley food mill.) Add all the other ingredients. Mix well. Pour into crumb crust. Sprinkle cinnamon and sugar on top, if desired. Bake at 350° for 45 minutes.

Millie Berman

Chocolate Cheese Cake

Crumb Crust

1 8½-ounce package chocolate wafers, crumbled
1/3 cup melted butter

2 tablespoons sugar
¼ teaspoon nutmeg

Cheese Filling

3 eggs
1 cup sugar
24 ounces softened cream cheese
12 ounces semi-sweet chocolate

bits, melted
1 teaspoon vanilla
⅛ teaspoon salt
1 cup sour cream

Blend crust ingredients and spread over bottom of spring form pan and as high on sides as possible. In a large bowl, at high speed, mix eggs and sugar until light. Beat in cream cheese until mixture is smooth. Add melted chocolate, vanilla, salt, and sour cream. Beat until smooth. Pour into crumb crust. Bake 1 hour, or until firm, at 350°. Cool overnight, covered. If desired, decorate with whipped cream, or shaved chocolate which is less sweet.

Lois Kuh

Chocolate Pineapple Cheese Cake

1 20-ounce can crushed pineapple, drained
4 large eggs
1 cup sugar
3 8-ounce packages cream cheese

1 tablespoon vanilla
½ teaspoon salt
1 square melted unsweetened chocolate
Graham cracker base

Beat eggs until thick and yellow. Beat in sugar until fluffy. In another bowl, beat cheese, vanilla and salt, and then beat into egg mixture until smooth. Beat in chocolate and fold in pineapple. Spread over graham cracker base prepared in a 9-inch spring form pan. Bake in 350° oven for 40 minutes. Remove from oven and spread with sour cream topping. Cool and refrigerator.

Sour Cream Topping

1½ cups sour cream

2 tablespoons sugar

Mix together.

Betsy Bobry

Pineapple Cream Cheese Cake

Graham cracker crust
3 8-ounce packages of cream
   cheese
5 eggs

1 cup sugar
½ teaspoon vanilla
1 small can crushed pineapple,
   drained

Topping
1½ pints sour cream
1 cup sugar

½ teaspoon vanilla

Prepare graham cracker crust and line the bottom of 13 x 9 pan. Beat cream cheese, one package at a time in mixer; add eggs, one at a time. Blend in sugar, vanilla and pineapple and pour into prepared crust. Bake at 375° for 30 minutes. Mix topping ingredients. Remove from oven, add topping and bake an additional 10 minutes.

Sora Lee Goldberg

Addie's Famous Chocolate Cake

2 cups sifted flour
½ teaspoon salt
1 teaspoon baking soda
½ cup boiling water
3 squares unsweetened chocolate
1 cup sugar

½ cup butter or margarine
½ cup brown sugar
2 eggs
2/3 cup sour cream or buttermilk
1 teaspoon vanilla

Sift together flour, salt, and baking soda. Melt chocolate in boiling water, stirring so it doesn't burn. Remove from heat; let cool. Cream shortening and sugars until light and fluffy. Add eggs and beat well. Then add chocolate mixture and blend. Add flour alternately with liquid, small amounts at a time, beating after each addition until smooth. Add vanilla. Bake in 2 greased 8-inch layer pans at 350° for 30 minutes or until done. Cool on rack for 10 minutes. Invert on rack and when cool, frost.

Addie Gallancy

Satin Smooth Chocolate Cake

½ cup butter
1½ cups sugar
3 eggs, separated
2 squares bitter chocolate
2 cups cake flour
1 teaspoon baking soda

½ teaspoon salt
1 teaspoon vanilla
2 heaping tablespoons sour
   cream
1 cup buttermilk

Cream butter and sugar; add egg yolks and beat well. Melt chocolate and add to above mixture with the vanilla. Sift and measure flour, salt and soda. Add sour cream to buttermilk and add, alternating with flour mixture, to creamed ingredients. Beat whites and fold into batter. Bake 40-45 minutes at 350° in 9 x 11 pan which has been lined with wax paper. Serves 10-12.

Rose Stein

Pareve Chocolate Fudge Cake

1 cup sugar
½ cup vegetable shortening
4 eggs

1 8-ounce can chocolate syrup
1¼ cups sifted all-purpose flour
1 teaspoon baking powder

Cream sugar and shortening. Add eggs, one at a time. Add syrup and flour, which has been mixed with baking powder, alternately. Bake at 350° for 30 minutes, or until done, in two 9-inch layer pans. This is such a rich cake, it can be served without frosting.

Ruth Drexler

Dutch Cocoa Cream Cake

2 cups sifted cake flour
1-2/3 cups sugar
4 teaspoons baking powder
1 teaspoon salt
5 tablespoons cocoa

2/3 cup soft shortening
1-1/3 cups evaporated milk (diluted with half water)
3 eggs
1-1/3 teaspoons vanilla

Sift together dry ingredients. Add shortening, milk and beat for two minutes. Add eggs, and vanilla and beat. Bake in preheated 350° oven, in two 9-inch layer pans which have been greased and floured, for 30 to 40 minutes. Note: Batter may appear to be "curdled". Do not worry. When cool, split layers and spread with 2 cups whipped cream between layers.

Milk Chocolate Icing

5 tablespoons shortening
½ cup cocoa
2-2/3 cups sifted confectioners sugar

7 tablespoons hot scalded milk*
1-1/3 teaspoons vanilla

Melt shortening and cocoa. Stir in sugar, milk and vanilla. *Can use evaporated milk.

Louise Vigdor

French Chocolate Cake

½ cup vegetable shortening
1½ cups sugar
2 eggs, beaten
½ cup milk
1¾ cups cake flour
¼ teaspoon salt

1½ teaspoons cream of tartar
2 squares melted chocolate
1 teaspoon baking soda dissolved in ¾ cup boiling water
1 teaspoon vanilla

Cream sugar and shortening. Add eggs and then add milk. Sift flour, salt and cream of tartar and add to mixture. Add chocolate and beat well. Add soda and boiling water mixture and stir lightly. Add vanilla. Grease two 9-inch cake pans and line bottoms with wax paper. Bake at 350° for 35 minutes.

May Lovenheim

Gateau au Chocolat

4 eggs
4 bars (4-ounce size) German's chocolate

¼ pound soft sweet butter
4 teaspoons sugar
4 teaspoons all-purpose flour

Preheat oven to 425°. Separate eggs, placing whites and yolks in large bowls. Let whites warm at room temperature about 1 hour. In top of double boiler, melt chocolate over hot, not boiling water, stirring occasionally. Remove from water, beat in butter with spoon. Meanwhile, beat egg whites until stiff and set aside. Beat yolks until thick, slowly add sugar, add flour and beat until just blended. Stir into chocolate mixture. Gently fold chocolate mixture into beaten egg whites. Turn into lightly greased 9 x 5 loaf pan, bottom of which has been lined with wax paper. Reduce oven temperature to 350° and bake 25 minutes. Let cake cool completely in pan on wire rack. Cake will settle like cheesecake. Refrigerate until well chilled. To serve, remove from pan by inverting on serving plate. Slice cake and serve with dollop of whipped cream. Serves 16.

Peggy Savlov

Grated Chocolate Cake

¼ pound butter
2 cups brown sugar
3 egg yolks
2 cups flour
1 teaspoon baking soda
3 teaspoons baking powder

½ cup milk
1 teaspoon vanilla
½ cup sour cream
2 squares chocolate, grated
3 egg whites, beaten

Cream butter and brown sugar. Add egg yolks. Gradually add sifted flour, baking soda, baking powder alternately with the milk. Add vanilla and sour cream. Stir in grated chocolate, then fold in beaten egg whites. Bake in two 9-inch greased tins in 350° oven for 30 minutes. Split each layer in two and frost with one pint of heavy cream, whipped. May add two or three tablespoons chocolate syrup, (to taste) for chocolate whipped topping. One teaspoon of instant coffee may be used in place of the chocolate syrup for a mocha flavored frosting.

Bea Horn

Hershey Cake

½ pound margarine
2 cups sugar
4 eggs
¼ teaspoon baking soda
1 cup buttermilk
2½ cups flour

¼ teaspoon salt
2 teaspoons vanilla
8 small plain Hershey bars,
  melted
1 cup Hershey syrup

Cream margarine and sugar. Add eggs, one at a time. Add baking soda to buttermilk. Sift dry ingredients together and add alternately with buttermilk. Add vanilla, melted candy and syrup. Bake in greased tube pan at 350° for 1 hour. Frost with chocolate frosting.

Lil's Favorite Frosting

1 heaping tablespoon vegetable
  shortening
1 whole egg
1 cup confectioners sugar, un-

sifted
1 teaspoon vanilla
3 heaping tablespoons cocoa
Few drops of milk

Beat all ingredients until smooth.

Lil Orlen

Chocolate Intrigue

3 cups all-purpose flour
2 teaspoons baking powder
½ teaspoon salt
1 cup butter
2 cups sugar

3 unbeaten eggs
1 cup milk
1 teaspoon vanilla
¾ cup chocolate syrup
½ teaspoon soda

Sift together flour, baking powder and salt; set aside. Cream butter and sugar. Blend in eggs, milk and vanilla. Add flour mixture and blend thoroughly. Pour 2/3 of batter into greased tube pan. Add syrup and soda to remaining batter and pour over white batter in pan. Do not mix. Bake at 350° for 45 minutes. Place a sheet of aluminum foil loosely on top of pan. Continue baking for 25 minutes. Cool completely before removing from pan.

Betty Bieber

Chocolate Macaroon Cake

Filling

1 egg white	1 teaspoon vanilla
¼ cup sugar	1 tablespoon flour
1 cup coconut	

In a small mixing bowl, beat egg white at high speed until soft peaks form. Gradually add sugar. Beat until stiff peaks form. Stir in coconut by hand, then add vanilla and flour. Blend well. Set aside.

Batter

2 cups flour	¾ cup cold water
1¾ cups sugar	½ cup shortening
½ cup unsweetened cocoa	½ cup dairy sour cream
1 teaspoon salt	4 eggs (reserve one egg white
1 teaspoon soda	for filling)
2 teaspoons vanilla	

Combine all ingredients for batter in large mixer bowl. Beat at low speed until moistened; continue beating for three minutes until well blended. Be sure to scrape the bowl occasionally. Pour chocolate batter in greased Bundt pan. Drop by teaspoonful coconut macaroon filling over chocolate batter. Bake in 350° oven for 55-65 minutes until top springs back when touched lightly. Cool for 20 minutes before removing from pan.

Chocolate Glaze

1 cup confectioners sugar	½ teaspoon vanilla
2 ounces pre-melted unsweeten- ed chocolate	1-2 tablespoons warm water

Combine all ingredients and enough water to be of glaze consistency. Drizzle over cake.

Mrs. Isadore Ouriel

Chocolate Mayonnaise Cake

1 cup sugar	½ teaspoon salt
2 cups all-purpose flour	1 cup cold water
4 tablespoons cocoa	1 cup mayonnaise
2 teaspoons baking soda	1 teaspoon vanilla

Sift dry ingredients together into bowl. Add water, mayonnaise and vanilla all at once, mixing well. Bake in a lightly greased 9 x 13 pan for 25-30 minutes at 350°, or until top cracks.

Dot McCrory

Chocolate Pound Cake

3 cups flour	1½ cups milk
3 cups sugar	3 teaspoons vanilla
1 cup cocoa	¼ cup light cream (or half and
2 teaspoons baking powder	half)
1 teaspoon salt	3 eggs
½ pound butter	

In large bowl of electric mixer sift together flour, sugar and cocoa, baking powder and salt. Make a well in center and add the soft butter, milk and vanilla. Beat mixture at medium speed for 5 minutes. Add eggs, one at a time, and the light cream, beating mixture thoroughly after each addition. Pour batter into well-greased large bundt pan and one small loaf pan. Bake in 325° oven for 1½ hours, or until cakes test done with toothpick. Small loaf pan will not take as long. Note: this chocolate cake has no baking soda.

Edith Perlman

Chocolate Souffle Roll

5 eggs, separated
1 cup confectioners sugar
3 tablespoons cocoa

Whipped cream
Chocolate sauce

Beat yolks, adding confectioners sugar slowly, until light and fluffy. Add cocoa. Fold in stiffly beaten whites. Bake 20 minutes at 350° in a small jelly roll pan. Turn out onto floured towel and roll to cool. When ready to serve, unroll, fill with whipped cream and reroll. Pour your favorite chocolate sauce over individual slices.

Leah Mermelstein

Chocolate Upside Down Cake

½ cup chopped pecans
1 6-ounce package semi-sweet
  chocolate bits
1 cup confectioners sugar
1/3 cup evaporated milk
¼ cup butter or margarine
¾ cup sugar

1 egg
1 teaspoon vanilla
1 cup plus 2 tablespoons flour
½ teaspoon salt
1½ teaspoons baking powder
½ cup milk

Line an 8 x 8 pan with waxed paper and sprinkle with nuts. Melt chocolate bits over hot water; gradually add confectioners sugar and evaporated milk, beating constantly. Spoon evenly over nuts. Beat margarine and sugar until light and fluffy; beat in egg and vanilla. Blend in sifted dry ingredients alternately with milk. Pour over chocolate mixture. Bake in 350° oven for 45-50 minutes. Let stand for 5 minutes before inverting on rack. Remove wax paper and cut into squares.

Frumel Ureles

Waldorf Astoria Chocolate Cake

2 cups sugar
½ cup butter
2 eggs
2 cups all-purpose flour (no
  substitutes)
½ teaspoon salt

2 teaspoons baking powder
1½ cups sweet milk
4 squares baking chocolate,
  melted
1 teaspoon vanilla
1 cup chopped pecans

Cream sugar and butter; add eggs, one at a time. Sift flour, salt and baking powder together, and add this alternately with milk to creamed mixture, beginning and ending with flour. Add melted chocolate and vanilla. Stir in chopped pecans. Pour into tube pan and bake for 50 minutes, or until done, at 350°. Do not invert pan after removing from oven. Let stand 24 hours before cutting.

Frosting

1½ squares chocolate
⅛ pound butter
¼ teaspoon salt
1-1/3 cups confectioners sugar

1 teaspoon vanilla
1 tablespoon lemon juice
1 egg, well beaten
1 cup pecans, coarsely chopped

Melt chocolate with butter and add salt. Add remaining ingredients except for nuts, beating until of spreading consistency. Add nuts.

Nina Olin

Fudge Surprise Cake

Filling

2 tablespoons butter	1 egg
8 ounces cream cheese	2 tablespoons milk
¼ cup sugar	½ teaspoon vanilla
1 tablespoon corn starch	

Batter

2 cups flour	½ cup butter
1 teaspoon salt	1-1/3 cups milk
1 teaspoon baking powder	2 eggs
½ teaspoon soda	4 envelopes Choco Bake
2 cups sugar	1 teaspoon vanilla

In a small bowl, blend filling ingredients and then beat at high speed until smooth and creamy. Set aside. In large mixing bowl, combine dry ingredients with butter and 1 cup milk. Blend well at low speed. Add 1/3 cup milk, eggs, Choco Bake and vanilla. Continue beating at low speed for about 1½ minutes. Pour batter into greased 13 x 9 pan. Spoon cheese filling mixture over batter, spreading to cover. Bake in 350° oven for 50-60 minutes or until done. Frost when cool.

Frosting

¼ cup milk	1 teaspoon vanilla
¼ cup butter	2½ cups confectioners sugar,
1 cup chocolate chips	sifted

Combine milk and butter in saucepan and bring to a boil; remove from heat. Blend in chips, sugar and vanilla. Beat until spreading consistency.

Brenda Moss

Beer and Kraut Fudge Cake

2/3 cup margarine	1 teaspoon baking soda
1½ cups sugar	1 teaspoon baking powder
3 eggs	¼ teaspoon salt
1 teaspoon vanilla	1 cup beer
½ cup cocoa	2/3 cup sauerkraut, rinsed,
2¼ cups unsifted all-purpose flour	drained and chopped

Cream margarine and sugar until light and fluffy. Beat in eggs and vanilla. Sift together cocoa, flour, soda, baking powder and salt. Add dry ingredients to the creamed mixture alternately with beer, starting and ending with dry ingredients. Stir in sauerkraut. Turn into 2 greased and floured 8-inch round or square pans. Bake in 350° oven for 40 minutes or until cake tests done. Frost with cream cheese frosting.

Chocolate Cream Cheese Frosting

2 4-ounce packages of German sweet chocolate	2 tablespoons light cream
	2 cups sifted confectioners sugar
2 3-ounce packages of cream cheese, softened	¼ teaspoon salt
	1 teaspoon vanilla

Melt chocolate in the top a double boiler over hot, not boiling water. Cool slightly and blend in cream cheese and light cream. Slowly add confectioners sugar, mixing well. Stir in salt and vanilla.

Millie Rosenbaum

Cocoa Cola Cake

2 tablespoons cocoa
½ pound margarine
1 cup Coca Cola
2 cups flour
2 cups sugar
¼ teaspoon salt

2 eggs
1 teaspoon vanilla
1 teaspoon baking soda
½ cup buttermilk or sour milk
1½ cups miniature white marshmallows

Melt margarine in small saucepan, add cocoa and Coca Cola. Bring to a boil, stirring. Set aside to cool, about 1½ hours. Sift together flour, sugar, and salt into a large mixing bowl. Pour cocoa mixture over flour and blend, then add eggs, vanilla, baking soda and buttermilk. Beat 3-4 minutes. Fold in marshmallows. Pour into well-greased and floured 11 x 7 pan and bake at 350° for 30-35 minutes. If a glass pan is used, grease and line bottom only with wax paper, then grease paper and flour and bake at 325° for 40-45 minutes. (Marshmallows will rise to top of cake and look bubbly.

Frosting

2 tablespoons cocoa
¼ pound margarine
6 tablespoons Coca Cola

2 cups confectioners sugar
1 cup chopped walnuts

In saucepan, bring cocoa, margarine and Coca Cola to a boil. Cool; add confectioners sugar and beat smooth. Add nuts. There is enough frosting to cover top and sides of cake.

Zelda Bilfield

Coconut Cake

3 eggs, separated
1½ cups sugar
¾ cup shortening
½ teaspoon vanilla
½-¾ cup fresh grated coconut

2½ cups cake flour
2¼ teaspoons baking powder
½ teaspoon salt
¾ cup coconut milk (from the
fresh coconut)

Beat egg whites until stiff but not dry, and gradually beat in ½ cup sugar. Set aside. Cream shortening with 1 cup sugar, add egg yolks and vanilla, beating well. Add coconut. Add sifted dry ingredients alternately with coconut milk. Fold in beaten egg whites. Bake in two 9-inch greased layer pans at 375° for 25-30 minutes. When cool, frost with lemon frosting.

Ida Gould

Crazy Cake

2 cups sugar
2 eggs
1 cup milk
2/3 cup cocoa
½ cup oil
½ cup butter or margarine

1 teaspoon salt
2 teaspoons soda
1 teaspoon baking powder
3 cups flour
2 teaspoons vanilla
1 cup boiling water

In a large mixing bowl, mix all ingredients in the above order, beating for 3 minutes. Bake in greased Bundt or 13 x 9 pan for 45-60 minutes at 350°, if metal pan is used. Bake at 325° if glass pan is used.

Joyce Beckerman

Mother Kuh's Cream Cake

3 eggs
1½ cups sugar
½ pint heavy sweet cream
2 cups self-rising flour, sifted
1 6-ounce package chocolate
chips, optional
2 tablespoons orange rind plus
1 tablespoon orange juice,
optional

Cream eggs and sugar at low speed. Add cream and beat until smooth. Slowly add flour and blend. Before baking, chocolate chips or orange rind and juice may be added. Bake at 325°-350° in spring form pan for 40 minutes, in 2 9-inch layer pans for 15-20 minutes, or in 18 cupcakes for 15-20 minutes.

Lois Kuh

Crumb Cake

4 eggs, separated
½ cup margarine
½-¾ cup sugar
2 cups stale cake crumbs
1 teaspoon baking powder
1 cup milk or milk substitute
1 teaspoon vanilla
½ can coconut, flaked

Beat egg whites until peaks form. Cream shortening, sugar and egg yolks. Alternate crumbs and baking powder with milk. Add vanilla, add coconut, and fold in egg whites. Bake in greased 9 x 9 pan at 350° for 45 minutes.

Lemon Frosting
2 tablespoons margarine
1 cup confectioners sugar
Lemon juice to spread

Combine ingredients and frost cake when cool.

Ruth Goldberg

Indio Date Cake

1 teaspoon baking soda
¼ teaspoon salt
1 cup boiling water
1½ cups dates, pitted, chopped
3 tablespoons butter
1 cup sugar
1 egg, separated
1½ cups flour
½ cup walnuts, chopped
Powdered sugar

Add baking soda and salt to boiling water. Pour over dates. Let stand twenty minutes. Meanwhile, cream together butter and sugar. Beat in egg yolk, flour and the date mixture. Combine thoroughly, then add walnuts. Finally, beat the egg white until stiff, but not dry, and fold into the mixture. Pour into a buttered 8 x 12 baking pan and bake at 350° for 30 to 40 minutes, or until it shrinks away from the edges of the pan. Cool, sprinkle top with powdered sugar and cut in squares to serve.

Ettie Rubenstein

Dump Cake

1 16-ounce can crushed pineapple
1 1-pound 5-ounce can cherry pie filling
1 box cake mix, white or yellow
1 8-ounce package coconut
1 8-ounce package chopped nuts
½ pound butter

Butter 9 x 13 cake pan. Pour crushed pineapple, juice and all into pan; add can of cherry filling. Dump cake mix directly from box over this. Add coconut and chopped nuts. Melt butter and pour on top of this mixture. Bake at 300° for 1¼ hours. Serves 12.

Eulah Feier

Fruit Cake

1 pound dates
1 pound candied cherries
½ pound Brazil nuts
½ pound walnuts
½ pound pecans
4 eggs, beaten

1½ cups sugar
1½ cups flour
2 teaspoons baking powder
1 cup crushed pineapple
1 ounce brandy, (optional)

Combine fruit and nuts whole. Combine with batter of eggs and dry ingredients. Add pineapple (not drained). Bake in two greased and floured loaf pans 9 x 5, at 350° for 1 hour. If desired, pour brandy over warm cake.

Stella Gelman

Funny Cake

1 9-inch pie crust, unbaked
1 cup flour
¾ cup sugar
1 teaspoon baking powder
½ teaspoon salt

¼ cup soft margarine
½ cup milk or pareve cream
½ teaspoon vanilla
1 egg

Stir together flour, sugar, baking powder and salt. Add soft margarine, milk or pareve cream, and vanilla. Beat 2 minutes at medium speed. Add egg and beat 2 more minutes. Pour into pie crust.

Chocolate Sauce

1½ squares baking chocolate
½ cup water
2/3 cup sugar

¼ cup margarine
1½ teaspoons vanilla
Chopped nuts

Melt chocolate with water and add sugar. Bring to a boil, stirring constantly. Remove from heat. Add margarine and vanilla. Pour over cake batter and sprinkle with nuts. Bake at 350° for 55 minutes.

Ruth Goldberg

Honey Cake

½ cup shortening
1 cup sugar
3 eggs
1 cup cold coffee
1 teaspoon baking soda
Pinch salt
2 teaspoons baking powder

3 cups flour
Rind of ½ orange
1 teaspoon cinnamon
1 full shot whiskey
1 cup honey
1 teaspoon vanilla
¾ cup chopped nuts

Cream shortening and sugar; add eggs one at a time. Combine coffee and baking soda — set aside. Sift together flour, baking powder and salt — set aside. Combine orange rind, cinnamon, whiskey and honey; add to creamed ingredients. Add the coffee mixture and dry ingredients alternately to the mixture. Beat slowly. Blend in vanilla and nuts. Pour into greased 9 x 13 pan. Bake at 350° for 1 hour.

Sylvia Wynar

One Bowl Honey Cake

1 cup sugar
3 cups sifted flour
1½ teaspoons baking powder
1½ teaspoons baking soda
1 teaspoon salt
1 teaspoon cinnamon
1 teaspoon allspice
1 teaspoon clove

1 teaspoon nutmeg
1 cup honey
1 cup strong coffee, cooled
¾ cup oil
1 teaspoon vanilla
3 eggs
½ cup raisins
½ cup chopped nuts

Sift all dry ingredients into large bowl. Make a well and add all liquid ingredients. Mix together thoroughly and add raisins and nuts. Bake at 350° for 45-60 minutes in a well-greased tube pan.

Carrie Roxin and Jill Musicus

Honey Chiffon Cake

3½ cups sifted flour
2½ teaspoons baking powder
1 teaspoon baking soda
½ teaspoon salt
1 teaspoon cinnamon
3 eggs, separated
1-1/3 cups hot tea

½ teaspoon ground cloves
¼ teaspoon ginger
1 cup sugar
¼ cup oil
1 pound honey
¼ teaspoon cream of tartar
1/3 cup chopped nuts, optional

Mix and sift dry ingredients. Make a well and add the egg yolks, oil, honey and tea; mix. Beat egg whites and cream of tartar until very stiff. Fold into the other mixture. Pour into ungreased 9-inch tube pan and bake at 350° for one hour. Invert until cold.

Lee Kucker

Honey Sponge Cake

6 eggs, separated
½ pound honey (1 cup)
2 cups flour
½ cup cooled black coffee

½ teaspoon baking powder
½ teaspoon soda
1 cup sugar
½ cup nuts (optional)

Beat egg yolks and add honey and sugar. Mix well. Add sifted dry ingredients alternately with coffee. Beat egg whites and fold in carefully. Add nuts. Bake in a tube pan for 45 to 60 minutes at 350°.

Mrs. Milton Hitter

Honey and Orange Cake

2 cups sifted cake flour
3½ teaspoons baking powder
½ teaspoon salt
½ cup sugar
½ cup vegetable shortening

2/3 cup honey
2 eggs, separated
½ cup orange juice
¼ teaspoon grated orange rind

Sift dry ingtedients together, set aside. Cream shortening, sugar and honey until very light. Beat in egg yolks, one at a time. Blend in dry ingredients alternately with juice and rind. Mix well, but do not overbeat. Fold in stiffly beaten egg whites. Bake in square pan or two 9-inch layer pans for 30 minutes at 350°. Cool, frost with orange confectioners frosting.

Ethel Simon

Honey Pecan Cake

1 tablespoon vinegar
1 scant cup milk
1 cup cooking oil
1½ cups sugar
3 eggs
1 teaspoon vanilla

2 cups sifted all-purpose flour
3 teaspoons baking powder
½ teaspoon baking soda
1 teaspoon ground cinnamon
¼ teaspoon ground cloves
½ cup chopped pecans

Honey Syrup
¼ cup honey
1 tablespoon water

1 tablespoon lemon juice

Combine vinegar and enough milk to make one cup; set aside. Stir cooking oil into sugar, add eggs and vanilla. Beat one minute at medium speed. Sift together flour, baking powder, baking soda, cinnamon and cloves. Add to creamed mixture alternately with sour milk. Beat one minute more. Stir in chopped pecans. Pour into greased ten-inch fluted tube pan. Bake in 350° oven for 40 minutes. Let stand 10 minutes. Meanwhile, boil together honey, water and lemon juice. Remove cake from pan. Prick holes in hot cake and drizzle with honey syrup.

Gigg Posner

Marble Chiffon Cake

¼ cup sugar
¼ cup cocoa
¼ cup boiling water
¼ teaspoon red food color
2 cups flour
1½ cups sugar
1 teaspoon salt

3 teaspoons baking powder
6 eggs, separated
½ cup vegetable oil
¾ cup water
2 teaspoons vanilla
½ teaspoon cream of tartar

Sift sugar and cocoa together and mix with boiling water and food color; set aside. Sift dry ingredients together into large bowl; make a well with a spoon and add egg yolks, oil, water and vanilla. Beat for 2 minutes; set aside. Beat egg whites with cream of tartar until stiff, but not dry; fold into egg yolk mixture. Take off ½ batter and mix it with cocoa mixture. Alternate layers of white and chocolate mixtures into ungreased 10-inch tube pan. Bake in preheated oven at 325° for 55 minutes, then 350° for 15 minutes. Invert until cool.

Ruth Bittker

Mocha Cake

2 cups flour
2½ teaspoons baking powder
1 cup butter (or ½ vegetable
   shortening, ½ margarine)
4 eggs, separated

1 cup cold black coffee
2 cups sugar
1 cup sweet cocoa
1 cup chopped nuts (optional)

Cream butter and sugar. Add beaten egg yolks. Add sifted dry ingredients, alternating with coffee. Add nuts and vanilla and fold in stiffly beaten egg whites. Bake at 375° in a 10-inch tube pan for 45 minutes or until done.

Bea Horn

Nut Cake

1 cup butter	2 cups sifted cake flour
1 cup sugar	1 teaspoon baking soda
3 eggs, separated	1 teaspoon baking powder
2 tablespoons orange and lemon rind	¾ cup sour cream or buttermilk
	1 cup ground walnuts or filberts

Cream butter and sugar. Add yolks and beat. Add orange and lemon rind. Sift flour, soda and baking powder. Add alternately with sour cream. Add ground nuts. Fold in stiffly beaten egg whites. Bake at 350° for 1 hour in greased tube pan.

Topping

¾ cup sugar	2 tablespoons lemon juice
2 tablespoons orange juice	

Bring ingredients to a boil. Prick cake with fork. Pour boiling glaze over top of cake.

May Lovenheim

Nut Roll

7 eggs	Sifted powdered sugar
¾ cup sugar	2 cups heavy cream, whipped
1½ cups ground walnuts	1 teaspoon vanilla
1 teaspoon baking powder	1 teaspoon confectioners sugar

Brush 10 x 15 pan with oil. Line with wax paper and oil the paper. Separate eggs, add sugar to yolks, and with a heavy beater mix until pale and thick enough to ribbon off the beater. Add nuts and baking powder. Beat egg whites until stiff. Fold egg whites into yolk mixture. Spread batter in pan and bake for 15-20 minutes at 350° or until golden. Cool cake right in pan. Cover with damp towel when cool and put in refrigerator for ½ hour. Take out and dust top of cake generously with sifted powdered sugar. Turn out on board covered with two sheets of wax paper (sheets overlapping). Carefully strip paper from bottom of cake and spread with whipped cream, flavored with vanilla and confectioners sugar. Roll cake (long side) with aid of wax paper. Place on a flat serving platter and sprinkle with sifted powdered sugar. Keep in refrigerator. May be frozen.

Zelda Bilfield

Orange Liqueur Cake

½ pound butter	1 teaspoon baking powder
1½ cups sugar	1 teaspoon baking soda
½ pint sour cream	Rind of 1 orange, grated
2 cups flour	2 ounces fresh orange juice
3 eggs, separated	1/3 cup orange liqueur

Mix butter with 1 cup sugar until light and fluffy. Add yolks to mixture and beat after each addition. Sift together flour, baking powder and soda. Add alternately to mixture with sour cream, beginning and ending with flour. Add rind. Beat egg whites until stiff but not dry. Fold into mixture, carefully. Grease 9-inch tube pan. Bake at 350° for 50 minutes. Mix ½ cup sugar, liqueur and orange juice. Pour over cake while still hot. Remove from pan when cool.

Martha Lovenheim

Fruity Orange Cake

2 cups all-purpose flour	1 cup seedless raisins
1 cup sugar	½ cup vegetable shortening
1 teaspoon salt	½ cup buttermilk or sour milk
1 teaspoon baking soda	¼ teaspoon lemon flavoring
1 medium unpeeled orange	2 eggs, unbeaten

Sift flour, sugar, salt and soda in large mixing bowl of electric mixer. Slice the orange and grind. Grind the raisins with the orange. To flour mixture, add shortening, milk and lemon flavoring and 1 egg. Beat 2 minutes and then add 2nd egg and beat 2 more minutes. Add orange and raisins and beat 1 minute at low speed. Pour into 8 inch tube pan, well greased and floured. Bake in 350° oven for 1 hour, 20 minutes. (It's a heavy cake.) Frost when cool.

Frosting

1 tablespoon vegetable shortening	1 teaspoon grated orange rind
1 tablespoon butter	2 cups confectioners sugar
½ teaspoon salt	2-3 tablespoons orange juice

Mix all ingredients well and frost.

Zelda Bilfield

Pareve Orange Cake

2 eggs	2 cups flour
¾ cup sugar	2 teaspoons baking powder
¾ cup vegetable oil	¼ teaspoon salt
¾ cup orange juice	Rind of one large orange

Beat eggs and sugar together thoroughly. Add oil and beat; add orange juice. Beat well. Sift flour, baking powder and salt together and add to mixture. Stir slowly until completely blended. Bake in greased 8- or 9-inch square pan at 325° for 30 to 45 minutes.

Sara Morris

Picnic Cake

½ cup shortening	½ teaspoon salt
1½ cups sugar	1 teaspoon vanilla
2 eggs	12 marshmallows
1 cup milk	½ cup brown sugar
2½ cups cake flour, sifted	½ cup chopped nuts
3 teaspoons baking powder	

Cream shortening, sugar and eggs well. Sift flour, baking powder and salt and add to shortening mixture alternately with milk. Add vanilla. Pour into greased and floured pan, 8 x 12. Cut marshmallows crosswise and arrange over batter. Sprinkle brown sugar and nut mixture over all. Bake at 350° for 45 minutes.

Mim Bogdonoff

Poppy Seed Cake

¾ cup shortening
1½ cups sugar
2 cups flour
1 teaspoon vanilla
½ cup poppy seeds soaked in

¾ cup water
2 teaspoons baking powder
2 egg yolks
3 egg whites
½ teaspoon salt

Cream shortening and sugar, add egg yolks, cream well. Add poppy seeds and water, then flavoring. Add sifted dry ingredients and fold in stiffly beaten egg whites. Bake in greased tube or bundt pan 50 minutes at 375° .

Mim Block and Carol Winterman

Poppy Seed Cake

1 cup butter
1½ cups sugar
12-ounce can or 1½ cups poppy
  seed filling
4 eggs, separated

1 teaspoon vanilla
1 cup sour cream
2½ cups sifted enriched flour
1 teaspoon soda
1 teaspoon salt

Poppy Seed Filling
2 cups poppy seed
1 cup milk
¾ cup honey

1 teaspoon grated lemon rind
½ cup seedless raisins

Grind poppy seeds (put through food chopper). Combine with milk and honey. Cook over low heat, stirring often until thick. Add lemon rind and raisins. Cool. Best made day ahead.

Cream butter and sugar until light and fluffy. Add poppy seed filling. Add egg yolks, one at a time, beating well after each addition. Blend in vanilla and sour cream. Sift together dry ingredients. Add gradually to mixture, beating well again after each addition. Fold in stiffly beaten egg whites. Pour into a well greased 9-inch or 10-inch tube pan, bottom lined with waxed paper. Bake in 350° oven for 1¼ to 1½ hours. Cool approximately 10 minutes. Remove from pan and peel off waxed paper. Sprinkle with confectioners sugar.

Fitzie Levine

Pound Cake

½ pound butter or margarine
2 cups sugar
4 eggs, separated
3 cups flour

1 cup milk or mocha mix
3 teaspoons baking powder
1 teaspoon vanilla or lemon

Cream butter, sugar and beaten yolks until light yellow. Add flour, baking powder and milk alternately. Add stiffly beaten egg whites and flavoring. Put in 2 greased loaf pans or a 10-inch tube pan. Bake 1 hour at 350° .

Lois Kwasman

Sour Cream Pound Cake

½ pound butter
3 cups sugar
¼ teaspoon baking soda
½ pint dairy sour cream

1½ teaspoons vanilla
6 eggs
3 cups sifted flour

Cream butter and sugar; add soda; add sour cream, vanilla. Add eggs two at a time, with one cup flour until all eggs and flour are added, beating well after each addition. Pour into 8-inch greased tube pan and bake in 325° oven for 1½ hours.

Alyne Phillips

Pumpkin Cake

4 eggs
2 cups sugar
1 cup oil
2 cups pumpkin pie filling
3 cups flour
2 teaspoons baking powder

2 teaspoons baking soda
½ teaspoon salt
½ teaspoon cinnamon
1 cup nuts or 6-ounce package chocolate chips

Cream eggs and sugar. Add remaining ingredients. Mix well. Pour into greased bundt or tube pan. Bake at 350° for 1 hour and 10 minutes.

Bea Horn

Chocolate Chip Raisin Cake

1 cup hot water
1 teaspoon baking soda
1 cup raisins
3 eggs
1 cup margarine or butter
1 cup sugar
3 cups flour

2 teaspoons baking powder
Pinch of salt
1 teaspoon vanilla
⅛-¼ cup orange juice
1 6-ounce package chocolate chips

Mix hot water, baking soda and raisins; refrigerate for 1 hour. Cream butter and sugar and add eggs. Drain raisins, reserving liquid which you add to vanilla and orange juice. Sift dry ingredients, adding raisins and chocolate chips; add to creamed mixture, then add liquid mixture. Bake in well-greased tube pan at 350° for 1 hour.

Nina Olin

Toffee Topped Cake

2 cups brown sugar
2 cups all-purpose flour
¼ pound butter
1 cup milk

1 teaspoon baking soda
Pinch salt
6 ¾-ounce Heath bars

Mix brown sugar and flour; cut in butter, as for pie crust. Reserve 1 cup for topping. Add milk, baking soda, and salt to first mixture, beat well. Spread in greased and floured 9 x 13 pan. Sprinkle with reserved cup of topping. Cut Heath bars into small pieces, then crush finely between two pieces of wax paper, with a rolling pin; sprinkle over cake batter. Bake at 350° for 30-35 minutes. Serve warm with ice cream.

T''Mahry Axelrod

Pistachio Cream Sponge Roll

4 eggs
¾ teaspoon baking powder
¼ teaspoon salt
¾ cup granulated sugar
1 teaspoon vanilla, or
½ teaspoon almond extract

¾ cup flour
1½ cups heavy cream
¼ cup confectioners sugar
2 tablespoons orange liqueur
¼ cup unsalted pistachio nuts
A little confectioners sugar

Brush a 15 x 10-inch jelly roll pan with shortening and then line with wax paper and grease a second time. Preheat oven to 400° . Beat eggs at room temperature with baking powder and salt. Beat until thick and light golden in color. Gradually beat in granulated sugar. Continue beating until mixture forms a ribbon when the beaters are lifted from the bowl. Add vanilla or ½ teaspoon almond extract. Beat briefly. Sift flour. Using a rubber spatula, fold the flour very gently but thoroughly into the batter. Pour batter into the prepared pan. Spread and smooth evenly. Bake 13 minutes or until done. (test with cake tester or toothpick.) Spread a clean towel on a flat surface. Sprinkle the center area generously with confectioners sugar. Immediately turn cake out onto sugared towel. Quickly remove the wax paper. Roll the cake jelly-roll-style, starting with the long side and enclosing the towel inside. Cool the roll on a rack. When cool, unroll. Whip heavy cream and add ¼ cup confectioners sugar, orange liqueur and unsalted pistachio nuts. Spread evenly. Reroll the cake, enclosing the filling. Sprinkle with additional confectioners sugar. Makes 8 or more servings. Any filling can be used.

Bea Horn

Lemon Frosted Walnut Cake

2 cups sifted cake flour
1 tablespoon instant coffee
1 teaspoon baking soda
¾ teaspoon salt
½ cup finely chopped walnuts
½ cup butter or margarine

1¼ cups sugar
2 teaspoons vanilla
2 eggs
¼ cup lemon juice
¾ cup light cream

Sift together flour, instant coffee, baking soda and salt. Combine with chopped nuts. Cream margarine and sugar and add vanilla. Add eggs and beat about 2 minutes, until fluffy. Combine lemon juice and cream. Add dry ingredients to creamed mixture alternately with liquids, beginning and ending with dry mixture. Beat well after each addition. Pour batter into 2 greased and floured 8-inch round layer cake pans. Bake at 375° for about 30 minutes. Cool before frosting.

Lemon Frosting

3½ cups confectioners sugar
½ cup butter or margarine
2 teaspoons light cream

½ cup chopped walnuts
Lemon juice

Cream butter and sugar. Add cream and enough lemon juice for spreading consistency. Spread frosting mixture between layers and over cake. Decorate with chopped walnuts or walnut halves.

Hattie Lipsky

Chocolate Nut Torte

5 eggs	2½ cups cake flour
2½ cups sugar	⅛ teaspoon salt
1 tablespoon butter or margarine	2½ teaspoons baking powder
1¼ cups milk, scalded	1 teaspoon vanilla

Beat eggs until light. Gradually add 1 cup sugar and beat well. Add remaining sugar and beat until light colored and fluffy. Combine butter and hot milk; add gradually to egg mixture. Add sifted dry ingredients and vanilla. Mix well. Bake in 2 waxed paper lined 9-inch layer pans at 350° for 30 minutes. Cool and cut layers in half.

Chocolate Nut Torte Frosting

2 cups milk	1 cup butter or margarine
½ cup granulated sugar	1 cup confectioners sugar
½ cup enriched flour	2 teaspoons vanilla
¼ cup cocoa	1½ cups chopped walnuts
1/3 cup cold milk	

Heat 2 cups milk in double boiler. Combine sugar, flour, cocoa and cold milk. Add to hot milk and cook over hot water until thickened, about 20 minutes, stirring constantly. Remove from heat, cover and cool to room temperature. Thoroughly cream butter and confectioners sugar. Add to cooked, cooled mixture. Beat smooth. Spread between layers and over entire cake. Sprinkle with chopped nuts on top and press to sides. Serves 16.

Lil Orlen

Dobos Torte

Batter

½ cup all-purpose flour	½ cup confectioners sugar
Dash salt	1 teaspoon vanilla
1 teaspoon baking powder	Rind of 1 lemon
8 eggs, separated	

Sift flour, salt and baking powder. Beat yolks until light and lemon colored. Gradually beat in sugar and with last addition, add vanilla and lemon rind. Gradually add flour and beat well. Beat egg whites until stiff, but not dry, and fold in lightly. Grease 4 layer pans and powder with flour. Spread ½ mixture thinly into pans. Reserve half batter for remaining 4 layers. Bake 5-7 minutes at 350°. Remove cake at once from pans. Grease and refill pans with remaining batter. Set layers aside to cool.

Filling

½ pound sweet butter	Instant coffee
½ cup confectioners sugar	2 tablespoons cocoa
1 teaspoon vanilla	2 egg yolks
Lemon juice	

Cream all ingredients together for rich pudding like consistency. Spread filling evenly between layers.

Mrs. E. Palage

My Mother's Torte

Fine dry bread crumbs
½ cup sifted flour
1 teaspoon baking powder
½ teaspoon salt
1 cup finely grated walnuts
¼ pound butter

1 cup granulated sugar
5 eggs
6 1-ounce squares semi-sweet
  chocolate
Confectioners sugar

Butter the bottom of a 9-inch spring form pan. Sprinkle lightly with bread crumbs. Sift together flour, baking powder and salt. Stir in walnuts and set aside. In large bowl, cream butter and sugar and set aside. Separate eggs. Beat egg yolks slightly. Add to butter mixture and beat well. Stir in sifted dry ingredients. With clean beaters, beat egg whites until straight stiff peaks form when beater is slightly withdrawn. Fold into flour mixture. Grate chocolate squares with Mouli hand grater. Fold into batter. Turn into prepared pan. Bake in pre-heated oven at 350° until cake springs back when lightly pressed with fingers, 50-60 minutes. Cool in pan on wire rack for 10 minutes. Remove sides of pan and continue cooling on rack. For serving, leave bottom of spring form pan under torte or loosen bottom with spatula and remove. Sprinkle with confectioners sugar or for a special occasion serve with a bowl of whipped cream.

Fritzie Levine

Trinidad Torte

2 cups flour
1 teaspoon baking powder
1 teaspoon baking soda
4 ounces chopped walnuts
½ pound butter or margarine
1 cup sugar
3 eggs, separated

¾ cup sour cream
2 tablespoons grated orange rind
2 tablespoons grated lemon rind
⅛ teaspoon salt
Fine dry bread crumbs or graham cracker crumbs

Sift together flour, baking powder and baking soda. Stir a few tablespoons of dry ingredients into walnuts. Set both mixtures aside. Cream butter or margarine and sugar together, beat in egg yolks one at a time. Add dry ingredients alternately with sour cream. Add nuts and stir in grated rinds. Beat egg whites with salt until they form a peak and fold into batter. Pour batter into greased spring form pan or bundt pan which has been coated with crumbs. Smooth top by shaking briskly back and forth. Bake 45-60 minutes at 350° or until cake tests done.

Glaze

¾ cup sugar
2 tablespoons orange juice

2 tablespoons lemon juice

A few minutes before removing cake from oven, prepare glaze by mixing juices in saucepan. Bring to a boil, stirring until sugar dissolves. When cake is done quickly prick top with sharp knife and brush hot glaze over hot cake. Let cake cool in pan. Serves 10.

Ruth Bloom

Nut Cake Torte

6 eggs, separated
1 cup sugar
1 teaspoon vanilla
1 cup graham cracker crumbs
⅛ teaspoon cocoa
⅛ teaspoon instant coffee
1 teaspoon baking powder
1½ cups ground fine walnuts

Beat egg whites until stiff but not dry. Set aside. In separate bowl beat egg yolks until light and fluffy. Beat sugar into yolks and then add vanilla. Fold egg whites into egg yolk mixture and then fold in graham cracker crumbs, cocoa, instant coffee and baking powder. Fold nuts gently into batter. Grease two 9-inch pans; cover with wax paper and grease again. Dust with flour. Pour ½ of mixture into each. Bake at 350° for 30 minutes. Test with cake tester or toothpick. Invert to cool. Trim with whipped cream.

Bea Horn

Apricot Filling

½ pound dried apricots
½ cup sugar
½ cup crushed pineapple drained
1 cup chopped nuts

Wash apricots; barely cover with water. Add sugar; cover and simmer slowly for 30 minutes, strain; add pineapple and nuts; Cool. Spread between layers.

Millie Rosenbaum

Fresh Coconut Filling

1 cup sugar
1 tablespoon cornstarch
Milk from one coconut
1 tablespoon lemon juice
1 fresh coconut, grated
1 cup chopped nuts

Mix sugar and cornstarch; add gradually to coconut milk. Cook over low heat until thick, stirring constantly. Add lemon juice, coconut and nuts; cool. Will fill one 3-layer cake.

Betty Tuchman

Strawberry Filling or Frosting

1 egg white
1 cup sugar
1 cup fresh strawberries

Whip all ingredients together until stiff enough to spread on cake layers. Will frost one 2 layer cake.

Sour Cream Filling

1 cup sugar
1 cup sour cream
1 cup chopped nuts
1 teaspoon vanilla flavoring

Combine sugar, cream and nuts. Cook to soft ball stage. Remove from heat. Add vanilla. Stir until slightly cooled. Will fill layers and top of 3 layer cake or will frost one 13 x 9 cake. Excellent for heavier cakes, such as raisin, pumpkin, walnut.

T'Mahry Axelrod

Boiled Frosting

½ cup boiling water
1 cup sugar
1 egg white
¼ teaspoon cream of tartar
1 teaspoon vanilla flavoring
Food coloring, if desired

Pour boiling water over sugar, egg white and cream of tartar. Beat with electric beater at high speed for several minutes. When frosting peaks, add vanilla. Add food coloring to all or part of mixture as desired. Will frost one 2 layer cake.

Betty Tuchman

Butter Cream Frosting

3 tablespoons butter
3 tablespoons milk
3 tablespoons brown sugar

1½ cups sifted confectioners sugar
1 teaspoon vanilla flavoring

Mix first 3 ingredients together and bring to a boil. Add sugar and mix well; stir in flavoring.

Chocolate Butter Cream Frosting

2 squares baking chocolate or
2 packets Baker's Redi-Choc
1/3 cup margarine
1 egg

3 cups sifted confectioner's sugar
¼ teaspoon salt
1 teaspoon vanilla

Cream margarine and egg. Add melted chocolate, sugar and salt. Add vanilla and beat until creamy. This frosting stays moist and soft.

Millie Rosenbaum

Chocolate Frosting

1 cup heavy cream
1 cup milk

1 package instant chocolate pudding

Beat above ingredients together. Frost cake when cool. For mocha flavor, add powdered instant coffee to taste. Vary flavor according to choice.

Bea Horn

Decorator's Frosting

1 large egg white
½ cup shortening
1 pound confectioners sugar

1/3 cup evaporated milk
½ teaspoon vanilla flavoring
½ teaspoon almond flavoring

Beat egg white and shortening with electric mixer. Add sugar alternately with milk. Add flavorings; beat well. Refrigerate until used. May be tinted with food coloring. Will cover 2 cakes.

Triple-Six Frosting

6 tablespoons hot strong coffee
6 tablespoons butter
6 tablespoons cocoa

1 teaspoon rum flavoring
1 box confectioners suger, sifted

Blend coffee, butter and cocoa, allow to cool for 20 minutes. Add rum flavoring. Gradually add sugar, blending after each addition; beat well. Will frost one 2-layer cake.

Margie Wiseman

Cherry Heering Glaze

½ cup Cherry Heering
½ cup water
1 tablespoon potato or corn

starch
2 tablespoons sugar

Cook until thick. Pour over cooled cake. May be used on sponge, white, coconut, lemon, and other cakes.

Bea Horn

Cheese and Eggs

Cheese Blintzes

Leaves	Filling
2 eggs	¼ pound cream cheese
2 tablespoons salad oil	¼ pound cottage cheese
1 cup milk	2 egg yolks
¾ cup flour	2 tablespoons sugar
½ teaspoon salt	1 teaspoon vanilla extract

Beat eggs, oil and milk together in a bowl. Add flour, salt and beat until very smooth. Chill for 30 minutes. Beat all ingredients of filling until smooth. Melt 1 teaspoon butter in 7-inch skillet. Pour 1 tablespoon of the batter into skillet, turning the pan quickly so batter will cover the bottom. Fry until lightly browned on one side only. Turn out onto a clean towel. Stack the blintzes, browned side up, until all the batter is used. Add additional butter as required. Place 1 tablespoon of the filling on each of the blintzes. Turn two opposite sides in a little bit, and then roll up. Fry the blintzes until lightly browned on both sides. Can be frozen.

Marcia G. Shapiro

Cheese Blintzes

Leaves	Filling
1 cup milk	1 pound pressed cheese
½ cup water	1 egg
2 eggs	¼ teaspoon white pepper
¼ teaspoon salt	2 tablespoons sour cream*
1 cup flour	

Put milk, water, eggs and salt into bowl. Add flour. With a fork moisten flour with liquid mixture. Mix at medium speed in electric mixer until thoroughly blended. Let stand for at least an hour until all bubbles are gone. Meanwhile, prepare cheese filling. Mix cheese, eggs, and pepper in a large bowl until thoroughly blended. *If dry, add sour cream. Set aside. Using a 9-inch frying pan, heat pan and then grease well with shortening. Pour ½ cup of leave mixture into frying pan. Keep turning until pan is coated. Pour off excess. Cook over medium heat until edges begin to curl. Turn out on board. Put 2 tablespoons of cheese mixture in middle. Fold over sides. Roll up. Place on platter until all are done. Continue above process until all ingredients are used. Fry on both sides until golden brown. Can be used immediately or frozen and reheated in oven.

Sarah Derman

Palacsinta (Hungarian Blintzes)

Batter	Filling
½ cup milk	1 pound farmer cheese
4 eggs	1 tablespoon butter or margarine
½ lemon rind, grated	2 tablespoons sugar
Dash salt	2 heaping tablespoons sour cream
2 tablespoons sugar	Vanilla
10 tablespoons flour	Grated lemon rind

To ¼ cup milk, add eggs and mix well with beater. Add lemon, salt, sugar and flour; mix well. Add rest of milk and mix thoroughly with beater. If still too thick, add more milk. Pour small amount into hot greased frying pan. When batter begins to fry, pour off excess. When shell is formed, turn out fried side up by inverting skillet over a towel. Fill with 1-2 tablespoons of filling. Fold edges to form a square, bake in a greased pan in 350° oven until **brown. Sprinkle with sifted confectioners sugar.**

Elizabeth Palage

Quiche Lorraine (Frozen)

One unbaked pie crust shell
1½ cups grated imported,
   Swiss cheese
4 tablespoons flour
¼ pound Nova lox

3 eggs
1 cup light cream
¼ teaspoon salt
Parsley
Pimento

Prepare one 9'' pie crust shell. Place in 9'' shiny pan only. Flute edges high. Do not bake. Combine grated Swiss cheese and flour. Sprinkle into pie shell. Place lox pieces over this mixture. Combine eggs, cream, and salt. Beat until smooth and pour over lox and cheese mixture. Partially fill and place in freezer; when cold, pour balance of filling from a pitcher. Freeze an hour and wrap carefully in foil or plastic bag. May be stored until used. Before serving, bake in 375° oven for 1¼ hours or until set. (Do not defrost — place in oven frozen). Protect crust with foil if it gets too brown. Cool slightly. Garnish with parsley and pimento. Serves 8.

Beula Sonders

Quiche Lorraine

Pastry shell

2 cups sifted flour
½ teaspoon salt
2 pinches sugar
¼ pound butter, in small pieces

3 tablespoons chilled shortening
5 tablespoons water
Bacos

Cut together first 5 ingredients. Add water and gather dough together into a ball and place on lightly floured pastry cloth. Using heel of hand, press pastry away from you in quick smears to fully blend flour and shortening. Gather dough again into a ball, sprinkle with flour, and refrigerate wrapped, for at least 1 hour. Roll dough into circle ⅛-inch thick about 2 inches larger than pie plate. When placing dough onto pie plate, make sides of shell a bit thicker and sturdier. Prick bottom with fork at ½-inch intervals. Press buttered foil on dough, and fill with dried beans (to prevent puffing up during baking). Bake at 400° for 8-9 minutes. Remove foil and beans. Prick bottom. Bake 2-3 minutes more. Remove from oven when beginning to brown and shrink from sides of mold. Sprinkle Bacos liberally into bottom of pastry shell.

Filling

3 eggs
1½-2 cups cream
½ teaspoon salt
Pinch pepper

Pinch nutmeg
½ cup grated Swiss cheese
½ tablespoon butter, in small
   pieces

Beat first 5 ingredients. Add Swiss cheese and pour into prebaked pastry shell. Sprinkle pieces of butter over top. Set pan in upper third of 375° oven. Bake 25-30 minutes or until quiche has puffed, jelled, and browned. Serve immediately for luncheon or for first course of dinner.

Judy Kaplan

Easy Quiche Lorraine

1 cup crushed saltine crackers	4 eggs
⅛ pound butter	1 cup milk
½ cup chopped onions	½ cup grated sharp cheese

Combine cracker crumbs and softened butter; pat into bottom and sides of 9'' pie plate to form crust. Saute onions and sprinkle over crust. Beat eggs, add milk and let settle a few minutes. Pour into crust over onions. Sprinkle with cheese. Bake in 350° oven for 25 minutes or until set. Serves 8.

Inez Lipman

Cottage Cheese Latkes

3 eggs	1 teaspoon salt
1 cup flour	¾ cup milk
1 tablespoon sugar	½ pound cottage cheese

Mash cottage cheese and combine with remaining ingredients. Heat oil in frying pan and drop in 1 tablespoon of mixture for each pancake.

Bunny Skirboll

Easy Cheese Souffle

6 eggs, separated	cheese soup
1 can condensed cheddar	Grated Italian cheese, optional

Beat egg whites until stiff; then beat egg yolks separately until thick and lemon colored. Heat soup and stir in egg yolks. Fold into egg whites. Put into greased 2-quart casserole. Sprinkle with cheese. Bake in slow oven at 300° for 1 hour or until firm. Serves 4-6.

Bunny Zigman

Egg Cheddar Souffle

2 cups croutons	½ teaspoon mustard, prepared
1 cup grated cheddar cheese	⅛ teaspoon onion powder
4 eggs, slightly beaten	Dash pepper
2 cups milk	Bacos
½ teaspoon salt	

Spread croutons and cheese in a 10 x 6 greased baking pan. Mix remaining ingredients together and pour over croutons and cheese. Sprinkle top liberally with Bacos. Bake at 325° for 55-60 minutes or until eggs are set. Serves 6.

Judy Kaplan

Cheese Souffle

6 slices white bread	3 large eggs
1 small jar blended American	1 pint Half and Half
cheese spread	Garlic salt to taste, optional

Remove crusts from bread and spread with cheese spread. Cut slices in halves or quarters and place in lightly greased souffle-type casserole. Beat eggs well; add Half and Half and garlic salt. Mix well. Cover bread with egg mixture and let stand in refrigerator overnight or for several hours. Bake uncovered at 350° for 50 minutes. Serves 4-5.

Mildred Feinberg

Cheese-Puff-Souffle

12 slices buttered bread, preferably challah
3 cups grated sharp cheddar
  cheese
1 pound fresh or 2 packages
  frozen broccoli, optional

1½ teaspoons dry mustard
6 eggs, well beaten
6 cups milk
1½ teaspoons salt
¼ teaspoon pepper

Cut crusts off bread and place enough bread in pan to cover bottom. Cover this with cheese, then broccoli, bread, cheese for 2 layers (or until used up.) Mix together rest of ingredients and pour over layers. Let stand overnight in refrigerator. Bake at 350° for 30-45 minutes, in a 9 x 13 greased pan.

Ruth Salesin

Cheese in Buns

½ pound American cheese
  slices, diced
1 cup chopped celery

1/3 cup minced dill pickles
2 tablespoons chili sauce
3 tablespoons mayonnaise

Mix ingredients together. Place spoonful into hamburger rolls. Put toothpicks at ends of rolls. Heat in slow oven about 20 minutes.

Esther Parsky

Welsh Rarebit

2 cans mushroom soup
½ soup can of milk
1½-2 cups sharp cheddar
  cheese
1 teaspoon dry mustard

2 teaspoons Worcestershire
  sauce
Cayenne pepper to taste
1 hard boiled egg per person
  (approximately 6)

Toast patty shells, or English muffins. Melt cheese in mushroom soup and milk in double boiler or chafing dish. Add seasonings. Add eggs, cut into halves. Serve on toast, patty shells or toasted English muffins. Serves 6.

Renee Rosenbaum

Savory Eggs for Brunch

2 cups American cheese, shredded or grated
¼ cup butter
1 cup Half & Half

½ teaspoon salt, scant
¼ teaspoon pepper
2 teaspoons prepared mustard
12 eggs, slightly beaten

Spread cheese in greased 13 x 9 baking dish. Dot with butter. Combine Half and Half, salt, pepper and mustard. Pour half mixture over cheese. Pour eggs into baking dish. Add remaining mixture. Bake at 325° until set, about 40 minutes. Serves 10-12.

Edith Perlman

Letchow

2 tomatoes, peeled and quartered
2 green peppers, cut up
2 medium onions, chopped
Pepper to taste

3 tablespoons butter or margarine
6 eggs
1 teaspoon coarse salt

Fry all vegetables slowly (about 15 minutes) in butter, drop in eggs and scramble until set.

Rachel Hyman

Verenikes

2 cups sifted flour
½ teaspoon salt
3 eggs
1 tablespoon water

Cottage cheese filling
½ cup melted butter or margarine
Sour cream

Measure flour and salt into bowl. Make a well in center of flour. Drop in eggs and water. With a fork, stir and blend mixture until smooth. Turn out onto a lightly-floured board. Knead until smooth and elastic. Cover with a bowl. Let stand about ½ hour. Divide into 4 portions. Roll each into a very thin sheet about 1/16-inch thick. Cut into 3-inch rounds. Place a spoonful of cottage cheese filling in center of each round. Fold in half, making a half moon, pressing edges together with tines of fork. Let dry on lightly-floured cloth until all are made. Drop into rapidly boiling, salted water. Lower heat, cook 20 minutes or until dough is cooked through. Remove with slotted spoon. Drain well. Place in a buttered baking dish or casserole. Spoon on melted butter. Bake, uncovered, in 375° oven for 30-40 minutes or until lightly browned. Serve hot with sour cream.

Cottage Cheese Filling

2 tablespoons French's Instant Mashed Potato granules
or
½ cup mashed potatoes
½ cup cooked kasha

½ cup pot cheese
2 tablespoons instant minced onions
½ teaspoon salt
1 egg, beaten

Prepare mashed potatoes according to directions on envelope. Combine all ingredients, mixing thoroughly. Use as filling for verenikes.

Cookies

Brownies

¼ pound butter or margarine
1 cup sugar
2 eggs
½ cup flour
Pinch of salt

2 squares baking chocolate, melted
1 teaspoon vanilla
1 cup broken nut meats

Cream butter and sugar. Add eggs, one at a time. Beat well. Add flour, salt and beat. Add melted chocolate, vanilla, nuts and blend. Pour into greased 10 x 6 pan and bake at 350° for 25-30 minutes.

Frosting

2 heaping tablespoons granulated sugar
2 tablespoons butter
1 egg

2 squares melted chocolate
Pinch of salt
½ teaspoon vanilla

Cream sugar and butter. Add egg, beat well. Add chocolate, salt, and vanilla. Blend well.

Rose Adelstein

Chocolate Brownies with Coconut

1/3 cup butter
2/3 cup sugar
1 egg
2 squares melted chocolate
¼ cup milk

1 teaspoon vanilla
¼ teaspoon lemon flavoring
2/3 cup coconut
1 cup flour
1 teaspoon baking powder

Cream butter and sugar together, add rest of ingredients all at once and beat for 2 minutes. Pour into 8 x 8 buttered pan. Bake 25 minutes at 350°. While warm cut into bars and roll in confectioners sugar.

Gertrude R. Greenstone

Chocolate Mint Brownies

¼ pound butter or margarine
2 squares chocolate
1 cup sugar

2 eggs
1 teaspoon vanilla
½ cup flour

Melt margarine and chocolate together. Cream sugar and eggs, add vanilla, flour and melted chocolate mixture. Bake 30 minutes at 350° in a greased 8 x 8 pan.

Mint frosting

¼ cup margarine, melted
2 cups sifted confectioners sugar
1½ teaspoons milk

1 teaspoon mint extract
Few drops green food coloring.

Blend sugar and margarine. Add milk, mint extract and food coloring and mix thoroughly. Spread over brownies and let frosting set 15 minutes.

Chocolate glaze

1 square chocolate

1 tablespoon butter

Melt chocolate and margarine. Pour over mint layer and spread evenly. Refrigerate 30-45 minutes. Cut into squares.

Esther Josephson

Fudgy Brownies

9 squares bitter chocolate	1 teaspoon salt
½ pound butter	6 eggs
1½ cups flour	3 teaspoons vanilla
3 cups sugar	1½ cups chopped nuts, optional

Melt butter and chocolate over hot water. Mix flour, salt, sugar. Add eggs, one at a time. Add vanilla. Pour in butter and chocolate gradually. Beat at medium speed until thoroughly mixed. Pour batter into well-buttered and floured 11 x 16 cookie sheet with sides. Bake at 350° for 20-25 minutes. The secret of fudgy brownies is to remove them from the oven while still underbaked. Cool slightly and cut into squares of desired size. You may frost with chocolate frosting if you wish before cutting into squares.

Sue Klein

Marshmallow Filled Brownies

2 cups sugar	1 cup flour
1 cup butter	1 cup nuts
4 eggs	1 jar marshmallow cream
4 squares bitter chocolate	

Beat sugar and butter, add eggs, add melted chocolate, add flour and nuts. Bake at 350° for 25-30 minutes in greased and floured jelly roll pan, 10 x 15. While warm spread marshmallow cream on top.

Frosting

3 cups powdered sugar	4 tablespoons hot milk
4 tablespoons cocoa	1 teaspoon vanilla
½ stick butter or margarine	

Mix thoroughly and spread over marshmallow cream.

Stella Gelman

Pudding Brownies

1 package chocolate pudding	½ cup sugar
½ teaspoon baking powder	1/3 cup melted butter
1/3 cup flour	1 cup chopped walnuts (optional)
2 eggs	

Sift together pudding, baking powder, and flour. Beat eggs until light, add sugar and melted butter. Add to dry ingredients. Add nuts. Grease 8 x 8 pan, line with wax paper and grease again. Pour batter into pan and bake at 325° for 40 minutes. Cut while warm.

Bea Horn

Viennese Brownies

1 package (8 ounces) cream cheese	½ cup margarine
1/3 cup sugar	2 eggs
1 egg	1 cup sugar
¼ teaspoon almond extract	¾ cup flour
2 1-ounce squares unsweetened chocolate or 2/3 cup cocoa	½ teaspoon baking powder
	½ teaspoon salt
	Sliced almonds

Combine the first 4 ingredients. Melt chocolate and margarine, cool. Beat eggs, add sugar and chocolate mixture. Sift together flour, baking powder and salt and add to chocolate mixture and mix well. Pour half of chocolate mixture into a greased 8 x 8 pan; spread with cream cheese mixture and top with remaining chocolate mixture. Sprinkle with almonds. Bake at 350° for 45 minutes.

Dolly Fishman

Butterscotch Meringue Squares

Batter
1 cup shortening
4½ cups sifted flour
1½ cups brown sugar
3 teaspoons baking powder
1½ teaspoons salt
6 egg yolks

Topping
6 egg whites
3 cups brown sugar
3 cups cut up nuts
1 cup shredded coconut
3 teaspoons vanilla
1 teaspoon salt

Cut shortening into the above dry ingredients to a meal texture and then add egg yolks until you get a crumbly texture (if you desire a more cakey texture, add a small amount of light cream). Pack into a greased 7 x 11 pan and cover with topping.

Beat egg whites until stiff, add sugar and the rest of the ingredients. Beat thoroughly and spread lightly over first mixture in pan. Bake at 325°, 20-25 minutes. Cool slightly and cut into squares. Makes about 60 pieces.

Anna Levine

Banana Chocolate Chip Bars

2 cups sifted flour
2 teaspoons baking powder
½ teaspoon salt
2/3 cup shortening
2/3 cup sugar
2/3 cup packed brown sugar

1 teaspoon vanilla
1 egg
1 cup ripe, mashed banana
1 6-ounce package semi-sweet chocolate chips

Sift together flour, baking powder, salt. Cream shortening, sugar, brown sugar until light and fluffy. Beat in vanilla and egg. Blend in bananas, then flour mixture. Stir in chocolate pieces. Spread batter in 9 x 13 greased, floured pan. Bake in preheated 350° oven for 20-25 minutes or until golden brown. Cool and cut into 2 x 2-inch bars. Store in tightly covered container.

Tillie Levinson

Chocolate Chip Meringue Bars

¾ cup butter or margarine
½ cup brown sugar
½ cup granulated sugar
3 eggs, separated
1 teaspoon vanilla
2 cups flour sifted
1 teaspoon baking powder

¼ teaspoon baking soda
¼ teaspoon salt
1 package (6 ounces) chocolate chips
¾ cup chopped nuts
1 cup brown sugar

Mix butter, brown sugar, and granulated sugar, egg yolks and vanilla; beat 2 minutes at medium speed. Sift flour, baking powder, baking soda and salt together and mix well with the butter and sugar mixture. Spread dough in a greased 13 x 9-inch pan and sprinkle with chocolate chips and nuts. Beat egg whites until frothy and add 1 cup brown sugar and gradually beat until stiff. Spread over chips and nuts. Bake 350° in preheated oven for 35-40 minutes. Cool and cut into squares or bars. Makes about 16-20.

Jill Musicus

Chocolate Scotcheroos

1 cup sugar
1 cup light corn syrup
1 cup peanut butter
6 cups Rice Krispies

1 6-ounce package semi-sweet
chocolate bits
1 6-ounce package butterscotch
bits

Combine sugar and syrup in 3-quart saucepan. Cook over moderate heat, stirring frequently until mixture boils. Remove from heat. Stir in peanut butter and mix well. Add Rice Krispies, stir until blended. Press mixture into buttered 13 x 9 pan. Melt chocolate and butterscotch bits over hot, but not boiling water, stirring until well blended. Remove from heat, spread evenly over Rice Krispies mixture. Cool until firm. Cut into bars. Makes 48 bars.

Lil Orlen

Chocolate Pineapple Squares

Batter

1 cup butter
1 cup sugar
1 egg
2 cups all-purpose flour, sifted
1 teaspoon baking powder

Pinch of salt
1 teaspoon vanilla
1½ squares unsweetened chocolate, melted
½ cup finely chopped pecans

Filling

1 #2 can crushed pineapple,
well-drained
2 eggs

2½ tablespoons flour
¼ cup sugar

Cream butter, sugar and egg. Sift dry ingredients and add to the creamed mixture. Add vanilla and chocolate and nuts. Press ¾ of batter into 8 x 8 pan. Mix all filling ingredients together and spread over batter. Place strips of reserved batter over top. Bake at 350° for 45 minutes or until done.

Selma Kay

Chocolate Malt Bars

1 1-ounce square unsweetened
chocolate
½ cup shortening
¾ cup sugar
2 eggs

½ teaspoon vanilla
½ teaspoon baking powder
1 cup flour
½ cup chocolate malt
½ teaspoon salt

Melt chocolate and cool. Cream together shortening, sugar, eggs and vanilla. Add melted chocolate. Sift dry ingredients; stir into creamed mixture. Bake in greased 8 x 8 pan at 350° for 20-25 minutes. Yields 32 bars.

Ellie Harris

Cinnamon Diamonds

1 cup butter or margarine
1 cup of brown sugar
1 egg yolk
½ teaspoon vanilla

2 cups sifted all-purpose flour
1 teaspoon ground cinnamon
1 slightly beaten egg whites
¾ cup chopped walnuts

Cream butter or margarine and brown sugar until light. Beat in egg yolk and vanilla. Sift together flour and cinnamon. Stir into creamed mixture. Pat out in ungreased 15½ x 10½ x 1 inch baking pan. Brush with egg white. Sprinkle with nuts, pressing lightly into surface. Bake in 350° oven for 18 to 20 minutes; cut into diamonds while warm. Makes about 4 dozen.

Rachel Hyman

Date and Nut Squares

½ cup butter, melted	¼ teaspoon baking powder
1 cup sugar	⅛ teaspoon salt
2 eggs	1 cup nuts, chopped
¾ cup flour	1 cup dates, chopped

Mix in order as listed, adding dates and nuts last. Spread in greased pan, 9 x 12. Bake at 350° for 30 minutes. Cut into bars and roll in confectioners sugar.

Myrna LaBaer

Holidate Chews

6 tablespoons butter or mar- garine	½ cup Nestle's Quik
¾ cup brown sugar	½ teaspoon baking powder
2 eggs, slightly beaten	1 cup dates, snipped
½ teaspoon vanilla	½ cup walnuts, chopped
¾ cup sifted all-purpose flour	½ cup coconut, flaked

In sauce pan, melt butter or margarine. Remove from heat; blend in brown sugar. Beat in eggs, one at a time, add vanilla. Stir in flour, Nestle's Quik and baking powder. Mix thoroughly. Fold in dates, nuts and coconut. Turn into 9 x 9 x 2 pan which has been greased and lightly floured. Bake at 350° for 25-30 minutes. Cool. Sprinkle with confectioners sugar or frost. This recipe may be doubled.

Chocolate frosting

1 tablespoon margarine	¼ teaspoon vanilla
1 cup confectioners sugar, sifted	1 teaspoon water
2 tablespoons Nestle's Quik	

Combine all ingredients. Use as frosting for cake bars.

Rachel Hyman

Dream Bars

Batter

¼ pound butter	1 cup flour
½ cup brown sugar	

Mix together the butter and brown sugar until creamy. Add flour. Pat into a greased 2-quart Pyrex pan, making sure that the mixture is spread evenly.

Topping

2 eggs	1 teaspoon baking powder
¾ cup brown sugar	1 cup chopped nuts
1 teaspoon vanilla	1 cup dark raisins
3 tablespoons flour	

Mix the ingredients in the order given. Pour this mixture over the base and bake 40 minutes at 325°. Cut into bars when cool.

Claire Taksen

Magic Cookie Bars

1½ cups corn flake crumbs
3 tablespoons sugar
½ cup margarine or butter,
   melted
1 cup chopped walnuts

1 cup chocolate morsels
1-1/3 cups flaked coconut
1 can Borden Eagle Brand
   sweetened condensed milk

In a 13 x 9 baking pan, mix together corn flake crumbs, sugar and margarine. Press mixture evenly on bottom of pan to form crust. Sprinkle nuts evenly over crust. Sprinkle chocolate morsels over nuts. Sprinkle coconut over morsels. Pour sweetened condensed milk evenly over coconut. Bake at 350° for 25 minutes. Cool and cut into bars

Shirley Jacobson

Fruit Layer Bars

Layer I
1½ cups sifted flour
1 tablespoon sugar
¼ teaspoon salt
6 tablespoons margarine or

butter
2 egg yolks
½ cup sour cream
½ teaspoon vanilla

Layer II
1 cup fine chopped dates
¾ cup sour cream

1/3 cup apricot preserves
2 tablespoons orange rind

Layer III
2 egg whites
7 tablespoons sugar

½ teaspoon cinnamon
½ cup chopped nuts

Sift together dry ingredients from layer I, then cream margarine into dry ingredients. Combine yolks, sour cream and vanilla and pat mixture into greased 13 x 9 pan and bake at 350° for 20 minutes. Combine the ingredients from layer II together and pour over baked crust. Then beat egg whites until stiff and add sugar and cinnamon and pour over layer II, top with the chopped nuts and bake another 30 minutes or until brown. Cool and cut into squares.

Lillian Schulman

Hungarian Pastry Squares

¼ pound margarine
½ cup sugar
2 egg yolks
1 teaspoon vanilla
1½ cups flour, sifted
½ teaspoon baking powder

Pinch of salt
Pinch baking soda
1 jar raspberry preserves
Chopped nuts
2 egg whites, beaten

Cream shortening and sugar. Add egg yolks, beat until light and fluffy. Add vanilla, then dry ingredients, well sifted. Pat into a 9 x 13 pan. Spread with preserves, sprinkle with nuts, spread beaten egg whites thinly. Sprinkle again with nuts. Bake at 350° for 25-30 minutes. Cut into squares when cool.

Beverly Chesler

Lebkuchen

4 eggs
1 pound brown sugar
1 teaspoon vanilla
2 cups flour
2 teaspoons baking powder
1 scant teaspoon each of all-

spice, cinnamon, nutmeg,
ground cloves
1 cup nuts, cut up
1 cup dates, cut up, or raisins
Candied fruit, optional

Glaze

1 cup confectioners sugar
½ teaspoon vanilla

Hot water

Beat eggs and sugar; add vanilla, flour, baking powder, spices and blend. Add nuts and dates. Candied fruit that has been floured may be added. Bake in a 10 x 15 inch pan at 325° for 30 minutes. Cut into strips while warm and frost when cold with a thin glaze. To make glaze, combine sugar and vanilla. Starting with 1 teaspoon of hot water, gradually add enough water until glaze is the proper consistency for spreading.

Ruth Bloom

Lemon Chooz

Dough

½ cup butter
1½ cups flour
1/3 cup firmly packed brown
    sugar

15-ounce can condensed milk
1½ cups graham cracker crumbs
½ cup flaked coconut
½ cup chopped walnuts

Cream butter, add flour and brown sugar. Make a crumb mixture. Press into 15 x 10 pan. Bake 5 minutes at 350°. Cool. Combine rest of the ingredients until well blended. Spoon over baked crust. Spread carefully with buttered or wet spatula. Bake at 350° for about 15 minutes until golden brown. Frost while warm.

Frosting

1 cup confectioners sugar
2 tablespoons lemon juice

1 tablespoon melted butter

Blend together. If consistency isn't thin enough, add water and more lemon juice. Frosting should be thin. It hardens on cake. Cut into squares or fingers.

Bea Horn

Lemon Layer Bars

1 cup sifted all-purpose flour
¾ cup brown sugar
½ cup margarine
1 tablespoon cornstarch
¼ cup frozen lemonade concen-
    trate

⅛ teaspoon salt
½ cup walnuts
2 beaten eggs
1-1/3 cups flaked coconut
1 teaspoon pure vanilla

Combine flour and ¼ cup brown sugar in mixing bowl. Cut in margarine until particles are fine. Press into greased 8 inch square pan. Bake at 350° for 10 minutes. In a small saucepan, combine ½ cup brown sugar, cornstarch, frozen lemonade concentrate and salt. Cook until mixture thickens. Add chopped walnuts, then spread over base. Combine eggs, coconut and vanilla. Spoon it over filling. Bake at 350°, 30-35 minutes until golden brown. Cool and cut into bars.

Rachel Hyman

Lemon Frosted Coconut Strips

Dough
1½ cups sifted all-purpose flour   ½ cup shortening or margarine
½ cup brown sugar

Combine and press mixture into 9 x 13 greased baking sheet. Bake 15 minutes at 275°.

Filling
2 eggs   ¼ teaspoon salt
1 cup brown sugar   2½ tablespoons flour
1½ cups coconut   ½ teaspoon baking powder
½ cup chopped nuts   1 teaspoon vanilla

Beat all ingredients together and spread this mixture over baked crust. Increase oven temperature to 350° and bake for 20 minutes. Cool for 5 minutes then frost.

Frosting
1 cup confectioners sugar   Lemon juice (enough to make thin
1 tablespoon melted margarine   icing)

Spread quickly and cut into narrow finger strips when cool. Yield 75 strips.

Helen Jassin

Bohemian Nut Slices

1 envelope dry granular yeast   2 eggs, separated
¼ cup warm water   ½ cup sugar
1 teaspoon sugar   1 teaspoon vanilla
2 cups sifted flour   ½ cup chopped nuts
½ teaspoon salt   Powdered sugar or icing
¾ cup butter or margarine

Sprinkle yeast over warm water, add 1 teaspoon sugar and let stand 10 minutes until softened. Sift together flour and salt, cut in butter until mixture resembles coarse meal. Blend in egg yolks, softened yeast mixture until a smooth ball is formed. Beat egg whites until stiff but not dry. Gradually beat in ½ cup sugar, continue beating until stiff and peaked. Fold in vanilla. Divide dough in half and roll out on lightly floured board into a 9 x 13-inch rectangle, spread with egg white mixture and sprinkle with nuts, roll as for a jelly roll. Place on greased baking sheet, repeat the same with other half of dough. Make a ½-inch deep cut down lengthwise on each roll. Bake right away (no rising) at 375° for 22 minutes or until lightly browned. Ice while hot or sprinkle with powdered sugar. Slice when cool.

Hetty Jacobson

Pecan Squares

1 cup dark brown sugar   1 egg, well beaten
1 cup shortening   2 cups all-purpose flour

Topping
1 egg, well beaten   ½ cup brown sugar
1 cup chopped pecans

Cream sugar and shortening. Add egg. Then work in flour gradually. Spread in well-greased 10 x 15 pan. For topping, spread egg, sprinkle with pecans and brown sugar. Bake at 350° for 20-25 minutes.

Claire Levison

Walnut Treasure Bars

½ cup shortening
1 cup brown sugar, packed
1 egg
¼ cup milk
¼ cup sherry
1-2/3 cups sifted all-purpose
flour

1 tablespoon instant powdered
coffee
½ teaspoon baking powder
½ teaspoon baking soda
1 cup coarsely chopped walnuts
1 cup semi-sweet morsels

Cream together shortening, sugar and egg. Add milk and sherry (batter may look curdled). Resift flour with coffee, baking powder and soda; add to creamed mixture. Stir in walnuts and chocolate morsels. Spread in greased 10 x 15 pan. Bake at 375° for 20 minutes. Cool in pan and spread with icing. Cut into bars or squares.

Icing

2¼ cups sifted powdered sugar
1½ tablespoons soft butter
2 tablespoons sherry

1 tablespoon milk
1 teaspoon instant coffee

Combine the above ingredients and beat until smooth. Spread on cake. May top with additional nuts.

Bea Horn

Pineapple Coconut Bars

½ cup margarine
¾ cup sugar, reserve ¼ cup for
topping
1¼ cups sifted all-purpose flour
1 3½-ounce can coconut

1 20-ounce can crushed pineapple, drained
1 egg
1 tablespoon melted margarine
½ teaspoon vanilla

Cream margarine with ½ cup sugar. Add flour until well blended. Press into bottom of 9 x 13 x ½ cookie sheet, greased. Bake 15 minutes at 350°. Remove from oven and sprinkle the coconut on top of crust. Spread pineapple on top of coconut. Mix remaining ¼ cup sugar, egg, melted margarine and vanilla. Spread over pineapple. Bake 20 minutes. Top should be golden brown. Cool and cut into desired size bars.

Helen Jassin

Pineapple Meringue Bars

1 can pineapple pie filling
½ cup shortening
1/3 cup sugar

2 egg yolks
1½ cups sifted flour

Topping

2 egg whites
½ cup sugar

½ cup sliced almonds

Beat shortening, sugar and egg yolks. Add flour and stir until blended. Spread crumbled dough on an ungreased 9 x 13 pan and bake for 15 minutes at 350°. Then spread pie filling and top with meringue made from the egg whites and sugar. Sprinkle with sliced almonds. Bake another 25 minutes at 350° and cut into squares when cool.

Trudy Boyar

Brown Rim Cookies

1 cup butter or margarine
1 teaspoon salt
2/3 cup granulated sugar
2½ cups flour

1 teaspoon vanilla (or lemon or orange juice)
2 eggs, well beaten

Combine salt, butter and vanilla. Add sugar and beaten eggs, then add flour and blend well. Drop by teaspoonfuls on greased cookie sheet. Let stand 5 minutes; flatten and bake at 375°, 10-12 minutes or until lightly browned around edge. You can put nuts, chocolate chips or jimmies on before baking.

Lillian Schulman

Chocolate Kisses

4 egg whites
1 cup sugar
12 ounces chocolate chips

1¼-1½ cups coconut
1 cup crushed walnuts
1 teaspoon vanilla

Beat egg whites until very stiff. Add sugar gradually, at high speed. Beat until marshmallow consistency. Melt chocolate chips and cool. To egg mixture, add coconut, walnuts, vanilla, and melted chocolate. Blend through. Drop by teaspoonfuls on cookie sheet lined with brown paper; form into round shapes with two spoons fitted together. Bake 10 minutes at 400°. Do not remove from sheet for at least 10 minutes. Makes 35-45 cookies.

Claire Levison

Chocolate Drop Cookies

½ cup margarine
1 cup brown sugar
1 egg
1 teaspoon vanilla
2 squares melted chocolate

2 cups sifted all-purpose flour
½ teaspoon soda
¼ teaspoon salt
¾ cup sour cream
½ cup chopped walnuts

Cream margarine and sugar until fluffy. Beat in egg and vanilla. Stir in chocolate. Sift together dry ingredients. Add to chocolate mixture, alternating with the sour cream. Mix well. Stir in nuts, drop from teaspoon 2 inches apart on a greased cookie sheet. Bake at 350° for 10 minutes. Remove and cool and frost. Makes 4 dozen.

Mocha Frosting

¼ cup margarine
2 tablespoons cocoa
2 teaspoons instant coffee
Dash of salt

3 cups confectioners sugar
3 tablespoons milk
1½ teaspoons vanilla

Cream margarine with cocoa, coffee and salt, then beat in confectioners sugar alternately with the milk, and vanilla. Beat until smooth.

Linda Ruda

Chocolate Chip Oatmeal Cookies

1¾ cups all-purpose flour
¼ teaspoon salt
2 cups rolled oats
½ cup coconut (optional)
1 cup butter
1 cup brown sugar

1 teaspoon vanilla
½ teaspoon baking soda
¼ cup boiling water
1 6-ounce package chocolate chips

Sift together flour and salt. Mix in rolled oats and coconut. Cream butter and sugar. Add sugar gradually and cream thoroughly. Add vanilla. Dissolve baking soda in boiling water and add water and soda. Add dry ingredients gradually, mixing well. Fold in chocolate chips. Drop from teaspoon on greased cookie sheet. Flatten with fork and bake in 350° oven, 15-20 minutes or until done. Cool on cookie sheet.

Selma Kay

Chocolate Crinkles

½ cup vegetable oil
4 squares unsweetened chocolate, melted
2 cups granulated sugar
4 eggs

2 teaspoons vanilla
2 cups flour
2 teaspoons baking powder
½ teaspoon salt
1 cup confectioners sugar

Mix oil, chocolate and granulated sugar. Blend in one egg at a time. Add vanilla. Stir in flour, baking powder and salt. Chill several hours or overnight. Drop dough by teaspoonfuls into confectioners sugar and shape into balls. Place 2 inches apart on greased cookie sheet. Bake at 350° for 10-12 minutes. Makes 6 dozen. Can be frozen.

Maxine Peters

Chocolate Macaroons

4 egg whites
1 cup sugar
1 12-ounce package melted

chocolate morsels
1 8-ounce package coconut

Beat egg whites until foamy but not stiff, add sugar and beat well. Add melted chocolate and coconut. Drop on greased cookie sheet by ½ teaspoonful each. Bake at 375°, not longer than 12 minutes. Makes about 5 dozen.

Joan Wheeler

Kichel

6 eggs
6 teaspoons sugar
1 teaspoon salt

¾ cup oil
2¼ cups flour

Beat eggs well. Add other ingredients and beat 5 minutes until thick. Drop by teaspoons on cookie sheet. Sprinkle top with sugar. Bake at 400° until golden brown.

Ida Krieger

Sour Cream Cookies

½ cup butter or margarine
1 cup sugar
2 eggs, beaten
1 teaspoon vanilla
1¾ cups flour, unsifted
½ teaspoon salt

¼ teaspoon baking soda
½ teaspoon nutmeg
½ cup sour cream
1 cup chopped nuts
1 teaspoon grated orange rind
  (optional)

Beat shortening and sugar together until creamy. Beat in eggs and vanilla. Stir flour, salt, baking soda and nutmeg together. Blend flour mixture, sour cream and nuts with the shortening mixture. Drop dough from teaspoon onto greased baking sheets. Space cookies about 2 inches apart. Bake in 375° preheated oven, 10-12 minutes or until lightly browned around the edges. Makes 4 dozen.

Idaire Leichtner and Myrna LaBaer

Brown-Eyed Susans

¾ cup soft butter or margarine	¼ teaspoon salt
½ cup sugar	1¾ cups sifted flour
1 egg	1 7-ounce package chocolate
1 teaspoon vanilla	mint candy wafers

Cream together butter, sugar, egg, vanilla and salt. Stir in flour. Chill about 1 hour. Shape in 1-inch balls, place 2 inches apart on ungreased baking sheet, flatten each by pressing a wafer in center. Bake in 400° oven 8 to 10 minutes. Remove immediately from pan. Makes 4 dozen.

Hetty Jacobson

Butter Cookies

1 pound butter or margarine	6 cups flour
1 cup sugar	1 teaspoon lemon juice
2 egg yolks	1 teaspoon vanilla
Rind of ½ lemon	1 teaspoon baking powder
2 tablespoons brandy	

Cream butter and sugar. Add yolks, slightly beaten, add rind of lemon, lemon juice, brandy and vanilla. Work in flour, sifting a little at a time. Add the baking powder to the flour after almost all of the flour has been added. The dough is very stiff. You will have to use your hands to finish mixing. Form into a round cake and put into refrigerator over night. Next morning cut into 4 or 5 pieces. Roll each piece very thin. Cut with cookie cutter. Brush the tops with either white of the egg or milk. Put a half pecan on each cookie, sprinkle with sugar and cinnamon. Bake at 350° for 10 minutes. Makes 12 dozen. This recipe may be cut in half.

Lucille Michel

Butter Fingers

½ cup butter	1 cup black walnuts, chopped
2 tablespoons confectioners	1 teaspoon cinnamon to 1 cup
sugar	confectioners sugar
1 cup flour	

Mix the first four ingredients together and chill. Roll into long rolls (size of a pencil). Cut into 2½-inch lengths. Bake on ungreased cookie sheet at 350° for 15 minutes. While hot, roll in confectioners sugar and cinnamon mixture.

Anna Levine

Caramel Sugar Cookies
(Chanukah Cookies)

1 cup shortening	3¾ cups flour
1 cup sugar	1 teaspoon salt
3 eggs, beaten	½ teaspoon soda
2 teaspoons vanilla	½ cup brown sugar

Combine shortening, granulated sugar, eggs and vanilla, then mix in dry ingredients. Chill dough overnight. Roll out ¼ inch thick. Cut with Chanukah cutters. Sprinkle with brown sugar and bake at 350° for 10-15 minutes. (Watch as they don't take long if thin).

Marsha Edelman

Cherry Surprises

1 cup butter or margarine
½ cup sifted confectioners sugar
2 cups sifted cake flour

1 teaspoon vanilla
½ cup chopped pecans
1 pound candied red cherries

Cream butter with confectioners sugar until light and fluffy. Add flour and vanilla and stir in chopped pecans. Wrap dough in waxed paper and chill, several hours. Roll enough dough around each cherry to make a ¾ inch ball. Place on ungreased cookie sheet and chill 15 minutes. Bake at 375° for 20 minutes. While still warm roll in confectioners sugar.

Marlene Elkin

Crescents

2 cups flour
1 cup butter

2/3 cup sour cream
1 egg yolk

Topping
1 tablespoon cinnamon
¾ cup sugar

½ cup nuts, finely chopped
Egg white, beaten

Mix flour, butter and add beaten egg yolk and sour cream. Divide this dough into 4 sections and wrap in wax paper and chill for 3 hours or overnight. Roll each section as you would for pie crust. Cut each section in ½ then ¼ and then ⅛. Sprinkle topping on each wedge. Roll from the larger end to make crescents. Place them on an ungreased cookie sheet, brush lightly with beaten egg white and top with cinnamon and sugar. Bake 20-25 minutes at 400°. Makes 32-64 crescents.

Rose Goldstein

Crescents with a Difference

1 package dry yeast
3 cups sifted flour, scant
1 cup butter
1 cup sour cream
3 egg yolks
1 cup sugar

1 cup chopped nuts
1½ teaspoons cinnamon
4 tablespoons butter, melted
12 ounces apricot preserves
Honey

Sprinkle yeast on flour; cut in softened butter and blend together with hands. Stir egg yolks into sour cream; add to flour mixture. Mix well until a stiff dough is formed. Roll dough into ball, wrap in wax paper and refrigerate overnight. Divide dough into 4 parts. Combine sugar, nuts and cinnamon. Sprinkle ¼ of this mixture on pastry board; roll one part of the dough on top of it into a 12 inch circle, ¼ inch thick. Brush with melted butter and spread with apricot preserves. Cut into 16 pie-shaped wedges; starting at wider edge, roll up each piece and gently curve into crescent shape. Repeat process for other 3 sections of dough. Bake on greased cookie sheet at 325° for 25 minutes. Brush tops with honey when warm, right out of oven. Makes 64.

T'Mahry Axelrod

Horn Crescents

3 cups flour	2 yeast cakes
1 cup coffee cream or Rich's Whip	3 egg yolks
	½ pound sweet margarine

Filling

1 cup chopped nuts	3 teaspoons cinnamon
1 cup sugar	1 cup raisins

Mix butter and flour together with pastry blender. Blend in cream, yeast and egg yolks, add to flour and butter mixture. Dough will be sticky. Place in refrigerator overnight. The next day, divide dough in 4 parts, roll each part in a circle about 16 inches in diameter. Mix filling and sprinkle each circle with ¼ mixture. Cut each dough circle into 16 pie-shaped wedges. Roll each wedge starting from the wide end. Form into crescents, place on greased cookie sheet at 400° for about 20 minutes or until lightly browned.

Bea Hoschander

Cheese Horns

¼ pound butter or margarine	1 egg yolk
¼ pound cream cheese	2 cups flour
3 teaspoons sugar	

Filling

Jam of your choice	Cinnamon and sugar
Chopped nuts	

Cream together butter, cheese, sugar and egg yolk, then add flour. It will form a soft ball. Chill over night. Three hours before making, take out of the refrigerator. Divide the dough into 4 pieces. Roll out thin on a floured board, spread with jam, nuts, cinnamon and sugar. Cut into 8 pie wedges and roll from the wide side to the narrow. Place on a cookie sheet covered with foil, brush with milk and sprinkle with cinnamon and sugar on top. Bake in 350° oven for 20 minutes. If smaller horns are desired, cut into 16 pie-shaped wedges. Makes about 32 horns.

Joan Wheeler

Yugoslavia Cookies (Kifle)

2 cups flour, sifted	margarine
1 cake compressed yeast	2 egg yolks
¼ pound unsalted butter or	½ cup commercial sour cream

Sift flour into large mixing bowl. Crumble in yeast. Cut in shortening with pastry blender until mixture is crumbly. Add yolks and sour cream and mix well. Form into a ball. On a slightly floured board, knead until smooth. (5 to 10 minutes). You can knead right in bowl. Divide dough into 3 equal parts. Wrap each in wax paper. Chill in refrigerator for 1 hour. On a board sprinkled with confectioners sugar, roll each part of the dough into an 8-inch circle. Cut each into 8 pie shaped wedges. Fill wide edge of each wedge with 1 tablespoon of walnut filling. Roll up from wide end to point. Place on greased baking sheet, curving ends to form crescent shape. Bake at 375° for 25 minutes.

Walnut filling

1 cup finely chopped walnuts	½ teaspoon vanilla
½ cup sugar	2 egg whites, stiffly beaten

Combine walnuts, sugar, vanilla. Fold in beaten egg whites.

Bea Horn

Coconut Slices

2 cups sifted all-purpose flour	1 cup sugar
½ teaspoon salt	2 cans angel flake coconut
1 cup butter or margarine	1 egg, slightly beaten

Cut butter in flour with pastry cutter until it looks like corn meal. Add sugar, coconut and slightly beaten egg. Knead until it holds together and all traces of egg disappear. Shape dough into rolls for slicing. Chill 1 or 2 hours, until firm enough to slice as thin as possible. Bake in 350° oven 10-12 minutes on ungreased cookie sheet.

Belle Lovenheim

Date Filled Cookies

½ cup shortening	2 cups flour
½ cup brown sugar	¼ teaspoon salt
½ cup white sugar	½ teaspoon baking soda
2 eggs	

Filling

1 cup chopped dates	1/3 cup water
¼ cup sugar	½ cup chopped nuts

Cook dates, sugar and water over low heat until thick, about 5 minutes; cool and add nuts. Thoroughly cream shortening and sugar. Add eggs and beat well; add sifted dry ingredients and mix thoroughly. Chill. Roll ⅛ inch thick on lightly floured surface. Cut with floured cookie cutter. Place teaspoon of filling on half of cookie, cover with remaining cookie dough and press edges together with fork. Bake on greased cookie sheet in hot oven at 400° for 10 minutes. If dough is a little too soft to roll out, add a bit more flour.

Ettie Rubenstein

Frosty Date Balls

½ cup soft butter or margarine	1¼ cups sifted flour
1/3 cup confectioners sugar	2/3 cup chopped dates
1 tablespoon water	½ cup chopped walnuts
1 teaspoon vanilla	

Cream butter and sugar thoroughly, stir in water and vanilla, add flour and mix well. Stir in dates and nuts. Roll in 1-inch balls. Place 2-inches apart on an ungreased baking sheet. Bake in 350° oven for 20 minutes. While warm, roll in confectioners sugar.

Mrs. Isadore Ouriel

Easy Cut-Out Cookie Dough

½ cup sugar	2½-2¾ cups flour
½ cup butter or margarine	2 teaspoons baking powder
2 eggs	1 teaspoon vanilla

Cream sugar and butter until light and fluffy, beat in eggs and add flour and baking powder and vanilla. Chill 3-4 hours before rolling. Bake 375° for about 10 minutes on ungreased baking sheet. Makes 40 2-inch cookies.

Maxine Straus

Esrog Cookies (Succoth Cookies)

3 cups unsifted all-purpose flour
1½ teaspoons baking soda
¼ teaspoon salt
2 teaspoons cinnamon
¾ cup vegetable shortening
1 cup firmly packed brown sugar
1 egg

1/3 cup light molasses
1 can (3½ ounces) flaked coconut
48 pitted California prunes
1 pound confectioners sugar
Lemon juice
Yellow food coloring

Mix flour, baking soda, salt and cinnamon. Cream shortening until fluffy. Stir in sugar, egg and light molasses. Stir in flour and coconut. Chill dough for 1 hour. Cut dough into 48 equal pieces. With floured hands flatten each piece of dough into a round. Place a prune on top of each and then pinch dough around prune to enclose it completely. Place seam side down on greased cookie sheets. Smooth tops and pinch ends to resemble a lemon half. Bake in a preheated 375° oven for 15 minutes or until puffed and firm to the touch. Cool on rack. To frost, mix confectioners sugar with enough lemon juice to make it the consistency of heavy cream. Add yellow food coloring until frosting is lemon colored. Spread a thick layer of frosting on the flat side of 24 of the halves. Press remaining halves against frosting to make 24 whole lemon shapes. Use remaining frosting to frost the outside of the cakes. Let stand at room temperature to allow frosting to dry well. Place on a platter surrounded with washed and dried lemon leaves, if desired.

Flaky Cream Cheese Cookies

1 cup flour
¼ pound butter or margarine

1 3-ounce package cream cheese
Pinch of salt

Mix all ingredients together at room temperature. Leave refrigerated overnight. Roll out dough (not too thin) cut with size of a sherbet glass. Put on buttered cookie sheet. Top with mixture of colored sugar and regular sugar. Bake at 425°, 6-8 minutes. Makes 1½ dozen. Cookie is light and flaky.

Ursula Gonsenhauser

Hamantaschen

½ pound butter or margarine
½ cup sugar
4 eggs
2 teaspoons vanilla
2 teaspoons baking powder
3½ cups flour
1 can Solo poppy seed

or prune filling
1 egg
½ cup sugar
3 tablespoons strawberry jam
1 cup raisins
1 cup nuts, chopped

Cream butter and sugar; add eggs one at a time. Add vanilla, baking powder and flour. When well mixed, add more flour gradually until no longer sticky. This could be 1-2 cups, more or less. Chill 1 hour. Roll out on floured board and cut in rounds, using plastic top of 1-pound coffee can as a pattern. Mix poppy seed or prune filling, egg, sugar, jam, raisins and nuts. Fill each round with filling and fold up 3 sides; pinch. Bake at 350° for 30 minutes, or until brown. Makes 30-40.

Sylvia Rickless

Hamantaschen

1 cup shortening or margarine	1 teaspoon lemon juice
1 cup sugar	¼ teaspoon salt
4 eggs	Grated rind of ½ lemon
3-4 cups sifted flour	Solo prune or apricot filling
2 teaspoons baking powder	

Cream shortening and sugar. Add eggs and remaining ingredients, except filling. Mix well and refrigerate. Roll out 1/3 of dough at a time to ⅛-inch thickness. Cut into 2½-inch circles. Place circles on lightly greased cookie sheet. Place ½-1 teaspoon filling in center and draw up 3 sides. Sprinkle with poppy seeds, if desired. Bake at 350° for 10 minutes.

Ina Rosenbaum

Hazelnut Balls

1½ cups hazelnuts	½ cup sugar
2 egg whites	Extra nuts for decorating

Grate nuts. Beat egg whites until frothy. Gradually add sugar and beat until stiff peaks are formed. Fold nuts into meringue. Drop with a teaspoon on lightly greased cookie sheet. Decorate each cookie with a piece of nutmeat. Bake at 300° for 25 minutes.

Trudy Boyar

Lemon Angel Halos

2 cups flour	1 teaspoon vanilla
1 teaspoon salt	1 egg
1 teaspoon soda	3 egg whites
2/3 cup shortening	¾ cup sugar (white)
1 cup brown sugar	2 teaspoons lemon juice.

Sift flour, salt and soda. Cream shortening, add brown sugar. Blend in vanilla and egg. Beat well. Add sifted dry ingredients; blend thoroughly. Chill while preparing meringue and filling. Beat 3 egg whites. Add sugar, blend in lemon juice. Shape dough into balls using 1 level teaspoon of dough for each ball. Place on greased baking sheet. Flatten to ⅛-inch thickness. Place 1 rounded teaspoon of meringue on each cookie. Hollow the center of each with back of teaspoon dipped in cold water. Bake at 300° for 10-12 minutes until cream color. When cool, fill meringue nest with ¼ teaspoon lemon filling.

Lemon Filling

3 egg yolks	1 teaspoon lemon rind
1 cup sugar	3 tablespoons butter
¼ cup lemon juice	

Combine first 4 ingredients in saucepan. Heat to boiling; stir. Remove from heat; add butter and cool.

Esther Parsky

Mandel Bread

1 cup peanut oil	1 teaspoon salt
1¼ cups sugar	2 teaspoons vanilla or
4 eggs at room temperature	1 teaspoon vanilla and 1 tea-
3½ cups flour	spoon orange juice
2 heaping teaspoons baking	1½ cups nuts or coconut
powder	Sliced almonds

Sift flour, baking powder and salt. Beat eggs until fluffy and pale. Add sugar, oil, flavoring. Add sifted dry ingredients. Add nuts or coconut. Flour board and shape dough into strips 2½-3 inches or scoop with large cooking spoon directly on ungreased cookie sheet and shape into strips with fingers. Decorate with sliced almonds or coconut or sugar. Bake at 350° - 375° for 20-25 minutes until golden brown. Remove and slice in desired size and lay pieces on side. Use extra cookie sheets, if necessary. Crisp in oven 5-10 minutes on each side. Pack in wax paper in tin or glass containers. Keeps for weeks. Suggestion: Save crumbs to use in strudel or kuchen.

Anne Relin

Chocolate Shot Kamish Bread

2 eggs	1 teaspoon baking powder
1 cup vegetable oil	½ teaspoon salt
1 cup sugar	4 ounces chocolate shot
1 teaspoon vanilla	1-1½ cups slivered almonds or
2 cups flour	cut-up walnuts

Beat eggs well; add oil and then add sugar and vanilla. Sift together flour, baking powder and salt. Stir in chocolate shot and slivered almonds. Chill 1 hour. Grease cookie sheet with sides very well. Make 3 rolls the long way and one across the short way. Bake 25-30 minutes at 350° . Slice with very sharp knife. Dry slices in oven at 200° for 1-1½ hours.

Jerry Morris Fineberg

Date Mandelbroit

2 eggs	2 teaspoons baking powder
½ cup sugar	Pinch of salt
¼ cup oil	½ cup cut-up dates
1 teaspoon lemon juice	Chocolate chips or nuts
2 cups all-purpose flour	

Mix ingredients in order given. Shape into 2 long loaves 2 inches thick. Place on greased cookie sheet and bake at 350° about 30 minutes. Ice with powdered sugar and lemon juice. Cut into ½-inch slices while warm.

Mrs. Harry Horwitz

Jellied Mandel Bread

½ cup oil	2 cups flour
½ cup sugar	1 teaspoon lemon juice
2 eggs	Dash of lemon and orange peel
2 teaspoons baking powder	1 cup nuts, chopped
¼ teaspoon salt	1 12-ounce jar marmalade

Blend oil and sugar, add eggs. Add dry ingredients and then lemon juice and nuts. Separate dough into 5 sections. Use Teflon cookie sheet. Pat each section flat with fingers and spread peach jam or orange marmalade down center of each section. Fold over, bringing long sides together and pinching ends so jam or marmalade is covered. Bake at 350° for 30-40 minutes or until done. Cool and slice.

Belle Garden

Mocha Balls

1 cup butter	1 tablespoon instant coffee
½ cup sugar	powder
2 teaspoons vanilla	1 cup finely chopped nuts
2 cups sifted flour	½ cup chopped marachino cherries
¼ cup cocoa	Confectioners sugar

In mixing bowl, cream butter, gradually add sugar and vanilla, beat until light and fluffy. Sift flour, cocoa, coffee powder and gradually add to creamed mixture. Blend in nuts and cherries. Chill dough for 1 hour. Shape into balls 1-inch in diameter and place on baking sheet. Bake in 325° oven for 20 minutes. Dust with confectioners sugar while warm.

Mrs. Isadore Ouriel

Nutty Cookie Rings

1 cup butter or margarine, softened	3 tablespoons orange or lemon flavored gelatin
½ cup sugar	1 cup chopped walnuts or pecans
2 cups all-purpose flour	

In large mixing bowl, cream butter and sugar. Blend in remaining ingredients. Chill dough for 1 hour. Shape dough by teaspoons into strips about the thickness of a pencil and 5 inches long. Shape into rings, place 1 inch apart on ungreased cookie sheets. Bake at 350° for 8-10 minutes until lightly browned. Cool cookies on cookie sheet about 2 minutes. Makes about 30 cookies.

Mrs. Isadore Ouriel

Oatmeal Icebox Cookies

1 cup sifted all-purpose flour	½ cup light brown sugar, firmly
½ teaspoon baking soda	packed
½ teaspoon salt	1 egg
½ teaspoon cinnamon	2 tablespoons honey
½ cup soft butter or margarine	1½ cups rolled oats
½ cup granulated sugar	

Sift flour with baking soda, salt, and cinnamon; set aside. In large bowl, with wooden spoon, or portable electric mixer at medium speed, beat butter until light. Gradually beat in sugars. Add egg and honey; continue beating until very light and fluffy. At low speed, gradually add half the flour mixture. Mix in rest, with hands, to form a stiff dough. Add oats, mixing to combine well. Refrigerate 30 minutes. Divide dough in half. On lightly floured surface, shape each half into a roll 7 inches long. Wrap in Saran or foil; refrigerate until firm, about 8 hours or overnight. (Rolls may be stored in refrigerator 7-10 days. Bake fresh as desired.) With sharp knife cut as many ⅛-inch slices as desired for baking at one time. Rewrap rest of roll; refrigerate. Place slices, 2 inches apart, on ungreased cookie sheets. Bake at 375° 8-10 minutes or until lightly browned. Remove to wire rack; cool. Makes about 7 dozen.

Julia Berlove

Pecan Puffs

½ cup butter
2 tablespoons sugar
1 teaspoon vanilla

1 cup cake flour
¼ pound finely chopped pecans
Confectioners sugar

Cream butter, sugar and vanilla. Add nuts and cake flour. Roll into large marbles and bake on buttered baking sheet at 300° for ½-¾ hour. Roll in confectioners sugar while hot. Roll again in sugar when cool. Makes 42.

Rose Adelstein

Poppy Seed Piroshkes

4 eggs
½ cup sugar
½ cup orange juice
1 cup oil
5 cups flour
2 teaspoons baking powder

1 teaspoon salt
Cinnamon and sugar
Raisins and nuts
Honey
1 tablespoon poppy seeds

Beat eggs and add sugar. Add oil and orange juice; mix well. Sift together flour, baking powder and salt. Add dry ingredients, 1 cup at a time, mixing well after each addition. Flour board heavily as dough will be quite soft. Divide dough into fourths. Roll dough thin, cover with oil and sprinkle with raisins, nuts, cinnamon and sugar. Roll like jelly roll. Slice into 1-inch slices. Lay on side on greased cookie sheet. Bake at 350° for approximately 30 minutes. After baking, immediately brush with honey and sprinkle with poppy seeds. Note: Use ½ pound butter in place of oil and ½ cup milk in place of orange juice, if desired.

Tillie Niewood

Queens Triangles

1 cup butter or margarine
1 cup cottage cheese
2 cups flour

⅛ teaspoon salt
Strawberry jam

Cream together butter and cottage cheese. Work in flour; add salt. Wrap dough in waxed paper. Refrigerate until firm. When cold, roll in thin sheets and cut in 3-inch squares. Place a teaspoon of jam in center of each square and fold into a triangle, pressing edges firmly together. Bake for about 15 minutes at 425° or until brown and crisp. Yield: 4½ dozen cookies.

Carolyn Steklof

Raggedy Ann Cookies

1 cup golden raisins
½ cup margarine
1 cup granulated sugar
2 eggs, beaten
1½ cups flour

½ teaspoon soda
1 teaspoon vanilla
4 cups uncrushed corn flakes
½ cup shredded coconut

Wash raisins, drain and dry on a towel. Cream margarine, add sugar and cream thoroughly. Add well-beaten eggs, flour sifted with soda; mix well. Add vanilla, raisins, cornflakes and coconut and mix, but do not crush cornflakes more than necessary. Form balls the size of a walnut. Place on ungreased cookie sheet and flatten slightly with hand. Bake at 400° for 12-15 minutes. Makes about 2½ dozen, medium size cookies.

Lois Kwasman

Raisin Walnut Crinkles

½ cup vegetable shortening
1-2/3 cups sugar
1 tablespoon vanilla
1 cup raisins, chopped
½ cup nuts, chopped
2 ounces premelted chocolate

2 cups sifted all-purpose flour
2 teaspoons baking powder
1 teaspoon salt
1/3 cup milk or orange juice
Confectioners sugar

Blend shortening, sugar and vanilla until fluffy. Stir in raisins, nuts and chocolate, mixing well until blended. Add flour, baking powder and salt alternately with orange juice. Cover, chill for several hours. Shape dough into 1-inch balls, roll in confectioners sugar until well coated. Arrange on lightly greased baking sheets about 2 inches apart. Bake at 350° for 10-15 minutes. The cookies will be soft, so be careful when removing to cool; they become crisp when cool. (This recipe has no egg in it.)

Ruth Drexler

Refrigerator Cookies

1¼ cups melted shortening (or salad oil)
2 cups brown sugar
3 eggs, well beaten
4½ cups cake flour

1 teaspoon cinnamon
½ teaspoon nutmeg
2 teaspoons soda
1 cup nut meats

Mix shortening and brown sugar, add eggs. Sift together flour, spices and soda. Add nut meats and add to first mixture. Shape into rolls and wrap in wax paper. Chill overnight. Slice very thin; place on greased cookie sheet and bake at 375° for 10-12 minutes.

Bea Horn

Sesame Cookies

1 cup soft margarine
¼ cup sugar
1 teaspoon almond extract
2 cups flour

Sesame seeds
Pure strawberry or red raspberry preserves

Cream margarine and sugar, blend in almond extract. Add flour, mix well. Shape tablespoonfuls of dough into balls, roll in sesame seeds. Place on ungreased baking sheet, flatten slightly. Indent center of each and fill with preserves. Bake at 400° for 10-12 minutes. Makes 3 dozen.

Mrs. Isadore Ouriel

Strudel

2 cups flour
½ cup softened butter or margarine
1 cup sour cream

Filling
12 ounces apricot perserves
6 ounces chopped nuts
1 cup chopped coconut

Cut butter into flour, add sour cream and form dough into ball. Refrigerate at least 4 hours or overnight. Divide dough into 4 parts and roll each part into a rectangle on a floured surface. Spread with preserves, sprinkle with nuts and coconut and roll as for a jelly roll. Bake at 350° for 45-60 minutes on lightly greased cookie sheet.

Lil Schulman

Grandma Lovenheim's Strudel

Dough

1½ cups all-purpose flour
¼ teaspoon salt
½ teaspoon sugar
1/3 cup warm water

1 egg, beaten
1 cup melted butter or margarine

Apple Filling

4 large apples
1 cup sugar and cinnamon

½ cup chopped walnuts
½ cup raisins

To mix and knead: Into large mixing bowl place salt, flour, sugar and egg. Add warm water, mixing dough quickly with a fork. Then knead on board, stretching it up and down to make it elastic until it leaves the board clean. Toss on a small well-floured board. Cover with a hot towel or bowl and keep warm ½ hour or longer.

To stretch dough: Lay dough in center of a well-floured tablecloth on a table about 30 x 48 inches. Flour dough, roll with rolling pin as thin as possible. Brush top of dough with ¼ cup melted butter or margarine. With hands under dough, palms down, pull and stretch the dough gradually all around the table, until it is as thin as paper. Cut off edges. Drip ¼ cup more butter or margarine over surface of dough.

To fill, roll and shape: Scatter filling mixture over ¾ of dough. Fold a little over one end and pick up cloth to roll into a large jelly roll. Trim edge again. Twist into greased 11 x 16 pan.

To bake strudel: Brush top with melted butter or margarine. Bake in hot oven (400°) ½ hour, reduce heat to 350° and bake ½ hour longer. Sprinkle top with confectioners sugar.

Barbara Lovenheim

Strudel Supreme

Dough:

½ pound margarine
½ pint sour cream

½ teaspoon almond extract
2 cups all-purpose flour, sifted

Cream together margarine, sour cream and almond extract. Slowly work flour into this mixture. Refrigerate overnight.

Filling:

1 pound golden yellow raisins
Hot water
7 cups bread crumbs
2 cups chopped nuts
¼ pound grated coconut

2 pounds orange marmalade
4 lemons, juice and rind
½ pound mixed candied fruit
1 cup sugar
¼ teaspoon cinnamon

Soak raisins in hot water for 3 minutes; drain and add to remaining filling ingredients. Mix thoroughly. (Should be moist; if not, add more marmalade.) Remove ¼ of dough from refrigerator. Roll out very thin on floured board into rectangle. Run filling along long edge of dough; make sure filling is about 1¼ inches in diameter. Roll over and over until all dough is used. Carefully place strip on well-oiled 9 x 13 baking sheet. 2 strips will fit on 1 sheet. Repeat process until dough and filling are used up. Make diagonal slashes about 1-inch deep, 1-inch apart, on each strip. Bake at 350° for 30 minutes or until nicely browned. Let stand in pan 3-4 minutes; sprinkle top with superfine sugar. (Left-over dough may be frozen. Strudel may be frozen after it is baked. May add grated apple or small can crushed pineapple to filling.) Makes 72 pieces.

Lee Kucker

Sugar Plums

½ cup shortening	½ teaspoon baking soda
½ cup sugar	¼ cup milk
2 eggs, well beaten	1 pound pitted dates
1 teaspoon vanilla	Walnut halves
1½ cups all-purpose flour, sifted	

Cream shortening, add sugar and blend well. Add eggs and vanilla. Sift flour with soda and add alternately with milk to first mixture. Stuff dates with walnut meats and dip into cookie batter. Bake on greased cookie sheet at 375° for 10 minutes.

Rose Goldstein

Swedish Ice Box Cookies

½ cup shortening	2 tablespoons caraway seeds
¾ cup confectioners sugar (or regular sugar)	1½ cups sifted flour, all purpose
	1 teaspoon vanilla
1 egg, well beaten	1 cup chopped nuts

Cream shortening, add sugar and beaten egg. Mix seeds with flour and nuts and blend thoroughly into first mixture. Form into rolls, wrap in wax paper and chill. Slice or form balls. Bake 12-15 minutes at 350° on lightly greased cookie sheet.

Fanny Frank

Thumbprint Cookies

½ cup soft shortening	¼ teaspoon salt
¼ cup brown sugar, packed	1 egg white, slightly beaten
1 egg yolk	¾ cup finely chopped nuts
½ teaspoon vanilla	Candied fruit, jam or frosting
1 cup flour, sifted	

Mix shortening, sugar, egg yolk and vanilla. Sift flour and salt together, stir into shortening mixture. Roll into 1-inch balls, dip in slightly beaten egg white, and roll in nuts. Place 1 inch apart on ungreased cookie sheet. Bake at 375° for 5 minutes. Remove from oven and quickly press thumb gently on top of each cookie. Return to oven and bake 8 minutes longer. Cool and place a piece of candied fruit or jam or frosting in thumbprint. Remove cookies very gently from cookie sheet as they crumble easily when warm.

Jill Musicus

Wine Cookies

2½ cups unsifted flour	3 tablespoons red wine
1 cup shortening	½ cup sugar
2 egg yolks	

Mix all ingredients with hands until dough is very pliable (one recipe at a time works best.) Make dough into small balls and decorate with nuts or cherries. For extra good taste, make a thumbprint in the cookie before baking and then fill with grape jelly. Bake at 350° for 15-20 minutes on greased cookie sheet. Makes about 6 dozen.

Mrs. Donald Friedman

Brazil Nut Fudge Balls

1 6-ounce package semi-sweet
   chocolate morsels
3 tablespoons light corn syrup
1/3 cup orange juice
2½ cups crushed vanilla wafers
1 cup finely chopped Brazil nuts

Melt chocolate morsels over hot, not boiling water. Remove from heat, stir in corn syrup and orange juice. Stir in remaining ingredients. Let stand about 30 minutes. Form into 1-inch balls. Roll in confectioners sugar, coconut or finely ground walnuts. Makes about 4½ dozen.

Rose Goldstein

Chocolate Nut Balls

1 small can evaporated milk
1 6-ounce package semi-sweet
   chocolate pieces
2½ cups crushed vanilla wafers
½ cup sifted confectioners
   sugar
1¼ cups chopped walnuts
1/3 cup brandy or orange juice

In saucepan, cook milk and chocolate pieces over medium heat, stirring until chocolate is melted and mixture is smooth. Remove from heat, add wafers, sugar, ½ cup nuts and brandy, mixing well. Let stand for 30 minutes. Shape into balls. Roll in remaining nuts. Refrigerate 1 hour or until firm.

Dottie Ring

Chocolate Rum Drums

1 8½-ounce package
   chocolate wafers
1 cup pecans, chopped
1 cup confectioners sugar
¼ cup light corn syrup
¼ cup dark rum
Confectioners sugar or sweetened
   cocoa mix

Combine crushed chocolate wafers, nuts, confectioners sugar, corn syrup and dark rum. Mix well, shape by teaspoonfuls into round balls. Let stand 10 minutes, roll in extra confectioners sugar or sweetened cocoa mix. Makes about 5 dozen.

Rose Adelstein

Date Coconut Balls

1 cup pitted dates
1 stick margarine or butter
1 scant cup sugar
½ teaspoon salt
1 egg
1 teaspoon vanilla
2 scant cups Rice Krispies
1 cup chopped nuts
Shredded coconut

Mix together dates, shortening, sugar, salt, egg and vanilla. Cook in saucepan for 10 minutes. Cool until workable. Add Rice Krispies and chopped nuts. Shape into balls about the size of quarters. Roll in coconut.

Ruth Bittker

Marshmallow Log Cookies

3 squares melted chocolate
1 cup confectioners sugar
½ cup chopped nuts
1 teaspoon lemon juice
¼ teaspoon vanilla
1 package miniature marshmallows
1 can coconut

Mix all ingredients well, except coconut. Sprinkle coconut on wax paper and roll mixture on coconut, into 2 log-shaped strips. Freeze. When ready to use, cut in slices.

Marlene Elkin

No-Bake Peanut Butter Cookies

1 cup light corn syrup
1 cup sugar
1 cup peanut butter

½ teaspoon almond extract
8-ounce box cornflakes

Heat corn syrup and sugar to boil. Remove from heat. Add peanut butter and almond extract. Pour mixture over cornflakes and combine quickly. Drop by teaspoons on waxed paper and let cool until firm. Makes about 7 dozen.

Lois Kwasman

Bite-Size Cheese Cakes

Topping:

½ cup sugar
1½ tablespoons corn starch
1 1-pound can red tart pitted

cherries
Few drops red food coloring

Filling:

½ cup chocolate cookie crumbs
    or ½ cup gingersnap crumbs
8 ounces cream cheese
1/3 cup sugar

1 egg, slightly beaten
2 teaspoons lemon juice
½ teaspoon vanilla

Combine sugar and cornstarch in sauce pan, stir in cherries and juice, stirring until mixture boils and thickens. Add red food coloring. Cool. Line miniature cup cake tins with paper cups. Spoon about 2 teaspoons crumbs into each cup. Beat cheese, sugar, egg, lemon juice and vanilla until smooth. Spoon into each cup. Bake 8-10 minutes until set in 375° oven. Cool. Top each with cherry sauce.

Frumel Ureles

Cherry Cream Cheese Tarts

1 3-ounce package cream
    cheese, softened
½ cup butter or margarine,
    softened
1 cup sifted enriched flour

¼ teaspoon salt
½ cup cherry preserves, cut up
½ cup chopped walnuts
1 teaspoon grated lemon peel

Blend cream cheese and butter, add flour and salt. Form dough into a ball. Chill 3-4 hours. Mix preserves, nuts and peel. Divide dough in half on lightly floured surface. Roll each half to approximately 12 x 12 inches. With glass, cut into circles; place ½ teaspoon preserve mixture in center of each circle. Moisten edges, fold, and seal with fork. Bake on ungreased baking sheet at 375° about 12 minutes. Dust with confectioners sugar. Makes about 40.

Eulah Feier

Glazed Cheesecake Puffs

1 pound cream cheese
¾ cup sugar
2 eggs
1 teaspoon vanilla

24 vanilla wafers
2 cans pie filling, cherry or
    blueberry

Whip cream cheese, sugar, eggs and vanilla with mixer. In 24 foil baking cups, put a wafer. Fill cups ¾ full of cheese mixture. Bake at 375° for 10 minutes; cover with pie filling and chill. Yields 24.

Maxine Peters

Cream Cheese Squares

Crust

16 graham crackers, crushed
3 tablespoons butter

¼ teaspoon cinnamon

Filling

1 pound cream cheese
3 eggs, beaten
½ cup sugar

½ teaspoon vanilla
½ teaspoon lemon juice

Topping

1 cup sour cream
2 tablespoons sugar

½ teaspoon vanilla

Mix crust ingredients and press into a greased 8 inch square pan. Mix filling ingredients and spread over crust. Bake 25 minutes at 375°. Cool slightly. Spread on mixed topping ingredients and bake 7 minutes more. Sprinkle chopped nuts after baking. Refrigerate when cool and cut before serving. Makes 25 squares.

Bertha Cravetz

Richie's Rich Cheese Squares

5 tablespoons butter or mar-
    garine
1/3 cup brown sugar
1 cup sifted all-purpose flour
¼ cup ground walnuts
½ cup granulated sugar

1 package (8 ounces) cream
    cheese, softened
1 egg
2 tablespoons milk
1 tablespoon lemon juice
½ teaspoon vanilla

Cream margarine and brown sugar together, add flour and nuts and mix well. Set aside one cup of above mixture for topping. Press remainder in bottom of 8 x 8 x 2 pan. Bake at 350° for 12-15 minutes. Blend granulated sugar and cream cheese until smooth. Add egg, milk, lemon juice and vanilla; beat well and pour over bottom crust. Sprinkle with topping and return to oven, bake 25 minutes more. Cool, chill and cut into squares. Makes about 16-20 squares.

Myrna LaBaer

Chocolate Eclairs

1 cup water
½ cup butter
1 cup flour

¼ teaspoon salt
4 eggs

Heat water and butter in saucepan until it boils. Pour flour and salt into hot mixture and beat thoroughly. Stir and cook over low flame until mixture forms stiff ball. Remove from heat and add unbeaten eggs 1 at a time. Beat thoroughly after adding each egg. Drop by teaspoon or tablespoon (depending on size desired) on greased baking sheet. Bake at 450° for 20 minutes, then at 325° for 20 minutes. Makes 1 dozen.

Vanilla custard filling

2 tablespoons cornstarch
½ cup sugar
2 eggs

2 cups milk
1 teaspoon vanilla
1 tablespoon margarine

Cook all ingredients except vanilla until thick. Cool, add vanilla. Fill puffs. Packaged vanilla pudding may be used. Frost with chocolate icing.

Myrna LaBaer

Chocolate Nut Tarts

Dough

1 cup sifted all-purpose flour	1 egg, beaten (cold)
¼ teaspoon baking powder	1/3 cup vegetable shortening
¼ teaspoon salt	

Filling

1 6-ounce package chocolate bits	1 teaspoon vanilla
	1 egg, beaten
1 tablespoon milk (or mocha mix)	Crushed walnuts, optional
	1/3 cup sugar
1 tablespoon butter	

Sift together dry ingredients, cut in shortening until the size of small peas. Sprinkle 3-4 tablespoons of beaten egg over dough and stir with fork to form dough. Roll out on floured board and cut to fit small tea-size cupcake tins. Mix filling together by melting chocolate and stirring in milk, butter and vanilla. Remove from heat and blend in egg. Add crushed walnuts to mixture, about 1 scant tablespoon for each pastry shell. Bake at 350° for 20-25 minutes.

Sylvia Kowal

Talglach

2 eggs, beaten	1 cup honey
2 tablespoons vegetable oil	½ cup sugar
1½-2 cups flour	½ teaspoon ginger
½ teaspoon salt	1 cup walnuts, chopped
½ teaspoon baking powder	

Prepare dough by mixing eggs and oil together; then add flour, salt and baking powder. Dough should be soft, but not sticky. Add more flour, if necessary. Knead until smooth. Roll and twist dough into a long strip about 1/3 inch thick. Cut into pieces about 1/3 inch in length. Either bake or boil in honey according to the following.

Bake: Combine honey, sugar and ginger and bring to a gentle boil, stirring constantly. When sugar is melted, pour syrup into baking pan and place the pieces of dough in this. Bake in 350° oven until dough puffs and begins to brown. This will take about 20 minutes. Do not open door before this time. When dough begins to brown, add nuts. Stir frequently with wooden spoon to separate the pieces. When taiglach sound hollow when stirred with a wooden spoon, place on a board wet with cold water. Pour the contents of the baking pan on this; with wet hands mold the taiglach into a cake about 8 inches square and 2 inches high. Cut into 2-inch squares or diamonds.

Boil: Bake the pieces of dough in a well-greased pan at 375° for about 10 minutes or until light brown. Shake pan to keep balls separated and to brown evenly. Boil honey, sugar and ginger gently for 5 minutes. Add dough and nuts. Boil gently over low heat, stirring constantly with wooden spoon, until mixture is a deep golden brown. Pour on board wet with cold water; shape and cut as for baked taiglach. Makes 3-4 dozen.

Desserts

Apple Crisp

6 apples
½ cup flour
1 cup brown sugar
1/3 cup butter

½ cup orange juice
Cinnamon
Whipping cream

Grease a 2-quart casserole. Peel and slice enough apples to fill it 2/3 full (about 6). In bowl combine flour, sugar and butter. Use pastry blender. Pour orange juice on apples. Top with sugar mixture. Sprinkle with cinnamon. Bake at 375° until apples are cooked and mixture bubbles. Serve warm with whipped cream or topping. Serves 6.

Enid Ryen

Peanut Butter Apple Crisp

1 quart sliced apples, (6-7 medium or 3 20-ounce)
½ cup white sugar
1/3 cup brown sugar
4 tablespoons flour

½ cup rolled oats (quick cooking)
1/3 teaspoon cinnamon
¼ teaspoon salt
3 tablespoons margarine
3 tablespoons peanut butter

Peel and slice apples into greased shallow pan, add white sugar and mix. Mix together the brown sugar, flour, oats, salt and cinnamon. Cut in margarine and peanut butter until crumbly. Sprinkle evenly over apples. Bake in 350° oven until apples are tender, about 40-50 minutes. Serve with ice cream.

Shirley Jacobson

Apple Krisp

6-8 apples
1 cup flour
½ cup sugar
1 teaspoon baking powder

1 egg
½ cup melted shortening
Cinnamon and sugar

Peel and slice apples into greased 9 x 12 baking pan. In a bowl, mix flour, sugar, baking powder and egg, stirring with fork until small balls form. Drop over apples. Pour melted shortening over dough. Sprinkle with cinnamon and sugar. Bake at 350° for 1 hour or until brown.

Bea Horn

Apple Squares

½ cup vegetable shortening
1 cup sugar
2 eggs
¼ teaspoon salt
2 cups all-purpose flour (enough

to handle dough)
2 cans sliced apples
½ cup sugar
2 teaspoons cinnamon

Blend shortening, sugar, eggs and salt; add enough flour to handle dough. Pat out half the dough in a 7½ x 11 baking dish. Spread apples over the dough. Cover with ½ cup sugar mixed with 2 teaspoons cinnamon, reserving 1/3 of it for top crust. Top crust will be difficult to spread so flour your hands, take small amounts of dough and flatten with your hands and set on top of apples until apples are covered. Sprinkle remaining cinnamon and sugar over top crust. Bake at 425° for 30 minutes.

Ruth Drexler

Ricky's Banana Pie Dessert

2 eggs, beaten	1 teaspoon baking powder
4 tablespoons butter	3 bananas
½ cup sugar	¼ cup coconut flakes
1 cup flour	¼ cup brown sugar
½ teaspoon salt	2 tablespoons lemon juice

Beat eggs. Cream butter and add sugar slowly, beating very well until fluffy. Add eggs and beat well. Sift flour, salt and baking powder and add to already beaten ingredients. Beat thoroughly. Grease and dust with flour an 8 inch or 10 inch square pan. Pour the mixture into the pan. Split bananas lengthwise and place the banana halves on top, sprinkle with the coconut flakes, brown sugar and lemon juice. Bake at 350° about 30 minutes. Let cool and serve with whipped cream. Serves 6.

Ricky Sands

Coconut Crunch

½ cup sugar	¼ cup lemon juice
2½ tablespoons corn starch	1 teaspoon grated lemon rind
¼ teaspoon salt	1 tablespoon butter
1 1/3 cups milk	½ teaspoon vanilla
1 egg	Coconut crust

Combine sugar, corn starch, salt. Stir in milk. Cook until thick, stirring constantly. Mix egg and lemon juice; stir in a little hot mixture, return to pan. Cook over low heat stirring constantly for 2 minutes. Add lemon rind, butter and vanilla. Pour into coconut crust.

Coconut Crust

1¼ cups shredded coconut	½ cup butter, soft
¾ cup graham cracker crumbs	½ cup flour
½ cup sugar	

Combine all ingredients. Place half in bottom of 8-inch square pan. Pour in filling, top with remaining coconut mixture. Bake at 400°, 25 minutes or until top is golden brown. Chill, cut in squares. Serves 9.

Beatrice DiMora

Cranberry Crunch Squares

1 cup quick cooking rolled oats	1/3 cup butter or margarine
¾ cup brown sugar	1 pound can whole cranberry
½ cup sifted flour	sauce
½ cup moist, shredded coconut	1 tablespoon lemon juice

Mix oats, brown sugar, flour and coconut. Cut in butter until crumbly. Place half in 8 x 8 x 2 greased baking dish. Combine cranberry sauce and lemon juice. Place on top of mixture in baking dish. Top with remaining crumbs. Bake in 350° oven for 40 minutes. Cut into squares and serve hot, topped with vanilla ice cream. Makes 9 servings.

Ettie Rubenstein

Date Squares with Meringue Topping

Batter

½ cup butter	1½ cups flour
½ cup brown sugar	1 teaspoon baking powder
2 egg yolks	

Mix butter, brown sugar and yolks for the base and cream very well. Mix in the flour and baking powder and pat into a 9-inch square pan.

Filling	**Topping**
1½ cups dates	2 egg whites
¾ cup water	1 cup brown sugar
1 teaspoon lemon juice	¼ cup chopped nuts

Boil the dates, water and lemon juice until the water has evaporated and the dates are soft. Spread on top of base. Beat egg whites until stiff. Add brown sugar and beat again. Gently fold in chopped nuts. Bake at 375° for 20-25 minutes. Cut into squares when cool.

Claire W. Taksen

Frosted Strawberry Squares

1 cup flour	2/3 cup granulated sugar
¼ cup brown sugar	1 10-ounce package frozen
½ cup chopped nuts	strawberries
½ cup melted butter	2 tablespoons lemon juice
2 egg whites	1 cup heavy cream, whipped

Combine the first 4 ingredients and spread on a cookie sheet. Bake 20 minutes at 350°, stirring occasionally to break up into small pieces. Beat egg whites on high speed, adding sugar gradually until stiff. Fold in partially defrosted berries, lemon juice and whipped cream. Place half of crumb mixture in the bottom of a 9 x 13 pan, then add all of the berry mixture; then sprinkle the rest of the crumbs and freeze. Serve frozen.

Maxine Strauss

Bananas a la Mode

2 ripe bananas, peeled	⅛ teaspoon cinnamon
1 tablespoon lemon juice	2 tablespoons banana liqueur
¼ cup brown sugar	¼ cup white rum
2 tablespoons butter	1 pint vanilla ice cream

Slice bananas in half length-wise; brush with lemon juice. Melt sugar in flat chafing dish or 10-inch skillet. Add bananas; saute until just tender. Sprinkle with cinnamon. Remove from heat; add liqueur and rum. Ignite at once. Baste bananas with liquid until flame burns out. Divide sauce and bananas over 4 servings of ice cream. (Eat and forget your weight — it's worth the extra pounds!)

Julia Berlove

Cherries Jubilee

¾ cup currant jelly	½ cup brandy
1 1-pound-13-ounce can pitted Bing cherries, drained	1½ quarts vanilla ice cream

Cut vanilla ice cream into 8 serving slices and freeze on wax paper. (This can be done several hours or day before serving.) In chafing dish, over direct heat, melt currant jelly, stirring gently. Add cherries to jelly, heat slowly until simmering, stirring occasionally. Pour brandy into center of cherries, heat undistrubed, then light with match. Quickly spoon flaming cherries over ice cream. Serves 8.

Sue Kiner

Orange Dessert

6 naval oranges
¾ cup orange juice
Juice of lemon
¾ cup sugar

1/3 cup water
Rind of ½ orange, cut in narrow strips.

Peel oranges. Either open in shape of flower or slice. Set aside. Cook the following until it boils: orange juice, lemon juice, sugar, water. Add orange rind. Simmer 45 minutes. Pour sauce over fruit. Serve with dessert fork and knife. Serves 6.

Marion S. Jacobstein

Baked Peach Halves

1 20-ounce can of peaches
1 scant cup brown sugar

Stick cinnamon (small amount)
Sour cream

Turn a can of peach halves into a baking dish. Sprinkle with brown sugar. Add stick cinnamon. Bake slowly at 325° until syrup is thick. Top with sour cream.

Anna Levine

Pineapple and Banana Fritters

1 cup flour
2 teaspoons baking powder
1¼ teaspoons salt
¼ cup sugar
1 egg, well-beaten
½ cup milk

1 tablespoon melted butter
1 teaspoon vanilla
4 small bananas
4 canned pineapple rings
Flour
Frying fat

Peel bananas and split lengthwise. Drain pineapple rings. Combine flour, baking powder, salt and sugar in bowl. Blend egg, milk, butter, and vanilla and add to dry ingredients. Mix until smooth. Batter will be thick. Coat fruit with flour. Dip in batter to cover. Deep fry in hot fat 375° until brown, about 4-6 minutes. May be served with these sauces:

Cardamon Orange Sauce

1½ cups orange juice
½ teaspoon grated orange rind
½ cup sugar

1½ teaspoons lemon juice
¼ teaspoon currant jelly
2 teaspoons ground cardamon

Blend all ingredients in sauce pan. Cook at rolling boil for 5 minutes. Chill.

Sour Cream Sauce

Chop maraschino cherries into sour cream

Eulah Feier

Elegant Strawberries Romanoff

½ pint heavy cream
1 pint softened vanilla ice cream

6 tablespoons Cointreau
2 quarts fresh strawberries, sugared

Whip heavy cream and mix with softened vanilla ice cream. Blend in Cointreau and sugared strawberries. Place in stem glass and garnish with more berries. Refrigerate until ready to serve.

Carol Goldberg

Strawberry Supreme

1 package (6 ounces) strawberry
  gelatin
1½ cups boiling water
1½ cups ice water

1 pint vanilla ice cream
1 package (10 ounces) frozen
  strawberries, thawed
2 teaspoons corn starch

Dissolve gelatin in boiling water. Add ice water and ice cream. Stir until thoroughly blended. Pour into 5-cup mold and chill until firm. Drain strawberries. Set aside. Combine syrup and cornstarch in saucepan. Cook over medium heat until mixture starts to boil. Remove from heat; add strawberries. Chill. To serve, unmold and serve with strawberry sauce.

Alyne Phillips

Compote Brulee

1 can (16 ounces) Freestone
  peaches
1 can (16 ounces) apricots, cut
  up or halves
1 can (16 ounces) black cherries

or fresh cherries
½ cup sugar
Juice of 1 orange
Juice of ½ lemon
Orange and lemon rind, grated

Drain fruit, place in oblong dish or casserole. Bake in oven, 325°, for one hour. Mix sugar, orange and lemon juice. Pour over fruit 3 minutes before finished and sprinkle rind over top. Serve hot or cold with whipped cream.

Anna Levine

Hot Fruit Compote

1 can peach slices, drained
  very well
1 can pineapple chunks, drained
  very well

1 small can mandarin oranges,
  drained very well
1 can cherry pie filling
2 tablespoons dry Tang

Put first three ingredients into greased casserole, and pour cherry pie filling over, and Tang. Mix gently. Heat in 325° oven, covered, for 20 minutes. A good side dish with meat or poultry. Can also be used over vanilla ice cream. Variations and additions are: 1 box dried apricots and/or 1 box dried pitted prunes which have been plumped in boiling water. Serves 6-8.

Jane Rubens and Marcia Isner

Fruit Compote Casserole

12 macaroons, crumbled
4 cups drained canned fruit
  (pears, apricots, peaches)
½ cup slivered almonds, browned
  in margarine (pareve)

¼ cup brown sugar
½ cup sherry
¼ cup melted butter or
  pareve margarine

Grease 2½-quart casserole. Cover bottom with crumbs. Alternate fruit and crumbs in layers ending with crumb layer. Sprinkle on almonds, sugar and sherry. Add melted butter or margarine before putting in oven. Bake at 350° for 30 minutes.

Lillian Schulman

Curried Fruit

1/3 cup pareve margarine
¾ cup brown sugar
2 teaspoons curry
1 can each of pears, peaches,

apricots, pineapple chunks
  (medium size)
1 jar Maraschino cherries

Melt margarine, add sugar and curry. Drain fruit. Put fruit in casserole. Pour sauce on top. Bake 1 hour at 325°.

Ellie Bernhardt

Fruit Supreme

1 large or 2 small fresh pineapples	Lemon juice
Sugar	1 cup slivered almonds, toasted
2 quarts strawberries	2 quarts lemon sherbet or vanilla ice cream
4-6 bananas	

Peel, core and cut pineapple in thin slivers. Sugar very lightly. It is important to have the fruit not too sweet, as the sauce is sweet. Wash and stem strawberries, leave whole. Near serving time, slice bananas and sprinkle with lemon juice; this keeps them from darkening.

Sauce:

½ cup butter	you like
3 cups brown sugar	2/3 cup pineapple or orange juice
Rum extract or light rum, if	

Melt butter in skillet. Add brown sugar, let this cook and bubble over moderate heat 2 or 3 minutes, but watch that sugar doesn't burn. Add juice. Cook until sugar dissolves and sauce is of syrupy texture but not too thick. Add more juice and rum extract. To serve: arrange sherbet or ice cream in center of large shallow bowl with the three fruits in groups around it. Or you could mix them just before serving. Sprinkle fruit with toasted slivered almonds. Heat the sauce and serve hot at the table after fruit and sherbet have been served. Serves 8.

Lucille Michel

Pareve Ice Cream

1 8-ounce container Rich's Whip, defrosted	2 eggs, separated
3 tablespoons sugar	1 teaspoon vanilla or any flavor you desire

Whip Rich's Whip at the highest whipping speed. Whip very well. Add sugar, 1 tablespoon at a time, then add egg yolks and flavoring. Whip egg whites and fold in. Freeze. Fruit may also be folded in after the egg whites.

Bea Hoschander

Pareve Chocolate Ice Cream

2 egg whites	2 tablespoons cocoa
2 8-ounce cartons whipped topping	1 teaspoon rum flavoring
1 small can (6 ounces) chocolate syrup	1 teaspoon almond extract
	¼ cup sugar

Beat whites until peaks form. Add topping and beat. Add rest of ingredients and continue beating for 15 or 20 minutes until thickened. Pour into freezer containers and freeze overnight or for about 5 hours. Serves 8.

Miriam Kolko

Pareve Chocolate Chip Ice Cream

1 8-ounce container Rich's Whip	1 teaspoon vanilla
3 whole eggs	1 6-ounce package chocolate bits
¼ cup sugar	

Beat Rich's Whip until full volume and add eggs, one at a time; beat well after each addition. Add sugar and vanilla and beat. Fold melted and slightly cooled chocolate bits gently into the whipped mixture and place in the freezer for several hours. This will freeze like chocolate chip ice cream.

Variations: 1. Fold in 1 can crushed pineapple, drained. 2. Add 1 teaspoon almond extract, tint with green food coloring and fold in toasted nuts.

June Cohen

Baked Alaska

1 9-inch yellow-cake layer	1 quart sherbet
1 quart vanilla ice cream,	8 egg whites
more ice cream if necessary	1 cup granulated sugar

A few days ahead: cut out piece of heavy brown paper at least ½ inch larger than cake layer; place on 14 x 10 cookie sheet. Center cake on paper; place in freezer to chill. Line 1½-quart mixing bowl with waxed paper or foil; along bottom and sides, pack vanilla ice cream. Then fill center with raspberry sherbet (or other sherbet). On top, place sheet of waxed paper; then press top flat with palm of hands. Freeze until firm. When ice cream is firm, make meringue. Beat egg whites until they stand in moist, drooping peaks when beater is raised. Slowly add sugar, 2 tablespoons at a time, beating until stiff and glossy. Invert ice cream onto cake layer. Peel off paper. Cover ice cream and cake completely with meringue. Return to freezer. 15 minutes before serving: heat oven to 500°. Remove Alaska from freezer. Bake 4-5 minutes until delicate brown. Remove from oven and serve immediately.

Elaine Simon

Ice Cream Cake Roll

5 eggs, separated	¼ cup sifted all-purpose flour
½ teaspoon cream of tartar	1 quart pink peppermint ice
1 cup sugar	cream, or any desired flavor
3 tablespoons cocoa	

Spread tea towel with confectioners sugar to receive cake. Beat egg whites and cream of tartar until stiff but not dry. Gradually beat in ½ cup sugar. Beat egg yolks until thick and lemon colored. Sift together remaining ½ cup sugar, flour, cocoa, and salt; fold into egg yolks until blended. Stir in vanilla. Carefully fold yolk mixture into egg white mixture. Line bottom of 15 x 10 jelly roll pan with waxed paper; grease paper lightly. Spread batter evenly in pan. Bake in slow oven at 325° for 25 minutes, or until cake springs back when lightly touched. Cool a few minutes. Cut carefully around edges. Turn out on towel. Peel off waxed paper quickly, but carefully. Cool for a few minutes. Roll cake with towel from short side of rectangle. When cool, unroll. Stir ice cream just to soften slightly; gently spread on cake. Roll again. Wrap carefully in foil and freeze. When cake is frozen, remove foil and spread with Chocolate Glaze. May be partially used at any time and returned to freezer.

Chocolate Glaze

6-ounce package chocolate	1 teaspoon vanilla
chips	½ cup broken pecans
6-ounce can evaporated milk	

In small sauce pan, combine chocolate chips and evaporated milk. Cook over low heat, stirring constantly, until blended and mixture comes to boil. Cook about 1 minute longer, stirring constantly. Add vanilla. Cool and spread on cake and sprinkle with pecans. Freeze uncovered until glaze hardens, then wrap.

Edith Perlman

Ice Cream Snow Ball

1 or 2 jelly rolls
1 pint vanilla ice cream
6 pints assorted colors and
flavors of ice creams or
sherbets
½ pint whipping cream

Slice jelly rolls into fairly thick slices. Line one or two bowls with the slices, cutting some pieces to fill all the empty spaces. Because the amounts of sherbet and ice cream make more than one bowl of dessert, it is better to make two at one time and freeze them to use as desired. Into bowl lined with jelly roll slices put alternate colors of ice cream and sherbet, varying the colors. Pour vanilla ice cream which has been melted at room temperature into the filled bowl. Cover with aluminum foil and freeze. Just before serving, take from freezer, run a spatula around inside of the bowl. Place dish over top of bowl; invert. Frost the contents with whipped cream. One bowl serves 8-10.

Julia Berlove

Orange Sherbet

2 cups water
½ cup sugar
½ cup corn syrup
⅛ teaspoon salt
1½ cups orange juice
1/3 cup lemon juice
Grated rind of 1 orange
2 egg whites, stiffly beaten

Mix water, sugar, corn syrup, and salt and cook for 5 minutes. Cool. Add orange juice, lemon juice, and orange rind. Pour into freezing trays and freeze to a firm mush. Beat until smooth and fluffy. Fold in the beaten egg whites. Return to freezer and freeze until firm. Can substitute ¾ cup lime juice for orange juice to make lime sherbet.

Nancy Moscov

Fudge Sundae Pie

1 cup evaporated milk
1 6-ounce package semi-sweet
  chocolate chips
1 cup miniature marshmallows
¼ teaspoon salt
Vanilla wafers
1 quart vanilla ice cream
Pecan halves

Combine milk, chocolate chips, marshmallows and salt. Stir over medium heat until marshmallows and chocolate chips melt and mixture thickens. Cool. Line bottom and sides of a nine inch pie plate (or two one-quart refrigerator trays) with vanilla wafers. Fill with half of the ice cream. Cover with half of the chocolate sauce. Repeat layers; garnish with pecans. Freeze.

Selma Kay

Apricot Mousse

4 egg whites
1-1/3 cups of apricot preserves

Beat egg whites until stiff. To ¼ of beaten egg whites, add apricot preserves. Stir vigorously. Fold the remaining egg whites carefully into the mixture. Pour into buttered 1-quart souffle dish. Place souffle dish in pan filled with 1-inch of water. Bake in 350° oven for 45 minutes. May be eaten immediately or left to cool.

Dr. Charles Solky

Chocolate Mousse

1 cup light cream	4 egg yolks
1 cup heavy cream	Dash of salt
½ pound bittersweet chocolate bits	1 teaspoon vanilla
	1 teaspoon instant coffee

Put bits in blender. Bring light cream to boil and pour over bits. Blend. Add yolks and blend (5 seconds). Add salt, vanilla, and coffee. Add heavy cream. Blend. Refrigerate for 24 hours or overnight. Pour into 5 or 6 sherbet cups.

Ellie Bernhardt

Pareve Chocolate Mousse

1 6-ounce package chocolate bits	4 eggs, separated
5 tablespoons hot coffee	2 tablespoons light rum

Over hot water, melt chocolate with hot coffee. Add rum and egg yolks and beat very well. Beat egg whites separately and fold chocolate mixture into whites. Pour into sherbet glasses and chill. Serves 6. The first 4 ingredients may be combined in blender and mixed on high speed for about 1 minute.

Mrs. Irwin Metzger

Coffee Mousse

24 marshmallows	½ pint stiffly beaten whipped cream
1 cup very strong coffee	

Melt marshmallows in coffee. Cool and fold in whipped cream. Chill and serve topped with a cherry or chopped nuts. Also good if you cut up an angel cake into 3 layers and put between layers.

Ellie Bernhardt

Mousse de Menthe

2 3-ounce packages lemon gelatin	¼ cup creme de menthe
1¾ cups hot water	2 cups whipped cream

Dissolve gelatin in hot water and add creme de menthe. Chill until mixture mounds, then whip until frothy. Fold in whipped cream. Chill in 5-cup mold. Note: Dessert topping may be used for a pareve dessert.

Sora Lee Goldberg

Diplomat Pudding

3 cups milk	5 ounces maraschino cherries
2 envelopes gelatin	½ pound almond macaroons, crumbled
¼ cup cold water	½ pint whipped topping
¾ cup sugar	
3 eggs, separated	

Bring milk to scald in double boiler. Dissolve gelatin in cold water. Add to milk and boil for about 5 minutes. Mix together sugar and egg yolks, and add to milk, boiling another 5 minutes. Beat egg whites and add to hot mixture. Cut cherries in quarters, draining and saving juice. In small greased Bundt pan begin to alternate layers — first macaroons, then quartered cherries, then mixture, then cherry juice. Continue until everything is used. Refrigerate at least 24 hours. Garnish with whipped topping. Serves 8-10.

Arline Wiseman

Raisin Bread Pudding

2 cups raisin bread (5-6 slices)
3 cups milk
1 tablespoon butter

2 eggs
2 teaspoons vanilla
Cinnamon

Remove crusts of bread and cut into 1 inch squares. Boil milk and pour over squares of bread. Add butter and cover. Beat eggs and slowly pour in the heated milk mixture. Add vanilla. Pour into lightly greased 8 x 12 pan. Sprinkle lightly with cinnamon. Place pan into another larger pan of water and bake at 350° for about 1 hour, or until knife comes out clean when inserted. Cool and serve. Serves 4-5.

Ida Handelman

Best-Ever Rice Pudding

½ cup raw rice
1 cup water
1 quart milk
¼ cup butter or pareve mar-
    garine

2 eggs, well beaten
½ cup sugar
½ cup raisins
½ teaspoon vanilla

Boil rice in water for 5 minutes. Drain water. Add milk and butter. Cover and cook on top of stove over low heat for 1 hour. Stir once every 15 minutes. Then add 2 well-beaten eggs, sugar, raisins and vanilla. Pour into serving bowl or custard cups. Serve hot or cold. Serves 8.

Sarah Ouriel

Heavenly Hash

2 cups cooked rice
2 cups miniature marshmallows
1 1/3 cups drained pineapple
    tidbits
¼ cup slivered almonds, toasted

½ cup heavy cream
¼ cup sugar
1 teaspoon vanilla
Maraschino cherries

Combine rice, marshmallows, pineapple tidbits and nuts. Whip cream, gradually adding sugar and vanilla. Fold into rice mixture. Chill. Garnish with cherries.

Selma Kay

Chocolate Angel Delight

2 6-ounce packages chocolate
    chips
4 tablespoons sugar
3 eggs, separated
2 cups heavy cream, whipped (or

pareve whip)
1 medium angel food cake
1 5-ounce package slivered
    almonds

Melt chocolate in double boiler. Add sugar and stir. Remove from heat. Add small amount of hot mixture to beaten egg yolks. Mixture will be grainy. Return yolk mixture to melted chocolate. Fold in stiffly beaten egg whites. Cool completely. Gently fold in whipped cream. Tear cake in bite-size pieces. Place layer of cake in 9 x 13 lightly buttered pan. Add layer of chocolate sauce. Lightly mix with fork. Repeat layers. Top with almonds. Refrigerate for at least 12 hours. Yields 15-18 servings.

Sharon Rosenbaum

Chocolate Chiffon Ice Box Cake

12 ladyfingers
1 envelope unflavored gelatin
½ cup sugar, divided
¼ teaspoon salt
3 eggs, separated
¾ cup milk

1 cup semi-sweet chocolate
pieces
1 teaspoon vanilla
2/3 cup evaporated milk, icy
cold and whipped

Split ladyfingers; cut off one end to stand upright and place around sides of 8-inch spring form pan. Mix gelatin, ¼ cup sugar, and salt in top of double boiler. Combine egg yolks and milk; add to gelatin mixture. Add chocolate pieces. Cook over boiling water, stirring occasionally, until gelatin is dissolved and chocolate is melted. Beat with rotary beater until blended. Remove from heat, and add vanilla. Chill until mixture mounds slightly when dropped from spoon. Beat egg whites until stiff but not dry. Gradually add remaining ¼ cup of sugar and beat until very stiff. Fold in chocolate mixture and thoroughly chilled, whipped evaporated milk. Turn into prepared pan. Chill until firm. If desired, top with additional whipped cream and chocolate shavings. Serves 8-10.

Margie Wiseman

Chocolate Ladyfinger Cake

4 packages German chocolate
3 tablespoons confectioners
sugar
3 tablespoons hot water
7 eggs

4 packages ladyfingers
2 pints heavy cream
Bitter chocolate or chocolate
jimmies

Melt chocolate on top of double boiler, adding sugar and water. Separate eggs, beat yolks and mix into chocolate. Beat egg whites until stiff and fold into chocolate mixture. Split ladyfingers and arrange a layer on bottom of a 9 inch spring form pan. Top with layer of chocolate mixture. Alternate layers of ladyfingers and chocolate; finish with ladyfingers. Refrigerate overnight. Can be frozen. Before serving, top with whipped cream and grate bitter chocolate over top or sprinkle with jimmies. Serves 16.

Claire Taksen

Chocolate Mousse Cake

Ladyfingers
½ pint whipping cream or ¾ of
a large container of pre-made
whipped topping

5 eggs, separated
1 10-ounce can chocolate syrup
1 tablespoon instant coffee
Chopped pecans

Line bottom and sides of 10 inch spring form with lady fingers. Whip cream. Set aside. Beat egg yolks. Add chocolate syrup and coffee. Fold chocolate mixture into whipped cream, then fold beaten whites into mixture. Pour into shell. Sprinkle with chopped pecans. Freeze, covered. Remove from freezer 20 minutes before serving. Serves 12.

Tillie Kolko

Angel Fruit Dessert

1 cup boiling water
1 package strawberry or rasp-
　　berry gelatin
1 package frozen strawberries
　　　　　or raspberries
½ pint heavy cream
Angel food cake (bar or ring)

Pour boiling water over gelatin; dissolve thoroughly. Stir in frozen strawberries. Chill. Whip heavy cream. When gelatin and strawberries are set, whip, then fold in half of the whipped cream. Tear cake into small pieces, put into tube pan. Pour gelatin-cream mixture over all. Work around cake, being careful not to mash. Chill thoroughly; unmold and frost with remaining whipped cream.

Merle Markus

Lemon Bisque

11 or 12 double graham crackers
6 tablespoons butter or mar-
　　garine, melted
6 tablespoons sugar
1 3-ounce package lemon gelatin
¾ cup sugar
¾ cup water
1 cup cold water
Juice and rind of one lemon
1 large can evaporated milk

Roll graham crackers fine. Stir in butter and sugar. Reserve 2 tablespoons crumb mixture. Pour remaining crumb mixture into greased 13 x 8 pan and press down to form crust. Refrigerate. (If desired, crust may be baked for 5 minutes at 325° before refrigerating). Bring gelatin, sugar and ¾ cup water to a boil. Add cold water, lemon rind and juice. Refrigerate lemon mixture until set. Whip evaporated milk until very thick. Add gelatin mixture by the spoonful to the whipped milk. Pour into crumb crust and sprinkle with reserved crumbs. Refrigerate.

Millie Berman

Elegant Lemon Refrigerator Cake

1½ envelopes unflavored
　　gelatin
1/3 cup cold water
6 egg yolks
¾ cup lemon juice
¾ cup granulated sugar
1 cup heavy cream, whipped
1 tablespoon grated lemon rind
6 egg whites
¾ teaspoon salt
¾ cup granulated sugar
2 dozen ladyfingers, split
½ cup toasted, shredded coconut

Day before: soften gelatin in cold water. In double boiler, beat egg yolks with lemon juice, stir in ¾ cup sugar. Cook over hot, not boiling water, stirring until mixture coats spoon. Remove from heat. Stir in gelatin with rind until dissolved. With electric mixer at high speed, beat whites with salt until they form soft peaks. Slowly add ¾ cup sugar, continuing to beat until whites form stiff peaks. Fold in lemon mixture. Line sides and bottom of 9 inch spring form cake pan with ladyfingers. Pour in lemon mixture. Refrigerate overnight. Just before serving, spread whipped cream on top of cake, garnish with coconut. Remove from pan. Serves 8-12.

Sue Kiner

Orange Blossom Bowl

1 pint whipped topping	12 double ladyfingers
2 tablespoons honey	1 small can mandarin oranges,
6 tablespoons frozen orange	drained
juice concentrate, thawed	

Combine honey and whipped topping in a large bowl. Beat until consistency of whipped cream. Fold in orange juice concentrate. Split ladyfingers; line bottom and sides of a glass serving dish (two-quart size). Pour cream mixture into dish. Refrigerate at least four hours before serving. Garnish with mandarin orange sections. Serves 8.

Margie Wiseman

Florida Snowball

2 tablespoons gelatin	1 cup sugar
4 tablespoons cold water	1/8 teaspoon salt
1 cup boiling water	1½ pints heavy cream
1 cup orange juice	1 large angel food cake
Juice of 1 lemon	1 package shredded coconut

Dissolve gelatin in cold water, add boiling water, juices, sugar, salt and mix well. Place in refrigerator to set until partially jelled (½-1 hour). Then add 1 pint cream, whipped, folding so that it is foamy looking. Take largest mixing bowl and line cross-wise with wax paper. Scrape brown crust from angel cake and break into bite size pieces. Alternate handfuls of cake with whipped cream mixture until bowl is filled. Chill until firm. Turn onto large platter. Frost with ½ pint whipped cream flavored with vanilla and sugar. Sprinkle entirely with coconut. Serves 12.

Joyce Beckerman

Caramel Sauce

1 tablespoon honey	3 tablespoons water
1 cup brown sugar	Cinnamon
3 tablespoons lemon juice	Nuts
3 tablespoons butter	

Mix ingredients. Cook ten minutes. Add cinnamon and nuts if desired.

Julia Berlove

Chocolate Sauce

1 cup sugar	Vanilla
1½ cups water	1½ tablespoons corn starch
1/3 stick butter	Dash salt
2 squares unsweetened chocolate	

Mix all ingredients in sauce pan. Stir over medium heat until it boils. Cool. Serve over cake or ice cream. Can be stored in refrigerator.

Renee Rosenbaum

Rum Sauce

6 egg yolks	¾ cup dark rum, cognac, or
1 cup sugar	kirsch

Beat the yolks until lemon colored, and slightly thickened. Gradually beat in the sugar. Then stir in half the rum and cook over boiling water, stirring constantly until mixture thickens. Do not allow to boil. Stir in the remaining rum. Yield: about 1½ cups sauce.

Ursula Gonsenhauser

Extra Treats

Iced Almonds

1 cup whole almonds, blanched	½ teaspoon vanilla
½ cup sugar	¾ teaspoon salt
2 tablespoons butter	

Heat almonds, sugar and butter in heavy skillet over medium heat. Stir constantly for 15 minutes or until almonds are toasted and sugar is golden brown. Stir in vanilla. Spread nuts on sheet of aluminum foil. Sprinkle with salt. Cool. Break into 2 or 3 nut clusters.

Millie Rosenbaum

Candied Apples

12 apples	¾ cup cold water
2 cups sugar	Few drops flavoring, anise
½ cup light corn syrup	Few drops red coloring

Wash, polish apples, insert sticks. Cook sugar, corn syrup in deep pan until 275° is reached on candy thermometer. Add flavoring and coloring. Stir as little as possible. If too thick, reheat slowly. Dip apples in syrup and place on lightly greased aluminum foil.

Sylvia Gertzog

Apricot Balls

2 packages dried apricots, chopped	1 cup condensed milk
1 cup chopped nuts	1/3 cup Grand Marnier, apricot
1 7-ounce package grated	brandy or apricot nectar
coconut	Confectioners sugar

Mix first 5 ingredients together in bowl. Form into small balls and roll in confectioners sugar. Chill 4 hours before serving.

Lillian Schulman

Apricot Candy

1 pound dried apricots	½ cup chopped nuts
3 cups water	Granulated sugar
3 cups sugar	

Cook apricots and water until mushy. Strain. Add sugar and boil for ½ hour, stirring constantly. Add nuts. Spread on wet board and let stand overnight. Cut into squares and roll in granulated sugar.

Evelyn Lubliner

Apricot Sweets

¾ cup dried apricots, washed and	1 tablespoon orange rind
drained	1 tablespoon lemon juice
¾ cup shredded coconut	Granulated sugar
½ cup nuts	

Put first 3 ingredients through food chopper. Add orange rind and lemon juice. Mix to a paste with your hands. Form into balls about the size of a hickory nut. Roll in granulated sugar. Keep in a covered jar in the refrigerator. Will stay moist and fresh a long time. Makes 35 balls.

Esther Lifshutz

Glazed Swedish Dunking Cherries

¼ cup light corn syrup
3 tablespoons currant jelly
1 tablespoon lemon juice
¼ teaspoon cinnamon

2 tablespoons maraschino
cherry syrup
1 cup red maraschino cherries,
well-drained

Combine first 4 ingredients in saucepan. Cook over low heat, stirring occasionally, until mixture spins a ¼-inch thread. Add cherry syrup and continue cooking over low heat, stirring occasionally, until mixture again spins a ¼-inch thread. Dip cherries, one at a time, into hot glaze. Drain on waxed paper. Makes 40 cherries.

Margie Wiseman

Coconut Balls

2¾ cups crushed vanilla wafers
¼ pound margarine, melted
½ cup chopped pecans

Powdered sugar
Orange juice
Coconut

Combine wafer crumbs, margarine, and pecans. Shape into small balls. Roll balls in powdered sugar; dip into orange juice. Roll in coconut and chill. Frozen juice, slightly diluted, may be used.

Millie Rosenbaum

Foolproof Fudge

¼ pound margarine or butter
2 packages chocolate pudding
mix (not instant)
½ cup milk

1 pound confectioners sugar
1 teaspoon vanilla
1 cup broken nut meats

Melt butter, add pudding as it comes from the package, and stir until well blended. Add milk and bring to a boil. Boil 2 minutes, stirring constantly. Remove from heat, add sugar, vanilla, nuts. Stir until batter is smooth. Place in buttered 8 or 9-inch square pan and chill thoroughly. Cut into squares.

Helen Gordon

Health Food Treats

¾ cup wheat germ
¾ cup powdered milk

½ cup peanut butter
½ cup honey

Combine all ingredients in a bowl and chill in refrigerator. Roll into 1-inch balls. Serve plain or roll in more wheat germ or shredded coconut.

Lois Kuh

Marzipan

1 pound almonds
1 pound confectioners sugar

1 egg white

Blanch almonds and grind very fine. Add sugar and egg white and mix to a smooth dough. As a sweet: Can be rolled into balls and eaten as is or can be dipped in chocolate. As a cookie: Brown in slow oven. As frosting: Roll into thin circles the size of cake used. Set on top. Delicious on whipped cream cake.

Nancy Berger Hauger

Peanut Brittle

1½ teaspoons soda
1 teaspoon water
1 teaspoon vanilla
1½ cups sugar
1 cup water

1 cup light corn syrup
3 tablespoons butter or
  margarine
1 pound shelled unroasted peanuts

Butter 2 baking sheets, each 15½ x 12; keep warm. Combine soda, water and vanilla; set aside. Combine sugar, 1 cup water and corn syrup in large saucepan. Cook over medium heat, stiring occasionally to 240° on candy thermometer (or until small amount of syrup dropped into very cold water forms a soft ball which flattens when removed from water). Stir in butter and peanuts. Cook, stirring constantly, to 300° (or until small amount of mixture dropped into very cold water separates into threads which are hard and brittle). Watch carefully so mixture does not burn. Immediately remove from heat; stir in soda mixture thoroughly. Pour half the candy mixture onto each warm baking sheet and quickly spread evenly about ¼-inch thick. Cool; break candy into pieces. Yield 2 pounds.

Mindy Hecker

Peanut Butter Bon-Bons

1 6-ounce package butterscotch
  pieces
½ cup peanut butter

2 cups chow mein noodles
½ cup chopped nuts

Melt butterscotch pieces and peanut butter in a double boiler or over low heat. Add noodles and nuts. Drop by spoonful onto waxed paper.

Margie Wiseman

Penuche

2 cups brown sugar
¼ teaspoon salt
1 cup milk or cream

1 tablespoon butter
1 teaspoon vanilla
1 cup nut meats

Stir sugar, salt and milk over low heat until sugar is dissolved. Boil until soft ball stage is reached, 230° on a candy thermometer. Add butter. Place saucepan in cold water. When bottom of saucepan is cool, begin to beat candy. Beat until soft and creamy. Add vanilla and nuts. Drop candy from spoon onto waxed paper or oiled surface.

Hyla Axelrod

New Orleans Cream Pralines

1 pound light brown sugar
⅛ teaspoon salt
¾ cup evaporated milk

1 tablespoon butter
2 cups (½ pound) pecan halves
½ teaspoon vanilla (optional)

In a 2-quart saucepan combine sugar, salt, milk and butter. Cook and stir over low heat until sugar is dissolved. Add pecans and continue cooking and stirring over medium heat to soft ball stage (234°). Remove from heat, stir in vanilla if desired, then let cool 5 minutes. Meanwhile, cover a large baking sheet with aluminum foil, or place a large sheet of aluminum foil on a flat surface in readiness for dropping patties. Stir rapidly until mixture begins to thicken and coat pecans lightly. Drop rapidly from a tablespoon onto foil to form patties. If candy becomes too stiff to handle easily toward the last, stir in a few drops of hot water. Let cool before serving.

Julia Berlove

English Toffee

1 cup sugar	1 teaspoon vanilla
1 cup butter	4 ⅞-ounce bars milk chocolate
3 tablespoons water	¾ cup finely chopped nuts

Combine sugar, butter, and water in heavy saucepan. Cook to 300° (hard crack stage), stirring constantly to prevent burning. Remove from heat and add vanilla. Pour into buttered 9 x 9 pan. Lay chocolate bars on top and spread evenly as they melt. While still warm, sprinkle on chopped nuts. Cool thoroughly and break into pieces.

Marsha Edelman

Quick Beet Preserves

3 1-pound cans shoestring beets	1½ tablespoons ginger powder
3 cups sugar	2 lemons, peeled and cut
1¼ cups water	Almonds or walnuts

Drain and wash beets. Mix all ingredients. Place in sauce pan and allow contents to come to a boil. Heat until thick. Turn off heat and allow to cool. Add nuts. Pour into sterilized jars and seal.

Julia Berlove

Peach Marmalade

3 pounds peaches	4 tablespoons lemon juice
2 large oranges (Sunkist), including rind	3½ cups sugar

Wash, peel, and slice peaches in ¼-inch slices. Grate rind of oranges. Peel orange and cut pulp into thin slices. Combine all ingredients in large preserving kettle. Cook until syrup is thick and fruit transparent, stirring frequently. Pour into sterilized jars. Seal. Makes 5 8-ounce glasses.

Esther Lifshutz

Rhubarb Jam

½ cup water	3 cups sugar
5 cups rhubarb	1 package red jello (3 ounces)

Cook water and rhubarb for twenty minutes; add sugar and jello. Keep in refrigerator for weeks or freeze in containers.

Stella Gelman

Tutti-Frutti Jam

1 cup cut fruit	3 oranges, peeled and cut into thin slices
1 cup sugar	

Cook fruit and sugar until thick, stirring often. Cool and pour into very large glass jar. Cover and place in refrigerator. As you cook each fruit, you add it and stir into this jar. When last fruit is added, add oranges and stir. Fill small jars and wax seal. Fruits that can be used: Strawberries, blueberries, blackberries, huckleberries, peaches, plums, apples, grapes, cantalopes, apricots, currants, pineapples, cranberries. Start in June with strawberries. Add each fruit as it comes into season.

Ann Levine

Kosher Dill Pickles

Washed pickles (about 3½ inches in length)
1 teaspoon pickling spices
1 red hot pepper (small or ½ large one)
1½ tablespoons coarse salt
1 flower or seed head of dill
1 clove garlic, crushed
1½ to 2 cups cold water

Pickles should be slim. One eight quart basket yields approximately 12 quarts of dill pickles. Quart size canning jars and covers should be ready. Soak pickles in cold water. Scrub and soak for about an hour in cold salt water. Sterilize jars and covers. Pack pickles in upright position into quart jars. Then fill each one with spices, dill, pepper and garlic. Dissolve coarse salt in cold water while placing other ingredients into jars. Fill jars with salt solution to about ½ inch from top. Seal tightly. Place jars in cool room. Ready as new dills in 4 days.

Sylvia Gertzog

Pickled Peppers

12 green peppers
Salt
1½ cups vinegar
1½ cups water
2 teaspoons pickling spices
½ cup sugar

Bake green peppers on hot grill. Keep turning until all sides are black. Peel off black skin under cold running water. Sprinkle with salt and let stand 15 minutes. Boil vinegar, water and pickling spices. After this comes to a boil, add sugar. Put peppers in large crock or several Mason jars; cover with cooled liquid. May be eaten in 3-4 days. (Roumanian side dish)

Ruthilyn Steinberg

Zucchini Pickles

4 quarts zucchini
6 white onions, sliced
2 green peppers, chopped
2 garlic cloves
½ cup salt
Cracked ice
5 cups white sugar
1½ teaspoons celery seed
1½ teaspoons turmeric
2 tablespoons mustard seed
3 cups vinegar

Do not pare zucchini; thoroughly wash and slice in ½-inch slices. Add onions, peppers, whole garlic and salt; cover with cracked ice. Mix thoroughly, let stand 3 hours; drain thoroughly. Combine remaining ingredients; pour over zucchini mixture. Heat juice to boiling, seal in hot sterilized jars. Makes 8 pints.

Beatrice Di Mora

Cranberry Relish made in Blender

1 pound fresh cranberries
Orange juice
2 oranges
1¼ cups sugar
Chopped walnuts (optional)

Wash cranberries and oranges. Pour enough orange juice in blender to just cover the blades. Cut up oranges and add a little at a time. Add cranberries a little at a time, until all are ground. Add sugar and let it stand overnight. Add walnuts after it has been set. The relish is always better the second day and keeps for weeks.

Stella Gelman

Fish

Gefilte Fish

2 pounds yellow pike, filleted	¼ teaspoon white pepper
1 pound white fish	1 cup cold water
3 eggs	2 medium onions
1 tablespoon salt	2 carrots, sliced

Grind fish and onions through food chopper. Put eggs in mixmaster bowl or use wooden chopping bowl. Beat well. Add ground fish and onion mixture. Add seasonings. Mix. Add water; chop thoroughly. Form into balls and drop into boiling water (almost enough to cover) to which has been added carrots, sliced onions, bones of fish, salt and pepper to taste. Cook slowly, covered, for about 2 hours. Remove fish from gravy carefully after cooling for an hour.

Ida Finn

Snow White Gefilte Fish

3 medium onions	3 pounds fillet white fish
1 large carrot, peeled and sliced	3 large eggs, beaten
3 stalks celery, cut up	3 tablespoons bread crumbs or
2 teaspoons coarse salt	challah
1 teaspoon white pepper	3 tablespoons matzo meal
Sugar, optional	

Place in large pot: 1 onion sliced, carrot, celery, 1 teaspoon course salt, ½ teaspoon pepper, sugar if desired. Grind or blend fish with remaining onions. Beat eggs well and mix thoroughly with fish. Add 1 teaspoon salt, ½ teaspoon pepper, bread crumbs, matzo meal. Form fish balls with wet hands. Place fish balls over vegetables and seasonings. Fill pot with cold water to cover fish. Bring to boil over medium heat. After it comes to a boil, cook 1½ hours more, covered. Cool; remove from liquid.

Rose Kroll

Economical Gefilte Fish Balls

1 pound frozen ocean perch, thawed	½ teaspoon pepper
Small onion	½ cup matzo meal
Small carrot	3 quarts water
Slice of white bread	1 large onion, diced
2 eggs, beaten	1 large carrot, diced
¼ cup peanut oil	2 stalks celery, diced
½ teaspoon salt	2 tablespoons parsley, chopped

Skin fish, rinse in cold water and grind with small onion, small carrot and slice of white bread. Mix well in a bowl, add well-beaten eggs, peanut oil, salt, pepper, and matzo meal. Refrigerate for 10 minutes. Fill large pot with 3 quarts of water, add onion, carrot, celery, and parsley. Bring to a boil, reduce heat to cook stock for 10 minutes. When stock is ready, remove fish from refrigerator and shape fish into balls. Add fish balls, any size to stock and simmer for 1¼ hours, covered. Serve stock as a fish chowder by adding cream or milk and serve with croutons. Serve either hot or cold for supper or as an entree. Serves 4

Betty Alpert

Mock Stuffed Fish

4 cups water
2 onions, sliced thin
2 carrots, sliced thin
2 stalks celery, diced
2 medium potatoes, sliced

1 pound can salmon
1 onion, grated
4 tablespoons matzo meal
3 eggs, separated
Salt and pepper to taste

Bring water to a boil in a large saucepan. Add sliced onions, carrots, celery, potatoes, and half of the salt and pepper. Remove skin from salmon, flake, and combine with grated onion, beaten egg yolks, matzo meal, and remaining salt and pepper. Fold in beaten egg whites. Form into balls. Place gently in the boiling water and vegetables. Reduce heat and simmer until it looks solid and done. Remove balls to a platter and cool, then chill. Serve with the vegetables and soup in which they were cooked. Serves 4.

Ricky Sands

Poached Salmon

Water
1 lemon, cut up
1 stalk celery, cut up
2 carrots, cut up

½ teaspoon pickling spices
2 bay leaves
6-6½ pound salmon

Mix enough water to cover fish with lemon, celery, carrot, spices and bay leaves. Put this in poacher or roasting pan and cook for ½ hour or longer. The longer you cook it, the better it is. This is called Court Bouillon. Wrap salmon in cheese cloth and place carefully in Court Bouillon. Cover and cook for 20-30 minutes on one side, then turn and cook other side for the same amount of time. When done, lift carefully to platter and remove skin from one side. Roll fish over in cheese cloth and remove skin from other side. Slowly work cheese cloth from under fish. The bone may be removed while it is hot. Garnish and refrigerate until ready to serve. Serves 10-12.

Sauce

½ cup sour cream
½ cup mayonnaise
¼ cup chili sauce
¼ cup Court Bouillon

10 pimento-stuffed olives, chopped fine
1 teaspoon horseradish
⅛ teaspoon dill seed

Blend in electric mixer.

Arline Wiseman

Pickled Yellow Pike or Georgian Whitefish

5-6 pounds or 10 pieces of fish
6 glasses water
1½ cups vinegar
6 large onions or 9 small onions

3 tablespoons pickling spices
½ cup sugar
½ teaspoon black pepper
2 tablespoons salt

Wash fish thoroughly and sprinkle kosher coarse salt on lightly. Place in refrigerator the night before or at least an hour before cooking. In a deep pan, cook water, vinegar, sliced onions, pepper, sugar, salt and pickling spices which have been tied securely in a small piece of cheese cloth. When this mixture starts to boil, place fish in slowly and cook for ¾ hour. Season to taste. When done, let cool. Remove fish very carefully to keep it whole. Put fish in a large glass bowl and cool. Strain stock, place onions in bowl with fish, throw away spices and pour stock over fish. Refrigerate and marinate a few days.

Jennie Levinson

Sweet and Sour Fish

3 pounds of salmon or 6 slices	1 tablespoon salt
2 large lemons	¼ teaspoon pepper
4 cups water	1 teaspoon ginger
½ cup seedless raisins	4 onions, sliced
½ cup brown sugar	4-5 ginger snaps

Wash fish; salt and allow to stand 1 hour; rinse. Boil lemon juice, water, raisins, sugar, salt, pepper, ginger and sliced onions. Season to taste. When this comes to a boil, add fish and cook slowly for 1 hour. While cooking, take a little of the fish stock and mix with ginger snaps to form a paste and then return to pan with fish. When fish has cooled, refrigerate.

Faye Levinson

Baked Fish—Creole

6 slices of fish fillet	1 tablespoon flour
2 tablespoons salad oil	1 cup tomato juice
1 cup chopped onions	1 teaspoon Worcestershire sauce
½ cup chopped green pepper	1½ teaspoons salt
1 clove garlic, minced	½ teaspoon pepper

Flounder, halibut or haddock may be used. Heat oil in large skillet, add onions, green pepper, garlic and saute 5 minutes. Blend in flour until smooth and add remaining ingredients. Simmer 5 minutes. Place fish in flat baking pan. Pour sauce over fish, covering all. Cover tightly with foil and bake in preheated oven 45 minutes at 350°. Serves 4.

Edna Wilcove

Baked Fish a la Italianne

2 pounds flounder	½ teaspoon oregano
½ cup butter	1 teaspoon lemon juice
3 tablespoons oil	1/3 cup white wine
1 teaspoon garlic powder, or minced garlic	Pepper, salt, paprika
	Bread crumbs

Melt butter, add oil, garlic powder, oregano, lemon juice, white wine, pepper, salt. Place fish in baking pan and sprinkle with paprika. Pour sauce over fish and sprinkle bread crumbs over all. Bake 30-45 minutes at 350° . Serves 4.

Sora Lee Goldberg

Fish and Peas Parnassus

1½ pounds fillet of sole	8-10 small cooked onions or small can mushrooms
Seasoned salt and pepper to taste	1 8-ounce can stewed tomatoes
Juice of ½ lemon	½ teaspoon seasoned salt
3 tablespoons butter	2 teaspoons cornstarch
1 17-ounce can early garden peas	

Roll up fish fillets into individual rolls. Arrange in baking dish, sprinkle with salt and pepper. Squeeze lemon over fish, dot with 1 tablespoon butter and bake in a 425° oven for 40 minutes, while preparing sauce. Pour off liquid from peas and save. Melt 2 tablespoons butter and add onions or mushrooms, tomatoes, ½ teaspoon seasoned salt. Stir and simmer 5 minutes. Mix ¼ cup liquid from peas with cornstarch, stir into sauce. Add peas, spoon mixture over and around fish, bake 10 minutes more or just till fish flakes with a fork. Serves 4.

Gert Greenberg

Swedish Baked Halibut

1 pound halibut
2 tablespoons melted butter
½ teaspoon salt
¼ teaspoon pepper
¾ cup canned tomatoes, drained

1 teaspoon confectioners sugar
½ onion, sliced thin
1/3 cup sour cream
Parsley

Place fish in shallow baking dish, sprinkle with salt and pepper. Brush with melted butter. Combine drained tomatoes with sugar and pour over fish. Cover with sliced onion. Bake at 400° for 20 minutes. Remove from oven, pour sour cream over fish and bake 10 minutes longer. Garnish with parsley.

Lil Schulman

Fillet of Sole a la Erdle

1 teaspoon salt
⅛ teaspoon fresh ground pepper
⅛ teaspoon mace
⅛ teaspoon thyme
6 fillets of sole (2 pounds)
½ cup dry vermouth
2 tablespoons lemon juice

2 tablespoons melted butter
1 tablespoon minced chives
2 tablespoons minced onions
24 mushroom caps
Chopped parsley
Lemon quarters

Preheat oven to 325°. Combine salt, pepper, mace, thyme and sprinkle on both sides of fillets. Place fish in buttered, heatproof skillet. Combine vermouth, lemon juice, butter and pour over fish. Sprinkle with chive and onion. Place mushrooms on and around the fish. Cover pan and very slowly bring to a boil over low heat. Immediately uncover pan and place in oven. Bake 15 minutes, basting often with the wine butter mixture. Garnish with parsley and lemon quarters. Serves 6.

Norma Erdle

Flounder Casserole

2 packages sour cream mix
2 onions, diced
2 tablespoons margarine
2 pounds fillet of flounder or sole

Garlic salt, and pepper to taste
½ cup bread crumbs
¼ pound grated Swiss cheese

Prepare sour cream mix according to directions. Saute onions in margarine until transparent. Place onions in greased baking dish. Place fish on top of onions and season with garlic salt and pepper. Pour sour cream mixture over fish. Bake, uncovered, at 350° for 25 minutes. Remove from oven and top with bread crumbs and grated cheese. Bake 10 minutes more. Serve with steamed brown rice.

Diane Axelrod Pariser

Baked Fish Roll-Ups

6 fillets of sole
1 cup sauterne
1 cup sliced onions

1 cup mayonnaise
1 cup sour cream

Marinate sole in sauterne for 2 hours. Drain fish and roll up, holding fish in place with a toothpick. Place rolled fish in a greased pan on the top of the sliced onions. Mix mayonnaise and sour cream and pour over fish. Bake ½ hour at 350°.

Millicent Tanenbaum

Fish Fillet Dinner

1½ cups all-purpose flour
¼ teaspoon baking powder
¾ teaspoon salt
¾ teaspoon pepper
¼ cup shredded sharp, yellow
    American cheese
¼ cup sesame seeds

½ cup butter
2 tablespoons onion flakes
1 pound fish fillets
1 large cucumber, sliced
2 tablespoons dry challah crumbs
2 tablespoons cooking oil

Topping
1 egg
1 cup sour cream

1 packet mushroom soup mix
½ cup shredded American cheese

Mix flour, baking powder, ½ teaspoon salt, ½ teaspoon pepper, cheese, sesame seeds, and butter. Mix at low speed until it forms coarse crumbs. Press into bottom of 12 x 8 pan. Place fish in pan and sprinkle with 1 tablespoon onion flakes and a layer of cucumber slices. Sprinkle with challah crumbs, ¼ teaspoon salt and ¼ teaspoon pepper. Drizzle with oil. Bake at 400° for 15 minutes. Combine topping ingredients, spread over fish and bake for 25 to 30 minutes longer

Rachel Hyman

Fillet of Flounder with Hazelnuts

4 fillets of flounder
Salt and pepper
Paprika

2 tablespoons lemon juice
1½ cups ground hazelnuts
4 tablespoons butter

Wipe fillets and season with salt, pepper, and paprika. Sprinkle with lemon juice. Coat both sides with ground nuts and let stand 15 minutes. Heat butter in chafing dish pan over direct flame until foamy. Saute fish until brown and crusty. Serves 4.

Pearl Albert

Fish Newburg

2 tablespoons butter or margarine
2 tablespoons flour
1 cup milk
1 cup Cheese Whiz

1 cup sherry wine
1½ pounds cooked fish
Salt and pepper to taste

In double boiler or saucepan, over low heat, melt butter; add flour, salt, pepper and stir until well blended. Slowly add milk, stirring constantly to avoid lumps. Add cheese and wine very gradually, stirring constantly. Add fish, broken into serving pieces, and heat through. Serve over toast points. Serves 4.

Sue Kiner

Halibut and Salmon Newburg

6 slices of halibut and salmon, mixed
Salt, pepper
Milk
1 can cheddar cheese soup

1 can cream of mushroom soup
1/3 cup cooking sherry
Sauteed mushrooms
2 hard boiled eggs, sliced

Place fish in buttered pan with little salt, pepper, and milk. Cover with aluminum foil and bake 30 minutes at 350°. Mix soups together, add sherry and heat in saucepan. Add sauteed mushrooms and eggs. When very hot, pour over fish which has been broken into bite size pieces. Heat all together in oven, and then serve over toast or in patty shells. Serves 12.

Lee Kucker

Salmon Bake

2 cups herb seasoned croutettes	4 eggs
2 cups (1 pound) salmon, drained and boned	2 cups milk
	½ teaspoon Worcestershire sauce
2 cups (½ pound) grated cheddar cheese	½ teaspoon dry mustard
	1 teaspoon salt

Place 1 cup croutettes in greased 2-quart casserole, cover with layer of 1 cup salmon and 1 cup cheese, repeat layers with remaining ingredients. In bowl beat eggs slightly, add milk, mustard, Worcestershire sauce, salt and blend together. Pour over salmon mixture. Bake 1 hour at 350°. Serves 6.

Tillie Kolko

Salmon Casserole

1 1-pound can salmon, drained	6 ounces narrow noodles, cooked
½ pint sour cream	1 4-ounce can peas, drained
1 egg	(optional)
1 can mushroom soup	Bread or potato chip crumbs

Mix all ingredients together except bread crumbs. Pour into a 2-quart greased casserole. Sprinkle top with bread crumbs or potato chip crumbs. Bake, uncovered, at 350° for 45 minutes. Serves 6.

June Rapowitz

Salmon Crepes

Filling

1 pound can salmon, reserve liquid	1½ cups liquid, salmon liquid and milk
1 teaspoon chopped onion	
3 tablespoons butter	2 egg yolks, beaten
¼ cup flour	2 tablespoons grated Parmesan cheese
¼ teaspoon salt	
⅛ teaspoon pepper	2 tablespoons sherry
⅛ teaspoon nutmeg	

Flake salmon, after removing liquid and bones. Cook onion in butter, until tender. Blend in flour, salt, pepper and nutmeg. Gradually add liquid and cook until thick, stirring constantly. Stir a little of this hot sauce into beaten egg yolks. Add back to remaining sauce and blend well. Add grated cheese, sherry and blend. Mix ½ cup of the sauce with the salmon and blend well. Reserve remaining sauce to serve with crepes. Spread about 2 tablespoons salmon mixture on each crepe. Roll as jelly roll. Place crepe on 12 x 15 cookie sheet and heat 10-15 minutes at 350°. Serve with heated sauce and garnish with lemon slices and parsley. Serves 6.

Crepes

¾ cup flour	2 eggs, beaten
¼ teaspoon salt	1 cup milk

Sift together flour and salt. Combine eggs with milk. Gradually add to flour mixture, stirring until smooth. Drop 2 tablespoons of batter on a hot greased 6-inch frying pan, tilting to distribute evenly. Fry about 2 minutes or until lightly browned. Turn and brown lightly on other side. Makes 12 crepes.

Judy Kaplan

Apple Salmon Loaf

½ cup crumbled corn flakes
½ cup shredded cheddar cheese
4 tablespoons melted butter
1 1-pound can salmon
Liquid from salmon plus milk to
  equal 1 cup
2 eggs

1 tablespoon lemon juice
1 cup shredded apple
1 cup bread crumbs
3 tablespoons minced onions
½ teaspoon salt
¼ teaspoon pepper

Line 8-inch cake pan with waxed paper. Combine cornflakes, cheese and 2 tablespoons butter. Spread on bottom of pan. Combine liquid with eggs, lemon juice, and remaining butter, add rest of ingredients and mix together. Pack into pan, bake 45 minutes at 350°. Let stand 5 minutes before unmolding. Serves 4-6.

Bunny Skirboll

Salmon Loaf

1 pound can red salmon, reserve
  liquid
¼ cup corn flake crumbs
2 eggs, beaten

1 large potato
½ cup milk
Salt and pepper to taste

Skin, bone and flake salmon. Add salmon liquid, crumbs and beaten eggs. Cook potato, drain and mash. When cool, add milk and add to salmon mixture. Pack into a greased 9 x 5 loaf pan. Bake at 350° for 45-50 minutes, or until browned. Serves 4-6.

Mary Kalin

Salmon-Tuna Loaf

1 cup herb bread stuffing mix
1 cup milk
2 eggs, beaten
1/3 cup sweet pickle relish
1 small onion, grated

½ teaspoon salt
1 can (7¾ ounces) pink or red
  salmon, undrained
1 can (7 ounces) flaked tuna,
  undrained

Remove skin and bones from salmon, then combine all ingredients and press into an 8-inch square greased pan. Bake 30 minutes in moderate oven, 350°, or until firm. May be served with tomato sauce. Serves 6.

Idaire Leichtner

Salmon Newburg

4 ounces cheddar cheese
¼ cup butter
¼ cup flour
2 cups tomato juice
½ teaspoon celery salt
1 teaspoon paprika

¼ teaspoon thyme
¼ cup chopped onion
¼ cup chopped green pepper
1 cup salmon (or tuna), drained
½ cup sliced mushrooms
4 hard-cooked eggs, sliced

Shred cheese. Melt butter in saucepan, blend in flour. Gradually add tomato juice, cook over medium heat, stirring constantly until thickened. Remove from heat; add cheese and stir until melted. Add other ingredients and blend thoroughly. Pour mixture into 1½-quart casserole and bake 10-15 minutes at 350°. Pour over pastry shells or toast.

Lil Orlen

Salmon and Potato Puff

1 tall can red salmon
4 medium sized potatoes
½ cup milk
1 teaspoon minced onion

1 tablespoon lemon juice
3 eggs, separated
1 tablespoon butter, melted
Salt and pepper to taste

Drain, skin, bone, and flake salmon. Boil and mash potatoes. Add milk, onion, lemon juice, and well-beaten yolks. Mix with salmon, add salt and pepper. Fold in stiffly beaten egg whites. Pile mixture lightly in buttered 1½-quart baking dish. Pour melted butter over top. Bake 45 minutes or until set in center and lightly browned, at 350°. Serves 4-5.

Mrs. Herman Handelman

Almondine Tuna

1/3 cup blanched almonds, halved
Salad oil
1 7-ounce can tuna
2 cups sliced celery, ½ inch thick
½ cup coarsely cut onions
1 cup hot water

1 teaspoon bouillon powder
½ teaspoon salt
1 teaspoon cornstarch
2 tablespoons cold water
1 teaspoon soy sauce
3 cups cooked rice

Place nuts in shallow pan and add ½ teaspoon oil. Heat in 300° oven for about 20 minutes until light brown. Drain and flake tuna. Heat 2 tablespoons oil in skillet; add vegetables. Saute lightly. Stir frequently. Add hot water, bouillon and salt; cook until tender crisp. Blend cornstarch, cold water and soy sauce. Stir into cooked mixture. Bring to boil. Add tuna. Heat thoroughly. Serve over rice, topped with the sauteed almonds. Serves 4-6.

Ruth Bittker

Chinese Casserole

1 small onion, diced
1 7-ounce can tuna
1 4-ounce can sliced mushrooms
1 16-ounce can chop suey

or chow mein vegetables
1 3-ounce can chow mein noodles
1 can cream of mushroom soup
½ cup milk

Saute onion in pareve margarine. Drain tuna, mushrooms, and vegetables. Place 1/3 can of noodles on bottom of 1½-quart greased casserole. Mix another 1/3 can of noodles into all other ingredients and pour into casserole. Bake 45 minutes, uncovered, at 350°. Remove from oven, put remaining 1/3 noodles on top and bake for another 10 minutes. Serves 4-6.

Marilyn Greenberg

Deviled Tuna Fish and Pecans

2 tablespoons butter
4 tablespoons flour
2 cups hot milk
½ teaspoon salt
¼ cup minced onion, sauteed
4 ounces grated cheddar cheese
1 can tuna, drained

1 teaspoon Worcestershire sauce
3 drops Tabasco sauce
1½ teaspoons dry mustard
3 hard cooked eggs, sliced
1 cup dry bread crumbs
½ cup chopped pecans

Melt butter over low heat, add and blend flour, stir milk in slowly, add salt. Cook and stir until smooth and thickened. Add onions, 3 ounces cheese, tuna, Worcestershire sauce, Tabasco, dry mustard, and egg slices. Mix together. Mix bread crumbs with pecans and remaining cheese. Place tuna mixture into 6 greased ramekins, or individual pie shells. Cover with crumb mixture. Bake 25 minutes at 375° or until crumbs become lightly browned.

Lee Kucker

Swedish Tuna Casserole

1 8-ounce package egg noodles	¼ cup margarine
1 jar (4¾ ounces) pimento olives	¼ cup flour
1 can tuna (7 ounces)	1 teaspoon salt
1 package American cheese slices	⅛ teaspoon pepper
(8 ounces)	2 cups milk

Cook noodles as directed. Drain olives and chop. Drain tuna and separate into chunks. Preheat oven to 375°. In sauce pan, melt margarine. Remove from heat. Stir in flour, salt, pepper until smooth, gradually stir in milk. Bring to boil, stirring constantly. Reduce heat and simmer 1 minute. Add about 2/3 of cheese and cook until cheese is melted, and blend. Combine noodles, olives and tuna in an ungreased 1½-quart casserole. Pour in sauce and blend. Top with remaining cheese. Bake uncovered 30-40 minutes, until brown. Serves 6.

Rita Koenig

Tater-Tuna Casserole

½ cup chopped onion	2 cans drained tuna (7 ounces)
½ cup chopped celery	¾ cup mayonnaise
½ cup chopped green pepper	½ cup milk
1 tablespoon butter	1 teaspoon Worcestershire sauce
½ teaspoon salt	½ package potato taters or puffs
Dash pepper	

Saute onion, celery, green pepper in butter until tender. Remove from heat and add salt, pepper and tuna (in chunks). Combine mayonnaise, milk, and Worcestershire sauce. Stir into tuna mixture. Pour into 1-quart baking dish and top with potato taters. Bake 15 minutes at 425°, or until potatoes are brown and crisp. Serves 4.

Myrna LaBaer

Tuna Broil

1 package fresh or 2 packages frozen spinach, chopped	4 tablespoons grated Parmesan cheese
10-ounce can frozen cream of potato soup	7-ounce can tuna, drained and flaked
¾ cup milk	2 tablespoons melted butter

Cook spinach until tender, drain well. Heat soup and milk, add cheese, stir until melted. Place spinach in 2-quart casserole and top with tuna. Pour sauce over tuna, drizzle with butter. Broil 5 minutes until sauce bubbles.

Lil Orlen

Tuna Cheesettes

1 cup (¼ pound) sharp cheddar cheese, diced small	¼ teaspoon Worcestershire sauce
3 hard cooked eggs, chopped	½ cup salad dressing or mayonnaise
1 can tuna (7 ounces)	½ teaspoon salt
2 tablespoons chopped green pepper	⅛ teaspoon pepper
2 tablespoons minced onion	½ cup chopped celery
2 tablespoons pickled relish	8 hamburger or other thick buns

Combine ingredients. Spread split buns with butter. Fill each bun with ⅛ of mixture. Wrap buns in aluminum foil. Place on cookie sheet, bake 30 minutes at 350°. Serve hot in foil wrappers if you wish.

Arlean Levinson

Tuna Egg Toast Sandwiches

1 7-ounce can tuna	½ teaspoon mustard
¾ cup grated cheddar cheese	8 slices bread
¼ cup green pepper	3 eggs
¼ cup celery	1½ cups milk
¼ cup olives, cut up	

Combine tuna, cheese, green pepper, celery, olives, mustard. Mix well. Trim crusts. Place 4 slices bread in greased pan. Spread tuna mixture over bread. Top with remaining slices. Combine eggs, milk, pour over sandwiches. Sprinkle with paprika. Bake at 325°, 50 minutes until puffy and light brown. Serves 4.

Bunny Skirball

Tuna French Toasties

7-ounce can tuna fish, flaked	8 slices bread
1/3 cup celery, chopped	3 eggs
¼ cup mayonnaise	2 tablespoons milk
1 tablespoon lemon juice	½ teaspoon salt
⅛ teaspoon salt	¼ cup shortening
Dash pepper	

Mix lightly together first 6 ingredients. Spread tuna mixture on 4 slices of bread and cover with remaining 4 slices. Cut in halves diagonally. Beat eggs slightly, stir in milk and salt. Heat half of shortening in skillet. Dip sandwiches quickly in egg mixture, coating evenly. Fry in skillet until golden brown on both sides, adding remaining shortening as needed. Drain on absorbent paper. Makes 4 servings.

Millie Rosenbaum

Tuna Hawaiian

2 tablespoons margarine	2 teaspoons soy sauce
1 cup sliced onions	½ teaspoon salt
1 cup sliced celery	2 cans tuna (7 ounces) drained
1 large green pepper, diced	½ cup water chestnuts, sliced
1 can pineapple chunks (#2 can)	1 can chow mein noodles
2 tablespoons cornstarch	(3 ounces)
1 cup vegetable bouillon	

Heat margarine, saute onion, celery, green pepper, until soft. Drain pineapple in bowl. Combine syrup, cornstarch, soy sauce, broth and salt in skillet. Cook over medium heat, stirring constantly until thick and bubbly. Add tuna, water chestnuts and pineapple, cover and heat thoroughly. Serve over chow mein noodles. Serves 6.

Linda Ruda

Tuna on Holland Rusk

8 Holland rusks	4 small packages cream cheese
8 slices tomato	Dash salt
8 slices American cheese	1 teaspoon Worcestershire sauce
2 cans tuna, 7-ounces each	1 small grated onion

Butter Holland rusk. Place slice of tomato on rusk. Combine tuna with cream cheese, salt, Worcestershire sauce and onion. Spread on rusk. Bake at 350° for ½ hour. Take out of oven. Criss cross pieces of American cheese and place under broiler until bubbly.

Stella Gelman

Tuna Miniatures

1½ cups cornflakes, crushed
1/3 cup milk
¼ cup mayonnaise
1 can tuna, drained and flaked
  (7 ounces)

1 tablespoon minced parsley, dried
¾ teaspoon lemon juice
¼ teaspoon Worcestershire sauce
¼ teaspoon salt
Dash pepper

Combine ½ of the cornflakes with milk in bowl until they get mushy. Mix in remaining ingredients and form into one-inch balls. Roll in remaining crumbs. Place on well-greased baking sheet. Bake 10-15 minutes or til thoroughly heated at 425°. Do not over bake. Makes about 15 small balls. May be used for luncheon or if made smaller, may be used as hors d'oeuvres.

Lil Schulman

Tuna Rice Casserole

1 onion, diced
¼ cup butter or margarine
1 7-ounce can tuna
½ cup raw rice
¼ cup parsley flakes

1 4-ounce can mushrooms
½ cup cheddar cheese, grated
1 10-ounce can mushroom soup
1 5-1/3 ounce can evaporated milk
Corn flakes or potato chips

Saute onion in butter or margarine. In 1½-quart casserole, add rest of ingredients and top with corn flakes or potato chips. Bake for 1 hour in 350° oven, uncovered. Serves 6.

Rose Goldstein

Tuna Tetrazzini

½ pound thin spaghetti
1 small onion, chopped
1 tablespoon salad oil
2 cans cream of mushroom soup
1-1/3 cups water
½ cup grated Parmesan cheese

3 cans (7 ounces) tuna, drained
1 small can mushrooms, drained
2/3 cup sliced black olives
1 teaspoon chopped parsley
2 tablespoons lemon juice

Cook spaghetti until tender; drain. Saute onion in oil. Add soup, water, ¼ cup cheese. Add tuna and remaining ingredients, except cheese. Combine with spaghetti. Pour into casserole. Top with remaining cheese and heat until golden brown at 350°.

Ruthilyn Steinberg

Tuna Tomato Casserole

4 tablespoons margarine
1/3 pound fresh mushrooms
1 onion, sliced or diced
2 tablespoons flour
1 can milk (use soup can)
¼ pound American or cheddar
  cheese, crumbled (reserve some
  for top)

½ can tomato soup (10 ounce)
  undiluted
Salt, pepper to taste
2 teaspoons lemon juice
2 teaspoons Worcestershire sauce
2 cans tuna (7 ounces) in chunks
½ cup frozen peas, not precooked

Melt 2 tablespoons margarine and saute mushrooms, and onions. In a large sauce pan, melt 2 tablespoons margarine, add flour, milk, cheese and soup, mix thoroughly until blended, over low heat. Combine cheese sauce with sauteed vegetables, add salt, pepper, lemon juice, Worcestershire sauce, tuna and peas. Place into a 1½-quart greased casserole, top with remaining cheese. Bake at 375° for 20 minutes or until bubbly. Serve over rice, toast points, egg noodles, or pastry sheells. Serves 4-6.

Enid Ryen

Low Calorie

Gefilte Fish

½ pound whitefish
½ pound carp
1 pound pike
1 stalk celery
2 tablespoons dried onion flakes
1 teaspoon garlic powder
2 tablespoons salt
1 teaspoon pepper

Artificial sweetener to equal
  2 teaspoons sugar
2 tablespoons unflavored
  gelatin
1 cup cold water
Romaine leaves
8 ounces sliced cooked carrots
8 teaspoons horseradish

Cut fish in small pieces; slice celery. Put fish and celery in grinder 3 times or blend at medium speed for 8 minutes. Add onion flakes, garlic powder, salt, pepper and sweetener; mix well. Mix gelatin into mixture. Add cold water ¼ cup at a time until no more water will be absorbed. Divide mixture into 4 oval loaves. Bake at 350° for 30 minutes. Use romaine, carrots and horseradish as garnish.

Carolyn Stekloff

Chopped Chicken Liver

1 onion, sliced
1 pound chicken livers, washed
  and halved
Salt
Freshly ground pepper
Pinch cayenne pepper or

Tabasco sauce
Pinch curry powder (optional)
Dash nutmeg (optional)
Lettuce
Radishes

In heavy, hot, dry frying pan make a layer of onion slices. Spread livers over onion. Cover and cook until liver is done but not dried out. (Cut one — it should be evenly tan, inside and out.) There should be a layer of liquid in the bottom of the pan. If there is more, remove livers and boil down remaining stock until you have about ¼ cup. Cool livers, onions and stock. Season with salt, pepper and a pinch of cayenne pepper or Tabasco. A pinch of curry powder or a pinch of nutmeg are optional. Put through fine blade of food grinder or puree in an electric blender with a little of the stock in which livers cooked to start it off. Serve on a lettuce leaf garnished with a slice of radish. Serves 2.

Miriam Rogachefsky

Chopped Chicken Liver

1½ pounds chicken livers
1 teaspoon salt
½ teaspoon garlic powder

½ teaspoon cayenne powder
¼ cup dehydrated onion flakes
½ cup chicken bouillon

Put chicken livers in Teflon pan, sprinkle with salt, garlic powder and pepper. Cook over medium heat, turning frequently for 10 minutes, or until livers are cooked. Grind livers with onion flakes through a fine blade or blend for about 5 minutes. Mix with chicken bouillon. Makes 4 servings.

Carolyn Stekloff

Diet Cheese Dip

3 ounces cottage cheese
1 tablespoon skim milk
½ clove garlic
¼ teaspoon salt

¼ teaspoon paprika
1 teaspoon Worcestershire
sauce

Put all ingredients in blender container and blend 20 seconds. Refrigerate until ready to use. A great dip for vegetables.

Gloria Brauer

Cranberry Dip

1 box cranberries
1 cup cottage cheese

Artificial sweetener
5-ounces horseradish

Place berries in pan almost covered with water. Bring to a boil. Add sweetener to taste and let cool. Add one cup cottage cheese and horseradish. Blend these all together. Serve with celery sticks or as a dressing.

Marg Abrams

Weight Watcher Fondue

1 egg
½ cup tomato juice

1 slice bread
1 slice cheese

Beat egg. Mix in tomato juice. Crumble and add bread and cheese. Bake at 350° for half an hour.

Gert Wynar

Pizza Crackers

4 egg whites
2/3 cup powdered skim milk
3 ounces grated cheddar cheese

2 tablespoons onion flakes
½ teaspoon pizza seasoning

Toast onion flakes in 325° oven for 5 minutes. Beat egg whites until stiff, fold in milk, cheese, 1½ tablespoons toasted onion flakes, and pizza seasoning. Drop by teaspoons on Teflon or Pam-sprayed cookie sheet. Top with a few toasted onion flakes and a sprinkle of paprika. Bake at 325° for 5 minutes and then at 250° for 20 minutes. For a crisper cracker, flatten each one with a knife before baking.

Diet Workshop

Borscht with Cabbage and Beets

1 cup celery finely diced, include leaves and stalks
½ cup carrots, finely diced
½ cup onions, diced
2 cups finely shredded cabbage
1 cup tomato juice
2 cups chicken stock or 3 chick-

en broth powder packets and
2 cups water
1 cup shredded canned beets
½ teaspoon liquid sugar substitute
Salt to taste

Cover celery, carrots and onions with boiling water (about 1½ cups.) Cook covered for 30 minutes. Add cabbage, tomato juice, chicken stock and beets. Cook 30 to 45 minutes more. Add sugar substitute and salt to taste. Stir and serve. Let soup cool uncovered (or with cover partly off.) Cover and refrigerate. It will last for days. If soup gets too thick stir in hot water and chicken stock. 4 servings.

Sarah Karchefsky

Borscht with Meat

3 pounds lean beef (shoulder or round steak)
1 large head cabbage, shredded
1 large onion
2½ cups canned whole tomatoes (no spices added) or fresh tomatoes
½ teaspoon salt
Sour salt (or lemon juice)
Sugar substitute to taste
½ to 1 teaspoon Gravy Master (for coloring)
Water to cover cabbage

Combine and cook in large soup pan for at least 3 hours on low flame or in pressure cooker for about 45 minutes. Prepare the day before serving. Refrigerate and remove any solidified fat. Slice meat and serve in hot borscht. Makes 6 servings.

Sarah Karchefsky

Calorie Free Soup

4 cups boiling water
4 packages seasoning and broth powder
1 #303 can French green beans, drained
1 4-ounce can mushrooms

Dilute powder in water. Add drained green beans and mushrooms with liquid. Simmer for 10 minutes to blend flavors.

Ruth Drexler

Gazpacho

1 clove garlic, minced
1 large can whole tomatoes
¼ cup minced green pepper
1 minced onion
2 cucumbers, thickly sliced
(washed, not peeled)
1 tablespoon wine vinegar
Salt, pepper to taste
Lime slices

Place all ingredients except lime slices in blender and blend until mixture is smooth. Chill. Serve in individual mugs over ice cubes. Garnish with lime.

Miriam Rogachefsky

Schav (Spinach Borscht)

1 quart water
1 teaspoon salt
1 pound fresh spinach
Juice of 2 lemons or 6 tablespoons lemon juice
Artificial sweetener to equal 2 tablespoons sugar
2 cups "sour cream"

Combine water and salt in pan. Chop spinach leaves. Add spinach to water and bring to a boil. Simmer 10 minutes. Add lemon juice; simmer 10 minutes. Remove from heat and add sweetener. Chill. Before serving add ¼ of "sour cream" into each portion of schav. Makes four servings.

Sour Cream

1-1/3 cups cottage cheese
6 tablespoons water
1 tablespoon lemon juice
½ teaspoon salt
¼ teaspoon onion powder

Combine all ingredients in blender at low speed for 3 minutes or until smooth. Chill. Makes two cups.

Carolyn Stekloff

Blintzes

½ cup liquid skim milk
½ cup skim milk powder
2 eggs

½ teaspoon salt
⅛ teaspoon pepper
1 package artificial sweetener

Mix the skim milk with the skim milk powder, and beat out all lumps. Beat eggs into mixture and add all remaining ingredients. Stir well. Pour batter into Teflon pan to make a thin pancake. Brown and turn. Makes six 8-inch pancakes.

Filling

6 ounces cottage cheese
½ pack artificial sweetener
Pinch salt

Pinch cinnamon
1 egg white

Blend all ingredients. Fill each pancake. Fold pancake into envelope shape. Heat in oven at 325°.

Evelyn Berlowitz

Low-Cal Cheese Blintzes

3 eggs

2 tablespoons water

Beat eggs and water. Make thin pancakes using three tablespoons batter in small Teflon pan. Turn pan in all directions to make even layer of batter. Brown only one side and flip out on clean cloth.

Filling

2/3 cup cottage cheese
1 egg, beaten

Small piece of orange rind
Sugar substitute

Combine filling ingredients; mix well. Put a heaping tablespoon on the edge of the browned side of each pancake. Roll up, tuck in ends. Broil or bake both sides in hot oven 10-15 minutes. Serves 3.

Marg Abrams

Sour Cream

2/3 cup cottage cheese
¼ cup water

¼ teaspoon salt (optional)
1 teaspoon lemon juice

Put all ingredients into blender container and blend until free from all lumps. If necessary, use a rubber spatula to turn cheese from sides of container into center where blades can get to it. Makes about 1 cup. Use slightly less or more water depending on desired thickness.

Evelyn Berlowitz

Pickled Fish

2 cups cold water
2 teaspoons onion powder
1 teaspoon salt

1½ cups vinegar
2 pounds fish
Artificial sweetener to taste

Bring water to a boil with onion powder, salt and vinegar. Add fish and cook for ¾ of an hour. Take fish out and cool. Add sweetener to liquid and pour over fish. Chill.

Marg Abrams

Salmon or Tuna Bake

1 slice bread	Lemon juice
Celery	1 egg
Green pepper	6 ounces canned salmon or
1 teaspoon onion flakes	tuna, drained

Blend bread to make crumbs and remove. Then put vegetables into blender and blend until pureed. Combine crumbs, pureed vegetables, lemon juice, egg and fish. Turn into baking pan. Bake in oven at 375° for fifteen minutes. 2 servings.

Mrs. Sarah Olles

Low-Cal Salmon Salad

1 1-pound can red salmon,	and chopped
drained	1 stalk celery, chopped
1 hard boiled egg, chopped	½ onion, chopped
1 cucumber, peeled, seeded	Realemon juice

Combine above ingredients with enough Realemon to bind together.

Ruth Bittker

Grilled Cheese and Tuna

2 ounces tuna, drained	1 ounce any hard cheese, cut
1 slice white bread	in small pieces

Spread tuna over one slice white bread. Put cheese on top. Bake at 350° or broil until cheese is melted.

Laurie Eisner

Barbecued Chicken

10 counces chicken — raw weight	¼ cup tomato juice
(including skin and bone)	½ teaspoon dehydrated parsley
¼ cup chicken bouillon	1 teaspoon onion powder
½ teaspoon Worcestershire	½ teaspoon dry mustard
sauce	1 pack artificial sweetener
1 teaspoon garlic powder	

Remove chicken skin and marinate chicken in remaining ingredients at room temperature for 1 hour before broiling. Broil for 15 minutes each side.

Norma Ouriel

Sweet and Sour Veal Balls

1¾ pounds ground veal	¼ teaspoon pepper
1 egg	¼ teaspoon salt
3 tablespoons minced onion	½ teaspoon ginger
½ teaspoon garlic powder	

Mix ingredients to form balls.

Sauce

2 cups tomato juice	¼ cup lemon juice
2 cups pineapple juice	10 packages artificial sweetener

Mix sauce ingredients. Cook at medium heat for 1 hour.

Marg Abrams

Stuffed Cabbage (Sweet and Sour)

1 pound lean ground beef
¼ teaspoon salt
⅛ teaspoon pepper
1 small green pepper, grated
Juice scraped from cut onion
1 clove garlic, pressed
1 tablespoon soy sauce
4 tablespoons ice water
1 medium sized cabbage
1½ cups tomato juice
1 cup whole canned tomatoes
¾ cup water
¼ teaspoon salt
⅛ teaspoon pepper
¼ teaspoon onion powder
1 packet bouillon
¼ teaspoon sour salt, to taste
½ teaspoon sugar substitute, or
 to taste
1 cup canned sauerkraut
¾ cup water

Mix first 8 ingredients well. Put aside. Cut middle core out of cabbage and place in bowl under very hot tap water until leaves are soft and separating. If water is not very hot, put cabbage into boiling water for a few minutes for the same results. Separate cabbage leaves and wrap around meat balls. (About 8 small balls). In bottom of cooking pot, mix remaining ingredients. Gently place cabbage rolls into this liquid and boil about 1 hour covered or until cabbage is very tender. By dividing the cabbage, you can serve 4 portions of 2 cabbage rolls each.

Beverly Kaufman

Baked Cauliflower

1 medium cauliflower
1 tablespoon tomato juice
1 tablespoon Parmesan cheese,
 grated
1 teaspoon oregano
1 teaspoon garlic salt
Dash seasoned pepper
Pimento

Steam cauliflower until half done. Remove to baking dish. Pour juice over cauliflower, then sprinkle cheese and rest of ingredients over it. Bake at 350° for 15 to 20 minutes. Garnish with pimento.

Sarah Karchefsky

Mock Sweet-Potato Pudding

1 package frozen squash
¼ teaspoon salt
Dash of pepper
1 teaspoon liquid sugar substitute
½ tablespoon grated orange
rind or juice

Put squash, salt, pepper, sugar substitute and orange rind or juice in baking dish. Sprinkle top with cinnamon and bake uncovered at 350° for ½ hour.

Gloria Brauer

Eggplant Gravy

1 medium eggplant
1 tomato
¼ cup chopped onion
¾ of a green pepper
½ lemon, juiced
1 teaspoon Sweet 'N Low
1 teaspoon salt

Bake eggplant until soft. Remove skin and add all ingredients. Chop all together or place in blender. Cook for 10 minutes. Serve with roasts.

Diet Workshop

Unlimited Bean Salad

1 16-ounce can yellow French style beans, drained
1 16-ounce can green French style beans, drained
1 4-ounce can mushrooms, drained

Dressing

¼ cup lemon juice
½ cup wine vinegar (white may be used)
½ teaspoon salt
½ teaspoon pepper
½ teaspoon garlic salt
3 packs Sweet 'N Low or liquid sweetener to equal 6 teaspoons of sugar

Combine beans and mushrooms in bowl. Mix dressing ingredients together, pour over beans. Refrigerate overnight, if possible, before eating. Store in a covered container in refrigerator. Salad is unlimited, delicious, and better make a double recipe because everyone enjoys it! Serves 6.

Diet Workshop

Green Bean Salad

2 16-ounce cans French style green beans, drained
1 16-ounce can French style wax beans, drained
1 8-ounce can stems, pieces mushrooms, drained
1 8-ounce jar of roasted peppers, diced
1 medium white onion, diced
1 large stalk celery, diced
¾ medium green pepper, diced

Marinate all ingredients overnight in dressing.

Dressing

1 cup cider vinegar
½ cup lemon juice or Realemon
Salt and pepper to taste
3 packages of Sweet and Low
½ teaspoon Italian seasoning
½ teaspoon instant garlic

Combine ingredients and blend thoroughly. Salad contains about 37 calories per cup.

Roz Richman

Blazer Salad

3 cups shredded red cabbage
3 cups shredded white cabbage
1 cup raw shredded or sliced beets or
1 cup French green beans
3 tablespoons lemon juice
1 teaspoon salt
Sweetener to taste
¼ teaspoon pepper
2 tablespoons white vinegar
Chopped chives

Combine lemon juice, salt, sweetener, pepper and vinegar. Pour over shredded vegetables. Cover and chill 24 hours. Garnish with chopped chives. Serves 6.

Diet Workshop

Cole Slaw

¼ cup hot water
3 tablespoons white vinegar
1 teaspoon liquid sweetener
1 teaspoon salt
1 egg, slightly beaten
1 medium head cabbage,
  shredded

Combine all the ingredients with the exception of the cabbage and cook over medium heat, stirring constantly, until thick. Pour over cabbage. Toss lightly and refrigerate. Note: You may add celery, onion and chopped green pepper. Serves 6.

Diet Workshop

Diet Potato Salad

2 10-ounce packages frozen
  cauliflower
2 stalks celery, chopped
½ green pepper, chopped
1-3 medium dill pickles, drained and chopped
3 tablespoons prepared mustard
1 tablespoon onion flakes (use
  fresh, if desired)
1 teaspoon parsley flakes
1 teaspoon salt
Artificial sweetener to equal
  2 teaspoons sugar
½ teaspoon Worcestershire
  sauce
½ teaspoon lemon juice

Cook cauliflower according to directions. Drain, cut into pieces and add rest of ingredients. Chill for several hours. Unlimited. Serves 4.

Diet Workshop

Cottage Cheese Mustard Dressing

2 tablespoons powdered non-
  dairy creamer (Pream)
Warm water
1 tablespoon sugar or four saccharin tablets
½ cup cottage cheese
3 tablespoons vinegar
1 egg yolk
1 teaspoon salt
Dash of pepper
1 tablespoon prepared mustard
2 cloves garlic, crushed

Place powdered non-dairy creamer in a cup and add warm water to make ½ cup liquid. Add saccharin tablets or sugar and dissolve. Place all ingredients in a blender until well-blended. Refrigerate. Makes one cup.

(15 calories per tablespoon, if made with sugar.)
(12 calories per tablespoon, if made with saccharin.)

Mae Calderon

French Dressing

¼ cup tomato juice
½ teaspoon dry mustard
Dash pepper
½ teaspoon salt
½ teaspoon liquid garlic
¼ cup wine vinegar
Dash celery salt
½ teaspoon liquid onion
½ teaspoon liquid sweetener

Combine all ingredients and shake. Refrigerate.

Mae Calderon

Roquefort Cheese Dressing or Dip

½ pound cottage cheese
1 tablespoon bleu cheese
Buttermilk
Garlic salt
Minced onion

Blend until creamy, using as much buttermilk as necessary to give consistency desired.

Lillian Bodner

Zero Dressing for Green Salads

2 cups tomato juice
½ cup lemon juice
2 teaspoons salt
4 teaspoons grated onion or
   1 tablespoon onion flakes
1 teaspoon garlic powder or

1 clove garlic, minced
2 teaspoons prepared mustard
2 teaspoons Worcestershire
   sauce
2 teaspoons liquid sweetener

Blend all ingredients, using high speed on blender. Store in refrigerator. Shake before using. Makes 2 cups.

Diet Workshop

Old Fashioned Bread and Butter Pickles

4 cucumbers, unpeeled, thinly
   sliced
2 tablespoons onion flakes
1 teaspoon garlic powder or 1
   clove garlic, crushed
10 ice cubes or 1 cup crushed ice
2 tablespoons salt
1 cup white vinegar

6 pack Sweet 'N Low or liquid
   sweetener to equal 2 tablespoons sugar
¼ teaspoon tumeric
½ teaspoon mustard seed
½ teaspoon celery seed
1 cup cauliflower buds (fresh
   or frozen)

Combine cucumbers, onion flakes, garlic powder. Mix well. Sprinkle with salt and ice. Cover. Let stand at room temperature for 3 hours. Drain well. Combine remaining ingredients. Pour over cucumbers in saucepan. Heat to a boil and simmer for 5 minutes only. Pour into 2 pint canning jars. Seal. Keep in refrigerator. Unlimited!

Diet Workshop

Apple Brown Betty

3 or 4 medium apples, sliced and
   pared
4 packages Sweet 'N Low
1 tablespoon lemon juice

½ teaspoon lemon rind, grated
1/3 cup hot water
2 teaspoons cinnamon
¼ teaspoon nutmeg

Spread half the apples in an 8 x 8 pan. Sprinkle with half the sweetener, lemon juice, rind, and cinnamon. Add remaining apples. Cover with rest of sweetener, lemon juice and rind. Pour hot water over mixture. Sprinkle with remaining cinnamon and nutmeg. Bake in 375° oven for about 15 minutes or until apples are tender.

Diet Workshop

Apple Muffins

3 apples
3 eggs
3 tablespoons sugar substitute
½ teaspoon orange extract

½ teaspoon vanilla
¼ teaspoon cinnamon
¼ teaspoon nutmeg
3 slices bread

Grate apples. Beat eggs and add spices. Break bread into small pieces and mix. Blend grated apples into mix. Place in 6-section muffin tin. Bake at 375° for 45 minutes.

Gloria Brauer

Bavarian Cream

1 package rasberry gelatin
  (diet may be used)
¼ cup sugar (or artificial powdered sweetener)

1 cup boiled water
¾ cup cold water or juice
1 package boxed whipped topping
1 package frozen raspberries

Dissolve gelatin and sugar in hot water. Add cold water or juice, and chill until thick. Whip topping as directed on package. Add berries to gelatin and whip on low speed until fluffy. Fold in whipped topping. Chill in mold until firm. (May also be served as frozen dessert by freezing for 4 hours.)

Dolly Fishman

Low Calorie Cheese Cake

1 pound farmers cheese
½ cup skim milk
2 tablespoons liquid sweetener
2 eggs
1 tablespoon lemon juice

1 teaspoon vanilla
1 1-pound 4-ounce can crushed
  pineapple, packed in its own
  juice

Beat all ingredients except pineapple together until creamy. Put in jello mold or 9 inch pie tin and bake in 375° oven for 20 minutes. While still hot, top with crushed pineapple that has been drained. Refrigerate. Serves 8.

Marge Gold

Danish Pastry

2 egg whites
1 slice bread

4 packs sweetener

Beat egg whites until stiff. Gradually add bread that you have toasted and blended to make crumbs. Add packs of sweetener. Drop by spoonfuls onto cookie sheet. Bake at 325° until hot. Serve with homemade blueberry jam.

Mae Calderon

Cantaloupe Ice Cream

½ cantaloupe peeled and cubed
4 ounces cold evaporated skim-

med milk
Artificial sweetener to taste

Put cubed cantaloupe in freezer until frozen. (About 24 hours.) When frozen, put in blender with 4-ounces of evaporated skimmed milk and sweetener. Blend until same consistency as soft ice cream. Can be stored in freezer.

Laurie Eisner

Cranberry Ice

1 jar low calorie cranberry
  sauce
1 teaspoon lemon juice
½ teaspoon orange flavoring

2 cups low calorie Wink or
  ginger ale
1/3 cup dry milk powder

Beat all ingredients until thoroughly blended; freeze until crystals form ½ inch around outer edge of container. Beat again; refreeze.

T'Mahry Axelrod

Key Lime Mold

1 package dietetic lime gelatin	4 ounces cottage cheese
1 package dietetic lemon gelatin	1 cup buttermilk
1 cup hot water	2 cups crushed pineapple
1 cup cold water	(packed in its own juice)

Dissolve gelatin in hot water and add cold water. Blend cheese and buttermilk. Add to gelatin. Add pineapple and juice. Pour into mold. Chill. Serves 4-6.

Diet Workshop

Instant Alba Mousse

1 cup boiling water	gelatin
1 package Alba	3 packages Sweet and Low
¼ cup cold water	1 teaspoon vanilla
2 packages unflavored	12 ice cubes

Put gelatin in blender with cold water, add boiling water to dissolve and blend on low for a few seconds. Add vanilla, Sweet & Low and chocolate Alba. Blend a few seconds. Turn blender to high speed and add ice cubes, 2 at a time. Blend until ice is mixed well. 6 servings, 69 calories each.

Mae Calderon

Mocha Mousse

3 tablespoons boiling water	ener
2 squares (2 ounces) unsweet-	1 tablespoon instant coffee
ened chocolate, cut up	2 eggs, separated
1 tablespoon non-caloric sweet-	

Put all ingredients, except eggs, in blender; cover and run on high until chocolate is liquified. Add egg yolks. Cover and run on high for one minute. Beat egg whites until stiff but not dry; fold in chocolate mixture. Chill until set. Serves 4. Approximately 91 calories per serving.

Faye K. Woocher

Mock Rice Pudding

2-2/3 cups small curd cottage	¼ cup sugar
cheese	½ teaspoon cinnamon
4 eggs, beaten	1 teaspoon vanilla
¼ teaspoon salt	Nutmeg
Artificial sweetener to equal	

Blend cottage cheese, beaten eggs, salt, sweetener, cinnamon and vanilla. Pour into shallow 8 x 12 baking pan. Sprinkle with nutmeg. Bake at 325° for 50 minutes or until knife inserted in center comes out clean. Serve chilled. Serves 6.

T'Mahry Axelrod

Diet Sponge Cake

4 eggs, separated
¼ teaspoon cream of tartar
1 teaspoon lemon juice

2/3 cup dry powdered milk
1½ teaspoons lemon Funny Face
(like Kool Aid)

Beat egg whites with cream of tartar until stiff. Mix lemon juice, powdered milk and Funny Face together and fold into beaten whites. Grease an 8 x 8 glass cake pan with ½ teaspoon lemon juice. Pour in blended mixture and bake at 300° for 30 minutes.

Lillian Bodner

Applesauce Candy

1 cup dietetic applesauce

1 package dietetic cherry gelatin

Boil applesauce. Dissolve gelatin in applesauce and spread in small pan. Cool, chill. Cut in squares.

Laurie Eisner

Low Calorie Candied Orange Peels

Orange peels
Low calorie ginger ale

Sweet 'N Low

Wash orange peels. Place in pot, cover with water and boil for 10 minutes. Throw off water, add fresh water and boil again. Repeat three times. After third time, drain and cover with low calorie ginger ale. Boil, uncovered, until all moisture has evaporated. Then cut peels into slices. Spread on cookie sheet, sprinkle with Sweet 'N Low and bake in 400° oven for 20 minutes or until crisp.

Diet Workshop

Low Calorie Soda

1/3 cup skim milk powder
¾ cup Cott's low calorie soda

4 ice cubes

Place in blender on low speed until ice is homogenized.

Diet Workshop

Coffee Milkshake

1 teaspoon instant coffee
½ cup liquid skim milk
½ teaspoon vanilla

1 ice cube
2 packages artificial sweetener
¼ cup powdered skim milk

Put all ingredients into blender and blend.

Norma Ouriel

Holiday Punch

Citrus slices
2 cups apple juice
2 cups diet cran-apple juice

2 small bottles Fresca (12 ounces)
1 cup orange juice

Mix together and chill. Toss in fruit slices. Add melon balls, if desired.

Gloria Brauer

Passover Matzo Pancakes

1 egg
½ board matzo

¼ cup skim milk
2 teaspoons liquid sweetener

Blend all ingredients. Pour batter in Teflon or heavy pan to make small round pancakes. Brown one side. Turn carefully and brown second side.

Diet Workshop

Fried Matzo

1 egg
½ board matzo

¼ cup skim milk
Salt and pepper

Soak matzo for 5 minutes in cold water and blot dry with paper towel. Beat egg, milk and seasonings together. Soak matzo in the batter. "Fry" on one side in heavy pan, flip and "fry" on other side.

Diet Workshop

Passover Pattie

½ board matzo, blended
3¾ ounces of fish, cooked
Dash of salt and pepper
Chopped green pepper and mush-

rooms
1 ounce tomato juice
Dash garlic powder
Dash parsley (optional)

Mix all ingredients and form into pattie. Pour tomato juice over it and sprinkle with garlic powder and parsley. Broil on one side 5 minutes, then turn and broil on other side 5 minutes. This recipe is delicious with flounder, halibut, whitefish, carp or any cooked left over fish.

Diet Workshop

Matzo Balls

½ sheet matzo
1 package instant broth
½ cup boiling water

1 egg
½ teaspoon dehydrated parsley

Pulverize the matzo in blender. Add 5 tablespoons of broth. Add egg and parsley. Mix well. Cover and refrigerate a few hours. Drop by teaspoons into fat-free soup.

Diet Workshop

Toasted Cheese Matzo

1 sheet of matzo
3 tablespoons milk
1 egg

¼ teaspoon salt
3 packets Sweet 'N Low
6 ounces cottage cheese

Break matzo to fit into small baking dish. Moisten matzo — do not make soggy. Mix egg, milk, Sweet 'N Low, and cheese. Place one half of the cheese mixture over one half of the matzo. Use second half of matzo and remainder of cheese. Cover and bake in 350° oven for 15 minutes. Serves 2.

Diet Workshop

Meats

KOSHERING MEAT

In the dietary laws of the Jewish people, the term "to kosher" is applied to the preparation of meat and poultry before preparing for the table. The animal must be slaughtered by a Shochet and purchased at a Kosher meat market.

The meat must be put in a utensil specifically reserved for this purpose, with enough water to cover completely, and left to soak for half an hour. Then the meat must be put on a board placed in a slanting position, or on a board with grooves or perforations to allow the blood to flow freely. Then the meat must be sprinkled on all sides with coarse salt and allowed to remain for one hour. It is then removed and rinsed with cold water three times until all salt is removed.

Liver cannot be koshered in this manner. It must be broiled in order to render it kosher, and it must be broiled before it can be sauted or used in any recipe. It should be washed, salted, then placed on a broiler. When it is finished, it must be washed in cold water to wash the blood away.

Meat that is served broiled, such as steaks, hamburgers and chops does not have to be koshered.

Mrs. Sol Cohen

Cholent

5 pounds small potatoes	1 large Kishka
2 1-pound boxes white navy beans	Pinch of salt
	Water

Peel potatoes. Place in bean pot with beans and kishka. Add salt and enough water to cover. Cook over night on low flame. Add more water in the morning, if needed. Bake in 200° oven all day until ready to serve.

Belle Kessler

Cholent

1 cup dried lima beans	Pepper
1 cup navy beans or pea beans	4 or 5 pounds brisket
2 quarts water	Monosodium glutamate
4 tablespoons chicken fat	1 cup medium barley
2 pounds sliced onions	4 tablespoons flour
2½ pounds peeled and quartered small potatoes	4 teaspoons paprika
	1 bottle rose wine
Salt	Boiling water

Wash and pick over dried lima beans and navy beans. Add the beans slowly to two quarts of rapidly boiling water and boil for four minutes. Turn off heat and let beans soak for three hours.

Use heavy ten-quart casserole. Over direct heat, melt chicken fat. Add sliced onions and potatoes and sautee until slightly golden. Turn off heat. Place brisket on bed of onions and potatoes, add the drained beans over and around the meat. Add salt, pepper and monsodium glutamate over and between the layers to taste. Add barley. Mix flour with paprika. Sprinkle over barley and beans. Add wine and then enough boiling water to just cover. Bring to simmer on top of stove.

Place in 175° -200° oven and roast covered for 18-24 hours. (Do not cook too rapidly or it will become mushy.)

Hannah Solky

Essig Fleisch

4 pounds chuck	1 cup hot beef bouillon
1 or 2 tablespoons oil or mar- garine	3 tablespoons tomato paste
4 cups chopped fresh onions or	2 tablespoons brown sugar
1 pound frozen chopped onions	2 tablespoons white wine vinegar
2 teaspoons garlic salt	1 cup raisins
¼ teaspoon black pepper	1 cup sherry

Brown chuck in oil or margarine. Add onions and brown over low heat. Add garlic salt, black pepper and bouillon. Cover and simmer two hours. Add tomato paste, brown sugar, vinegar and raisins soaked in sherry. (Soak the cup of raisins in cup of sherry for one hour. Then add both raisins and sherry.) Blend well and simmer until done, about thirty minutes more.

Dr. Charles Solky

Shale's Stuffed Derma

2 yards casing
½ pound breast fat, ground
2 cups corn flakes, crushed
1 cup quick oats
2 cups coarse grits

3 cups flour
2 onions, medium, grated
1 teaspoon salt
½ teaspoon pepper

Get casing from butcher. Scrape and clean well on both sides. Sew one end and reverse. Fat must be at room temperature. To fat, add other ingredients (except flour). Mix thoroughly, then add flour, one cup at a time and continue blending well. Stuff casing very loosely and sew other end. Put stuffed derma in boiling water and keep piercing with a fork to let air out. Boil two hours. Remove from stove and place derma in roasting pan with a little water or chicken soup and brown in 350° oven. Keep turning derma from time to time until nicely brown.

Shale Gans

Mock Kishka

¼ pound margarine, melted
1 box (12 ounces) Tam Tam
   crackers, crushed
1 onion, large, sweet

1 carrot, large
1 stalk of celery
Salt and pepper
Lawry salt, to taste

Grate carrot, onion and celery very fine. Roll crackers as fine as possible with a rolling pin. Add melted margarine. Divide mixture into 3 parts. Make each part into a roll. Place each roll on aluminum foil. Wrap each roll securely and place on cookie sheet. Bake for 45 minutes at 350°. Unwrap and slice into 1½-inch pieces. Serve hot. Kishka may be frozen and baked before serving.

Mim Block and Tillie Kolko

Carrot Tzimmes

2 pounds carrots
1 pound sweet potatoes
1 small onion
1 cup sugar
1-2 pounds meat (brisket,

   flank or short ribs)
2½ cups water
½ cup flour diluted in ¼ cup
   water
1 tablespoon salt

Scrape carrots and grate on course grater. Peel and slice sweet potatoes. Cut onion fine. Put meat in center of carrots and sweet potatoes which have been placed in a large pot. Add salt, sugar and water. Cook on top of stove on slow fire for 2 hours. Remove from heat. Remove meat. Cream Tzimmes with the flour which was diluted with water. Taste for salt and sweetness. Put meat back in center of tzimmes. Put dumplings around sides of pot, bake 2 hours at 300°.

Potato Dumplings

3 medium potatoes
1 egg
¼ cup boiling water
1 teaspoon salt
½ cup bread crumbs or matzo
   meal

¼ teaspoon pepper
¼ teaspoon salt
1 small onion, chopped fine
1 tablespoon chicken fat or
   pareve margarine

Grate potatoes, put in linen towel and squeeze well to remove water. Season with salt and pour boiling water over. Add egg and mix well. Divide mixture into 4 equal parts. Mix bread crumbs with onion, salt and pepper. Add fat and divide also into 4 parts. Put one part of bread mixture into center of one part of potato and make into a ball. Drop into tzimmes, if desired.

Sarah Derman

Flomen Tzimmes—Potato and Prune Tzimmes

1-3 pounds fat brisket or short ribs, cut up	1 cup sugar
	Coarse salt, several tablespoons
3-4 pounds potatoes	Water
2 pounds prunes	

Place pieces of meat in a 5-quart Dutch oven. Peel and quarter the potatoes and put a few around the meat. Add prunes over and around meat and potatoes. Sprinkle with salt and sugar. Repeat layers. Add water to one inch of top of pot. Bring to a boil and then simmer, covered, for about 1 hour. Place in 325° oven and roast for 3-5 hours. Serves 16.

Addie Gallancy

Standing Rib Roast

3-6 pound standing rib   Salt and pepper

Place roast, fat side up, on rack in open pan. Rub in salt and pepper. Insert meat thermometer in the center of the thickest part of the meat, not touching bone nor resting on fat. Place in pre-heated 325° oven. For rare meat, roast 26 minutes per pound or until meat thermometer reaches 140%; for medium meat, roast 30 minutes per pound or until meat thermometer reaches 160° ; for well done, roast 35 minutes per pound or until meat thermometer reaches 170°.

Inez Lipman

Brisket of Beef

5 pound brisket	4 celery stalks
2 teaspoons salt	1 cup chili sauce
¼ teaspoon pepper	¼ cup water
2 onions, sliced	1 can beer (12 ounce)

Season meat. Place in pan, fat side up. Place onions, celery and chili sauce over beef. Add ¼ cup water in bottom of pan. Allow 1 hour per pound for roasting at 325°. Roast uncovered, basting often, with drippings until meat is well browned, then cover. After meat has baked for 3½ hours, pour beer over it. Re-cover and cook 1½ hours, or until tender. Remove meat, cool and strain gravy. Skim off fat, slice meat and reheat in gravy. Add ½ cup of water if gravy is too thick.

Rose Goldstein

Barbecued Brisket

5-7 pound brisket	Monosodium glutamate to
Salt, pepper, garlic salt,	taste

Sauce

1 14-ounce bottle ketchup	6 tablespoons brown sugar
2 teaspoons prepared mustard	1 cup celery, diced
¾ cup water	½ cup gravy from the brisket
6 tablespoons Worcestershire sauce	

Roast brisket, covered, seasoned with salt, pepper, garlic salt and MSG. Do not add water to roasting pan. Roast at 300° -350° until tender. Combine ingredients for sauce in pot. Simmer for 1 hour. Slice brisket. Let sit in sauce, refrigerated, for 24 hours. Bake at 300°, covered, about 1 hour before serving. Can be served over buns or plain.

Ruth Salesin

Roast Brisket

4-5 pound double brisket	¼ teaspoon Accent
1 clove garlic, quartered	¼ teaspoon paprika
½ teaspoon salt	¼ teaspoon garlic powder
1/8 teaspoon black pepper	

Pierce meat with small knife and insert garlic in four areas. Season top and bottom of meat. Cover and roast at 325°, about 2¼ hours. Slice meat against the grain on the double part. The single part must be cut against the grain at another angle. This roast is not for rare or medium rare cuts. It must be well done to be tender. 8 servings.

Adeline Evans

Sweet and Sour Brisket

6 pound single brisket	1 cup ketchup
2 onions, sliced	1 cup water
1 clove garlic, minced	1 tablespoon salt
¾ cup brown sugar	Freshly ground pepper
½ cup vinegar	

Place brisket in heavy skillet and brown on all sides. Add and brown onions and garlic. Add remaining ingredients. Cook, covered, until meat is tender, about 2¼ to 3 hours. Serves ten.

Maxine Peters

Glazed Corned Beef

5 pound corned beef	1 10-ounce jar preserves
1 20-ounce can sliced pineapple	(apricot, peach, pineapple)
1 cup dark brown sugar	

Place beef in pot with enough water to cover and bring to boil. Cook for approximately three hours or until tender. Drain water and place meat in baking pan. Pat with brown sugar, pour half of pineapple juice over meat, place pineapple rings on top of and around meat. Roast at 350° for ½ hour covered; pour preserves over meat, baste with remaining juice if necessary, and bake uncovered for another ½ hour or until sauce is syrupy and thick.

Inez Lipman

Creole Pot Roast

4 pound brisket	sauce
1 large onion, sliced	1 teaspoon salt
¼ cup chopped green pepper	¼ teaspoon pepper
½ cup chopped celery	6 medium potatoes, peeled
1 can tomato and mushroom	

Brown meat in a Dutch oven. If meat is very lean, use a little fat for browning. Add sliced onion, green pepper and celery; saute until tender. Add tomato and mushroom sauce, salt and pepper. Cover and simmer 2½-3 hours, or until tender. Cut potatoes in half and add during last half hour of cooking. Serves 6-8.

Priscilla Brown

Pot Roast with Pineapple Sauce

3½-4½ pound pot roast   pineapple
Salt and pepper   2 tablespoons brown sugar
1 15-ounce can tomato sauce   2 teaspoons salt
1 13½-ounce can crushed   1 large onion, thinly sliced

Heat oven to 325°. Place pot roast in 12 x 9 pan. Sprinkle with salt and . pepper lightly. Arrange onion over meat. Mix together tomato sauce, pineapple, brown sugar and salt. Pour over meat. Cover pan with foil and bake three hours until fork tender. Uncover last ½ hour. For thick gravy, remove meat to warm platter. Blend ½ cup water and ¼ cup flour and stir into gravy. Cook until thickened. Serves 6.

Eulah Feier

Soul Beef Roast

4 pound chuck roast   ½ pound spinach, stems removed,
1 large onion, sliced   (optional)
1 cup pineapple juice   Mushrooms
¼ cup soy sauce   Sliced almonds
1½ teaspoons ground ginger   2 tablespoons cornstarch
¼ teaspoon salt   ¼ cup water
1 cup sliced celery   1 can pineapple chunks
4 carrots cut into 3-4 inch   (optional)
     lengths

Roast meat uncovered until lightly browned. Then mix the pineapple juice, onion, soy sauce, ginger and salt and add to roast. Continue roasting covered for 2½ hours, or until meat is tender. Add celery, carrots and pineapple chunks; continue to roast uncovered (if there is enough gravy, or covered if there is not), for 20 minutes. Arrange spinach and mushrooms on top of meat and simmer until spinach wilts about 10 minutes. Place meat on platter and sprinkle with sliced almonds. Blend together cornstarch and water, stir into meat juices and simmer a few moments to thicken gravy. May be cooked on top of stove if desired.

Ettie Rubenstein

Cherried Roast

4-5 pounds boneless chuck roast   bouillon
1 1-pound can pitted tart red   2 tablespoons shortening
     cherries   ¼ teaspoon pepper
1/3 cup vinegar   ½ cup hot water
½ cup brown sugar   ½ cup cold water
1 tablespoon instant beef   ¼ cup flour

Slice beef part way down into ¾ inch slices. Place meat into a glass or enamel dish. Drain cherries and set aside. Combine cherry juice, vinegar, sugar, and instant bouillon; pour over meat. Cover and allow to marinate at least four hours, turning meat occasionally. Remove meat from marinade and allow to drain well. Reserve marinade. In a Dutch oven, brown meat on all sides in hot shortening. Season with salt and pepper. Add hot water. Cover. Roast in 325° oven or on top of stove, low, about 2½ hours or until tender. When tender, remove to a hot platter. Skim most of the fat from the pan juices. Add reserved cherries and marinade. Put ½ cup cold water and ¼ cup flour in a shaker and shake well. Stir into juices. Cook, stirring constantly, until gravy boils. Adjust seasoning. To serve: spoon cherries into slits in meat and serve with remaining cherry gravy. Makes 6 to 8 servings.

Merle Markus

Chuck Steak Roast

4 pound shoulder or middle   ¼ envelope onion soup mix
chuck steak, 1 inch-1½ inch thick   Ketchup to taste

Place large sheet of aluminum foil on shallow baking pan. Place meat in center. Sprinkle on the onion soup mix and ketchup to taste. Fold up foil and seal ends well, so meat is completely wrapped. Bake in 325° oven for 2½-3 hours, depending on desired tenderness.

Helen Jassin

Foiled Steak

4 shoulder steaks, cut very thin   ½ cup matzo meal
Salt   2 eggs
Pepper   2 tablespoons mushrooms
Garlic powder   2 tablespoons margarine
Parsley   ½ cup chicken soup

Season steaks with salt, pepper, garlic powder and parsley. In a small bowl, mix matzo meal, eggs, mushrooms, margarine, more parsley, salt and pepper. Spread ¼ of this mixture onto each steak. Roll and secure with skewer or toothpick. Wrap each steak in foil, pouring chicken soup over each one before wrapping securely. Place in any flat pan and bake in 350° oven for 2 hours. Serves 4.

Ireene Morris

Beef Bourguignon

10 small or 5 medium onions   Thyme
2 pounds lean beef, cubed   ½ cup beef bouillon
2 tablespoons oil   1 cup dry red wine
1½ tablespoons flour   ½ pound fresh mushrooms,
Salt and pepper to taste   sliced
Marjoram

Peel, slice and fry onions in oil until brown. Remove onions to a separate dish. Saute beef cubes in same oil, adding more, if necessary. When beef is brown on all sides, sprinkle with flour and a generous pinch each of salt, pepper, marjoram and thyme. Add bouillon and red wine. Stir the mixture well and let simmer as slowly as possible for 3¼ hours. If liquid cooks away too much, add a little more bouillon and wine (1 part bouillon and 2 parts wine) to keep beef barely covered. Return onions to skillet, add mushrooms, stir well and cook for another ¾ hour. (The sauce should be thick and dark brown). Serves 6.

Debby Goldman

Beef Burgundy

2 pounds steak, cut into 2 inch cubes   1 large green pepper
1 cup Burgundy   1 8-ounce can mushrooms,
1 teaspoon oregano   reserve liquid
Garlic salt and pepper   Margarine or shortening
2 medium onions

Marinate steak cubes in Burgundy, oregano, garlic salt and pepper for at least 2 hours. Slice onions. Cut green peppers into ¼ inch strips and saute with onions and mushrooms in margarine until light gold, not brown. Remove vegetables. Brown meat quickly in same pan, turning constantly. Add sauteed vegetables and reserved liquid. Cook for 20 minutes over low heat. Serve over rice or broad noodles. May be frozen.

Evelyn Berlowitz

Beef Stew with Wine

2 pounds boneless chuck
1 teaspoon salt
½ cup flour
1 teaspoon garlic salt
¼ teaspoon pepper
½ cup margarine
1 onion, chopped
2 cans (4 ounces each) sliced
  mushrooms

2 stalks celery, cut in
  ½ inch pieces
3 carrots, cut in ½ inch pieces
1 cup water
1 cup red wine
1 can (10½ ounces) consomme
1 carton frozen peas (optional)
3 potatoes, cubed (optional)

Have butcher cut meat into 2-inch cubes. Combine flour, salt, garlic salt and pepper. Dredge meat in flour mixture. Brown meat in margarine. Add onion and drained mushrooms. Cook over low heat until onions are tender. Add, celery, carrots, water, wine and consomme. Cover, simmer and stir occasionally for 2 hours or until tender. Peas may be added during last ½ hour of cooking. Potatoes may be added during last hour of cooking.

Ann Lib Kozel

Wine Juice Stew

2 onions, thinly sliced
2 cloves garlic
1 pound chuck, cubed

½ cup orange juice
½ cup malaga wine
3 parboiled potatoes

Saute onions and garlic. Brown chuck. Add orange juice and wine. Simmer 2 hours or longer. Add parboiled potatoes 5-10 minutes before serving.

Judy Kaplan

Carbonnades a la Flammande

Flour for dredging
Salt and pepper to taste
2 pounds boneless beef, cut
  into 1-inch cubes
¼ cup oil
6 medium onions, sliced
1 clove garlic, finely chopped

1 12-ounce can of beer
1 tablespoon chopped parsley
1 bay leaf
¼ teaspoon thyme
½ pound fresh mushrooms,
  sliced (optional)

Combine flour, salt and pepper. Dredge meat in seasoned flour. Heat oil in skillet. Add onion slices, optional mushrooms and garlic and cook until tender, but not brown. Remove onions and mushrooms from skillet. Add meat to skillet and brown on all sides, adding a little more oil if necessary. When meat has browned, return onions and mushrooms to skillet. Add remaining ingredients. Cover and cook over low heat until meat is tender, about 1¼ hours. Serve with rice. 4-6 servings.

Debby Goldman

Carbonnades de Bouef

4 tablespoons oil
2 pounds beef, cut up
2 medium onions
¼ cup flour
1¼ cups hot water
1 cup beer
1 clove garlic

1 bay leaf
2 teaspoons salt
½ teaspoon sugar
1½ teaspoons vinegar
1/8 teaspoon nutmeg
¼ teaspoon oregano

In large skillet, heat 2 tablespoons oil. Add beef a little at a time and brown. Remove meat. Add 2 tablespoons oil and onions. Brown well. Stir in flour, then hot water, until boiling. Add remaining ingredients. Return meat to pot. Bring to boil and turn into a 2½ quart casserole. Cover and bake 2 hours at 325°. Serve with Chinese noodles or rice.

Tillie Levinson

Five-Hour Stew

2 pounds cubed chuck
½ green pepper, cubed
2 onions, cubed
4 carrots, fingered
1 cup chopped celery
2 cups stewed tomatoes
1 6-ounce can tomato sauce
4 tablespoons Minute tapioca
1 tablespoon brown sugar
1 cup Burgundy wine (or ½ cup)
Salt, pepper
2 beef bouillon cubes

Combine in covered casserole. Bake at 265° for 5 hours. Serve with rice, noodles or potatoes.

Betty Reif

Hungarian Goulash

2 large onions, chopped
1 tablespoon fat or oil
2 pounds chuck steak, cubed
Salt
1 fresh tomato or 1 tablespoon
tomato sauce
½ green pepper, cut up
1 tablespoon paprika
Water
4 large potatoes, cubed

Brown onions in oil, add meat, salt, tomato and green pepper. Simmer for 30 minutes. Add paprika and cover with water. When meat is almost done, add potatoes.

Elizabeth Palage

Beef Ragout

2½ pounds stew meat
2 tablespoons oil
1 teaspoon soy sauce
½ cup dry red wine
¾ cup condensed beef bouillon
2½ cups water
1 large onion, sliced thin
2 cups mushrooms
¼ tablespoon chopped parsley
½ teaspoon thyme leaves
¾ teaspoon salt
1 10-ounce package frozen peas

Season meat. Heat oil 325° add soy sauce. Gradually add meat, brown and remove. Reduce heat 225 . Return meat to pan and add wine, water , bouillon, onion, mushrooms, parsley, salt and thyme. Cover and cook 4 hours. Add peas and cook till tender.

Beverly Chesler

Beef Stroganoff

1 pound filet of beef
1 onion, sliced
8 mushrooms
3 tablespoons chicken fat
or margarine
2 fresh tomatoes,
cubed and skinned
1 tablespoon flour
½ cup chicken soup
1 egg yolk
¼ cup white wine
Salt and pepper to taste

Fry sliced mushrooms and onion in one tablespoon fat. Cut meat into thin slices and pound. Fry in one tablespoon fat, then add to onions and mushrooms. Blend flour in one tablespoon fat over low heat, then add chicken soup and boil. Blend well-beaten egg yolk into this mixture (with heat off). Then return to low heat, add wine and tomato. Cook for a few minutes — season and pour over meat and serve. Serves 3-4.

Ireene Morris

Sweet and Sour Beef Stew

3 pounds chuck, cubed
1 cup flour
1/8 teaspoon salt
1/8 teaspoon pepper
3 tablespoons shortening
½ cup chopped onion
3 tablespoons sugar

1 tablespoon prepared mustard
3 tablespoons Worcestershire sauce
1 cup ketchup
1 cup water
¼ cup vinegar

Dredge meat in a mixture of flour, salt, and pepper until flour is absorbed into meat. Brown in shortening with onions. Mix the remaining ingredients and bring to slow boil. Simmer about 10 minutes. Add meat to this mixture and bake at 300° -325° for 3½ hours or until tender. Mixture may be simmered on top of stove for 1½ hours.

Renee L. Serling

Barbecued Short Ribs

8 pounds short ribs
Marinade
3 cups beer
1 cup honey
1½ teaspoons dry mustard
2 teaspoons chili powder

2 teaspoons crumbled sage
4 tablespoons horseradish
1 tablespoon salt
2 tablespoons lemon juice

Place ribs in large shallow pan. Pour marinade over ribs and let stand several hours. Turn periodically. Broil over charcoal about 15 minutes. Turn frequently, brush with marinade. Serves 8.

Helen Gordon

Barbecued Short Ribs

2 pounds short ribs of beef
Garlic salt
½ cup vinegar
1 teaspoon salt
1 teaspoon dry mustard
4 teaspoons celery seed

1½ teaspoons chili powder
1 cup ketchup
¼ cup sugar
1 teaspoon paprika
½ teaspoons pepper

Have butcher cut ribs into serving pieces. Sprinkle ribs generously with garlic salt. Place in baking pan. Combine all remaining ingredients and pour over ribs. Bake in 325° oven for 2½ hours. Spoon sauce over ribs frequently; turn often. Serves 4.

Gert Wieder

Islander Beef Short Ribs

3-4 pounds beef short ribs
½ teaspoon salt
1 can (15¾ ounces) pineapple tidbits
½ cup catsup
¼ cup vinegar
¼ cup water

½ cup chopped onion
¼ cup finely chopped green pepper
3 tablespoons brown sugar
½ teaspoon dry mustard
Flour for gravy (optional)

Brown short ribs in own fat. Pour off drippings. Cover tightly and cook slowly 1½ hours. Pour off drippings again. Combine remaining ingredients and pour over short ribs. Cover and continue to cook an additional 30 minutes. Place in oven at this point at 325°. Thicken liquid with flour and water for gravy. Serve with rice. 4-6 servings.

Merle Markus

Marinated Shoulder Steak

¾ cup tomato sauce
2 pounds shoulder steak
¼ cup molasses
2 tablespoons plus 1 teaspoon
vinegar
1 tablespoon oil

1 tablespoon Worcestershire
sauce
1 tablespoon minced onion
½ teaspoon mustard
Salt and pepper

Mix all ingredients except steak together. Pour over steak and marinate overnight. Barbecue or broil steak. Serves 4.

Bunny Skirboll

Shish Kabob

2 pounds beef cubes
1 cup Italian salad dressing
1 cup red wine
12 baby white onions
3 green peppers

12 firm white mushroom caps
3 firm tomatoes
½ cup melted margarine
4 cloves garlic, crushed
Salt and pepper

Prepare marinade from salad dressing and red wine. Marinate beef cubes over night. Blanch baby white onions—and drain. Cut green peppers in eighths, blanch and drain. Quarter tomatoes. Shake mushrooms in sauce made from margarine, garlic, salt and pepper. Arrange drained meat and add vegetables on skewers. Broil for three minutes on each side, brushing once or twice with the melted margarine mixture.

Judy Kaplan

London Broil

2 pounds London broil
1 tablespoon salad oil
2 teaspoons chopped parsley
1 clove garlic, crushed

1 teaspoon salt
1 teaspoon lemon juice
1/8 teaspoon pepper

Trim excess fat from meat. Combine remaining ingredients. Brush half of mixture over steak and let stand 45 minutes. Place steak, oil side up, on lightly greased broiler pan. Broil about 4 inches from heat for 5 minutes. Turn steak, brush with remaining oil mixture, broil 4-5 minutes longer. The steak will be rare the way London broil should be. Remove steak to board, slice very thinly on diagonal. 4 servings.

Maxine Peters

Steak Nino

1½ pounds shoulder steak, sliced
paper thin
Few drops olive oil
2 tablespoons margarine
1 teaspoon dry mustard
2 teaspoons chopped chives

2 tablespoons margarine
2 teaspoons Worcestershire
sauce
1 tablespoon lemon juice
2 tablespoons minced parsley

Cut meat into 2-inch squares. Brush with olive oil and sprinkle with salt and pepper. In large skillet, place olive oil, margarine, mustard and chives. Add steak and cook for 1-2 minutes on each side. Remove to warm platter. Add to skillet margarine, Worcestershire sauce, lemon juice and parsley and cook until all ingredients are well mixed. Pour sauce over steak pieces and serve immediately.

Judy Kaplan

Steak au Poivre

1 or 2 tablespoons peppercorns   2 teaspoons salt
Steaks

Crush (don't grind) peppercorns. Press steaks into the crushed pepper and work it into the meat on both sides with heel of your palm. Sprinkle bottom of a heavy skillet with salt. Preheat pan and brown the steaks on high heat. Reduce to medium and turn the meat to cook until done.

Sauce

¼ cup pareve margarine,   sauce
  melted   2 tablespoons lemon juice
1 teaspoon Worcestershire   2 ounces cognac

Remove steaks to a heated metal sizzler and pour melted margarine and seasonings over meat. Flambe with cognac. Steaks may be marinated in red wine before preparing.

Carole Goldberg

Party Beef Fondue

2-2½ pounds diced rib or   Peanut oil, sufficient to place
  shoulder steak (enough for   in fondue pots
  six people)

Fill each fondue pot with peanut oil. Heat on stove until oil boils and begins to brown. Transfer fondue pot to flame over fondue burner. Place between every two guests bowl of bite sized pieces of raw tender meat and variety of sauces. Each guest, using the long handled fork, spears a piece of beef and plunges it into the hot oil and cooks it until done as desired (1-2 minutes.) When done, he uses a table fork and dips beef into one or more of the offered sauces, thus allowing for pieces of meat to be cooking at all times. Provide a small bowl of rice for each guest.

Sauces for Fondue

Garlic Sauce

½ cup softened margarine   Salt and pepper to taste
3 cloves garlic, minced

Combine and beat with fork. Refrigerate or freeze. Serve at room temperature; makes ½ cup.

Tomato Sauce

1 8-ounce can tomato sauce   2 tablespoons brown sugar
1/3 cup steak sauce   2 tablespoons salad oil

Combine. Refrigerate or freeze. When ready to serve, bring to boil. Serve hot; makes 1½ cups.

Horseradish Sauce

1 cup mayonnaise   ¼ teaspoon salt
3 tablespoons white horseradish   Dash paprika

Combine. Refrigerate until serving time. Makes 1¼ cups.

Curry Sauce

1 teaspoon curry powder   ½ teaspoon lemon juice
1 teaspoon grated onion   1 cup mayonnaise

Suggested Condiments

Radishes, celery, carrot sticks, chives, salted peanuts, slivered almonds, pineapple chunks, parsley, chutney, cocktail onions, olives, pickled relish.

Maxine Peters

Beef and Chicken Fondue with Broth

4 chicken breasts, skinned,
   boned and sliced very thin
   across grain
1 pound beef, any tender cut,
   sliced very thin across grain
3 14-ounce cans chicken broth
3 bouillon cubes

Skin chicken breasts and bone. Put beef and chicken in freezer until partially frozen to make slicing easy. Or have butcher do this for you. Shortly before cooking time, arrange meat and chicken on large tray or in foil-lined baskets. Heat broth with bouillon cubes in sauce pan until bubbling. Transfer to fondue pot. Let each guest cook his own meat on fondue fork and dip in variety of sauces. Serve rice in the broth after cooking. Serves 4.

Sauces

Catsup with horseradish
Hot Mustard Sauce
Sweet and Sour Sauce

Eulah Feier

Chinese Beef and Peppers

2 pounds lean beef
2 tomatoes
2 green peppers
2 tablespoons salad oil
1 clove garlic, crushed
1 teaspoon salt
Dash pepper
¼ cup soy sauce
½ teaspoon sugar
1 1-pound can bean sprouts
1 tablespoon cornstarch
¼ cup water

Cut meat into thin strips (julienne style) across grain. Cut tomatoes into eighths, peppers into 1-inch squares. Heat oil in large skillet. Add beef, garlic, salt and pepper. Brown over high heat. Add soy sauce and sugar, cover and cook slowly for 5 minutes. Add tomatoes, peppers, drained bean sprouts. Bring to boil, cover and cook briskly for 5 minutes. Make paste of starch and water. Add to beef mixture; cook until sauce thickens slightly. Simmer until done, stirring occasionally. Water may be added at any time. Serves 6.

Veda Rubin

Sukiyaki

2 tablespoons nyafat
3 stalks chinese celery, cut
   in 1-inch pieces
1 onion, thinly sliced
1½ pounds beef tenderloin,
   cut in paper-thin strips
¼ pound ground beef
1 4-ounce can water chestnuts
1 small carrot, thinly sliced
¼ pound fresh spinach

Melt nyafat in skillet. Add celery and onion, cook 5 minutes. Add tenderloin and ground beef, brown. Add remaining ingredients.

Sauce

2 tablespoons soy sauce
2 tablespoons beer
½ cup beef broth
2 teaspoons sugar

Mix sauce ingredients and add to skillet. Continue cooking for about 20 minutes. Serve immediately.

Ireene Morris

Sukiyaki

1 pound shoulder steak cut into
   2-inch pieces
3 stalks celery, sliced
2 large onions, thinly sliced
½ pound mushrooms, thinly
   sliced
1 8-ounce can bamboo shoots,
drained
1 bunch scallions, cut in
   1½ inch lengths
3 tablespoons water
1/3 cup soy sauce
½ cup strong chicken bouillon
3 cups raw spinach leaves

Brown shoulder steak pieces; add celery and onions, cook 3-5 minutes. Add mushrooms, bamboo shoots, scallions, water, soy sauce and chicken bouillon. Simmer until vegetables are tender, about 10 minutes. Add spinach leaves and cook 5 minutes. Serve on rice. Serves 4-6.

Judy Kaplan

Teriyaki

3 pounds shoulder steak
Vegetable oil
1 6-ounce can frozen concentrated pineapple juice
2 tablespoons honey
2 tablespoons soy sauce
¾ teaspoon ginger
1 clove garlic, crushed

Cut steak paper thin, then into strips 1-inch wide. In large heavy skillet or Dutch oven, heat oil and brown meat rapidly. Combine thawed pineapple juice concentrate with remaining ingredients and pour over meat; bring to a boil, stirring carefully. May be served immediately, without further cooking, over browned or fluffy white rice. Serves 4. Note: if desired, shoulder steak may be sliced ¼ inch thick; if so, then simmer gently 10-15 minutes longer.

T'Mahry Axelrod

Steak Teriyaki

2 pounds shoulder steak
1 tablespoon salad oil
½ cup soy sauce
¼ cup sugar
2 tablespoons dry sherry wine
1 teaspoon ginger
1 clove garlic, crushed

Cut and roll strips of steak, pinwheel style. Fasten with turkey tie pin. Combine remaining ingredients, pour over meat and marinate 1-1½ hours. Broil 7 minutes on each side for rare, 10 minutes each side for medium, and 13 minutes on each side for well done. Heat sauce and serve separately.

Suzie Horwitz

Rolled Cabbage

1 head of cabbage
1½ pounds ground meat
1 teaspoon salt
Pepper
1 egg

Sauce
1 #2½ can tomatoes
Juice of 2 lemons
½ cup brown sugar
¾ cup apricot jam

Steam cabbage 5 minutes; separate leaves. Mix meat, salt, pepper and egg. Place tablespoon of meat mixture on each leaf, roll up and place rolls in pan. Mix sauce ingredients and pour over cabbage rolls. Roast at 350° for 2½ hours; first 1½ hours covered, last hour uncovered.

Selma Soloway

Stuffed Cabbage

1 pound ground meat	1 large head of cabbage
2 onions	1 green pepper
1 cup uncooked rice	1 tablespoon flour
2 apples	1 tablespoon fat
2 tablespoons fat	2 4-ounce cans tomato sauce
Salt and pepper to taste	2 tablespoons sugar
Paprika	

Finely chop onions and apples. Mix together with meat, rice, fat and seasonings. Wash whole head of cabbage. Remove center core. Place in boiling water to separate leaves. When leaves are soft, put 1 tablespoon of meat mixture on each leaf. Roll up, tuck corners and fasten with toothpick. Cut up any remaining small pieces of cabbage and place in bottom of pot. Wash and remove center of green peper and stuff with meat mixture. Put pepper in center of pot. Add stuffed cabbage leaves around pepper. Cover half way with water. Start cooking over medium heat. Brown flour and fat and add tomato sauce and sugar. Pour over cabbage and cook for two hours. Tip: Freeze cabbage for three days so leaves will separate easier.

Rachel Hyman

Quick Stuffed Cabbage

1 head cabbage	Dried prunes, optional
3-4 onions, sliced	Paprika

Filling

2 pounds ground beef	2 tablespoons matzo meal
1 onion, grated	1 teaspoon lemon juice
1 egg	½ teaspoon salt
¼ cup rice	

Sauce

Juice of 1 lemon	1 tablespoon honey
2 tablespoons sugar	1 8-ounce can tomato sauce

Immerse cabbage in boiling, salted water 5-10 minutes, until leaves are limp; separate them. Mix all filling ingredients together. Place 2 tablespoons of meat mixture near stem end of leaf and roll up like an envelope. Steam sliced onions, sprinkled with paprika, in pressure cooker. On layers of onions, with some dried prunes, if desired, place layers of cabbage rolls. Mix together sauce and pour over contents of cooker. Cover and steam at high pressure for 20 minutes. Before eating, place in large roasting pan and brown uncovered in 300° oven for 30 minutes.

Mrs. Aaron Karp

Stuffed Peppers

1½ pounds ground beef	½ cup cooked rice
1 onion, grated	4 green pepers
1 tablespoon salt	1 8-ounce can tomato sauce
Dash of black pepper	1 tablespoon sugar
2 eggs	Salt to taste

Mix ground beef, onion, salt, pepper, eggs and rice. Scoop out centers of 4 green peppers and stuff with this mixture. Bring tomato sauce to a boil, adding sugar and salt. Place green peppers in a casserole, pour over prepared tomato sauce. Make meat balls from remaining meat and add to casserole. Bake for one hour in a 350° oven.

Mrs. Elizabeth Palage

Oriental Meat Balls

1 pound hamburger
1 can (5 ounces) water chestnuts, diced
1/3 cup bread crumbs
1 egg

½ teaspoon soy sauce
¼ teaspoon Tabasco
Salt and pepper to taste
¾ teaspoon ground ginger
Olive oil for frying

Mix together first 8 ingredients and shape into meat balls. Brown in olive oil in large skillet. Pour off oil.

Sauce

½ cup vinegar
3½ tablespoons Soy sauce
¼ cup molasses or honey
1/3 cup ketchup
1 can (9 ounces) pineapple
  chunks and syrup

1 jar kumquats
1 jar pickled watermelon rind
1 jar (10 ounces) maraschino
  cherries and juice
Green pepper rings

Mix together all sauce ingredients except green peppers and pour over meatballs. Cook 1 hour. Add green pepper rings about 10 minutes before serving.

Judy Kaplan

Meat Ball Special

1 pound lean ground beef
½ cup bread crumbs
1 egg
¼ cup tomato sauce
1 teaspoon salt
1/8 teaspoon pepper
1/8 teaspoon allspice
1 teaspoon onion juice

2 tablespoons fat
3 cups water
¾ cup tomato sauce
1 package onion soup mix
1¼ cups sliced carrots
1 10-ounce package frozen peas
½ green pepper, chopped
3 medium potatoes, cubed

Combine first eight ingredients, mix well and form into 12 meat balls. Brown meat balls in fat in Dutch oven or large pot. Add next seven ingredients and bring to a boil. Cook over low heat until tender. Add a little more water if desired.

Hetty Jacobson

Some Spicy Meatballs

2 pounds ground meat
1 teaspoon garlic powder
Salt and pepper to taste
2 16-ounce cans jellied cran-

berry sauce
2 8-ounce cans tomato sauce
1 teaspoon oregano

Season meat with garlic powder and salt and pepper; form into small balls, the size of a walnut. Melt cranberry sauce over low heat until jelly-like consistency; blend in tomato sauce and oregano. Add meat balls to sauce and simmer slowly, in a covered pot, about 1 hour. Serves 6-8.

Sharon Axelrod

Swedish Meat Balls

Sauce

1 large onion, sliced	1/3 cup ketchup
½ cup raisins	¼ cup vinegar
½ cup brown sugar	¼ teaspoon salt

Mix above ingredients and bring to a boil. Lower heat to simmer for 5 minutes. Add meat balls, cover and cook for 1½ hours. Shake pot occasionally.

Meatballs

2 pounds ground beef	Small onion, grated
1 egg	1 heaping tablespoon oatmeal
1 teaspoon salt, or other seasoning	3 tablespoons warm water to soften oatmeal
¼ teaspoon pepper	2 tablespoons ketchup

Mix above ingredients and make meatballs the size of a walnut. Add gradually to the sauce while simmering.

Alice Lipsetts

Aunt Rose's Swedish Meat Balls

2 pounds chopped beef	jelly
1 bottle chili sauce	¼ cup white raisins
1 bottle water	¼ cup cut-up almonds
2 heaping tablespoons grape	

Combine all ingredients, except meat, in saucepan and simmer for 15 minutes. Add a little water to meat, shape into balls and drop into simmering sauce and cook, covered, for ½ hour. Serve over rice, mashed potatoes or noodles. Good for hors d'oeuvres.

Selma Soloway

Spaghetti and Meat Balls

Sauce

½ onion, chopped	½ cup water
1 teaspoon garlic salt	1 tablespoon sugar
1 tablespoon shortening	¼ teaspoon pepper
1 1-pound can tomato puree	1 teaspoon oregano
1 6-ounce can tomato paste	

Cook onion and garlic salt in shortening until tender, but not brown. Add remaining ingredients. Simmer 30 minutes. Add meat balls and continue cooking 30 minutes longer.

Meat Balls

2 slices bread	½ teaspoon oregano
1 pound hamburger	1 teaspoon salt
2 eggs	Dash pepper
1 teaspoon garlic salt	

Soak bread in water 2-3 minutes, then squeeze out moisture. Combine soaked bread with remaining ingredients. Form meat balls, brown, add to spaghetti sauce and cook 30 minutes. Serves 4-6.

Bernice Sklar

Meat Balls and Spaghetti Sauce

1 pound hamburger
1 egg
2 teaspoons chopped parsley
1 tablespoon bread crumbs
Salt, pepper and garlic powder
   to taste
1 chopped onion
Vegetable oil
1 1-pound 13-ounce can tomato

puree
1/3 can cold water
1 1-pound 13-ounce can tomatoes
1 6-ounce can tomato paste
1 small can cold water
½ bunch parsley
4 bay leaves
19 fennel seeds

Mix meat with egg, parsley, bread crumbs and seasonings to taste. Form into balls. Saute chopped onion in oil until transparent. Use small amount of oil. Brown meat in this mixture until lightly brown. Strain canned tomatoes, reserving 2 tomatoes which are cut up and added to sauce. Add tomato puree, water and tomatoes as described, tomato paste with water, seasonings, parsley, bay leaves and fennel seeds. Simmer for 2 hours, lightly covered.

Norma Erdle

Inside-out Ravioli Casserole

1 pound ground beef
½ cup chopped onion
1 clove minced garlic
1 tablespoon salad oil
1 10-ounce package chopped
   spinach
1 1-pound can spaghetti sauce
   with mushrooms
1 8-ounce can tomato sauce

1 6-ounce can tomato paste
½ teaspoon salt
Dash pepper
2 cups shell macaroni, cooked
   (7 ounces)
½ cup soft bread crumbs
2 well-beaten eggs
½ cup salad oil

Brown ground beef, onion and garlic in salad oil. Cook spinach and drain. Reserve liquid and add water to make 1 cup. Stir spinach liquid and spaghetti sauce, tomato sauce, tomato paste, salt and pepper into the meat mixture. Simmer ten minutes. Combine spinach with remaining ingredients. Spread in a 13 x 9 pan. Top with meat sauce. Bake at 350° for 30 minutes. Let stand 10 minutes before serving. Serves 8-10.

Arlean Levinson

Chow Mein Burgers

1 pound ground beef
½ cup chopped onion
1-pound can chop suey vegetables,
   drained
1/3 cup water
3 tablespoons soy sauce

2 tablespoons cornstarch
8 hamburger buns, split and
   toasted
1 3-ounce can chow mein
   noodles

In medium size skillet, combine meat and onion and cook until meat is brown. Add chop suey vegetables. Stir water and soy sauce into corn starch, add to beef mixture. Cook 1-2 minutes, stirring to coat vegetables and meat. Spoon onto bottom halves of buns, add crumbled chow mein noodles over each sandwich. Cover with top of buns.

Bunny Zigman

Barbecued Beefburgers

1 pound hamburger	sauce
2 tablespoons oil	3 tablespoons water
1 8-ounce can tomato sauce	1 tablespoon chopped onion
2 tablespoons chili sauce	1 tablespoon brown sugar
2 tablespoons vinegar	1 tablespoon prepared mustard
1 tablespoon Worcestershire	

In fry pan, brown ground beef in oil. Add rest of ingredients. Reduce to simmer and let cook 15 minutes. Serve on toasted hamburger buns.

Shirley Jacobson

Easy Meat Loaf

2 eggs	1 package onion soup mix
1/3 cup catsup	1½ cups matzo meal
¾ cup warm water	2 pounds ground beef

In a large bowl, beat eggs lightly. Stir in catsup, warm water and onion soup mix. Add matzo meal and beef. Mix well. Form into a loaf, bake in greased pan for 1 hour at 350°. Makes 6-8 servings.

Priscilla Brown

Easiest Ever Meat Loaf

2 pounds ground meat	½ cup water
2 eggs, slightly beaten	1 11-ounce can tomato
1 3-ounce package potato pan-	mushroom sauce
cake mix	

Combine all ingredients with ½ cup sauce. Put into greased 9 x 5 x 3 loaf pan. Top with remaining sauce. Bake at 350° for one hour. Serves 6.

Gert Greenberg

Meat Loaf

2 pounds ground beef	drained
1 can French-style green beans	1 can small potatoes
1 can vegetarian vegetable soup	Paprika
1 4-ounce can mushrooms,	

Drain off half of the liquid from the can of string beans. Mix mushrooms, beans and soup together. Place meat into flat pan (approximately 9 x 13), Pat out meat until flat, leaving enough room to put the vegetable mixture and potatoes around the meat. Sprinkle paprika on top and bake for 1½ hours at 350°. Serves 4.

Joyce Axelrod

Meat Loaf

1½ pounds hamburger	1 cup bread crumbs
1 egg	1 4-ounce can tomato onion
1 teaspoon salt	sauce
¼ teaspoon pepper	

Mix above ingredients together and place in loaf pan.

Sauce

1 cup hot water	2 tablespoons prepared mustard
2 tablespoons vinegar	1½ tablespoons brown sugar

Mix together and pour over top of meat loaf. Bake at 350° for 1 hour basting every 15 minutes with sauce.

Marge Gold

Party Pinwheel Roast

2 large onions, diced
½ cup hot oil
1 cup quick-cooking oats
1 cup fine bread crumbs
1 teaspoon salt
¼ teaspoon pepper
1 cup soup stock or water

2 pounds ground beef
1 medium onion, chopped fine
1 teaspoon herb seasoning
½ teaspoon garlic salt
¼ teaspoon pepper
¼ cup bread crumbs

Saute onions in hot oil. When browned, remove from heat; add oats, bread crumbs, salt, pepper and soup stock or water. Mix well and cool in refrigerator before spreading on meat. Mix all remaining ingredients. Roll out meat on 13 x 9 aluminum foil. Spread cooled stuffing over all. Roll up as for jelly roll in aluminum foil. Place on rack in shallow pan in 350° oven for 1½ hours. Remove foil and place on platter with tiny boiled potatoes, dipped in melted margarine and chopped parsley and canned asparagus tips.

Betty Alpert

Quick Chile Con Carne

1 pound ground beef
3 tablespoons flour
2 teaspoons salt
1 teaspoon sugar

2 teaspoons chili powder
2 cups canned tomatoes
2 cups canned kidney beans

Brown ground beef. Stir in flour, salt and sugar. Add chili powder, canned tomatoes and kidney beans. Cover and simmer for ½ hour or until done.

Ruth Drexler

Shepherd's Pie

1 pound ground beef
1 teaspoon salt
¼ teaspoon pepper
1 teaspoon onion powder
¼ cup bread crumbs

½ cup water
1 egg
4 servings instant mashed
   potatoes

Mix together meat, salt, pepper, onion powder, bread crumbs, water and egg. Spread in 9-inch pie plate and bake at 350° for 35 minutes. Prepare instant potatoes according to directions, spread on meat and bake additional 10 minutes.

Linda Rock

Texas Hash

2 large onions, sliced
2 green peppers, cut fine
3 tablespoons shortening
1 pound ground beef

2 cups canned tomatoes
½ cup uncooked rice
1 teaspoon chili powder
¼ teaspoon pepper

Cook onions and green pepper in shortening until onions are yellow. Add ground beef and saute until mixture falls apart. Add tomatoes, rice and seasoning. Arrange in casserole and bake at 350° for 45 minutes or until done. Serves 6-8.

Edna Berman

Lamb a la Mouradean

¼ cup olive oil
½ garlic clove, minced
½ teaspoon oregano
½ teaspoon salt
¼ teaspoon freshly ground
  pepper
Lamb chops or lamb roast

2 tablespoons Dijon-style
  mustard
1 tablespoon anchovy paste
Juice of ½ lemon
1 teaspoon ground oregano
½ garlic clove, mashed

Combine first 5 ingredients. Put meat in this marinade and let stand at least 4 hours, turning frequently. In a bowl, mix together remaining ingredients. Remove meat from marinade, spread mustard mixture on sides and broil chops 3-4 minutes on each side or bake roast at 350° until meat thermometer reaches lamb temperature, 185° .

Carole Berlove

Lamb Chops with Soy Sauce Marinade

1 cup soy sauce
½ cup oil
½ cup honey

Garlic salt
Lemon-pepper seasoning
12 lamb chops, rib or shoulder

Day before, liberally sprinkle lamb chops with garlic salt and lemon-pepper. Arrange chops in a shallow baking pan. Combine soy sauce, oil and honey and pour over chops. Turn chops frequently in marinade. When ready to cook, broil chops for 4-5 minutes on both sides, or more, depending on thickness and desired doneness. This marinade is also delicious on a thick family steak, punctured with holes so the marinade seeps in.

Nancy Hoffman

Crown Roast of Lamb with Rice Stuffing

5 pound crown roast of lamb
1 6-ounce package long grain
  and wild rice mix
1½ pounds ground lamb

1 teaspoon salt
½ teaspoon pepper
1 cup pureed cooked chestnuts
1 cup chicken bouillon

Have crown prepared at market by tying together a rack of lamb ribs from shoulder joint down and cutting down 2 inches between ribs and into other portion. Cook rice according to package directions. Saute ground lamb, salt, pepper, and chestnut puree until meat is lightly browned. Drain off drippings. Mix in cooked rice and place this mixture in center of roast; cover tips of roast with foil to prevent charring. Bake at 325° for 1½ hours, basting occasionally with bouillon. Replace foil with paper frills. Garnish with carrots, spiced crab apples, and parsley. Serves 8-10.

Eulah Feier

Lamb Stew

2 pounds lamb, cubed
¼ cup flour
Salt and pepper to taste
2 onions, sliced
3 tablespoons oil

1 cup boiling water
4 carrots, diced
4 potatoes, diced
1 green pepper, diced

Roll meat in flour. Sprinkle with salt and pepper. Fry onions in oil in a Dutch oven. Add meat and brown. Add water, cover and simmer for 1 hour. Add vegetables and cook for ½ hour longer.

Selma Soloway

Shish Kebab

20 small onions
3 boxes cherry tomatoes
1½ pounds large mushrooms
6-8 large green peppers
Coarse salt
3-4 pounds lamb or veal roast, cubed

1 teaspoon rosemary
1 teaspoon chervil or freshly chopped parsley
Salt and pepper to taste
½ cup red wine
½ cup olive oil
2-3 cloves crushed garlic

Par bake green peppers and cut into large pieces; remove seeds and core. Par boil small onions; remove skin. In a large bowl, add all above vegetables and coarse salt. Refrigerate over night. Place lamb cubes in a marinade made of rosemary, chervil or parsley, salt, pepper, wine, olive oil and crushed garlic. Marinate over night. Day of cooking, bring vegetables to room temperature. Alternate meat and vegetables on skewers and barbecue. Serves 6-8.

Carole Berlove

Number 7 Short Ribs

2 pounds lamb or veal ribs
7 tablespoons brown sugar
7 tablespoons soy sauce

7 tablespoons water
Crushed garlic, to taste

Brown ribs in dry skillet to remove excess fat. Combine remaining ingredients. Add ribs and bake at 350° for 1 hour. Serve hot over Chinese rice. This same recipe may be used for chicken wings.

Inez Lipman

Veal Roast

Shoulder of veal
2 large cloves garlic

¼ pound margarine
Salt and pepper

Slice garlic lengthwise into several pieces. Make gashes in veal shoulder and insert garlic. Melt margarine in Dutch oven. Brown veal in melted margarine. Add salt and pepper. Reduce heat and cover pot. Simmer ½ hour per pound. Test for tenderness. Remove from stove. Let stand before slicing. May add large chunks of celery or Belgian endive to pot for last ½ hour and braise with meat.

Annette Lee

Marinated Veal Roast

4-5 pound rolled and tied veal

Marinade
½ cup soy sauce
½ cup dry sherry
2 cloves garlic, crushed

1 tablespoon dry mustard
1 teaspoon ginger
½ teaspoon thyme, crushed

Combine all marinade ingredients and beat with mixer or in blender. Place roast in large, double, clear, plastic bag. Set in deep bowl to steady. Pour in marinade and close bag tightly. Let stand 2-3 hours at room temperature or overnight in refrigerator. Occasionally press bag against meat in several places to distribute marinade evenly. Remove meat from marinade. Place roast on rack in shallow roasting pan. Roast uncovered in slow oven at 325° for 2½-3 hours or until meat thermometer registers 175°, basting occasionally with marinade during last hour of roasting time. Serves 10-12.

Edna Wilcove

Veal French

1 pound thin slices of veal	Juice of 1 lemon
1 cup flour	½ teaspoon dried parsley
1 teaspoon salt	½ pound margarine
¼ teaspoon pepper	1 cup white wine
2 eggs + little water	Oil

Dip veal in flour, mixed with salt, pepper and parsley, then beaten eggs, then flour again. Brown in oil on both sides. Drain on paper toweling. Make sauce by melting margarine, adding wine and lemon juice. Put cutlets back in sauce and cover. Simmer ½ hour.

Beverly Chesler

Veal Marengo

6 tablespoons oil	3 cups chicken broth
3 pounds veal, cut in pieces	1 6-ounce can tomato paste
2 small onions, diced	6 carrots, cut up
Salt and pepper to taste	1 can mushrooms
Generous dash paprika	1 package frozen peas
5 tablespoons flour	Chopped parsley

Heat oil in large pot. Add veal and brown. Add chopped onions, salt, pepper, paprika; cook until onions are limp. Sprinkle flour over mixture, stir thoroughly. Add chicken broth and tomato paste. Stir, cover and simmer 30 minutes. Add mushrooms, carrots and peas. Cook 30 minutes more. Sprinkle with parsley.

Beverly Chesler

Veal and Peppers

¼ cup sliced onions	2 green peppers, sliced
½ cup sliced mushrooms	Paprika
2 tablespoons oil	Garlic salt
1 pound veal, cubed	1½ cups chicken broth

Brown onions and mushrooms in oil. Add veal and brown. Add green peppers and season everything with paprika and garlic salt. Pour in chicken broth and cover pan. Allow to simmer until meat is tender. Serve over rice.

Ireene Morris

Tangy Veal Saute

½ pound veal steak, ¼ inch thick	½ teaspoon rosemary
1 lemon, juice and rind	½ teaspoon salt
1 egg, slightly beaten	Dash pepper
1/3 cup bread crumbs	3 tablespoons oil

Arrange veal steaks in a shallow dish. Sprinkle both sides with grated rind and juice of lemon. Refrigerate for 1 hour. Turn once. Dip veal in egg, then in seasoned crumbs. Saute in hot fat on both sides until golden brown. Serve at once. Delicious with spaghetti. 2 servings.

Veal Scallopini

1 pound veal, sliced very thin	1 4-ounce can sliced mushrooms
1 cup beef or chicken bouillon	Parsley
½ cup dry white wine	

Pound veal, roll in flour and saute in pareve margarine or oil until lightly browned. Add bouillon and wine and simmer uncovered, stirring occasionally, for about 20 minutes. Add mushrooms. Sprinkle with parsley. Serve over noodles or rice. Serves 4.

Sue Kiner

Braised Veal Shanks

2 tablespoons margarine
2 tablespoons vegetable oil
3 veal shanks (5-6 pounds) cut
   in 2½ inch pieces
1 cup chopped onion
1 large garlic clove, minced
1 cup dry white wine
2 cans (8-ounce) tomato sauce

1 tablespoon dried rosemary
2 tablespoons dried marjoram,
   crumbled
1 teaspoon salt
Dash of pepper
2 tablespoons chopped parsley
Dash of dry mustard

Heat margarine and oil in heavy sauce pan over medium heat. Add shanks and brown on all sides. Remove from pan. Add onions to fat left in pan. Cook 5 minutes, stirring occasionally. Return shanks to pan, add remaining ingredients, except chopped parsley. Cover, bring to full boil, simmer 1-1½ hours. Remove shanks. Serve over plain rice or bulgar pilaf. Add strained sauce and sprinkle with parsley. Serves 4.

Carole Berlove

Breast of Veal

5 or 6 pound breast of veal
Onion salt
Garlic salt
Paprika
½ cup water
2 tablespoons margarine

2 chopped onions
12-ounce jar apricot preserves
2 tablespoons soy sauce
½ teaspoon ginger
1 teaspoon prepared mustard
¼ cup vinegar

Sprinkle veal with onion and garlic salts and paprika. Put in roasting pan with the water. Bake, uncovered, at 350° for 1 hour. In saucepan, melt margarine and saute onions until tender. Add apricot preserves, soy sauce, ginger, mustard and vinegar. Blend until smooth. When veal has cooked 1 hour, brush with sauce. Return to oven and cook 1 more hour. Turn veal over and brush with sauce again. Return to oven and cook remaining 45 minutes. Total cooking time 2 hours 45 minutes. Serves 6.

Ireene Morris

Roast Breast of Veal with Grated
Potato Stuffing

1 breast of veal
6 medium potatoes
1 onion
2 eggs
½ cup flour

1 teaspoon salt
½ cup hot melted shortening
1 clove garlic
Flour

Have butcher cut a deep pocket in veal. Grate pared potatoes into a deep bowl. Squeeze out excess water. Grate onion into bowl. Add eggs, flour, salt and pepper. Stir until well combined. Heat shortening in roasting pan and pour into potato mixture, stirring rapidly until combined. Fill pocket in veal breast. Fasten with skewers or toothpicks. Rub meat with cut clove of garlic, dredge with flour and place in greased roasting pan. Roast in oven at 350° for 2½-3 hours. Test with fork for tenderness.

Lillian Cohen

Chicken Liver Saute

1 pound chicken livers
2 large onions, sliced
1 4-ounce can sliced mushrooms
1 8-ounce can stewed tomatoes
Salt and pepper to taste

Saute onions; add livers and brown. Season. Cover and stew for 20 minutes. Add mushrooms and tomatoes. Simmer 15 minutes. Serve over rice.

Ellie Harris

Chicken Livers with Mushrooms

1 pound mushrooms
1 pound chicken livers
6-8 tablespoons oil
1 medium onion, sliced
½ cup sauterne or any white wine
Salt and pepper to taste

Wash mushrooms. Paper towel dry and slice. Saute mushrooms and sliced onion in oil until brown, stirring occasionally. Add chicken livers and cook for 5 minutes more. Season with salt and pepper, add wine and cook for about 1 minute. Don't let it boil. Serve hot over toast for appetizers or rice for main dish. Serves 4.

Ricky Sands

Chicken Livers and Rice Casserole

3 cups cooked rice
1 teaspoon salt
Dash dried thyme leaves
1 tablespoon minced parsley
2 tablespoons margarine
1 pound chicken livers
¼ cup margarine or chicken
fat
1 onion, chopped
1 clove garlic, minced
½ teaspoon salt
Dash pepper
2 tablespoons sherry

To hot cooked rice, add salt, thyme, parsley and 2 tablespoons margarine. Melt ¼ cup margarine or chicken fat in frying pan, cook 5-10 minutes until chicken livers are lightly browned and onion is tender. Add garlic, salt, pepper and sherry to chicken livers. Mix rice into chicken livers and bake at 375° for 15 minutes. Serves 4-6.

Irene Friedman

Bokharin Pilaf

10 chicken livers
½ cup chicken fat
1 cup coarsely grated carrots
2 onions, chopped
2 tablespoons parsley
4½ cups water or stock
1½ cups rice, raw
1½ teaspoons turmeric
Salt and pepper to taste
2 large tomatoes, diced
Dash garlic salt

Lightly fry livers in chicken fat. Dice. Lightly fry carrots, onions and parsley. Put all ingredients, except tomatoes, in covered saucepan. Cook 30 minutes. Add diced tomatoes and heat through.

Eve Mendelson

Israeli Liver and Eggs

1 pound sliced liver   1 egg
1 small onion   Coarse salt
¼ cup oil

Sprinkle coarse salt over liver and broil on both sides until all blood is gone. Wash each slice and cut into 2-inch squares. Cut onion into small pieces and fry until golden brown. Dip pieces of liver in beaten egg and add to fried onions. Fry on both sides until egg is done. Remove to hot platter. Serve with cooked rice on which you pour left-over onion (or cinnamon and sugar). Even if you omit the rice, the liver is delish!

Mrs. Aaron Solomon

Lungen Stew

1 beef lung, cubed   About 4 teaspoons brown sugar
½ cup diced onions   1½ teaspoons salt
1 clove garlic, minced   ¼ teaspoon pepper
3 tablespoons cooking fat   1½ cups diced carrots
2 cups canned tomatoes

Trim veins from lung before cutting into small cubes. Lightly brown onions and garlic in hot fat. Add lung and brown lightly on all sides. Add tomatoes, brown sugar, salt and pepper. Cover and simmer over moderate heat until meat is tender. Add carrots and, if desired, other diced or cubed vegetables after stew has cooked about 15 minutes. Total cooking time is about 1½ hours. Thicken stew with 1 tablespoon flour mixed to a paste with cold water. Blend with ½ cup stew sauce and then add to stew. Cook 5 minutes longer.

Sora Lee Goldberg

Baked Tongue

Beef tongue   1 cup ketchup
2 large carrots, sliced diagonally   ¼ cup water
2 large onions, thinly sliced

Boil tongue until tender. Cool, peel and slice. In roasting pan, place onions; cover with sliced carrots; add sliced tongue in layers. Cover all with ketchup; add water. Cover and bake at 350° for 30 minutes. Stir and continue baking 30 minutes more.

Helen Hecker

Pickled Tongue or Brisket

5 pounds tongue or brisket   4 or 5 cloves garlic

Pickling solution
4 quarts cold water   1 tablespoon brown sugar
1½ pounds coarse salt   1 tablespoon mixed whole spices
½ ounce saltpeter (purchased   10 bay leaves
  at drugstore)

Combine ingredients for pickling solution and boil 5 minutes. This amount is enough to cover 5 pounds of meat or tongue. Place meat in stoneware crock that has a tight cover. Add garlic and when solution is cool, pour over meat. Weight the meat with a heavy plate or flat rock. Be sure meat is well under solution. Cover top of crock with double layer of muslin tied around. Place cover over muslin and store in cool place 10 days — 2 weeks. The crock cover need not be tight and can be adjusted so that air circulates between it and muslin cover.

Lillian Cohen

Pickled Tongue in Raisin Sauce

1 pickled tongue	2 tablespoons lemon juice
½ cup light brown sugar	1½ cups water
1 teaspoon dry mustard	½ cup raisins
2 tablespoons cornstarch	2 tablespoons margarine
2 tablespoons vinegar	

Cook tongue in boiling water until tender. Cool, peel and slice thin. Mix brown sugar, dry mustard and cornstarch; slowly stir in vinegar. Add lemon juice, water, raisins, and margarine. Stir over low heat until thickened. Pour over tongue and serve hot.

Ruth Salesin

Roast Tongue

1 fresh tongue	¾ teaspoon salt
1 teaspoon salt	¼ teaspoon pepper
2 cloves garlic	Ginger
2 onions, sliced	4 ounces V-8 juice
½ teaspoon peppercorns	2 sliced onions
½ teaspoon basil	2 split garlic cloves
½ teaspoon thyme	½ cup water
½ teaspoon rosemary	

Bring fresh tongue to boil in enough water to cover. Add next 7 ingredients and cook 2-3 hours, until tender. Remove tongue from liquid, and peel. Place tongue in roaster and sprinkle all over with salt, pepper and ginger. Add juice, onions, garlic cloves and water. Roast at 350° for 2-3 hours, basting often.

Judy Kaplan

Sweet and Sour Tongue

3 pound pickled tongue	6 ginger snaps, broken
1 12-ounce can tomato juice	2 onions, sliced
Juice of 1 lemon	2 cloves garlic
1 tablespoon mixed spices	Salt and pepper to taste
1 cup dark brown sugar	½ cup white raisins, optional

Cook tongue in boiling water until tender. Peel immediately. Let stand until cold. Cut into ¼-inch slices. (If thinner, meat will fall apart when heated.) Combine remaining ingredients. Simmer together until onions are tender. Strain over sliced tongue. Add raisins, if desired. Place in refrigerator for 24 hours to marinate. Reheat at 350° and serve over rice.

Zelda Bilfield

Sweet and Sour Tongue

2½-3 pound beef tongue	3 bay leaves or celery tops
Water to cover	1 10-ounce jar currant jelly
½ tablespoon salt	6 ounces chili sauce
1 onion, sliced	

Boil fresh tongue in salted water, to which onion and bay leaves have been added, until fork tender. Cool, peel, and slice tongue. Mash jelly with fork in saucepan over low heat until liquified. Add chili sauce, simmer for 5 minutes and remove from heat. Place a thin layer of sauce in bottom of casserole. Alternate layers of sliced tongue and sauce, ending with sauce. Seasoning may be added to taste. Refrigerate overnight or longer. (May be frozen for a short time). Bake at 350° for 1 hour.

Jeanette Presberg

Molds and Salads

Almond Gelatin Mold

1½ cups slivered almonds	1 cup cold milk or milk substitute
1 large can pineapple tidbits	1 cup scalded milk
1 pound miniature marshmallows	1 pint whipped cream
2 packages unflavored gelatin	

Soak marshmallows in pineapple juice overnight. Dissolve gelatin in cold milk. Add hot milk. Combine marshmallows and pineapple. Stir in gelatin and add almonds. Fold in whipped cream. Pour in 10-cup mold. Serves 10-12.

Betty Loeb

Avocado Salad Ring

1 package (3 ounces) lime gelatin	¾ cup riced hard boiled egg
1 cup hot water	¾ cup mayonnaise
3 tablespoons chopped parsley	½ teaspoon salt
2 cups mashed avocado (3 pears)	Onion juice, if desired
1 tablespoon lemon juice	

Put lemon juice on avocado as soon as it is peeled and mashed. This prevents discoloration. Dissolve gelatin in hot water, chill until it begins to jell. Add remaining ingredients. Place in 5-cup mold until it hardens. Serve on a bed of lettuce. Serves 10.

Julia Berlove

Blueberry Gelatin Mold

2 packages (3 ounces) rasp- berry gelatin	1 pint sour cream
3½ cups grape juice	1 cup blueberries

Dilute gelatin in warm grape juice. Refrigerate until set. Whip in mixmaster or high speed for 15 minutes. Fold in sour cream and blueberries. Pour into 5 cup mold. Serves 6-8.

Betty Loeb

Cherry Mold

2 packages (3 ounces) black cherry gelatin	1 2-pound can pitted bing cherries
2 cups boiling water	½ cup heavy sweet wine
	½ cup chopped walnuts

Dissolve gelatin in 2 cups boiling water. Drain cherries and add enough water to juice to make one cup. Combine with sweet wine and add to dissolved gelatin. Refrigerate until partially set and add cherries and nuts. Pour into 1½-quart mold. Serves 6-8

Judy Kaplan

Cranberry Salad Mold

2 packages (3 ounces) raspberry gelatin	1 11-ounce can mandarin oranges
2 cups water	1 1-pound can bing cherries
2 1-pound can whole cranberry sauce	(optional)

Dissolve gelatin in water. Add whole cranberry sauce. Drain other 3 cans of fruit and add to gelatin mixture. Pour into 2-quart mold and refrigerate.

Gloria Cohen

Cranberry Hearts Salad

1 envelope gelatin
¼ cup cold water
1 can whole cranberry sauce
1 tablespoon lemon juice
¼ teaspoon salt
¾ cup crushed pineapple
(undrained)
2 packages (3 ounces)
cream cheese
or 2/3 cup cottage cheese
½ cup cream, whipped

Add gelatin to cold water and allow to stand 2 minutes. Place cup in pan of boiling water until gelatin dissolves, add to cranberry sauce. Stir in lemon juice and salt. Beat cheese until soft. Combine with pineapple and blend. Fold into whipped cream. Pour into 1½ quart mold and chill. Serves 6-8.

Florence Margolius

Frozen Gelatin Mold

1 package (3 ounces) gelatin
1 cup boiling water
1/3 cup mayonnaise
¼ cup lemon juice
1 package non-dairy dessert topping
1 cup nuts
1 small can mandarin oranges
1 small can crushed pineapple
1 can (16 ounces) fruit cocktail
1 small jar maraschino cherries

Dissolve gelatin in boiling water. Add mayonnaise and lemon juice. (Mixes easier in blender). Thicken. Make dessert topping with milk or non-dairy milk substitute. Add drained fruits and fold in dessert topping. Freeze in loaf pan. To serve, unmold and let stand 10 minutes and slice. Serves 6-8. Note: Lime gelatin good with crushed pneapple, nuts, cherries and mandarin oranges. Orange gelatin good with mandarin oranges, fruit cocktail, nuts.

Beverly Chesler

Ice Cream Gelatin Mold

2 packages (3 ounces) strawberry
gelatin
1½ cups hot water
1 pint vanilla ice cream
1 package (16 ounces) frozen strawberries, thawed

Dissolve gelatin in water. Soften ice cream by stirring. Add ice cream to gelatin. Stir in strawberries. Pour into 1½-quart mold. Chill. Serves 8-10.

Marilyn Greenberg

Jewelled Dessert

1 package (3 ounce) pineapple-
grapefruit, orange or orange-pineapple gelatin
1 tablespoon sugar
⅛ teaspoon salt
1 cup boiling water
1 can (11 ounces) mandarin oranges
1 can (8¾ ounces) pineapple tidbits
1 cup sour cream
1 cup coconut
1 cup miniature marshmallows
1 cup seedless grapes

Dissolve gelatin, sugar and salt in boiling water. Drain oranges and pineapple, measuring combined syrups. Add water to make 1 cup, if necessary, and add to gelatin mixture. Stir in sour cream. Chill until very thick. Stir in drained fruits, coconut, marshmallows and grapes. Chill 15 minutes, then spoon into a 1½-quart mold. Chill until firm. Garnish with additional coconut and several seedless grapes, or maraschino cherries. Serves 6-8.

Marlene Elkin

Lemon Pineapple Ring

2 packages (3 ounces) lemon gelatin   pineapple
2 cups boiling water   1½ cups cream-style small curd
1 pint lemon sherbet   cottage cheese
1 can (8¾ ounces) crushed

Dissolve gelatin in boiling water. Add sherbet a spoonful at a time stirring until melted. Add undrained pineapple. Chill until partially set. Fold in cheese. Pour into 6½-cup ring mold. Chill until set, about 5 hours. Unmold and fill center with sliced strawberries. Serves 6-8.

Mrs. Isadore Ouriel

Lime Whip Salad

1 package (3 ounces) lime gelatin   ½ cup mayonnaise
¼ teaspoon salt   ¾ cup diced grapefruit
1 cup boiling water   ¾ cup diced celery
½ cup cold water   1 tablespoon chopped onion
1 tablespoon vinegar

Dissolve gelatin and salt in boiling water. Add cold water, vinegar, mayonnaise. Blend with beater. Quick freeze in freezer tray until firm, 1 inch from edge. Beat until fluffy. Fold in grapefruit, celery and onion. Pour into 1½-quart mold and chill until firm. Serves 6.

Hattie Lipsky

Mango Gelatin Mold

3 packages (3 ounces) lemon gelatin   1 large package cream cheese
4 cups boiling water   1 large can mangos

Dissolve gelatin in boiling water. Let cool. Blend mangos and juice and add cream cheese. Blend again. Add to gelatin mixture and pour into 2-quart mold and chill. Refrigerate 4-6 hours before serving. Serves 8-10.

Frumel Ureles

Orange Mold

2 packages (3 ounces) orange gelatin   1 can (11 ounces) mandarin
2 cups hot water   oranges, undrained
1 6-ounce can frozen orange juice,   1 can (16 ounces) chunky apple
  undiluted   sauce

Dissolve gelatin in hot water. When cool, add orange juice, oranges and apple sauce. Pour into 2-quart mold. Serves 12-14.

Mim Greenberg

Orange Pineapple Mold

1 can (11 ounces) mandarin oranges   1 can (13½ ounces) crushed
2 packages (3 ounces) orange gelatin   pineapple
1 pint orange sherbet

Drain oranges. Add water to syrup to make 1½ cups liquid. Bring to a boil in saucepan. Remove from heat and add gelatin. Add sherbet and stir until melted. Chill until like unbeaten egg whites. Fold in oranges and pineapple. Pour into 2-quart mold. Serves 8-10.

Beverly Chesler

Peach Mold

1 package (6 ounces) strawberry-
   banana gelatin
2 cups boiling water
1 cup orange juice

1 cup Cool Whip
1 cup sliced fresh peaches
3 bananas, sliced

Add boiling water to gelatin and stir gently until dissolved. Add orange juice, chill slightly. Fold in Cool Whip, peaches and banana slices. Pour into medium sized mold. Serves 8-10.

Marcia Isner

Pear Gelatin Mold

1 3-ounce package lemon gelatin
2 cups boiling water
1 8-ounce package cream cheese

1 3-ounce package lime gelatin
2 cups boiling water
1 large can bartlett pears

Dissolve lemon gelatin in 2 cups boiling water and refrigerate until syrupy. Mash cream cheese and add to gelatin. Beat with mixer until smooth and set into 5 cup mold. Make lime gelatin with 2 cups boiling water and pour over lemon gelatin. Add drained pears and refrigerate. Serves 8.

Mrs. Louis Friedman

Pink and White Salad Mold

1 package (3 ounces) strawberry or
   raspberry gelatin
1 cup boiling water
1 cup canned fruit juice (such as pine-

apple, orange, peach, cherry or
   cranberry)
1 cup cottage cheese (large curd)

Dissolve gelatin in hot water; add fruit juice and blend well. Allow to cool in refrigerator until it starts to congeal (consistency of unbeaten egg white). Beat with rotary beater until foamy in appearance, fold in cottage cheese and spoon into individual molds. Unmold on lettuce or other greens.

Carolyn Steklof

Rainbow Mold

1 3-ounce package each of raspberry,
   orange, lemon, lime, strawberry
   gelatin

1 2/3 cups boiling water for each
   package
Whipped topping

In separate bowls, dissolve each flavor of gelatin in boiling water. Chill until partially set, the consistency of egg whites. Whip one flavor at a time, starting with raspberry, on high speed on electric mixer. Pour into a 10" tube pan. Return to refrigerator while whipping second flavor; pour second flavor on top of first. Repeat procedure for all flavors. When set, unmold on large serving platter. "Frost" as you would a cake, with whipped topping of your choice, or serve as is, with all colored stripes showing. Serves 16-20.

T'Mahry Axelrod

Raspberry Mold

1 package (16 ounces) frozen
   raspberries (slightly thawed)
2 packages (3 ounces) raspberry
   gelatin

1½ cups boiling water
1 small can crushed pineapple
1 mashed banana
½ pint sour cream

Dissolve gelatin in hot water. Add undrained raspberries, pineapple and mashed banana. Pour ½ mixture in an oiled 6-cup mold. Refrigerate until firm. Cover top of hardened gelatin with sour cream and add remaining gelatin. Serves 10-12.

Joan Markus

Raspberry Mold

1 large package raspberry gelatin
　(6 ounces)
2 cups hot water
1 package frozen raspberries (16

ounces)
1 medium can apple sauce
½ pint sour cream
2 cups miniature marshmallows

Combine gelatin and water. Add raspberries and apple sauce. Pour into
9 x 13 pan. Chill 24 hours. Mix together miniature marshmallows with sour
cream, or low calorie sour cream. Spread on top.

Stella Gelman

Rhubarb Mold

1 pound box frozen rhubarb, thawed
2 3-ounce boxes strawberry gelatin
1 pound box frozen strawberries,
　thawed

½ cup boiling water
1 16-ounce can crushed pineapple,
　drained

Heat rhubarb slowly until mushy. When dissolved, add remaining
ingredients. Pour into 1½-quart mold and chill. Serves 8-10.

T'Mahry Axelrod

Stadium Salad

1 package (3 ounces) strawberry
　gelatin
1½ cups boiling water
1 #2½ can chilled peach
　slices

2 packages (3 ounces) lemon gelatin
2 cups boiling water
⅛ teaspoon salt
½ cup cold water
¼ cup diced green pepper

Dissolve strawberry gelatin in 1½ cups boiling water. Turn into 9 x 5 loaf
pan or shallow casserole. Chill until firm and cut into cubes. Dissolve lemon
gelatin and salt in 2 cups boiling water. Add cold water and ½ cup reserved
peach syrup. Arrange a few peaches on bottom of 2-quart mold. Fold
remaining peaches, strawberry cubes and green pepper into lemon gelatin.
Pour into mold and chill until firm. Serves 10-12.

Hattie Lipsky

Creamy Waldorf Mold

1 package (3 ounces) pineapple
　gelatin
1 cup boiling water
2 cups chopped apples

1 cup chopped celery
½ cup chopped walnuts
½ cup raisins
1 package non-dairy dessert topping

Pour boiling water on gelatin to dissolve. Cool until stiff. Add apples, celery,
raisins, and nuts. Whip dessert topping until in firm peaks. Fold into fruit
and gelatin. Pour into 6-cup mold. Serve on lettuce with a few chopped nuts
on top. Serves 6-8.

Eunice Goldman

Wine Gelatin

3 packages unflavored gelatin
1½ cups cold water
1½ cups sugar

½ cup lemon juice
3 cups dry red wine

Sprinkle gelatin over water in medium saucepan. Place over low heat,
stirring constantly until gelatin dissolves. Remove from heat. Add sugar,
stir until dissolved. Stir in lemon juice and wine. Pour into 8-cup mold and
chill. Serves 8-10.

Beverly Chesler

Cottage Cheese Tuna Mold

1 package (3 ounces) lime gelatin
1½ cups hot water
3 tablespoons vinegar
½ teaspoon salt
8 ounces cottage cheese
½ cup chopped celery

1 can (7 ounces) tuna, drained and flaked
3 tablespoons chopped or grated onion
½ cup thinly sliced radishes
¼ cup mayonnaise

Dissolve gelatin in hot water. Stir in vinegar and salt. Chill until slightly thickened. Fold in remaining ingredients. Pour into 8-inch ring mold. Chill until firm. Unmold on greens, garnish with more cottage cheese and radishes. Serves 6.

Idair Leichtner

Green Cheese Mold

1 package lime gelatin
1 cup hot water
¾ cup shredded cucumber
2 tablespoons grated onion

1 cup creamed cottage cheese
1 cup mayonnaise
½ cup slivered blanched almonds

Dissolve gelatin in water and chill until syrupy. Combine cucumber, onion, cheese, and mayonnaise. Blend in gelatin. Add almonds. Pour into greased round 5-cup mold.

Esther Parsky

Pimento Cheese Pineapple Mold

1 package (3 ounces) lemon gelatin
½ cup boiling water
1 jar pimento cream cheese

1 #2 can crushed pineapple and juice
1 package non-dairy dessert topping

Combine gelatin and water and let cool for 15 or 20 minutes. Cream cheese and crushed pineapple, mixing well, and add to gelatin. Beat dessert topping mix according to instructions on package and fold into above mixture. Pour into 2 or 2½-quart mold. Serves 6-8.

Edna Berman

Deviled Egg Mold

1 package (3 ounces) lemon gelatin
½ teaspoon salt
1 cup hot water
¾ cup cold water
4 deviled eggs

Olive slices
1 tablespoon vinegar
Dash of hot pepper sauce
1/3 cup chopped olives
¼ cup chopped parsley

Dissolve gelatin and salt in hot water. Add cold water and pour into a 9 x 5 loaf pan to a depth of ¼ inch. Chill until almost firm. Chill remaining mixture until slightly thickened. Spread tops of deviled eggs with slices of olives, then small amount of thickened lemon gelatin. Carefully invert egg halves on firm gelatin in pan. Add balance of ingredients (vinegar, pepper sauce, chopped olives, and parsley) into remaining mixture and cover eggs. Chill until firm. Unmold and slice. Serves 6-8.

Florence Margolius

Chicken Salad

2 cups cooked diced chicken
French dressing
¼ cup crushed pineapple
½ cup diced celery
1 teaspoon grated onion
½ cup chopped toasted almonds
Salad dressing

Marinate chicken in French dressing for 1 hour. Drain, if necessary. Add remaining ingredients with enough salad dressing to moisten. Chill and serve. Serves 6.

Millie Rosenbaum

Party Chicken Salad

2 cups cubed, cooked chicken
2 tablespoons lemon juice
½ teaspoon salt
1 cup sliced celery
1 cup seedless grapes
2 chopped cooked eggs
½ cup mayonnaise
¼ cup toasted slivered almonds

Sprinkle chicken with lemon juice and salt. Add remaining ingredients and toss lightly. Serves 4-5.

T'Mahry Axelrod

Fish Salad

4 halibut steaks
½ onion
3 stalks celery
4 hard boiled eggs, chopped
1 cup celery, chopped
¼ cup sweet pickle, chopped
1 cup mayonnaise
Salt and pepper
Juice of ½ lemon
¼ cup stuffed olives, sliced

Cook halibut with onion and celery in small amount of water. Cover and cook only until done. Remove from water. Cool, flake and remove all bones. Mix the flaked fish with chopped eggs, celery, relish, mayonnaise, lemon juice and sliced olives. Season to taste. Serves 4-6. Can be shaped in a fish mold.

Rachel Hyman

Fresh Seafood Salad

2 cups cooked haddock, flaked
2 cups cooked halibut, flaked
1½ cups celery, finely chopped
½ cup sweet pickles, drained
and finely chopped
½ teaspoon dry mustard
1 teaspoon salt
1 cup mayonnaise or
¾ cup mayonnaise plus ¼ cup
French dressing

Combine ingredients and mix well. Chill. Place on bed of lettuce and trim with watercress and sliced cucumbers.

Ruth Bittker

Halibut Salad — Mock Whitefish

1-1½ pounds halibut steak
4 hard boiled eggs
2 3¼-ounce cans smoked kipper-
ed snacks, drained
4 rounded tablespoons mayonnaise
1 cup finely chopped celery
Juice of ½ lemon

Salt and pepper and broil halibut until flaky. Remove skin and bone when fish is done. Flake halibut and kippers well with fork. Mash eggs with mayonnaise and lemon juice. Add celery and fish. Mix and garnish.

Dora Morgenstern

Herring Salad

1 8-ounce jar herring in cream
   sauce
2 cold cooked potatoes
½ sour pickle
2 apples, peeled

4 tablespoons beets, cubed
¼ cup walnuts, chopped
3 tablespoons beet juice
Mayonnaise to bind

Dice the potatoes, pickle, apples and beets and herring. Add cream sauce from herring, beet juice, chopped nuts and mayonnaise. Chill. Serve with party rye bread.

Lil Schulman

Smoked Whitefish Salad

3 pounds smoked whitefish
1 cup chopped celery
1 cup chopped green pepper
Juice of 1 lemon

1 cup mayonnaise
1 4-ounce jar pimento, drained
   and chopped

Skin, bone and flake fish. Add remaining ingredients, with pimento carefully folded in last. Pack tightly into 5-cup fish mold, coated with mayonnaise. Unmold by running knife along edge and inverting. Garnish with olive slices and pimento strips to resemble a fish.

T'Mahry Axelrod

Salmon Salad

1 can salmon, drained and
   boned
2 tomatoes, chopped and peeled
1 cucumber, diced and peeled

3-4 tablespoon sour cream
2 tablespoons French dressing
1 tablespoon dill
⅛ teaspoon pepper

Mix together and chill.

Shirley Jacobson

Tuna Salad

1 10-ounce package frozen green
   beans (Italian style), cooked
1 7-ounce can tuna fish
1 cup celery, chopped fine
½ cup mayonnaise

1 tablespoon lemon juice
1½ teaspoon soy sauce
Dash garlic powder
1 cup chow mein noodles

Mix together. Just before serving, add chow mein noodles. Serve cold.

Stella Gelman

Apple Tuna Toss

1 head lettuce in bite-size pieces
2 cups diced apples
1 can drained mandarin oranges
   (11 ounces)
1 can drained tuna, broken up

1/3 cup chopped nuts
½ cup mayonnaise
2 teaspoons soy sauce
1 teaspoon lemon juice

Toss first five ingredients together. Mix last three ingredients together and mix through salad. Serves 6.

Helen Gordon

Tuna Fruit Salad

2 tablespoons gelatin	drained
1 cup cold water	1½ cups pineapple tidbits,
1 cup boiling water	drained
1 package (8-ounce) cream	1 cup chopped pecans
cheese softened with ¼ cup	½ teaspoon salt
apricot nectar	1 teaspoon paprika
2 cans (7-ounces) tunafish,	

Soften gelatin in cold water. Add boiling water and dissolve. Add cream cheese with apricot nectar, blend in and mix well. Chill until slightly thickened. Break tuna into pieces. Fold in tuna, pineapple, pecans, salt and paprika into gelatin mixture. Turn into quart mold and chill until firm. Unmold and surround with salad greens and garnish as desired. Serves 8.

Florence Margolius

Tuna Salad Luau

1 13-ounce can tuna	½ cup walnuts, chopped
1 cup pineapple chunks,	½-¾ cups mayonnaise
drained	Walnut halves
1 cup celery, chopped	

Combine flaked tuna with pineapple chunks, celery, and chopped nuts. Blend in mayonnaise and season to taste. Top with walnut halves. Serves 4-5.

Lil Schulman

Salad Nicoise

1 9-ounce package frozen	8 pitted ripe olives
French-style green beans	2 tablespoons olive or salad oil
2 medium green peppers	1 tablespoon red wine vinegar
1 2-ounce can anchovy fillets,	1 teaspoon salt
drained	¼ teaspoon pepper
1 red onion, thinly sliced	3 hard boiled eggs, quartered
1 7-ounce can chunk-style tuna,	1 large tomato, thinly sliced
drained	

Cook beans as directed, drain well and cool. Clean and cut green peppers into thin strips. Rinse anchovies and drain well on paper towels. In a large salad bowl, combine beans, green pepper, anchovies, onion, tuna and olives. Toss to mix well. Add oil, vinegar, salt and pepper. Toss lightly until well combined. Garnish with eggs and tomatoes. Serves 6.

Leah Mermelstein

Ambrosia

1½ large cans pineapple chunks	1 package miniature marsh-
3 small cans mandarin oranges	mallows
3 regular oranges, cut up	Coconut
1 pint sour cream	

Mix together and refrigerate overnight.

Ellie Harris

Frozen Salad

¼ pound grated mild cheese
1 large can pineapple, tidbits
1 medium size bottle of cherries
1 cup nuts, chopped

1 cup small marshmallows
1 cup whipped cream
1 cup mayonnaise or salad
   dressing

Mix together well and freeze.

Julia Berlove

Medley of Fruit in Cream

1 cup pineapple tidbits, drained
½ cup mandarin oranges, drained
1 cup miniature marshmallows
½ cup sliced peaches, drained

1 package frozen raspberries or
   strawberries, drained
1 cup sour cream

Combine fruits in large bowl. Using a rubber spatula, gently fold in sour cream. Refrigerate 1 hour or more to mellow. Serves 6.

Lil Schulman

Fantastic Orange-Pineapple Salad

1 11-ounce can pineapple chunks
1 11-ounce can mandarin
   oranges
2 tablespoons chopped walnuts

2 tablespoons shredded coconut
½ cup miniature marshmallows
Prepared topping

Drain pineapple and oranges very well. (The secret of this recipe is to have the fruit completely free of juice and dry to the touch). Store, preferably in toweling, in the refrigerator overnight. Mix remaining ingredients together with drained fruit and add whipped topping to hold it together. This is delicious as a salad alone or as a center filling for a pineapple or orange ring mold. Serves 4-6.

Sue Kiner

Waldorf Salad

1/3 cup salad dressing
2 tablespoons cream
3 cups diced apples
2 cups diced celery

1 cup pecans
1 cup seedless grapes,
   halved
1 cup small marshmallows

Thin salad dressing with cream. Combine all other ingredients. Toss with salad dressing. Serve in lettuce cups. Serves 6.

Phyllis Lippman

Five Bean Salad

1 #303 can green beans
1 #303 can yellow beans
1 #303 can lima beans
1 #303 can kidney beans

1 #303 can chick peas
1 green pepper, diced
1 red onion, sliced

Marinade

¼ cup sugar
½ cup vinegar
½ cup oil

1 teaspoon oregano
½ teaspoon garlic salt
Salt and pepper

Drain beans. Combine in large bowl. Add all ingredients and chill overnight in marinade.

Elaine Hoffman

Bean Salad with Dill Mayonnaise

1 10-ounce package frozen
small lima beans
1 1-pound can green beans,
drained
1 small onion, thinly sliced
1 egg

1¼ teaspoon dill weed
3 tablespoons lemon juice
½ teaspoon salt
Dash pepper
½ cup salad oil

Cook and chill lima beans. Break egg into blender, add salt, dill weed and pepper. Whirl 30 seconds. Add lemon juice; blend. Turn to high speed, pour in oil in a slow steady stream. Mix limas, string beans and onions with dressing and chill. Marinate several hours. Serves 4-6.

Maxine Straus

Caesar Salad

1 clove garlic, split
1/3 cup vegetable oil
1 head romaine lettuce or
fresh spinach
1 head iceberg lettuce
2 cups hot seasoned
croutons
2 tablespoons vegetable
oil
¾ teaspoon salt

½ teaspoon pepper
¼ teaspoon dry mustard
1 tablespoon Worcester-
shire sauce
1 egg, coddled one minute
2 or 3 tablespoons lemon
juice
½-ounce can anchovies,
drained

Place garlic in oil, cover and refrigerate one hour. Wash greens, drain and dry thoroughly. Tear into medium size pieces in large bowl. Chill about one hour. Heat 2 tablespoons oil in fry pan. Add croutons, cook over moderate heat, stirring gently until lightly brown and oil is absorbed. Set aside. Remove garlic from chilled oil, add salt, pepper, mustard and Worcestershire sauce. Pour seasoned oil over lettuce, tossing gently. Add egg and lemon juice. Toss lightly. Sprinkle toasted croutons over salad, toss again. Serve immediately in chilled salad bowls. Garnish with anchovies.

Rhoda Ann Herzog

Caesar Salad

1 clove garlic
¾ cup salad oil
1 head romaine lettuce
1 head iceberg lettuce
1/3 cup Parmesan cheese
1 tablespoon Worchester-
shire sauce

¾ teaspoon salt
¼ teaspoon pepper
1 raw egg
¼ cup lemon juice
2 cups croutons, seasoned
and unseasoned

Place garlic in ¼ cup salad oil and refrigerate. Separate and wash lettuce; dry in refrigerator one hour. Tear greens into large salad bowl and sprinkle with cheese. Combine remaining ½ cup salad oil, Worcestershire sauce, salt and pepper. Drizzle over greens and toss gently. Break raw egg over greens. Pour on lemon juice and toss until egg specks disappear. Toss croutons with the ¼ cup salad oil after removing garlic. Serves 8-10.

Gail Cahn

Cucumber Marinade

4 cucumbers, peeled and
  thinly sliced
2½ teaspoons salt
3 scallions

½ cup cider vinegar
3 tablespoons cold water
½ teaspoon sugar
¼ teaspoon pepper

Sprinkle cucumber slices with salt and let them stand for one-half hour.
Slice the scallions, using some of the tops also. Add to cucumbers and mix
everything thoroughly. Refrigerate for 3-4 hours before serving. Serves 5-6.

Ricky Sands

Gourmet Company Salad

1 head endive, broken in
  chunks
1 head escarole, broken in
  chunks
2 packages bleu cheese,
  crumbled

3 large cans artichoke
  hearts, drained
2 avocados, skinned and
  cut up in chunks
2 bottles Caesar salad
  dressing

Toss well and serve. Serves 15 with scant seconds. To prepare ahead, keep
artichoke hearts separate until the last minute when you put on the dressing.
Do not cut up avocados until last minute, or it turns.

Nancy Hoffman

Israeli Sallattah

¼ cup green onions
¼ cup celery
¼ cup lettuce
¼ cup cucumber
¼ cup tomato
¼ cup radishes

1 pinch salt
Dash pepper
2 black olives
Small piece of herring, cut up
1 teaspoon oil

Cut vegetables into quarters. Toss with oil. Top with olives and herring.

Esther Solomon

Macaroni Salad

3 cups macaroni
½ cup shredded carrot
½ cup diced cucumber
½ cup diced celery
½ cup sliced radishes
1 medium red onion,
  chopped
3 hard boiled eggs, diced

¼ cup chopped olives,
  optional
1 8-ounce can dilled green
  beans
1 8-ounce can julienne beets
Salt and pepper to taste
½ teaspoon lemon juice
Mayonnaise

Cook macaroni according to directions on package, drain and rinse with cold
water. Drain thoroughly. When dry, place in large bowl and stir in all other
ingredients, using as much mayonnaise as is necessary to moisten salad.

Kathy Ureles

Meat and Potato Salad

2½ cups diced cooked
  beef or veal
3 tomatoes, quartered
2 cups diced cooked potatoes
2 tablespoon chopped par-
  sley

3 sweet pickles, diced (or 3
  tablespoons sweet India
  relish)
2 tablespoons chopped chives
¾ cup French dressing

Combine in a bowl, diced meat, tomatoes, parsley, pickles and chives. Mix
in the dressing. Serve on watercress or lettuce. Serves 6.

Julia Berlove

Patio Salad

Garlic
Salt
2 jars marinated artichoke
  hearts
1-2 cups tongue, salami,
  chicken, turkey
8 cups salad greens

2 tablespoons capers
1 cup garlic croutons
2 tablespoons white tarragon vinegar
10 radishes, sliced
¼ teaspoon dry mustard
Olive oil

Rub bowl with garlic. Sprinkle with salt. Add greens, capers, radishes,
croutons and artichoke hearts (save oil). Toss lightly in oil from artichokes
and olive oil to make ¼ cup. Add vinegar and mustard. Toss again. Top with
cold meat.

Arlean Levinson

Sour Cream Potato Salad

7 medium potatoes, cooked
  in jacket, peeled and sliced
  (6 cups)
1/3 cup clear French or
  Italian dressing
¾ cup sliced celery
1/3 cup sliced green onions
  and tops

4 hard cooked eggs
1 cup mayonnaise
½ cup dairy sour cream
1½ teaspoons prepared
  horseradish mustard
Salt and celery seed to
  taste
1/3 cup diced, pared cucumber

While potatoes are warm, pour dressing over. Chill 2 hours. Add celery and
onion. Chop egg whites; add. Sieve yolks; reserve some for garnish. Mix
rest with mayonnaise, sour cream, horseradish mustard. Mix thoroughly
while adding salt and celery seed. Mix in diced cucumber.

Edith Perlman

Fresh Spinach Salad

2 packages fresh spinach   ½ thin sliced red onion

Break spinach into bite-size pieces. Wash and drain well. Add red onion.
Chill.

Dressing

1½ cups sour cream
2-3 tablespoons lemon juice
2-3 tablespoons Parmesan
  cheese
Pinch salt, pepper

1 teaspoon garlic powder
½ teaspoon each basil,
  thyme
Garlic croutons or Bacos

Combine all of the ingredients. Adjust to taste. You may add garlic croutons
or Bacos. Toss with salad just before serving. Serves 8-10.

Carol Goldberg

Cold Rice Stuffed Tomatoes

½ cup raw rice
¼ cup oil
1 tablespoon vinegar
Salt and pepper to taste

1 teaspoon minced onion
1 tablespoon minced parsley
6 medium tomatoes
Lettuce leaves

Cook rice according to package directions. When tender and still hot, add oil and toss lightly. Add vinegar, salt, pepper, onion and parsley. Toss lightly and let stand, covered, at room temperature for three hours. At serving time, cut the stem ends from the tomatoes. Hollow them out and mix the tomato flesh with the rice. Pile the rice mixture lightly into the tomato shells and set on a bed of lettuce. Serves 6.

Debby Goldman

Vegetable and Rice Salad Bowl

½ cup cold water
½ cup Italian-style dressing
1 cup packaged pre-cooked rice
1 10-ounce package frozen peas, cooked and drained
4 tablespoons slivered green onions and tops
½ cup canned sliced mushrooms,

drained
½ cup cut up cucumber
4 tablespoons stuffed olives, sliced crosswise
2/3 cup mayonnaise or salad dressing
Lettuce leaves
2 tomatoes

In small saucepan, combine ½ cup cold water and Italian-style dressing; bring to boil. Remove from heat. Add rice; let stand, covered, 5 minutes. Fluff rice with fork. Turn into medium bowl. Add peas, mixing with fork; refrigerate until cold. Add onions, mushrooms, cucumber, olives, and mayonnaise; mix well with fork. Refrigerate, covered. To serve, toss salad again in bowl; garnish edge with lettuce leaves and tomato wedges. Makes 6 generous servings.

Hank Stoler

Winter Salad Bowl

¼ bunch curly endive
1 small head lettuce
2 oranges, pared and sliced

½ mild white onion or red sweet onion
1 avocado, sliced

Garlic Dressing
2 teaspoons orange rind
1½ teaspoons salt
1 teaspoon sugar
½ teaspoon dry mustard

1/3 cup wine vinegar
2/3 cup salad oil
1 clove garlic, minced

Wash, drain and tear endive and lettuce in bite-size pieces. Slice onion in rings. Arrange vegetables and fruits in salad bowl. Combine garlic dressing ingredients in a jar and shake vigorously. Remove garlic before serving. Save a few orange slices for top. Note: ½ teaspoon garlic powder may be used in place of clove garlic. Mandarin oranges may be used.

Hattie Lipsky

Salad Dressing

1/3 cup white vinegar
¼ cup oil
¼ cup sugar

1 teaspoon salt
1 teaspoon grated onion

Mix together and chill.

Jill Musicus

Bleu Cheese Salad Dressing

2 cups mayonnaise
2 tablespoons wine vinegar
1 teaspoon salt
½ teaspoon Lawry's salt
¼ teaspoon white pepper

1 tablespoon Worcestershire
  sauce
1¼ tablespoon sugar
¼ teaspoon Accent salt
2 ounces bleu cheese

Mix together well.

Beverly Chesler

Depot Salad Dressing

1 package Good Seasons bleu
  cheese
1 bottle Roquefort dressing
½ cup mayonnaise
1 teaspoon sugar

1 tablespoon tarragon vinegar
1 tablespoon water
Salt and pepper to taste
Bacos

Prepare Good Seasons dressing according to directions. Blend with Roquefort dressing and mayonnaise; add remaining ingredients and mix well. Add croutons and Bacos to salad greens.

Lois Kuh

French Dressing

¾ cup vinegar
1 cup vegetable oil
1 cup catsup
1 cup sugar
1½ tablespoons Worcester-
  shire sauce

1 teaspoon paprika
2 teaspoon salt
1½ teaspoons dry mustard
1 small onion, grated
4 cloves garlic, minced

Mix thoroughly. Pour into quart jar. Keeps indefinitely in refrigerator.

T'Mahry Axelrod

Fruit Dressing

1 package Lucky Whip
1 3-ounce package cream cheese
1 small jar Maraschino cherries,
  cut

2 tablespoons Maraschino juice
2 tablespoons mayonnaise
2 tablespoons lemon juice
1 tablespoon milk

Prepare Lucky Whip according to directions. Blend with remaining ingredients. Serve with fruit platter. May add red food coloring for more color.

Beverly Chesler

Dressing for Fruit Salad

1 pint sour cream

2 tablespoons honey

Mix well and use over any fruit mold or fruit salad.

Julia Berlove

Noodles and Rice

Apple Noodle Kugel

1 pound noodles
10 tablespoons pareve
  margarine or butter
4 eggs, slightly beaten
½ cup sugar
Scant teaspoon cinnamon
1 teaspoon vanilla

½ cup orange juice or milk
2 large apples, sliced
Raisins
Frosted flakes, crushed or
  sugared cereal
Cinnamon

Cook noodles about 8 minutes. Stir margarine into hot noodles until melted. Add eggs, sugar, cinnamon, vanilla and orange juice or milk. Stir well into noodles. Add apples and raisins. Pour into greased 9 x 12 pan. Cover with frosted flakes or sugared cereal. Sprinkle cinnamon on top and dot with margarine or butter. Bake on second shelf in oven at 350° about 1 hour until brown. Serves 10-12.

Sylvia Kowal

Applesauce Noodle Pudding

1 12-ounce package noodles
¼ cup butter or pareve
  margarine
6 eggs, beaten

⅛ cup brown sugar
1 pint applesauce
Corn flakes
Peach or apricot jelly or jam

Boil noodles 5-8 minutes in salted water. Drain, add butter, beaten eggs and sugar. Add applesauce. Spread in 9 x 13 greased pan. Top with cornflakes. Bake one hour in 350° oven. Spread with jam or jelly and return to oven for ½ hour. Serves 12.

Claire Cohen

Applesauce and Pineapple
Noodle Kugel

1 16-ounce box medium noodles
2 tablespoons sugar
Juice of ½ lemon
2 eggs, separated
2 cups applesauce

½ cup margarine, melted
½ cup raisins
1 8-ounce can pineapple chunks
  or crushed pineapple

Cook noodles as package directs. After cooking, mix in all ingredients except pineapple and egg whites. Beat egg whites until stiff and fold in. Bake in buttered 13 x 9 pan at 350° for 1 hour. Pour pineapple chunks over top of casserole with some juice, and return to oven for 10 minutes. Serves 12.

Shirley Nozik

Apricot Noodle Pudding

1 package (8 ounces) medium
  noodles
4 eggs
1 pound jar applesauce

¾ cup cut-up dried apricots
¾ cup sugar
¼ cup melted butter or pareve
  margarine

Preheat oven to 350°. Melt butter in 8 x 10 baking pan while warming the pan. Cook noodles as directed for baking. Beat eggs well. Combine all ingredients and bake at 350° approximately 1 hour or until done. Serves 6-8.

Bea Apple

Fluffy Pecan Noodle Pudding

1 tablespoon salt
3 quarts boiling water
8 ounces wide egg noodles
4 eggs, separated
½ cup sugar

¼ teaspoon cinnamon
¼ cup butter or margarine,
 melted
½ cup seedless raisins
¼ cup chopped pecans

Add salt to rapidly boiling water. Gradually add noodles so that water continues to boil. Cook uncovered, stirring occasionally until tender, about 10 minutes. Drain thoroughly. Beat egg yolks, add sugar, cinnamon and butter; beat until blended. Combine with drained noodles. Mix in raisins and pecans. Beat egg whites until stiff and fold into noodle mixture. Turn into a greased 1½-quart casserole. Bake at 325° for 1 hour. Serves 8.

Pearl Albert

Moist Boston Noodle Pudding

1 pound wide noodles
½ pound cream cheese
 (preferably whipped)
¾ cup sugar
4 eggs
2 cups milk
1 teaspoon vanilla
2 tablespoons orange juice
½ pint sour cream substitute

¾-1 cup prepared banana pudding
Dried apricots or canned apricots
 (pre-soaked in hot water or
 brandy for 15 minutes)
Corn flakes
Pareve margarine, melted
Sugar
Cinnamon

Cook noodles according to package directions. Wash off with cold water. While noodles are boiling, cream the cream cheese with sugar. Add eggs, milk, vanilla, orange juice and sour cream substitute and mix together, in an extra-large mixing bowl. Add banana pudding and cream into mixture. Mixture will be very soupy. Do nothing to make it thicker or you will spoil pudding. Add noodles to above mixture. Pour ½ of above mixture into greased 9 x 13 glass casserole dish. Cover with apricots (if desired). Add other half of noodle mixture. Top with corn flakes, melted margarine, sugar and cinnamon. Can be frozen at this point or when half baked. Bake at 350° for 1-1¼ hours. Do not overbake or pudding will become dry. Serves 10-12.

Nancy Hoffman

Onion Noodle Pudding

1 pound wide noodles
¼ pound butter, melted
8 ounces whipped cream cheese
1 pint sour cream
1 onion, chopped

4 eggs, beaten
Salt and pepper to taste
Bread crumbs
Paprika
Butter

Cook noodles as directed on package; drain and rinse. Combine and mix well butter, cream cheese, sour cream, onion, eggs and salt. Use salt liberally. Stir into noodles and place in a buttered 2-quart casserole. Sprinkle with bread crumbs and paprika and dot with butter. Bake at 350° for 1 hour. Serves 8-10.

Veda Rubin

Pineapple Noodle Pudding

½ pound medium noodles, cooked
¼ pound butter
½ cup sugar, scant
1 cup cottage cheese
1 cup sour cream

3 eggs
1 8-ounce can crushed pineapple, including juice
1 cup crushed corn flakes
¼ cup sugar
½ teaspoon cinnamon

Cook noodles; drain. Add butter to hot noodles. Add beaten eggs, sugar, cheese, cream, pineapple and juice. Mix thoroughly, cover and refrigerate over night in mixing bowl. Before baking, remove from refrigerator, keep at room temperature 15 minutes, stir thoroughly and put into greased 7 x 11 baking pan. Top with crushed corn flakes and mixture of sugar and cinnamon. Bake uncovered at 350° for 1 hour. Can be frozen.

Shirley Axelrod

Prune Lukshen Kugel

1 package wide noodles
3 eggs
½ cup shortening, margarine or chicken fat
1 cup brown sugar, well packed

1 cup raisins
2 teaspoons cinnamon
Bread crumbs
Prune juice

Boil noodles in salted water as directed on package, increasing cooking time to 20 minutes. Drain and mix cooked noodles with rest of ingredients, except bread crumbs and prune juice. Put into greased 8 x 12 pan and sprinkle top with bread crumbs and cinnamon. Baste with prune juice several times while baking. Bake for 1½ hours at 350°.

Sarah Derman

Ruth's Noodle Torte

½ pound medium wide noodles
½ pound farmer cheese
½ pound cottage cheese
½ pound cream cheese
2 cups milk
1 cup sour cream

1 teaspoon salt
1 teaspoon vanilla
6 eggs, well beaten
½ cup sugar
6 tablespoons melted butter or margarine

Cook noodles in boiling water and drain. Blend together farmer cheese, cottage cheese and cream cheese. Add remaining ingredients, in order listed. Pour over noodles and blend well. Pour mixture into greased spring form pan or 13 x 9 pan. Bake in 350° oven for ½ hour. Remove from oven and sprinkle with topping. Bake 1 hour longer; if not firm, bake another 10 minutes. Serve 20.

Topping

½ cup slivered almonds
¾ cup brown sugar

½ cup melted butter or margarine

Combine all ingredients. Sprinkle over torte. Note: May be made in advance. Leave mixture in bowl; blend mixture just before baking and proceed as above. May be frozen after baking.

Ruth Axelrod

Sweet Noodle Kugel

½ pound wide noodles
4 eggs
⅝ cup brown and white sugar, mixed

1 jar (15 ounces) chunky apple and cherries
Pareve margarine
Cinnamon

Cook noodles and drain. Beat 4 eggs into noodles, then add sugar mixture and apples and cherries. Pour into well-greased 9 x 12 pan. Sprinkle with cinnamon and dot with margarine. Bake at 350° for 45 minutes covered with aluminum foil, then uncover for 15 more minutes. Serves 12.

Marilyn Greenberg

Tip Top Noodle Kugel

1 pound noodles, cooked
2 eggs
1 teaspoon vanilla

¼ cup sugar
¼ pound butter

Topping
½ pound cottage cheese
1 cup sour cream
1 teaspoon lemon juice

¼ cup milk
2 eggs

Mix noodles, eggs, vanilla, sugar and butter together. Pour into ungreased 8 x 16 glass pan. Mix cottage cheese, sour cream, lemon juice, milk and eggs together in blender. Pour on top of noodle mixture. Bake at 350° for 1 hour. Serves 10.

Barbara Glickman

Upside Down Noodle Kugel

8 ounces medium egg noodles
3 quarts boiling water
1 tablespoon salt
1/3 cup butter or margarine
3 eggs
½ cup sugar
1 teaspoon grated lemon peel
¼ teaspoon salt

2 cups milk
2 tablespoons toasted blanched slivered almonds
½ cup firmly packed dark brown sugar
1 20-ounce can pineapple slices, drained
9 maraschino cherries

Cook noodles in boiling salted water until tender; drain in collander. Toss with 3 tablespoons butter. Beat together eggs, sugar, lemon peel and salt; stir in milk and almonds. Toss noodles with egg mixture. Melt remaining butter in bottom of 9-inch square pan. Sprinkle brown sugar in bottom of pan; arrange pineapple slices in pan and place a cherry in the center of each. Add noodle mixture. Bake in 350° oven 40 minutes or until set. Cool slightly. Turn out onto platter. Serve with sweetened whipped cream or sour cream.

Alyne Phillips

Walnut and Raisin Noodle Pudding

1 pound wide noodles
3 eggs, separated
½ pint sour cream
1 pound cottage cheese
½ cup milk

½ cup sugar
¼ pound butter
¾ cup brown sugar
Walnuts
Raisins

Boil noodles. Beat egg yolks and whites separately. To the yolks, add sour cream, cottage cheese, milk and sugar. Mix this into drained noodles and fold egg whites into this mixture. Melt ¼ pound butter in 8 x 16 pan. Sprinkle with brown sugar, walnuts and raisins. Pour in noodle mixture. Bake at 350° for 1 hour or until done. Invert when done. Serves 8-10. Freezes well.

Helen Gordon

Baked Lasagna

Oil
1 cup minced onions
2 cloves garlic, minced
1 green pepper, chopped,
 optional
1½ teaspoons salt
¼ teaspoon pepper
½ teaspoon oregano
2 tablespoons chopped parsley
1 can (29 ounce) tomato puree

9 lasagna noodles
1½ pounds cottage cheese
¼ cup sour cream or low-fat
 sour dressing
1 egg
Cheeses: 1 pound Swiss or mozzarella or combination*
Grated Parmesan or romano
 cheese

Saute onion and garlic in oil. Add salt, pepper, oregano, parsley and tomato puree sprinkled with a bit of grated cheese. Cover and simmer while preparing lasagna noodles. Cook noodles as directed, about 15 minutes, adding a touch of oil to the water to prevent noodles from sticking. Combine cottage cheese, sour cream and egg in a bowl. Cut up cheese in another bowl. Spread 1/3 of the sauce on the bottom of a 12 x 8 baking dish. Arrange alternate layers of the lasagna, cheeses, cottage cheese mixture and sprinkling of grated cheese. Spread the sauce and repeat the process to make two more layers. Save a bit of sauce and grated cheese for the top. Bake at 350°, 1 hour. *Gouda also is good, if available.

Tamar Bronstein

Baked Lasagna

1 pound lasagna noodles
1½ pounds ricotta cheese
¾ pound mozzarella cheese
2 eggs

Grated Parmesan cheese
1 quart marinara sauce
Salt and pepper to taste

Mix ricotta cheese with eggs, salt and pepper. Cook noodles according to package directions. Put marinara sauce in bottom of ungreased 8 x 13 pan just to cover bottom. Put layer of noodles over sauce and then pour more sauce over them. Spread ricotta cheese mixture over sauce, then cut chunks of mozzarella cheese over that and sprinkle with Parmesan cheese. Cover with another layer of noodles, ricotta cheese, mozzarella, sauce and Parmesan. Repreat layers until pan is full. On top layer omit ricotta cheese. Bake at 350° for 45 minutes. Let stand 15 minutes at room temperature before cutting. Serve with sauce poured over top. Serves 8-10.

Phyllis Kasdin

Lasagna

9 lasagna noodles
1 pound small curd cottage
 cheese
1 quart spaghetti sauce

1 pound sliced mozzarella cheese
1 egg
Grated Parmesan cheese

Cook noodles. In a separate bowl, combine cottage cheese and egg. Arrange ingredients in ungreased, 2-quart, rectangular glass casserole as follows: sauce first and then noodles, cottage cheese mixture, sauce, Parmesan cheese and slices of mozzarella cheese, arrange to cover the layer. Repeat from the noodles and cottage cheese mixture to mozzarella cheese, two more times. Bake at 350° for 45-60 minutes uncovered. Cool 20 minutes before cutting and serving. Serves 8. Can be frozen.

Myrna Davidson

Macaroni Parmigiana

2 cloves garlic, minced
2 tablespoons vegetable oil
1 can (8 ounces) tomato sauce
1 16-ounce can tomatoes
1 small onion, minced
1½ teaspoons salt
¼ teaspoon pepper

1½ teaspoons oregano
1 package (8 ounces) elbow
   macaroni, cooked
1 pound cottage cheese
½ pound mozzarella or Swiss
   cheese
½ cup Parmesan cheese

Brown minced garlic in oil. Add tomato sauce, tomatoes, minced onion, salt, pepper, and oregano and simmer 15-20 minutes. Grease 3-quart casserole. Alternate layers of macaroni, cottage cheese, tomato mixture, mozzarella and Parmesan cheeses. Bake at 375° for 20-25 minutes. Serves 6-8.

Mim Bogdonoff

Summer Spaghetti

1/3 cup margarine
1/3 cup olive oil
3 small cloves garlic, minced
1 pound mushrooms, sliced
½ teaspoon salt

¼ teaspoon dried oregano
¼ cup parsley flakes
1/3 cup dry red wine
½ pound thin spaghetti
Grated Parmesan cheese

In 10-inch skillet over moderate heat, cook margarine, olive oil and garlic for about 1 minute. Do not brown garlic. Add mushrooms and cook turning often until softened (about 5 minutes). Sprinkle with salt, oregano and parsley. Add wine and stir well. Cover and remove from heat. Meanwhile, cook spaghetti according to package directions. Drain well and return to clean pot. Add mushroom sauce and toss well. Serve on hot plates with Parmesan cheese. Serves 6.

Hattie Lipsky

Fettucini

1 pound green noodles
1-2 cloves garlic, crushed
1 cup butter, cut in small pieces
2½ teaspoons basil
1 teaspoon salt

½ teaspoon pepper
½ cup heavy cream, heated
1 cup grated Parmesan or
   Swiss cheese

Cook green noodles as directed. Drain and place in hot serving dish. Toss thoroughly with rest of ingredients. Serve immediately on very hot plates. Serves 8.

Judy Kaplan

Garlic Noodles

1 pound fusilli pasta
¼ pound margarine
½ pint cream

Garlic powder to taste
Grated Parmesan cheese

Cook pasta according to package directions. When still firm but cooked, drain in collander. Melt margarine in pot. Return drained pasta to pot and toss until all pieces are coated. Add cream, garlic powder and Parmesan cheese to taste. Toss and taste until all margarine and cream are absorbed. Serve immediately. Serves 6-8.

Annette Lee

Poppy Seed Noodles, Dutch Style

1 8-ounce package wide noodles,
  cooked
3 tablespoons margarine
3 teaspoons poppy seeds

½ cup slivered almonds, toasted
1 tablespoon lemon juice
Salt and pepper to taste

Melt margarine and add poppy seeds, almonds and lemon juice. Pour over noodles and toss lightly. Add salt and pepper to taste. Serves 6.

Judy Kaplan

Armenian Pilaf

2 tablespoons pareve margarine
¼ cup orzo or Rosa Marina #35
  (a type of noodle)
¼ cup finely chopped onions

¾ cup raw rice
2½ cups chicken stock
Salt to taste

Melt margarine in heavy 1½-quart saucepan, add orzo or Rosa Marina, and onions. Saute until onions and orzo are golden brown (do not let margarine turn brown; pilaf will be bitter). Add rice, salt and chicken stock. Do not stir. Bring to a full boil, turn to simmer and cook 20 to 30 minutes. Mix well before serving. Serves 6. **Variations:** 1. Leftover lamb or veal may be added when stock is added. 2. Mushrooms and raisins may also be added. 3. Add toasted almonds just before serving and mix well.

Carole Berlove

Baked Rice with Noodles

3 onions, chopped
½ cup raw fine noodles
Chicken fat
1 cup raw rice
1 cup white raisins, scant

2 cups canned chicken soup,
  undiluted
½ cup slivered almonds
Salt and pepper to taste

Saute onions and noodles in fat, allowing noodles to become brown. Add raw rice, soup, raisins, almonds, salt and pepper. Bake covered for 1½ hours at 350° in ungreased casserole. Uncover the last 10 minutes to brown. If rice becomes too dry while baking, add a little water. Serves 6.

Adelaide Weinberg

Green Rice

4 cups cooked rice
1 onion, chopped
1 can (5 ounces) evaporated
  milk
¾ cup vegetable oil
2 cans mushroom soup
2 cans (4 ounces each) mush-

rooms and juice
2 eggs, well beaten
1½ cups mild cheddar cheese,
  grated
2 cups chopped parsley
Seasonings to taste

Cook chopped onion in oil and add to rice. Add all other ingredients, except cheese, and mix well. Sprinkle grated cheese on top. Bake in 3-quart casserole, lightly greased, for 1 hour at 350°. Serves 20.

Lucille Michel

Kosher Rice-A-Roni

2½ tablespoons shortening or chicken fat
1 cup raw rice
¼ cup raw vermicelli (broken up in small pieces)
2¼ cups water

Salt to taste
1 teaspoon onion powder
2 tinfoil packets G. Washington Brown Seasoning & Broth Mix

Melt fat in large frying pan and brown raw rice and raw vermicelli. To 2¼ cups of water in a 2-quart saucepan add onion powder and packets of seasoning mix. Bring this to a boil and add browned rice and vermicelli. Stir once, then cover pot and reduce heat. Simmer until all liquid is absorbed. Serves 4.

Ireene Morris

Onion Rice Casserole

1 cup raw rice
3¾ cups water

1 envelope onion soup mix
¼ cup margarine

Stir all ingredients in uncovered 2-quart casserole. Put in 350° oven for 1¾ hours, stirring at the end of the first 45 minutes. Serves 6-8.

Daisy Cherry

Polynesian Rice

1 package onion soup mix
4½ cups boiling water
4 cups pre-cooked rice, raw
4 large stalks pascal celery
2 large onions
1 large green pepper
½ to 1 pound fresh mushrooms
1 3-ounce jar stuffed olives, cut

1 4-ounce jar small pitted ripe olives, cut
1 #2 can bean sprouts
½ cup slivered blanched almonds
4 or 5 raw chicken livers or or several cups cooked diced chicken or meat.

Pour onion soup mix into boiling water and add rice. Cover and remove from heat; let stand. Slice onions, celery and peppers thinly. Saute in small amount of oil over low flame, stirring occasionally. When onions look clear, remove from flame and add to rice. Clean and slice mushrooms thinly, saute in oil, season to taste and add to rice. Drain and add stuffed olives, pitted ripe olives, bean sprouts and almonds.

Cut up chicken livers, saute in oil, season to taste and add to rice. Or, if using chicken or meat, add to rice. Mix together thoroughly, and put 1/3 into well-greased 3-quart casserole; dot with margarine. Put 1/3 more in casserole; dot with margarine. Put the rest of mixture in and dot again. Bake 1 hour, covered, at 375°. Serves 16.

Sue Klein

Raisin Orange Rice

1 cup diced celery
3 tablespoons melted margarine
1½ cups water
2 teaspoons grated orange rind
½ cup orange juice

1 teaspoon salt
2 tablespoons brown sugar
1 cup uncooked rice
¾ cup raisins

Cook celery in margarine until tender. Add water, orange rind, orange juice, salt and sugar. Heat to boiling. Add rice and raisins. Stir. Cover, reduce heat and simmer for 30 minutes or until rice is tender and liquid is absorbed. Serves 6.

Irene Shapiro

Rice Braised in Chicken Stock

1/3 cup finely chopped onions	Salt and pepper to taste
2 tablespoons parve margarine	Herbed bouquet (2 parsley sprigs,
1 cup raw white rice	½ bay leaf, 1/8 teaspoon thyme,
2 cups chicken stock	tied in washed cheesecloth)

Cook onions slowly in margarine until soft. Add rice and stir over moderate heat for 2 to 3 minutes until rice becomes milky white. Stir in the chicken stock and season lightly with salt and pepper. Add herb bouquet. Stir briefly until simmer is reached, then cover tightly and cook at moderate temperature on stove or in preheated 375° oven. Rice should absorb liquid in about 18 to 20 minutes. Do not stir rice until liquid is absorbed. Remove bouquet. Fluff lightly with fork, adding more salt and pepper if necessary.

Hattie Lipsky

Rice Casserole

1 onion, diced	(pieces, stems and liquid)
1 can mushroom soup	1 cup raw rice
1 can water	Butter
1 can (4-ounces) mushrooms	

Saute onion in butter until yellow. In well-greased 1½-quart casserole add all ingredients and mix well. Bake 1 hour at 350°. Serves 4-5.

Jane Rubens

Barley-Mushroom Casserole

2 tablespoons margarine	1 can (4 ounces) sliced mushrooms
¼ cup diced onions	½ cup barley
1 can chicken broth (13¾ ounces)	¼ teaspoon salt

Melt margarine in 1½-quart casserole. Add onions and cook until wilted. Add broth to measuring cup and add liquid from mushrooms until total liquid measures 2 cups, and add to onions. Add mushrooms, barley and salt. Bake uncovered at 350°, stirring several times, for 1 hour. Cover tightly and bake ½ hour more. Serves 4.

Maxine Straus

Farfel Special

1 8-ounce package Cohen's Haymisha Farfel	1 4-ounce can chopped mushrooms
1 4-ounce can French fried onion rings	2 tablespoons chicken fat

Cook farfel as directed. Drain thoroughly. In casserole, mix farfel, onions, mushrooms and fat. Bake at 300° until top is crisp. Serves 4-5.

Helen Hecker

Kasha Varnishkas

1 cup medium buckwheat groats	3 cups boiling water
Salt	1 tablespoon shortening
1 egg	1 cup cooked bow knot noodles
1 small onion, minced	

Put groats, salt, egg and minced onion in baking pan and mix until groats are slightly moistened. Roast in 350° oven about 10 minutes, stirring once or twice until groats are brown. Add boiling water and cover. Cook until water is absorbed. Add shortening and bow knots. Serve with meat gravy.

Pies

Angel Pie

Meringue Crust

4 egg whites
1 cup sugar

¼ teaspoon cream of tartar

Beat egg whites until stiff, slowly adding sugar and cream of tartar. Bake in 9-inch pie tin at 275° for 1 hour.

Filling

4 egg yolks
½ cup sugar
1 tablespoon lemon rind
3 tablespoons lemon juice
Pinch of salt

1 pint whipping cream
1 9-ounce package frozen strawberries, thawed
2 tablespoons toasted coconut

Cook first five ingredients over boiling water 8-10 minutes. Cool and add ½ pint whipping cream, whipped. Place drained berries in pie crust. Cover berries with cooled filling mixture. Whip remaining ½ pint cream and place in dollops along outer edge of pie. Garnish with toasted coconut.

Lil Orlen

Apple Pie with Sour Cream

1 unbaked and chilled 9-inch pie shell

Filling

2 tablespoons flour
¾ cup sugar
¾ teaspoon cinnamon
⅛ teaspoon salt

1 egg
½ teaspoon vanilla
1 cup sour cream
6 medium apples, pared, cored,
sliced

Preheat oven to 400°. Sift together flour, sugar, cinnamon and salt. Stir in the egg, vanilla and sour cream. Fold in the apples and spoon into the pie shell. Bake for 15 minutes. Reduce oven to 350° and bake 30 minutes longer.

Topping

1/3 cup flour
1/3 cup sugar

½ teaspoon cinnamon
¼ cup butter

Combine flour, sugar and cinnamon and with a pastry blender or the finger tips, blend in butter until mixture is crumbly. Sprinkle over the pie and bake at 400° ten minutes longer. 6 servings.

Bea Horn

Cookie Dough Apple Pie

Crust

1 2/3 cups flour
1 teaspoon baking powder
½ cup butter

½ cup sugar
1 egg

Sift flour and baking powder together. Cream butter and sugar and beat in egg. Stir and knead dry ingredients into above. Divide dough into two parts. Cover bottom of spring form pan with one half of dough, spreading dough with hands.

Filling

7 tart apples, peeled and sliced
½-¾ cup sugar to taste
1 teaspoon cinnamon

¼ teaspoon nutmeg, optional
2 tablespoons flour
1 tablespoon butter

Mix sugar, cinnamon and flour together, and stir into the apples. Turn into springform pan. Dot with butter and cover with second half of dough. Bake at 350° for 60 minutes. Serve warm or cold with whipped cream.

Sophie Bernstein

Never-Fail Dutch Apple Pie

1 9-inch unbaked pie shell

Topping

2/3 cup sifted all-purpose flour
1/3 cup light brown sugar, firmly
  packed
1/3 cup butter or margarine

Filling

2 pounds tart cooking apples
1 tablespoon lemon juice
2 tablespoons flour
¾ cup granulated sugar
Dash of salt
1 teaspoon cinnamon

Prepare pie shell; refrigerate until used. To make topping, combine flour and sugar in medium bowl. Cut in butter with pastry blender until mixture is consistent. Refrigerate. To make filling, core and pare apples, slice thinly into a large bowl. Sprinkle with lemon juice. Combine flour, sugar, salt and cinnamon and mix well. Toss lightly with apples. Turn filling into unbaked pie shell, spreading evenly. Cover with topping. Bake at 400° 40-45 minutes or until apples are tender.

Sue Kiner

Cognac Apple Flan

Pastry

1 cup flour
2 tablespoons sugar
¼ teaspoon salt
¼ cup butter

2 tablespoons shortening
Grated rind of 1 lemon
1 egg, slightly beaten
Ice water

Place flour, sugar and salt in bowl. Cut in butter and shortening with pastry blender. Add lemon rind, egg and enough ice water to mix pastry into a ball. Roll out on a lightly-floured pastry cloth to about ¼-inch thickness to fit an 8 or 9-inch flan ring. Fit pastry in without stretching. Trim by rolling the pin across the top of the flan form. Chill pie shell thoroughly in refrigerator or freezer. Preheat oven to 400°. Line shell with aluminum foil and fill with dried beans or rice. Bake 8-10 minutes or until pastry is set. Remove foil and beans or rice and return to oven for 3 minutes.

Filling

6 cups Golden Delicious apples,
  pared and thinly sliced
2/3 cup apricot perserves
2 tablespoons cognac
½ cup plus 1 tablespoon sugar
2 tablespoons butter

1 teaspoon grated lemon rind
¼ teaspoon nutmeg
¼ teaspoon cinnamon
2 tablespoons golden raisins
2 cups thin, even apple slices
1 teaspoon lemon juice

Place 6 cups apples in a pan, cover and stew over low heat until soft and mushy, adding a tablespoon or two of water only if necessary to prevent sticking. Stir occasionally. Stir in ¼ cup apricot perserves (strained, if too lumpy), cognac, ¼ cup sugar, butter, lemon rind, nutmeg, cinnamon and raisins. Continue to cook, stirring continuously, until mixture resembles applesauce.

Toss thin apple slices with lemon juice and 2 tablespoons of the remaining sugar. Spread the warm applesauce mixture in flan shell. Arrange tossed apple slices neatly over the surface to make a pattern, sprinkle lightly with 1 tablespoon sugar and bake about 25-30 minutes until pastry is cooked and apple slices are glazed slightly. Heat the remaining preserves with the rest of the sugar until it boils; simmer, stirring for 30 seconds. Brush this glaze over apple slices as soon as tart is removed from oven. Serve warm or at room temperature with whipped cream if desired. Serves 6-8. Note: Golden Delicious apples are a must in this recipe.

Helen Hecker

Apple Dumplings

1 cup sugar
2 cups water
⅛ teaspoon cinnamon
⅛ teaspoon nutmeg, if desired
2 or 3 drops red food coloring
2 tablespoon butter or margarine

8 medium apples, pared and cored
2 cups all-purpose flour
2 teaspoons baking powder
1 teaspoon salt
2/3 cup shortening
½ cup milk

Combine sugar, water, cinnamon, nutmeg, food coloring; bring to a boil. Add butter, set aside. Sift together flour, salt, baking powder; cut in shortening. Add milk all at once and stir until moistened. Divide in two parts. Roll each part on floured pastry cloth to make 4 6-inch squares. Place 1 whole apple in center of each pastry square. Sprinkle generously with sugar, cinnamon and nutmeg, dot with butter. Fold corners to center and pinch edges together. Place 1 inch apart in 1 greased 11 x 7 pan and 1 greased 9-inch square pan. Spoon syrup over dumplings; sprinkle with sugar. Bake in moderate oven 375° about 35 minutes, or until light brown. Make and add more syrup while baking if it becomes needed.

Edith Perlman

Banana Split Pie

1 baked 9-inch pie shell
1 quart soft vanilla ice cream

2 bananas
1 can cherry pie filling

Add ice cream to pie shell, freeze. Slice banana on frozen ice cream. Add pie filling. Decorate with long diagonally sliced bananas. Serve at once

Maxine Straus

Black Bottom Pie

12 gingersnaps
½ cup margarine
1 envelope unflavored or orange
  gelatin
¼ cup cold water
1 cup sugar
1½ tablespoons corn starch
⅛ teaspoon salt
2 eggs, separated
1¾ cups scalded non-dairy

coffee cream
2 squares unsweetened chocolate,
  melted
1 teaspoon vanilla
⅛ teaspoon cream of tartar
1 tablespoon rum or Grand Marnier
½ cup whip topping or Cool Whip
1 tablespoon confectioners sugar
1 tablespoon grated bitter or semi-
  sweet chocolate

Roll gingersnaps into fine crumbs, blend in margarine. Press mixture into 9-inch pie plate. Bake 375° for 8 minutes. Soak gelatin in cold water. Mix ¾ cup sugar, cornstarch and salt, add egg yolks, beat well. Add milk slowly, stirring constantly. Cook over boiling water until mixture coats spoon. Add gelatin stirring until dissolved. Divide mixture in half, to one half add chocolate and vanilla. Mix well; spoon into crust. Cool. Cool remaining ½ pudding. Beat egg whites foamy, add cream of tartar. Beat until stiff. Gradually add remaining ½ pudding. Add rum. Spread over chocolate mixture. Chill overnight. Before serving whip topping, add confectioners sugar, mix well. Spread over pie, sprinkle with grated chocolate. Serves 6-8.

Helen Berger

Black Bottom Pie

1 cup vanilla wafer crumbs
½ cup chopped pecans
1/3 cup melted butter
1 6-ounce package semi-sweet
   chocolate bits
½ cup milk

1 package vanilla pudding
1½ cups milk
1 tablespoon rum
½ cup heavy cream, whipped
1 cup miniature marshmallows

Combine wafer crumbs, chopped pecans and butter and pat into 9-inch pie plate. Bake at 375° for 5 minutes. Combine chocolate bits, milk and marshmallows over low heat. Stir until melted. Pour into crust. Prepare pudding using only 1½ cups milk and rum. Cover and chill. Fold in whipped cream. Pour over chocolate mixture in pie plate. Chill.

Beverly Chesler

Blueberry Cream Pie

1 baked 8-inch pie shell
1 package vanilla pudding
1½ cups milk
½ cup heavy cream, whipped
1 package thawed frozen unsweetened

or 2 cups fresh blueberries
1 tablespoon cornstarch
2 tablespoons granulated sugar
1 tablespoon lemon rind
1 tablespoon lemon juice

Early in day, make pudding as package directs, using 1½ cups milk; refrigerate until cold. Fold whipped cream into pudding; turn into baked pie shell. Refrigerate until firm. Meanwhile, make blueberry topping. In saucepan, place 1 cup berries. Add combined cornstarch and sugar, lemon rind and lemon juice. Cook over low heat, mashing and stirring, until mixture thickens and clears. Add rest of berries, cool slightly, then carefully spoon over pudding in pie shell. Refrigerate until serving time.

Elaine Simon

Brandy Alexander Pie

1 9-inch graham cracker crust
1 envelope unflavored gelatin
½ cup cold water
2/3 cup sugar
⅛ teaspoon salt

3 eggs
¼ cup brandy
¼ cup creme de cacao
2 cups heavy cream, whipped or
   pareve substitute

Sprinkle gelatin over cold water in saucepan. Add 1/3 cup sugar, salt and egg yolks. Stir and heat over low heat until gelatin dissolves and mixture thickens. Do not boil. Remove from heat and add brandy and creme de cacao. Chill until mixture slightly thickens. Beat egg whites until stiff adding 1/3 cup sugar slowly. Fold into mixture. Fold in 1 cup whipped cream. Pour into crust. Chill several hours or overnight. Spread other cup whipped cream on top. Garnish with shaved chocolate or chocolate curls.

Gloria Cohen

Apricot Cheese Pie

1 pastry shell
1 cup dried apricots
3 eggs
½ teaspoon grated lemon peel
1 teaspoon lemon juice

¾ cup sugar
1 tablespoon flour
½ teaspoon salt
1½ cups cottage cheese

Rinse and drain apricots, cut into small pieces and distribute over bottom of pastry shell. Place everything else in blender, gradually add eggs one at a time, alternately with cottage cheese. Pour over apricots. Bake at 375° for 35 minutes. Test with knife.

Dolly Brenner

Lemon-Strawberry Cheese Pie

Spiced Crumb Crust

1¼ cups graham cracker crumbs
2 tablespoons brown sugar
¼ teaspoon cinnamon
1/3 cup melted butter or margarine

Combine all ingredients and mix thoroughly. Pat crumbs firmly on bottom and sides of a buttered 9-inch cake pan. Bake about 6 minutes, or until lightly browned, at 400°.

Lemon Cheese Filling

1 package lemon pie filling
1 egg, beaten
1¾ cups water
½ cup sugar
⅛ teaspoon salt
½ pound cream cheese

Combine pie filling with egg, water, sugar, and salt. Stir well and cook over moderate heat until mixture boils and thickens; stir constantly. Mash cream cheese; stir in lemon mixture; beat with rotary beater until smooth. Pour into crust; chill until firm.

Fresh Strawberry Topping

1½ teaspoons unflavored gelatin
2 tablespoons cold water
2½ cups strawberries, washed and
hulled
½ cup sugar
¼ cup water

Soften gelatin in 2 tablespoons cold water. Slice 1 cup strawberries and cook with sugar and ¼ cup water for 5 minutes. Strain; immediately stir in gelatin. Add 1½ cups whole berries and chill. When slightly thickened, spread over filling. Chill until set.

Helen Hecker

Pecan Cream Cheese Pie

2 3-ounce packages of cream cheese
¼ cup plus 2 tablespoons sugar
2 teaspoons vanilla
4 large eggs
¾ cup dark corn syrup
Unbaked 9-inch pie shell
1¼ cups chopped pecans

Beat cream cheese with ¼ cup sugar, 1 egg, and 1 teaspoon vanilla until thick and smooth, reserve. Beat remaining 3 eggs slightly, add corn syrup, remaining 2 tablespoons sugar and remaining 1 teaspoon vanilla. Beat only until blended. Spread reserved cream cheese mixture in bottom of pastry shell, sprinkle with pecans, gently pour syrup mixture over pecans. Bake at 375° below center of oven until middle is firm to touch. 35-40 minutes. Cool.

Dolly Brenner

Uncooked Cheese Pie

1 9-inch baked graham cracker pie crust
½ pound cream cheese
1 cup confectioners sugar
1 pint Cool Whip
½ can cherry or strawberry pie filling

Cream cheese well. Fold in sugar and Cool Whip and blend well. Pour into crust and top with pie filling. Chill.

Lillian Schulman

French Cherry Pie

1 9-inch baked pie shell or   3 ounces cream cheese
  graham cracker crust   ½ cup confectioners sugar
1 can cherry pie filling   ½ teaspoon vanilla
1 cup heavy cream, whipped   ⅛ teaspoon salt

Soften the cream cheese, then whip the heavy cream and combine with the softened cream cheese. Whip them together until fluffy and then add sugar, salt and vanilla. Turn cream cheese mixture into pie shell and spoon cherry pie filling on top of it. Refrigerate. Serves 8.

Jill Musicus

Chocolate Almond Pie

1 8-inch graham cracker or baked crust
Filling
6 chocolate almond 10¢ bars   ½ cup milk
16 marshmallows, cut up   ½ pint heavy cream

Melt chocolate bars, milk and marshmallows in double boiler. Cool. Fold in whipped heavy cream into the chocolate mixture. Pour into the graham cracker crust. Refrigerate for a few hours. May be garnished with whipped cream or shaved German chocolate.

Mabel Bogoly

Chocolate Dream Pie

Crust
3 egg whites   ⅛ teaspoon cream of tartar
½ cup sugar   ⅛ teaspoon salt
½ teaspoon vanilla   ½ cup walnut meats

Beat together above ingredients and fold in walnut meats. Grease pie plate well and pour in mixture. Make an indentation in the middle, higher on the sides. Bake at 300° for 50-55 minutes.

Filling
1 bar German sweet chocolate   1 pint heavy cream
½ teaspoon vanilla

Melt chocolate in double boiler. Remove from heat and add vanilla and cool. As it cools, it will thicken. Beat in heavy cream until thick. Pour into cool meringue shell. Top with Dream Whip or Cool Whip.

Susan Horwitz

Easy Chocolate Pie

1 6-ounce package semi-sweet   4 eggs, separated
  chocolate pieces   1 teaspoon vanilla
2 tablespoons sugar   1 9-inch baked pie shell
3 tablespoons milk

Melt and blend together chocolate, sugar and milk. Cool. Beat in egg yolks, one at a time, and vanilla. Beat egg whites until stiff and fold in chocolate mixture. Pour in cooled baked 9-inch pie shell. Chill. Garnish. This pie can be made pareve by using pareve milk substitute. Can also be frozen.

Marcia G. Shapiro

French Mint Chocolate Pie

Crust

1 cup graham cracker crumbs	3 tablespoons melted butter
2 tablespoons powdered sugar	

Combine ingredients and bake in 8-inch pie plate for 5 minutes at 325°. Chill.

Filling

½ cup butter	2 eggs
1 cup powdered sugar	¼ teaspoon peppermint extract
2 squares melted chocolate	1 teaspoon vanilla

Cream butter and powdered sugar until fluffy. Slowly add melted chocolate. Add eggs, one at a time, beating well after each addition. Add peppermint and vanilla. Spread into shell. Chill 6 hours.

Stella Gelman

Frozen Chocolate Cream Pie

Crust

1½ cups chocolate wafers, crushed   ½ cup melted margarine

Mix wafers and margarine, pat into 10-inch pie plate and bake at 325° for 10 minutes.

Filling

1 ounce cream cheese	1 6-ounce package mint choco-
½ cup sugar	late chips, melted
1 teaspoon vanilla	1 cup heavy cream, whipped
2 eggs, separated	¾ cup nuts

Combine soft cream cheese, ¼ cup sugar and vanilla and mix until blended. Stir in beaten egg yolks and melted chocolate chips. Beat egg whites. Gradually add ¼ cup sugar. Fold egg whites and whipped cream into chocolate mixture. Nuts may be added or used as garnish. Freeze. (Let stand 10 minutes before serving.)

Beverly Chesler

Caribbean Fudge Pie

¼ cup butter	1 teaspoon rum extract
¾ cup brown sugar, packed	¼ cup all-purpose flour
3 eggs	1 cup walnuts or pecans
1 12-ounce package semi-sweet	1 unbaked 9-inch pie shell
chocolate chips, melted	½ cup pecans or walnut halves
2 teaspoons instant coffee	

Cream butter with sugar. Beat in eggs, one at a time. Add melted chocolate chips, instant coffee, rum extract. Stir in flour and broken nuts. Turn into pie shell. Top with remaining ½ cup nuts. Bake at 375° for 25 minutes. Cool and top with whipped cream.

Annette Waldman and
Dolly Brenner

Coffee Chiffon Pie

1 9-inch chocolate cookie
   crumb crust
1 envelope unflavored gelatin
¼ cup cold water
2 tablespoons instant coffee

¾ cup hot water
¼ teaspoon salt
½ cup sugar
3 eggs, separated

Soften gelatin in cold water. Dissolve the coffee in hot water in the top of a double boiler. Add salt and ¼ cup sugar. Cook over direct heat until the sugar is dissolved. Beat the egg yolks slightly. Slowly add hot liquid, stirring constantly. Return to top of double boiler and cook over hot water, stirring constantly, until the mixture is slightly thickened. Remove from heat and add softened gelatin. Stir until it is dissolved. Chill until mixture is the consistency of unbeaten egg whites. Beat the egg whites until stiff — then gradually beat in the remaining ¼ cup sugar. Fold in chilled coffee mixture. Put into cookie crumb crust and chill until firm. Garnish with whipped cream and shaved chocolate, if desired.

Ricky Sands

Grasshopper Pie

30 chocolate icebox cookies
4½ tablespoons melted butter
30 large marshmallows
1 cup cream (light or heavy)

½ ounce green creme de menthe
½ ounce white creme de cocao
1 cup heavy cream, whipped

Roll cookies into crumbs and mix with melted butter. Line 9-inch pie plate with crumbs, bake 5 minutes at 300°. Chill thoroughly. Melt marshmallows in cream in double boiler. Cool until thick. Add creme de menthe and creme de cocao. Fold green mixture into whipped heavy cream. Pour into shell and freeze. Remove 5-10 minutes before serving. May be garnished with shaved chocolate. Serves 8.

Leah Mermelstein

Ice Box Pie

18 chocolate sandwich-style
   cookies
1/3 cup melted butter
1 quart coffee or peppermint ice
   cream, slightly softened

2 squares bitter chocolate
1 small can evaporated milk
½ cup sugar
2 tablespoons butter

Crust

Crush cookies (not too fine). Mix with melted butter and pat into 9-inch pie pan. Spread with quart of slightly softened ice cream. Place in freezer until ready to cover with fudge sauce.

Fudge Sauce

Cook and stir bitter chocolate, evaporated milk, sugar and butter over low flame until thick. Cool before spreading on top of ice cream. After frosting with sauce, place in freezer again and when solid, cover with foil and keep in freezer until ready to serve. Keeps well for several days. Serves 8-10.

Mildred Feinberg

Lemon Chiffon Pie

1 cup sugar	1 tablespoon plain gelatin
½ cup lemon juice	¼ cup cold water
½ teaspoon salt	1 teaspoon grated lemon rind
5 eggs, separated	1 baked 10-inch pie shell

Add ½ cup sugar, lemon juice, and salt to beaten egg yolks; cook over boiling water until custard consistency. Soften gelatin in cold water for 5 minutes. Add to hot mixture and stir until dissolved. Add grated lemon rind and cool. When mixture starts to thicken, whip egg whites with remaining ½ cup sugar until it stands in stiff peaks. Fold gently into custard mixture. Put into pie shell. Chill. Garnish with whipped cream.

Esther Josephson

Lemon Meringue Pie

1 baked 9-inch pie shell

Filling

6 tablespoons cornstarch	3 unbeaten egg yolks
¼ teaspoon salt	2 tablespoons butter or margarine
1 cup sugar	2 tablespoons lemon rind, grated
2 cups water	5 tablespoons lemon juice

In double boiler, combine cornstarch, salt, water, ½ cup of sugar. Stir slowly until thick, about 10 minutes. In separate bowl, combine yolks and rest of sugar. Spoon 3 tablespoons of hot mixture into egg mixture. Mix until smooth, then pour back into hot mixture. Cook until thick. Stir in butter, lemon juice and lemon rind. Cool to room temperature without stirring. Pour into pie shell.

Meringue

3 egg whites (at room temperature)	6 tablespoons sugar

Beat egg whites until they stand up in peaks. Sprinkle lightly with sugar and beat until glossy. Spread meringue from center to edge — seal to crust. Bake for 15-20 minutes at 325°. Cool.

Dorothy Rubens

Lemonade Chiffon Pie

1/3 cup sugar	1 6-ounce can frozen lemonade, thawed
¼ teaspoon salt	
1 envelope unflavored gelatin	1 cup whipping cream, whipped
¾ cup water	1 9-inch baked pie shell

Combine sugar, salt, and gelatin in saucepan, add water and stir over low heat until gelatin is dissolved. Remove from heat, add undiluted lemonade. Chill until mixture begins to thicken, then fold in whipped cream and pour into pie shell. Chill and garnish with whipped cream.

Lil Orlen

Key Lime Pie

9-inch baked pie shell
4 egg yolks
1 can sweetened condensed milk
½ cup lime juice
½ teaspoon cream of tartar
6 egg whites
¾ cup sugar

Beat egg yolks until lemon colored, blend in condensed milk slowly. Add lime juice and mix well. Add cream of tartar to egg whites and beat until foamy. Continue beating, adding sugar, 1 tablespoon at a time, until the egg whites peak. Fold 6 tablespoons of the meringue into the filling mixture. Pour into a 9-inch baked pie shell. Top with the meringue and bake in a slow oven, at 330° until golden brown.

Lil Schwartz

Mandarin Angel Pie

Crust

3 egg whites
¼ teaspoon cream of tartar
1 cup sugar

Beat egg whites and cream of tartar to soft peaks. Gradually add the sugar, beating to stiff peaks. Spread on bottom and sides of well greased 9-inch pie plate. Bake at 275° for 1 hour. Turn off heat and let dry for 2 hours.

Filling

1 package lemon pudding
½ cup sugar
¼ cup water
3 egg yolks
1 8-ounce can mandarin
oranges
½ cup whipped cream
1 tablespoon lemon juice

Combine pudding, sugar and water. Blend in yolks. Drain oranges, save syrup. Add lemon juice and enough water to syrup to make 1¾ cups. Stir into pudding mixture. Cook and stir over medium heat until boiling. Cool completely. Fold in whipped cream and ¾ cup oranges. Spoon into crust. Chill overnight. Garnish with rest of oranges and whipped cream.

Beverly Chesler

Mocha Pie

1 9-inch graham cracker crust
½ cup sugar
1 square bitter chocolate
1 tablespoon instant coffee
3 tablespoons flour
1 tablespoon cornstarch
1 cup milk
1 teaspoon vanilla
1 cup heavy cream, whipped

Cook sugar, chocolate, coffee, flour, cornstarch and milk in double boiler, stirring constantly. When it thickens, remove from heat and cool. Add vanilla. Fold in two-thirds of whipped cream. Partially fold in remaining whipped cream. Refrigerate several hours before serving.

Bea Horn

Peach Creamy Pie

18 large marshmallows
¼ cup milk
1 cup heavy cream, whipped
3 cups fresh peaches, diced,
5-6 medium
Pie crust — baked or crumb

Melt marshmallows in milk in double boiler. Cool until set, and beat until smooth. Fold in heavy cream and peaches. Chill. Pour into pie crust.

Maxine Straus

Peachy Blueberry Pie

Pastry for 2-crust
  9-inch pie
5 cups sliced fresh peaches
1 cup fresh, cleaned blueberries
½ cup sugar, or to taste

1 teaspoon lemon juice
2 tablespoons flour
¼ teaspoon cinnamon
1½ tablespoons butter

Line 9-inch pie plate with pie dough. Sprinkle lightly with corn flake crumbs to avoid soggy crust. Stir together flour, sugar, and cinnamon. Mix with fruit and add lemon juice. Turn into unbaked pastry and dot with butter. Cover with lattice top and bake 35-45 minutes at 425°.

Lattice Top

Roll dough as for pie crust. With a sharp knife or a pastry wheel, cut strips about ½-inch wide. Place criss-cross over pie, being sure to seal with outer fluted edge. Baste the strips with milk and sprinkle with a little sugar. Do not baste the outer edge. Cover fluted edge with foil for part of the baking time. Remove last 15 minutes.

Edith Perlman

Peach Parfait Pie

3½ cups sliced fresh peaches
  or 1 #2½ can
1 package lemon gelatin
½ cup cold water

1 pint vanilla ice cream
1 baked pie crust — pastry or
  graham cracker

Let sliced fresh peaches stand fifteen minutes — or drain canned peaches, saving syrup or juice. Add water to juice or syrup to measure one cup and heat to boiling. Add gelatin and dissolve. Add cold water. Cut ice cream and add to hot liquid, stirring. Chill fifteen minutes in refrigerator. Line pie crust with peaches. Pour in liquid, refrigerate to set.

Frumel Ureles

Peanut Butter Ice Cream Pie

1 prepared graham cracker crust
½ cup crunchy peanut butter

½ cup Cool Whip
1 quart vanilla ice cream

Let ice cream soften slightly, just enough to blend in peanut butter and Cool Whip. Do not let ice cream become soupy. When all three are blended thoroughly, pour into pie crust and keep in freezer. Note: this can be made and stored in freezer indefinitely. It's nice to have on hand.

Judy Schwartz

Pecan Pie

1 cup corn syrup
3 eggs, slightly beaten
1 cup sugar
2 tablespoon melted butter or
  pareve margarine

1 teaspoon vanilla
¼ teaspoon salt
1 cup pecans, halves or chopped
1 unbaked 9-inch pastry shell

Mix all ingredients for filling together, adding pecans last. Pour into pastry shell. Bake in 400° oven for 15 minutes. Reduce heat to 350° and bake for 30-35 minutes longer. Outer edges should be set, center slightly soft.

Ruth Drexler

Pineapple Icebox Pie

10 ounces vanilla wafers
¼ pound butter
1 cup sugar
3 eggs, beaten
1 #2 can drained crushed pineapple
½ pint heavy cream, whipped

Cream butter and sugar, add eggs. Add drained pineapple. Fold in whipped cream. Crush vanilla wafers with rolling pin or use blender. Spread in greased 10-inch pie plate. Save remaining crushed wafers. Pour mixture into pie shell. Cover with remaining crushed wafers. Refrigerate for 24 hours. May be frozen.

Bea Horn

Pumpkin Pecan Pie

3 slightly beaten eggs
1 cup canned pumpkin
1 cup sugar
½ cup dark corn syrup
1 teaspoon vanilla
½ teaspoon cinnamon
¼ teaspoon salt
1 cup chopped pecans
1 unbaked 9-inch shell

Combine eggs, pumpkin, sugar, syrup and spices. Mix well. Pour into shell. Top with pecans and bake at 350° for 40 minutes or until knife inserted in pie comes out clean. Chill. Top with whipped cream.

Ruth Kravetz

Rum Chiffon Pie

Crust
¾ package chocolate covered graham crackers

Put crackers through food chopper. Press crumbs into a 9-inch pie plate
Filling

1½ cups milk
2 tablespoons cornstarch
3 egg yolks
1 cup sugar
1 envelope plain gelatin dissolved in
¼ cup cold water
5 egg whites
⅛ teaspoon salt
1 tablespoon rum flavoring

Place milk in top of double boiler and dissolve cornstarch in a small amount of milk before it gets hot. Add mixture to the remainder of milk and cook over hot water until thickened. Separate eggs. Put yolks in small bowl, add 3 tablespoons of cornstarch-milk mixture. Blend well, add to the remainder of the cornstarch-milk mixture. Cook for about 4 minutes. Add ½ cup sugar and softened gelatin. Stir until dissolved and set aside to cool. Refrigerate until thick. Beat 5 egg whites with salt until peaks form. Add remaining ½ cup sugar and beat for several minutes longer. Do not overbeat. Take beaters from whites and beat cooled congealed mixture right in top of double boiler until smooth. Fold in egg whites very gently with rubber spatula. Add rum flavoring and pour into prepared crust. Chill. Decorate with whipped cream and chocolate curls.

Sarah Derman

Festive Sherry Pie

1 3½-ounce package vanilla flavor
  whipped dessert mix
½ cup very cold milk
¼ cup very cold water
¼ cup very cold sherry
2 tablespoons finely chopped

candied cherries
2 tablespoons finely chopped
  candied pineapple
¼ cup finely chopped walnuts
1 baked 8-inch graham cracker
  crust

In a small deep bowl, thoroughly blend dessert mix with cold milk at low speed. Whip at high speed 1 minute. Blend in cold water and sherry at low speed. Whip at high speed 2 minutes until fluffy and soft peaks form. Gently fold in candied fruit and nuts. Turn into baked crumb shell. Chill several hours or overnight. If desired, garnish with small swirl of whipped cream and candied cherry halves. Serves 5-6. Chocolate variations: use 1 package of chocolate flavored whipped dessert mix.

Julia Berlove

Half 'N' Half Strawberry Pie

1 baked 9-inch pastry or
  graham cracker crust
1 quart strawberries

1 cup sugar
3 tablespoons cornstarch
¼ cup water, scant

Place ½ quart strawberries, sugar, cornstarch and water in a pot. Cook slowly to make a thick syrup; then cool to lukewarm. Slice remaining ½ quart of berries into baked pie shell. Pour cooked mixture over the top. Chill thoroughly. May be served with whipped cream.

Linda Rock

Mile-High Strawberry Pie

Crust

1½ cups flour
½ teaspoon sugar
1 teaspoon salt

½ cup salad oil
2 tablespoons milk

Sift dry ingredients into 10-inch spring form pan. Combine oil and milk and pour over mixture in pan. Blend well, then press firmly on bottom and about 1-inch up sides. Bake at 425° 12-15 minutes until lightly browned. Set aside.

Filling

2 egg whites
1 16-ounce package frozen strawberries drained
2 tablespoons cornstarch
¼ to 1/3 cup Cointreau (or rum,

kirsch, sherry)
2/3 cup sugar
1 tablespoon lemon juice
1 teaspoon vanilla
1 cup heavy cream, whipped

Heat strawberry juice and cornstarch until thick and clear, then thin with liqueur and cool. Beat eggs slightly in large bowl; add strawberries, sugar and lemon juice. Beat at high speed 15 minutes until firm peaks. Add vanilla to whipped cream and fold in strawberry mixture. Pile lightly in spring form pan and place in freezer for 12 hours. Remove 15 minutes before serving. Remove rim with sharp knife. Border with berries. Serves 8-10.

Frumel Ureles

Strawberry Rhubarb Pie

Pastry for 2-crust 10-inch pie
4 cups rhubarb
2 cups strawberries, fresh
1/3 cup flour

1 1/3 cups sugar
½ teaspoon cinnamon
6 dots of butter, about 1 tablespoon

Cover 10-inch pie plate with dough, and sprinkle lightly with corn flake crumbs to avoid a soggy crust. Clean, wash and dry rhubarb and strawberries. Cut rhubarb in ½-inch slices. Cut strawberries in half if they are large. Mix together flour, sugar, and cinnamon and mix thoroughly with fruit. Turn into unbaked pie shell and dot with butter. Cover with upper crust and seal edges carefully by fluting. Cut slits in upper crust to allow steam to escape. Cover outer edge of pie with narrow strip of aluminum foil until last 15 minutes of baking. Then uncover. Bake in hot oven at 425° for 40-50 minutes until fruit bubbles through slits in crust.

Edith Perlman

Tangerine Bavarian Pie

1 tablespoon unflavored gelatin
¼ cup cold water
½ cup sugar
¼ teaspoon salt
3 eggs, separated
½ cup milk
2 tablespoons fresh lemon juice
1 teaspoon grated lemon peel

1 teaspoon grated tangerine peel
1 teaspoon vanilla
1 cup diced tangerine sections
½ cup heavy cream, whipped
¼ cup sugar
1 9-inch baked pie shell
Whipped cream for garnish

Soften gelatin in cold water. Combine ½ cup sugar, salt and egg yolks in saucepan or top of double boiler. Stir in milk. Cook over hot water until custard coats metal spoon, stirring constantly. Remove from heat and stir in softened gelatin. Chill until mixture just begins to thicken. Stir in lemon juice, lemon peel, tangerine peel, vanilla and tangerine sections. Fold in whipped cream. Beat egg whites until they stand in soft peaks. Gradually beat in ¼ cup sugar, a tablespoon at a time. Fold into gelatin mixture. Turn into pie shell. Chill until firm. Garnish with whipped cream. 6-8 servings.

Hattie Lipsky

Heath Bar Toffee Pie

1 unbeaten egg white
2/3 cup brown sugar
2 teaspoons instant coffee
1½ teaspoons vanilla

1 teaspoon lemon juice
1 cup whipping cream
4 ¾-ounce Heath bars
1 9-inch baked pie shell

Beat together egg white, brown sugar, coffee, vanilla and lemon juice. Beat whipping cream, then fold into egg mixture. Crush Heath bars and fold in, saving some for garnish. Pour into baked pie shell. Freeze until firm.

Stella Gelman

Pie Crust

2½ cups all-purpose flour
½ teaspoon salt

¾ cups shortening
5-7 tablespoons chilled water

Cut shortening into flour and salt until size of peas, with pastry blender. Add chilled water and blend with a fork until smooth. Makes 2 9-inch pie crusts or 1 covered pie. Prick pastry with fork — chill for 1 hour and bake at 450° on upper shelf for 15 minutes or until lightly browned.

Ruth Drexler

Pie Crust

1½ cups sifted flour	3 tablespoons cold milk
1/3 cup oil	½ teaspoon salt

Sift flour and salt together. Measure oil and milk into same cup — don't stir. Pour into flour. Stir until mixed. Press into ball and flatten slightly. Place between 2 sheets of waxed paper (12 inch square). Roll out gently to edges of paper. Dampen counter top to prevent slipping. Peel off top paper. Lift paper and pastry by top corners. Place paper side up in 8 inch or 9 inch pie plate. Peel off paper. Flute edges. If used for shells, pierce pastry with fork and bake at 475° for 8-10 minutes.

Bea Horn

Pie Crust

3 cups all-purpose flour, sifted	shortening
½ teaspoon salt	7 tablespoons orange juice
1 cup + 2 tablespoons vegetable	Pastry cloth, rolling pin cover

In large bowl cut ½ shortening into the flour with pastry blender, then other half of shortening. Sprinkle orange juice over all and blend. Divide in 3 parts. Roll on floured pastry cloth with covered rolling pin. Bake as described for specific pie. For pie shell — prick crust all over with fork. Do not do so for covered pie. Makes 1 2-crust pie and 1 shell.

Edith Pearlman

Pat a Pie Crust

1½ cups sifted flour	2 tablespoons cold milk (or Mocha
1½ teaspoons sugar	mix)
½ teaspoon salt	½ cup oil

Sift dry ingredients into 9 or 10-inch pie plate. Make well and pour milk and oil in well. Blend and make into ball. Pat into place on sides and bottom of pie pan. Bake at 400° for 12-15 minutes.

Pie Crust Shell

1 cup flour	3 tablespoons ice water
1/3 cup vegetable shortening	1/3 cup ground toasted nuts,
¼ teaspoon salt	almonds, walnuts, pecans

Sift flour and salt. Cut in shortening with pastry blender. Add ice water and toss lightly with fork. Add nuts last. Fit into 9-inch pie shell and flute edges. Place extra pie plate inside shell and bake at 425° for 12 minutes.

Bea Horn

Never Fail Meringue

2 tablespoons sugar	⅛ teaspoon salt
1 tablespoon cornstarch	½ teaspoon vanilla
½ cup water	6 tablespoons sugar
3 egg whites	

Combine 2 tablespoons sugar and cornstarch in small sauce pan. Add water. Cook over medium heat, stirring constantly until mixture is thick and clear. Cool. Beat egg whites with salt and vanilla until stiff but not dry. Add six tablespoons sugar gradually, beating well after each addition. Add cornstarch mixture. Continue beating until meringue stands in stiff peaks. Spread meringue on pie, bake at 375° for 10-12 minutes.

Edith Perlman

Poultry and Stuffings

Methods of Cooking Poultry

Broiling Chicken

Cut a small bird (1½ to 2 pounds) in half, and break at the three or four major joints. Lay in a shallow pan, brush thoroughly with melted fat. Leave skin side down. Place on rack 2-5 inches from direct heat. Turn chicken several times as it browns, basting each side with fat. When nicely brown and done, in 40-60 minutes, season. Turn heat off. Let chicken finish cooking on retained heat to insure thorough doneness. Transfer to warm platter. Pour drippings over the chicken, or prepare gravy from the drippings. Garlic or onion flavor is a delicious addition.

Roasting Chicken

Large chickens are roasted about 30 minutes to the pound, while 35-45 minutes of cooking is necessary for small or medium birds. Lay breast side up in the roasting pan. Roast at a moderate temperature 325° — 350°. Roasting birds weigh 3-6 pounds.

Frying Chicken

Preheat oven to 500° and put in enough fat to cover bottom of pan. When fat is hot, put in the pieces of cut-up chicken, which have been dipped in a coating of seasoned bread crumbs. Put the thick, meaty pieces in first — add rest of chicken. Turn chicken when browned on one side (about 20 minutes) and continue cooking for about 15 minutes after turning. Reduce temperature to 300° and cook for 15-20 minutes longer.

Roast Turkey

How to Stuff Turkey

Salt the inside cavity — ⅛ teaspoon salt per pound of bird. Don't pack the stuffing. An overstuffed bird makes a soggy dressing, and bird may burst during roasting. If you're not planning to roast the bird right away, chill stuffing before roasting bird.

How to Truss

Bind legs and wings closely to body of the bird. It will cook more evenly, look better on the platter and carve more easily. After stuffing bird, skewer neck skin to back. Fold wings so tips hold neck skin. Close body cavity openings with skewers and cord. Tie legs to tail.

How to Roast

Grease skin with melted cooking fat. Place bird breast side down in shallow pan. Use flat rack or V rack. Unless bird has generous layers of fat underneath the skin, cover with aluminum foil or cheese cloth. Do not cover pan, do not sear bird; do not add water. When bird is approximately three-fourths done according to timetable, turn it breast up, and replace cloth.

How to Tell if Turkey is Done

1. Drumstick will turn easily in socket.

2. Meat on heavy part of leg feels soft when touched with paper towel. With some roasted turkeys the meat around the bone is pink. This may be due to the feed given the turkey. If turkey has been roasted according to weight, the meat will be cooked.

Chicken Fat

Fat and fatty skin of one chicken   3 small onions, sliced

Cut clean fat and fat skin of chicken into small pieces. Place in sauce pan. Put sliced onions on top of fat. When onions turn golden brown, chicken fat is done. Drain fat and keep in covered jar in refrigerator. The pieces are called Grieben, and are delicious mixed with chopped hard boiled eggs as an entree.

Jennie Levinson

Mock Chicken Fat

1 medium onion   1 teaspoon instant chicken soup
1 cup oil

Saute onion in oil until lightly browned, stirring occasionally. Add chicken soup. Strain into jar. Yields one cup.

Lillian Markus

Chicken Fricasse

1 4-pound chicken   2 medium onions
1 tablespoon salt   4 celery stalks

Combine above ingredients in pot with enough water to barely cover all ingredients. Bring to a boil and cook slowly until tender. Remove chicken from pot; skin, bone and cut into desirable pieces. Strain broth clear from all vegetables and put back into pot.

2 pounds of ground meat   2 teaspoons salt
½ cup wheat germ or bread crumbs   Dash of pepper
      1 medium onion
1 cup tomato sauce   2 eggs

Combine above ingredients, form into small balls and drop into chicken broth that has been brought to a boil. Reduce heat and boil for approximately 1 hour. Remove from heat, strain and set aside.

½ pound sliced mushrooms, include stems   Salt
      Pepper
2-3 tablespoons flour   Curry powder
Garlic salt   2 tablespoons fat

Add seasonings to flour. Sprinkle mushrooms with flour mixture. Saute in fat until tender and slightly browned. Gradually add strained broth and cook until slightly thickened. Combine chicken chunks and meat balls in sizable pot and pour gravy with the mushrooms over it and cook over low flame for about a ½ hour or longer. Serve over mashed potatoes, rice or biscuits.

Jeanette Komesar

Chicken in Mandarin Sauce

1 chicken, quartered
2 tablespoons oil
2 tablespoons margarine
Seasoned flour
4 tablespoons lemon juice

½ cup orange juice
2 tablespoons honey
½ tablespoon soy sauce
½ teaspoon powdered ginger
1 can mandarin oranges

Dust chicken pieces with seasoned flour; saute in oil and margarine until slightly browned. Add sauce made by combining remaining ingredients and simmer gently in covered pan about 30 minutes, or until chicken is tender.

Sora Lee Goldberg

Chicken with Orange Soy Sauce

3 pounds chicken breasts
1/3 teaspoon pepper
1 teaspoon salt
½ cup flour
1 tablespoon ginger
½ cup salad oil

Orange Soy Sauce
½ cup orange juice
¼ cup lemon juice
3 tablespoons soy sauce
1 teaspoon honey
½ cup chicken stock
½ cup dry sherry

Bone chicken breasts and cut in half, removing skin. Combine pepper, salt, ginger and flour in a bag. Shake the pieces in the bag until well coated. Cook the chicken in hot oil until both sides of each piece are browned. Put browned chicken in casserole and pour sauce over chicken. Cover and bake at 300° for 1 hour. Check to see if tender and serve. Serves 4.

Hattie Lipsky

Chicken in Pineapple Juice

1 3½-4 pound fryer, cut up
Salt and pepper
2 cups pineapple juice

½ cup sauterne or vin rose
1 teaspoon arrowroot or flour
Chicken fat

Season chicken with salt and pepper. Broil quickly until golden brown, using small amount of chicken fat. When almost done, heat pineapple juice with wine in casserole. Thicken with arrowroot or flour. Add broiled chicken. Cover. Bake at 350° for 30-40 minutes, until tender. Serve with rice.

Esther Lifshutz

Sweet and Sour Chicken

6 chicken breasts
½ teaspoon salt
3 teaspoons cornstarch
1 tablespoon water
1/3 cup oil
2 cloves garlic, crushed

1 can (8 ounce) pineapple chunks
1 jar (4 ounce) sweet mixed
  pickles
2 teaspoons soy sauce
½ cup green pepper strips
1 tomato, cut in wedges

Cut chicken into strips; mix with salt and 1 teaspoon cornstarch. Saute garlic in oil; remove garlic, add chicken, stirring continuously for 15 minutes over high heat. Add juice from pineapple, liquid from pickles and soy sauce. Bring to a boil; add pineapple chunks, pickles and green pepper. Blend in 2 teaspoons cornstarch dissolved in 1 tablespoon water. Add tomato. Serves 4-6.

Edith Parker

Chinese Chicken

1 medium sized chicken,
   quartered
8 ounces honey
¾ cup oil
2 tablespoons soy sauce
2 tablespoons Worcestershire

sauce
Salt, pepper, garlic salt, paprika
   to taste
Duck sauce — about ½ jar
4 pineapple slices
4 Maraschino cherries

Combine honey, oil, soy sauce, Worcestershire sauce and seasonings. Mix well. Dip chicken in sauce. Place chicken, skin side down, in pan with remaining sauce. Cover pan and bake 40 minutes at 325° . Turn chicken pieces and bake 30 minutes more. Brush with duck sauce and bake 20 minutes more. Place 1 canned pineapple slice and 1 cherry on each slice. Bake another 20 minutes. Serve over rice.

Maddy Rubens

Chicken Chop Suey

1 cup shredded green pepper
1 cup shredded onion
3 tablespoon chicken fat
2 cups shredded celery and tops
2 cups diced cooked chicken
2 cups drained bean sprouts

1½ cups chicken soup
1 tablespoon cornstarch
1 cup water chestnuts, drained
1 cup bamboo shoots, drained
¼ cup soy sauce

Add pepper and onion to hot fat in Dutch oven. Allow to cook several minutes without browning. Add chicken and cook 5 minutes. Add celery, bean sprouts, bamboo shoots and water chestnuts. Make paste of chicken soup, soy sauce and cornstarch. Add to chicken and vegetable mixture; cook gently 10 minutes, stirring frequently. Serve with hot rice and Chinese noodles.

Mollie Rossberg

Easy Chow Mein

2 cups diced cooked chicken
1 can chicken soup
1 9-ounce can pineapple tidbits,
   drained
1 tablespoon soy sauce

1 cup celery, sliced
2 tablespoons chopped scallions
   or green onions
1 3-ounce can chow mein noodles

Combine all ingredients except noodles. Gently fold in 1 cup noodles. Place in 8 x 8 x 2 baking dish. Sprinkle with remaining noodles. Bake for 50 minutes at 350° or until hot. Serves 5.

Stella Gelman

Turkey Sukiyaki

½ cup sauterne
¼ cup soy sauce
1½ teaspoons onion, minced
1 clove garlic, minced
¼ teaspoon ginger
2 cups cooked turkey

2 tablespoons margarine
1/6 cup flour
1 cup chicken bouillon
½ cup sliced mushrooms
½ cup chopped celery
½ pound fresh spinach, cooked

Combine sauterne, soy sauce, onion, garlic and ginger. Pour over turkey and marinate for 1 hour. In saucepan, melt margarine, add flour and chicken bouillon. Add celery, mushrooms and turkey with marinade. About 5 minutes before serving, add spinach. Serves 4.

Judy Kaplan

Coq au Vin

4 chicken breasts, boned and
  split
½ cup white or any dry wine
¼ teaspoon saffron
¼ teaspoon sage
½ teaspoon parsley flakes
¼ teaspoon minced garlic

Salt and pepper to taste
1 pound fresh or frozen asparagus or broccoli
1 can condensed mushroom
  soup, pareve
Bread crumbs
Paprika

Mix wine, saffron, sage, parsley, garlic, salt and pepper. Pour over chicken
and marinate for 1 hour. Arrange asparagus or broccoli in bottom of
casserole. Place chicken on top of vegetables. Pour marinade and
mushroom soup over all, carefully. Do not stir. Cover top with bread crumbs
and paprika. Bake 1 hour at 325° until bubbly and brown. Can be frozen.
Serves 4.

Evelyn Berlowitz

Special French Chicken

3 whole chicken breasts
1 onion, thinly sliced
1 carrot, thinly sliced
¼ teaspoon dried tarragon
½ cup white wine
Boiling water

3 tablespoons margarine
3 tablespoons flour
½ teaspoon salt
Dash of pepper
2 tablespoons margarine
1 egg yolk, slightly beaten

Cut breast in half along breast bone. Pull off skin. Place chicken, onion,
carrot, tarragon and wine in large sauce pan. Add boiling water to cover.
Cover and simmer about 25 minutes until chicken is tender. Remove chicken
and keep warm. Strain liquid. Boil gently until liquid is reduced to about 2
cups, about 1 hour. Then melt the 3 tablespoons margarine. Stir in flour, salt
and pepper. Gradually add the 2 cups of chicken broth, cook, stirring
constantly until mixture is smooth and thickened, add 2 tablespoons of
margarine, stir until melted. Stir in egg yolk. To serve, pour sauce over
chicken breasts. Decorate with parsley. Serves 6. May be made ahead of
time and warmed up in oven.

Eulah Feier

Chicken Kiev

3 large chicken breasts, boned
½ pound margarine
6 mushrooms, finely chopped
1 clove garlic
2 tablespoons chopped parsley

Salt and pepper
2 eggs
1 tablespoon vodka
Bread crumbs

Separate chicken breast halves and pound thin. Let margarine come to room
temperature and cream together with the sauteed chopped mushrooms,
garlic and parsley. Chill in refrigerator until firm enough to handle, then
shape into six oval rolls about 2½-3 inches long and ¾-1 inch wide at the
thickest part. Place rolls in ice water until hard. Sprinkle salt and pepper on
each flattened breast half. Dry margarine rolls and place one roll on each
flattened breast half. Roll the chicken around the margarine roll, folding the
ends in so the margarine is completely encased. Secure with toothpicks.
Beat 2 eggs with vodka. Roll the rolled-up chicken in breadcrumbs, then in
eggs with vodka, and again in bread crumbs. Fry in margarine until rolls are
golden brown, making certain that the margarine is not too hot. Drain and
place in hot oven for 5 minutes. This dish can be frozen before frying and can
be fried directly from the freezer. Serves 6.

Sue Kiner

Chicken Cacciatore

2 small broilers, quartered	1 20-ounce can tomatoes
½ cup flour	1 6-ounce can tomato paste
¼ cup oil	1 bay leaf
1 onion, sliced	1 teaspoon salt
1 green pepper, sliced	1 teaspoon thyme
1 4-ounce can mushrooms,	½ teaspoon oregano
drained	½ cup cooking sherry
2 cloves garlic, minced	

Coat chicken with flour. Brown in hot oil on all sides. Remove chicken and saute onions, green pepper, mushrooms and garlic in remaining oil. Add remaining ingredients. Simmer sauce for 15 minutes. Place chicken in casserole; pour sauce over chicken and bake covered, at 300° for 1 to 1½ hours, or until tender.

Selma Soloway

Easy Chicken Cacciatore

2½ to 3 pound frying chicken	1 1½ ounce envelope spaghetti
¼ cup salad oil	sauce mix
1¾ cups water	¼ cup onion flakes
1 6-ounce can tomato paste	1 4-ounce can mushrooms

Cut chicken into serving pieces. Brown in hot oil in a heavy skillet. Add water, tomato paste, spaghetti sauce mix and onion flakes. Cover and cook slowly until chicken is tender, about 30 minutes. Add mushrooms just before serving. Serves 4-6.

Beatrice DeMora

Broilers a la Italienne

1 envelope Italian salad dress-	2 tablespoon lemon juice or
ing mix	vinegar
½ cup light molasses	¼ cup minced onion
¼ cup salad oil	3 small broilers, cut in half or
1 cup tomato sauce	quarters

Combine salad dressing mix, molasses, salad oil, tomato sauce, lemon juice and onion, blend well. Pour over chicken; cover and place in refrigerator to marinate overnight. When ready to cook, remove chicken from marinade. Place chicken parts in shallow pan. Bake in 350° oven for about 1 hour; pour marinade over chicken and continue baking until tender.

Hannah Dankoff

Oregano Chicken

2½-3 pound fryer, cut up	1 can (6 ounce) frozen orange
1½ teaspoons salt	juice, thawed
½ cup flour	1 juice can water
1 cup shortening	2 tablespoons dark brown sugar
⅛ teaspoon pepper	½ teaspoon oregano

Sprinkle chicken pieces with 1 teaspoon salt. Mix flour, remaining salt and pepper in a bag. Add chicken. Shake several times to coat chicken pieces evenly. Brown chicken in shortening and spoon off excess fat. Combine remaining ingredients. Add to chicken. Cover. Simmer about ½ hour turning several times. If sauce is too thick, add water. Accompany with hot rice.

Edna Berman

Chicken Marengo

1 fryer (2½-3 pounds) cut up
1/3 cup flour
1½ teaspoons salt
¼ teaspoon pepper
2 tablespoons oil
1 4-ounce can sliced mushrooms, drained

1 clove garlic, minced
¼ teaspoon thyme
1 package golden G. Washington seasoning
1½ cups hot water
1 6-ounce can tomato paste
1/3 cup dry white wine

Coat chicken with mixture of flour, salt, and pepper; in large skillet brown chicken in oil. Add mushrooms, garlic and thyme. Cook 5 minutes. Pour off fat. Dissolve seasoning in hot water; combine with tomato paste and pour over chicken. Simmer, covered 30 minutes. Add wine; simmer 15 minutes more. Serves 4-6.

Arlean Levinson

Stuffed Chicken Breasts Roma

6 10-ounce boned chicken breasts
2 tablespoons chopped green onion
½ cup margarine

1½ cup soft bread crumbs
¼ pound chopped salami
Garlic salt

Saute onion in 3 tablespoons margarine until soft. Stir in crumbs and salami. Spoon stuffing into breasts. Secure with toothpicks. Grill over charcoal fire. Baste with melted margarine. Sprinkle with garlic salt.

Maxine Straus

Waterzooi
(a peasant dish from Belgium)

1 stewing chicken cut into serving pieces or a broiler-fryer, adjusting the cooking time
1¾ cups water
1 teaspoon salt
¼ cup margarine
¼ teaspoon thyme
1 bay leaf

4 medium carrots, peeled and quartered
3 stalks celery, cut in three-inch pieces
4 leeks, peeled and cut in three-inch pieces
8 small white onions, peeled
3 egg yolks, beaten

Place chicken in a deep kettle with 1½ cups water and salt. Cover. Bring to a boil; reduce heat and simmer about 1 hour or until chicken is tender. Meanwhile, bring margarine and remaining ¼ cup water to boil in a saucepan. Add thyme, bay leaf, and prepared vegetables. Cover tightly and bring to a boil. Reduce heat and simmer about 30 minutes or until vegetables are tender. (Additional water may be added during cooking to prevent sticking). Remove bay leaf. When chicken is tender remove from broth; set aside. Stir about ¼ cup chicken broth into beaten egg yolks; return to pot and gradually stir over medium heat until broth is slightly thickened. Add chicken and hot vegetables with juices. Serve at once in soup plates. May be served with rice if desired. Serves 4-5.

Beatrice DiMora

Barbecued Chicken

3½ pound frying chicken   Salad oil

Cut chicken into serving pieces. Place in shallow baking dish, brush with oil and bake in moderate oven 375° for 45 minutes, or until browned. In the meantime, prepare the following barbecue sauce:

¼ cup salad oil	1 tablespoon Worcestershire
¼ chopped onions	sauce
1 tablespoon brown sugar	¼ cup lemon juice
½ teaspoon salt	½ cup water
¼ teaspoon paprika	1 cup chili sauce

Place salad oil and onion in saucepan. Cook over low heat, stirring frequently, for 10 minutes. Add remaining ingredients and simmer 15 minutes, stirring occasionally. Remove from heat. When chicken is brown, pour sauce over it and continue baking 45 minutes. Baste frequently.

Priscilla Brown

Barbeque Sauce for Chicken

1 8-ounce can jellied cranberry	2 tablespoons brown sugar
sauce	¼ teaspoon salt
1 8-ounce can tomato sauce	1 tablespoon lemon juice
1 tablespoon vegetable oil	

Combine all ingredients in a sauce pan and heat until everything is blended and smooth. Pour on chicken and baste.

Marlene Elkin

Marinade for Chicken

¾ cup oil	Few drops Tabasco sauce
¼ cup vinegar	3 tablespoons brown sugar
1 clove fresh garlic, chopped	2 tablespoons prepared mustard
fine	

Mix together in a jar. Pour over chicken. Marinate several hours.

Lil Orlen

Cumberland Sauce

1 cup red currant jelly	1 teaspoon dry mustard
1 can frozen orange juice	⅛ teaspoon ginger
4 tablespoons sherry	¼ teaspoon Tabasco sauce

Simmer all together until hot and smooth, stirring constantly. Use with any kind of poultry.

Julia Berlove

Apricot Glazed Chicken Breasts

4 boned chicken breasts	4 whole pitted apricots
½ bottle Italian salad dressing	4 teaspoons apricot preserves
1 cup corn flake crumbs	

Dip each chicken breast in dressing and then in crumbs. Place one apricot inside of breast and fold over. Top each with 1 teaspoon of preserves. Bake on cookie sheet 1 hour at 350°.

Jill Musicus

Marinated Glazed Chicken

2 chickens, in eighths or quarters
1 jar orange marmalade (9-12 ounces)
1 envelope onion soup mix
1 bottle Russian or Thousand Island dressing

Mix last three ingredients. Marinate chicken in sauce overnight or a few hours. Use all of the sauce in baking. Bake in open pan at 350° for 1 hour or until nicely brown. Baste while baking. Serves 8.

Bea Apple

New Jersey Chicken

1 cup tomato sauce
½ cup red wine
1 package dry onion soup mix
3-3½ pound chicken, cut up

Combine first three ingredients and pour over chicken. Bake, uncovered, at 350° for 1½ hours. Serves 4.

Linda Rock

Crispy Baked Chicken

4 whole chicken breasts or 8 halves
8-ounce bottle French dressing
Salt and pepper
Lemon juice

Marinate chicken overnight in French dressing. Next day, shake off French dressing until only film remains on chicken. Salt and pepper chicken lightly. Put in single layer in foil-lined pan. Bake one hour in 450° oven. To the remaining French dressing, add equal amount of lemon juice and baste chicken with this mixture three times during baking. Should puff up and brown nicely. (Diet French dressing may be used instead of regular bottled French dressing.)

Helen Berger

Chicken in Corn Flakes

2 cut-up chickens
3 cups crumbled corn flakes
¾ cup melted margarine
1 teaspoon garlic powder
½ teaspoon salt
Dash pepper

Wash and dry chickens. Combine corn flakes, garlic powder, salt & pepper in bowl. Dip chicken in melted margarine and roll in corn flake mixture. Place on cookie sheet. Bake at 350°, 1½ hours.

Linda Ruda

Chicken Diable

3 pound fryer, quartered
¼ cup pareve margarine
½ cup honey
¼ cup prepared mustard
1 teaspoon salt
1 teaspoon curry powder

Wash chicken pieces and dry. Melt margarine, honey, mustard, salt and curry powder together. Roll chicken pieces in mixture and arrange, cut side down, in a single layer in a shallow baking pan. Bake at 375° for 1¼ hours, or until tender and richly glazed. Serve with boiled rice.

Fritzie Levine

Chicken a la Puff

1/3 cup flour
2 teaspoons salt
¼ teaspoon pepper
2½-3 pound fryer, disjointed
¼ cup oil
1 cup sifted all-purpose flour
1 teaspoon baking powder

1 teaspoon salt
3 well-beaten eggs
¾ cup non-dairy cream diluted
 with ¾ cup water
¼ cup margarine, melted
¼ cup chopped parsley

Combine 1/3 cup flour, salt and pepper. Coat chicken pieces with mixture; brown in hot oil. Place chicken in 2-quart casserole or 11 x 7 x 2 bake-and-serve dish. Sift flour, baking powder and salt together. Combine remaining ingredients, add to dry ingredients and beat until smooth. Pour over chicken. Bake at 350° for 1 hour or until batter turns golden brown. The batter puffs up around the chicken as it bakes. 4-5 servings.

Bertha Goldstein

Sesame Chicken

3 tablespoons margarine
3 tablespoons oil
1 cup flour
1 cut-up chicken

1 small box sesame seeds
¼ cup chopped scallions
1 cup white wine

Melt together the margarine and oil; let cool. Flour chicken parts and coat with oil mixture. Place skin side down in baking dish. Sprinkle with ½ box of sesame seeds. Bake at 400° for 30 minutes. Turn chicken over and sprinkle on the rest of the sesame seeds and scallions. Pour wine into pan; continue baking at 375° for 45 minutes, basting often. Serves 4.

Linda Rock

Chicken Shrevesport

4 cut-up chickens
Flour
1 14-ounce bottle tomato ketchup
1 6-ounce bottle root beer
1 teaspoon celery salt
1 teaspoon onion salt

Cayenne pepper to taste
1 tablespoon Worcestershire
 sauce
2 onions, cut up
2 celery stalks, cut up

Dip chicken pieces in flour and fry in skillet in oil, not too well done. Place chicken in roaster. Mix ketchup, root beer, celery salt, onion salt and pepper and pour over chicken. Cover and steam slowly in 300° oven for about 1 hour; add Worcestershire sauce, onions and celery to gravy and continue steaming until tender about 30-45 minutes longer. Serves 8-10.

Julia Berlove

Chicken Sweet and Hot

2 fryers, quartered
½ cup margarine
¼ cup Worcestershire sauce
1 clove garlic, minced
½ cup red currant jelly

1 tablespoon Dijon mustard
1 cup orange juice
1 teaspoon ginger
3 dashes Tabasco

Combine all ingredients except chicken, heat and stir until jelly is melted and sauce is smooth. Put chicken into baking dish and cover with marinade for 3 hours. Cook covered in preheated oven, for 1 hour at 350° . Uncover, increase oven temperature to 400°. Baste frequently until chicken is an even brown, about 45 minutes. Serves 4-6.

Arlean Levinson

Country Captain's Chicken

6 chicken breasts, boned, skinned and halved
¼ cup flour
1 teaspoon salt
¼ teaspoon pepper
3 tablespoons oil
2 small onions, minced
1 green pepper, minced
1 clove garlic, minced or pressed

1-2 teaspoons curry powder
2 tablespoons chopped parsley
Pinch of thyme
2 cups Italian pear-shaped
tomatoes
¼ cup, or more, dried currants
Almonds, blanched, split and
toasted

Shake chicken breasts in a bag with flour, salt and pepper. In a large skillet, saute chicken in oil until slightly browned. Remove breasts and keep warm (150° oven.) In remaining fat, saute onions until golden. Add pepper and garlic; simmer for 3-4 minutes. Stir in parsley, thyme, curry powder and tomatoes. Simmer sauce 15 minutes. Add chicken; cover; simmer until tender. Five minutes before finished cooking, add dried currants. Sprinkle with almonds. Serve with rice.

Dr. Charles Solky

Chicken Breasts Almondine

4 boneless chicken breasts
¼ cup chicken fat or pareve
margarine
3 tablespoon cognac
1 clove garlic, minced
½ cup sliced mushrooms
1 tablespoon cornstarch

½ cup beef broth or water
½ cup wine
Salt and pepper to taste
½ teaspoon paprika
½ cup blanched, slivered almonds
1 tablespoon pareve margarine

Brown chicken slowly in hot fat. Heat cognac. Ignite with a match and pour over chicken. When flame dies down, remove chicken and set aside. Add garlic and mushrooms to skillet and cook for 3 or 4 minutes. Dissolve cornstarch in broth. Add, with wine, to skillet. Simmer 3 minutes, stirring. Return chicken to skillet. Season, cover and simmer 25 minutes. Remove to a heated serving platter and garnish with almonds which have been browned in margarine.

Selma Soloway

Pecan Stuffed Chicken Breasts

4 small whole chicken breasts
Lemon juice
6 tablespoons melted margarine
3 cups toasted bread crumbs
½ cup diced celery
1/3 cup chopped onion

¾ cup chopped pecans
¾ teaspoon Accent
1 teaspoon salt
⅛ teaspoon pepper
¼ cup water

Brush each chicken breast on both sides with lemon juice and 2 tablespoons of melted margarine. Combine remaining margarine with other ingredients. Toss lightly. Make four mounds of stuffing and arrange on four squares of double thickness aluminum foil. Place on baking sheets. Place a whole chicken breast, skin side up on mound of stuffing. (The breast covers the stuffing). Fold foil around chicken to make individual packages. Bake at 350° for 40 minutes; increase oven to 400°, open foil and bake 10 minutes longer or until brown. Serves 4.

Eulah Feier

Rudy's Chicken Breasts in Wine

8 chicken breasts, skinned and
   boned
¼ pound pareve margarine
Salt and pepper to taste

½ cup chicken soup
½ cup sherry or sauterne wine
½ cup pareve milk substitute
½ pint fresh mushrooms

Pound chicken breasts flat if preferred. Saute breasts in margarine. Add salt and pepper to taste. When almost cooked remove from pan. Add soup, wine and milk substitute to pan and simmer until blended. Saute mushrooms. Place chicken in casserole. Pour over sauce and mushrooms. Bake, covered, at 350° about 1 hour or until tender.

Ruth Salesin

Easy Roast Chicken

3-3½ pounds chicken legs and
   breasts
½ cup Catalina dressing

¼ cup boiling water
Salt, pepper, onion salt, paprika
to taste

Line deep cookie sheet or glass baking dish with aluminum foil. Place legs or breasts of chicken skin side up on foil. Mix Catalina dressing with ¼ cup boiling water. Pour over chicken parts and season. Roast in 350 degree oven for 1-1½ hours, depending on size of pieces. Serves 4.

Daisy Cherry

Roast Chicken Burgundy

4-4½ pounds chicken
Salt and pepper
½ cup soft pareve margarine
½ teaspoon dry mustard
½ teaspoon powdered ginger

⅛ teaspoon garlic powder
Dry crumbs
1 can mushrooms
2 cups Burgundy wine

Salt chicken well, rubbing inside and out. Sprinkle with pepper. When margarine is soft, mix in mustard, ginger and garlic. Spread over bird, inside and out. Tie legs and wings. Dust surface with fine dry crumbs. Place in roasting pan, breast side up. Roast uncovered at 350°, adding wine and mushroom at end of first ½ hour. Baste every 20 minutes. Bake until chicken is tender. Serves 6-8.

Rhoda Ann Herzog

Southern Fried Chicken

3 pound fryer, cut up
1 cup flour
1 teaspoon baking powder

2 teaspoons Lawry's seasoned
salt
½-¾ cup oil or fat

Coat pieces of chicken heavily with mixture of flour, baking powder and seasonings. Brown on both sides in very hot fat, to a depth of 1½ inches. Reduce heat, and cook slowly about 1 hour, turning pieces to brown evenly on all sides. Serves 4.

Millie Rosenbaum

Elegant Chicken Casserole

4 cups cooked chicken	½ teaspoon tarragon
2 teaspoons salt	1 tablespoon lemon juice
1 teaspoon pepper	2 cups mayonnaise
¼ cup extra dry vermouth	1 cup sliced, blanched, toasted
4 cups celery, finely chopped	almonds
¼ cup grated onion	1 cup crushed corn flakes

Season chicken parts with salt and pepper. Bake in a 325° oven, one hour or until tender, basting with extra dry vermouth several times during baking. Allow to cool in vermouth. Remove chicken from bone, skin and cut into ¾-inch cubes, (the dark meat slightly smaller). Thoroughly combine chicken with remaining ingredients, except corn flakes. Allow to stand at least 1 hour. Add additional seasoning, if desired. Spoon into a greased shallow glass baking pan 8 x 12.** Top with crushed corn flakes and bake in a 350° oven for 25 to 30 minutes, or until heated through and lightly browned. Approximately 12-15 servings *4-5 pounds chicken parts — 4 breasts and 4 or 5 thighs, depending upon size. **Casserole can be refrigerated at this point until baking time.

Arline Wiseman

Chicken and Chips Casserole

2 cups diced cooked chicken	½ cup mayonnaise
1 cup diced celery	¼ cup bottled French dressing
½ cup chopped walnuts	1 teaspoon lemon juice
2 tablespoon minced onion	½ teaspoon salt
½ cup pimento stuffed green	¼ teaspoon pepper
olives	1 cup pareve mocha
3 hard boiled eggs, chopped	2 cups crushed potato chips

Combine all ingredients except potato chips. Place in greased two quart shallow casserole. If desired, cover and chill overnite. Top with potato chips, bake at 450° for 20 minutes. Serves 6.

Inez Lipman

South of the Border Casserole

½ cup chopped onion	¼ of a bay leaf
2 tablespoons margarine	3 tablespoons chopped parsley
1 or 2 minced garlic cloves	¼ teaspoon cloves
2 pounds cooked chicken chunks	¼ teaspoon marjoram
1 cup raw rice	½ teaspoon chili powder
1 large can tomatoes	Dash of cayenne
2 cups consomme, beef or	1 tablespoon salt
chicken	⅛ teaspoon pepper

Brown onion and garlic in margarine, then put in bottom of large casserole. Add chicken chunks, raw rice, tomatoes and consomme. Add remaining ingredients and mix thoroughly. Cover and bake for 1½ hours at 350°. Serves 6-8. Excellent buffet dish. May be kept on "warm" in oven for an hour without drying. Double recipe fits 6½-quart casserole. Serves 16.

Ireene Morris

Curried Chicken

4 cups diced, cooked chicken
½ cup finely chopped onion
½ cup finely chopped celery
¼ cup margarine
1/3 cup flour
2 cups chicken broth

1 cup tomato juice
3 teaspoon Worcestershire
  sauce
Salt and pepper
2 teaspoons curry powder

Saute vegetables in margarine. Add flour and blend. Add hot broth and cook until thick, stirring constantly. Add tomato juice, Worcestershire sauce, seasonings and chicken. Heat thoroughly. Serve over rice with chutney. Serves 4.

Ellie Harris

Chicken Divan

5 or 6 pound chicken
1 bunch broccoli
½ cup flour
2 cups chicken broth

1 cup mayonnaise
1 teaspoon lemon juice
1 teaspoon curry
Bread crumbs

Cook chicken until tender. Cook broccoli. In sauce pan, combine flour and chicken broth until thickened. Remove from heat, add mayonnaise, lemon juice, curry and stir well. You may want to add a little more lemon juice. Place chicken and broccoli in layers in casserole. Pour sauce over all, top with bread crumbs and bake for 45 minutes at 400°. Serves 6-8.

Hattie Lipsky

Chicken Pilaf

1 cup rice, raw
2 cups chicken soup or cold
  water
½ teaspoon salt if water is used
1 medium onion, chopped
2 tablespoons vegetable

shortening
2 cups diced cooked chicken
1 cup tomato juice
4 tablespoons hot melted shortening

Rinse rice and drain. Cook in chicken soup or water in double boiler until liquid is absorbed. Saute onion in fat and add diced chicken as soon as onion is light brown. Stir lightly for one minute over moderate heat. Add cooked rice and tomato juice. Turn into well-greased baking dish, topping with hot melted fat. Bake 20 to 30 minutes at 350° until lightly browned. Serves 4.

Eleanor Chiger

Chicken Ring

1 cooked, diced chicken
2 cups soft bread crumbs
5 beaten eggs
1 teaspoon salt
¼ cup chicken fat, melted

3 cups soup stock
2 teaspoons chopped parsley
1 teaspoon chopped onion
1 cup rice, cooked and drained
Pepper to taste

Mix ingredients in order named. Pour into greased ring mold. Bake in slow oven 1 hour. Let stand 10 minutes, then turn out on platter. Fill center with heated peas and mushrooms.

Bea Horn

Duck a la Schwartz

1 duck	1½ cups orange juice
Kosher salt	1½ cups apricot juice
1 green apple, peeled	1 29-ounce can peaches
1 orange, peeled	½ pound fresh cranberries

Rub duck inside and out with salt. Place on rack. Place peeled apple inside body; sew up. Place peeled orange in neck; sew up. Mix orange juice and apricot juice. Prick duck all over with fork. Pour one-half of juices over duck. Bake in 325° oven for 2 hours. Continue to baste with remaining juice, if necessary. 20 minutes before duck is done, place canned peaches on rack and fill peaches with whole cranberries. Baste. Cut duck into four parts with poultry shears. Serve immediately. Serves 4 amply.

Hedy Bagatelle

Easy Duck a l'Orange

1 average size duckling	1 11-ounce can mandarin oranges,
1 6-ounce can concentrated	drained
orange juice, thawed	Sherry wine (6-ounce juice can)

Clean duck and pat dry with paper towels. Score breast diagonally on either side of breastbone at 90° angles. Bake on rack uncovered, at 350° for 2 hours. Cool. Discard fat. Cut into serving pieces and marinate, covered, overnight in refrigerator, in orange juice and juice can full of sherry, turning once or twice. Add mandarin oranges and bake at 350° until crispy, (about ½ to ¾ hours). Serves 3-4.

Sue Kiner

Orange Broiled Duck

1 large duck, cut in halves or	¼ cup sauterne wine
quarters	¼ teaspoon ginger
6 tablespoons orange marmalade	

In a broiler pan with a rack, place duck, skin side down, with top surface 6 inches from the heat. Broil 40-50 minutes, turning several times for even browning. If some spots start to brown too fast, cover them with aluminum foil. Combine marmalade, wine and ginger. During last 10 minutes of broiling, brush one side of duck with sauce, broil 5 minutes. Turn, brush with sauce, broil 5 minutes more. Serves 2-4.

Marcia Isner

Rock Cornish Hens

8 Rock Cornish hens	Paprika,
Salt and pepper	1 10-ounce jar currant jelly
¼ pound pareve soft margarine	Parsley

Wash and dry hens, sprinkle with salt and pepper and tie legs together. Rub hens with softened margarine and sprinkle with paprika. Roast in large shallow roasting pan at 425° for about 1 hour, or until tender and well browned, basting with melted margarine. When hens are done, spoon some melted currant jelly over each. Serves 8. Garnish with parsley.

Rose Adelstein

Bread Crumb Dressing

1 large onion
4 tablespoons chicken fat
3 stalks celery, cut fine
½ cup chopped walnuts
1 challah
1 teaspoon poultry seasoning

1 teaspoon salt
½ teaspoon pepper
4 heaping cups grated stale challah or other white bread
2 eggs

Saute onion in melted fat for 2 minutes. Add celery and nuts and stir while cooking over moderate heat for 5 minutes. Add bread, which has been soaked in cold water and squeezed, poultry seasoning, salt and pepper, grated challah crumbs; stir for one minute. Beat eggs in a bowl, add to cooked mixture in frying pan, stir well. If mixture is too dry, add more fat.

Jennie Levinson

Stuffing or Kugel

2 large onions, sliced
1 8-ounce can mushrooms,
drained
1 envelope G. Washington
broth
1½ large challahs, cubed and

toasted
6 eggs
¼ teaspoon oregano
¼ cup hot water
2 tablespoons margarine

Saute onions in small amount of margarine. Add mushrooms when onions are golden. Pour envelope of broth over challah cubes. Beat eggs, add oregano and hot water and pour this mixture over challah cubes. Add onions and mushrooms. Melt margarine in casserole and pour in challah mixture. Bake at 350° for ½ hour or use as stuffing. Salt and pepper may be substituted for broth mixture.

Mary Weltman

Rice-Pecan Stuffing or Casserole

2½ cups brown rice
7½ cups water
7½ teaspoons instant
chicken soup mix
½ cup margarine or chicken fat
1 cup chopped onion
1 cup chopped celery

¼ cup minced parsley
2 cups chopped pecans
1½ teaspoons salt
1 teaspoon thyme
½ teaspoon poultry seasoning
½ teaspoon pepper
Fresh mushrooms, optional

Wash rice, cook in water to which you have added the soup mix, bring to a boil, turn down flame, cover and cook about 40 minutes. Water should all be absorbed. Melt margarine in skillet, add onion, celery and parsley. Saute over low heat until tender, stirring frequently. Add mushrooms and cook a few minutes longer. Combine with cooked rice, pecans and seasonings, toss lightly together. This is enough to stuff a 12 pound turkey. For casserole, put in lightly greased casserole and bake until crisp on top.

Ida Gould

Wild Rice Stuffing

1 package wild and long-grained rice mix
½ cup celery, diced
5 ounce-can water chestnuts, sliced

3 ounce-can chopped mushrooms, drained
4 tablespoons melted margarine
1 tablespoon soy sauce

Prepare rice according to directions. Add remaining ingredients and mix well. Makes 4 cups of stuffing.

Linda Rock

Stuffing for 10-Pound Turkey

2 medium onions, diced
¼ pound parve margarine
¾ loaf sliced bread, cubed
¼ cup water
1½ cups diced celery

¼ teaspoon salt
⅛ teaspoon pepper
½ teaspoon sage
2 tablespoons brown sugar
½ pound chestnuts, optional

Saute onions in margarine until soft and golden. In large bowl, put bread cubes and water. Add sauteed onions and margarine, raw celery, sugar and seasonings. Toss lightly, add chestnuts and stuff bird. Any leftover dressing may be baked in separate pan covered with aluminum foil. If chestnuts are used, they may be prepared in advance. Slit and bake at 350° for 15-20 minutes. Shell and chop fine. Store in refrigerator until ready to use.

Adeline Evans

Turkey Giblet Stuffing

Giblets
1 loaf sliced white bread
2 large diced onions
1½ cups diced celery
1 pound mushrooms

1 turkey liver
Margarine
Salt
Pepper

Cook giblets as one would for soup. Allow to cool, then grind or cut fine. Reserve stock. Toast sliced bread in oven, then cube and put aside. Saute onions, celery, mushrooms and liver in margarine. Add ground giblets, and sauteed ingredients to cubed bread. Add stock from giblets to moisten. Season to taste. Stuff turkey just before roasting. Will fill 12-14 pound turkey.

Verna Braverman

Turkey Gravy

4 tablespoons fat from turkey pan
2 tablespoons flour
2 cups hot stock or boiling water

Salt
Pepper
Cooked gizzards
Chopped parsley

Pour fat in pan. Add flour and brown. Add water or stock; cook 5 minutes. Season with salt and pepper. Add gizzards and parsley.

Hattie Lipsky

Sephardic

THE ROCHESTER SEPHARDIC COMMUNITY

The term Sephardim literally means Jews with a Spanish background. When used in connection with Jews of today, it applies to descendants of those who, after their expulsion from Spain in 1492, found their way eastward to Italy and countries in the Eastern Mediterranean area or northward to towns such as Amsterdam and London and from there sometimes westward to North and South America.

The earliest Jewish settlers in both North and South America were predominantly Sephardim. It is not improbable that Christopher Columbus came from a Sephardic Jewish background. Today, in this country, there are a number of communities of Sephardim, one of which is in Rochester.

In 1906, a stream of Jews began to arrive in Rochester about a week before Passover. They were strange because they did not speak Yiddish as all the other Jews did. Although they adhered to the traditional in religious matters, their customs, language and national origin, marked them off as a distinct group. These were Sephardic Jews, who came from Monastir in Serbia, then a part of the Turkish Empire, now within the borders of Yugoslavia. They spoke Turkish, in addition to a jargon, Judeo-Spanish or Ladino, common to most Mediterrean Jews. There was a great stir in the Jewish community in Rochester over these strange people who were so different from them.

For the first three or four years, the community consisted only of men. They boarded in various homes in the Joseph Avenue area. Time passed, and now we have a flourishing Sephardic community, with a new synagogue dedicated in 1965.

Through the endless wanderings of the Sephardic Jews, their recipes reflect the influences of the countries in which they lived. Those who lived in the Middle East absorbed the cuisine of that culture, and so on. In this section of the cook book, we have attempted to bring you a cross section of Sephardic recipes prepared by experts of the community.

Mrs. Sol Cohen

Cold Cucumber Soup

1 pint plain yoghurt
1 pint sour cream
½ cup buttermilk
1 mashed garlic clove

3 tablespoons oil
Salt and pepper
3 cucumbers, finely chopped

Mix all together and chill. Serve with French bread or crackers. Note: 2 pints of sour cream may be used, omitting yoghurt.

Dora Levy

Greek Lemon Soup

2 quarts chicken soup
1 cup matzo meal
Salt to taste

3 eggs
2 lemons
¼ cup chopped walnuts, optional

Warm chicken soup, add matzo meal slowly, stirring constantly. Have ready 3 eggs, beaten well, and gradually beat in juice of 2 lemons. Add chicken broth slowly to egg mixture, mixing all the time. Be sure the soup is not hot so it will not curdle the eggs. Return to stove and heat very slowly, stirring constantly. This soup is better when prepared in the morning and reheated later. For a specially delicious and gourmet touch, add chopped walnuts when the egg mixture is added. Note: Rice, fine egg noodles or egg farfel may be used instead of matzo meal.

Dora Levy

Cheese Bourekas

1 pound Feta Cheese
2 pounds pressed cheese or
  pot cheese
4-5 eggs

1 teaspoon salt, or to taste
1 pound Filo sheets
Oil

Crumble Feta cheese into small pieces; add pressed cheese and blend well with eggs and salt. Pastry sheets should be put between 2 sheets of waxed paper and covered with a damp towel so they will not dry out. Take out 2 sheets at a time and place on a flat surface; brush with oil very lightly. Each strip should be about 3½ inches wide; double fold, oil again. Place a heaping tablespoon of cheese mixture in bottom right hand corner of strip and fold into triangular shape; continue folding, making sure with each fold that the bottom edge is parallel with the alternate side edge; lightly oil top of finished triangle. Continue until all pastry sheets and cheese mixture are used. Bake at 425° for 20-25 minutes or until golden brown. If not quite brown, put pan on top shelf of oven. Serve warm.

Variations: 1. 3 boxes of frozen chopped spinach may be added to the above recipe. Thaw spinach and squeeze out as much water as possible and mix with the cheese. Proceed as above. 2. Oil 13 x 9 pan very generously. Line pan with pastry sheets and oil each sheet lightly. Use about ½ of the sheets on bottom pan. Add cheese mixture and spread carefully over sheets. Top cheese mixture with other half of pastry sheets. Bake at 375° for 30 minutes and about 10 minutes on top shelf of oven to a golden brown. Cut into 3-inch diamond shape pieces. Serve warm as an hors d'oeuvre.

Dora Levy

Cottage Cheese and Eggplant Pie

1 medium eggplant
2 eggs, beaten
Matzo meal
Oil

2 pounds farmers cheese
6 eggs
Salt and pepper

Peel and slice eggplant. Dip into egg and roll in matzo meal. Fry in oil until brown. Lay a flat layer in 10 x 12 greased dish. Mix cheese, eggs and seasonings. Spread over eggplant. Dot with oil. Bake at 350° until top is brown, about 40 minutes.

Bess Kopen

Cottage Cheese and Spinach Pie

1 10-ounce package fresh
  spinach
2 pounds dry cottage cheese
4 eggs, beaten

Salt and pepper
6 matzos
Oil

Chop spinach. Mix cheese, eggs and seasonings; add to spinach. Soak matzo until soft and squeeze dry. Place layer of matzo in bottom of greased 10 x 12 pan, spread with cottage cheese and spinach mixture. Top with layer of matzo. Spread oil over top. Bake at 350%until brown.

Bess Kopen

Peta-de-Spinoche
(Matzo Spinach Pie)

2 10-ounce packages fresh
  spinach
4 eggs, beaten
1 teaspoon salt

1 10-ounce box matzo
1 5-ounce package walnuts,
  chopped

Wash spinach, cut off stems, let drain. Cut spinach in small pieces into large bowl; add beaten eggs, salt and chopped nuts. (Save part of nuts to put on top of Peta.) Soak matzos until pliable. Line a greased 13 x 9 pan with ½ of matzos; spread with spinach mixture; cover with balance of matzos. Sprinkle top with remainder of chopped walnuts and bake at 400° for 1 hour.

Betty Hurvitz

Casa cum Webo
(Cheese and Eggs)

Cooking oil
2 small jars roasted red peppers
1 pound pressed cheese
½ teaspoon salt

1 teaspoon crushed hot red
  pepper seasoning
5 eggs, slightly beaten
½ small can tomato paste

Cover bottom of large skillet with oil and heat; add peppers and cook until soft; break up with fork. Add pressed cheese, to which salt has been added; mash cheese and peppers; sprinkle hot red pepper seasoning over top. Blend beaten eggs into tomato paste; pour over cheese and pepper mixture. Cover and continue cooking slowly until egg sets. May be put in 350° oven and baked until egg sets — comes out like a fluffy omelet. Serves 4-6.

Marilyn Aroesty

Wevos Haminadoes
(Turkish Eggs)

1 dozen eggs   5 or 6 quart pot with cover

Place eggs in large pot and fill with water to the top. Cover and cook on very low heat for 7 to 8 hours. Note: If brown shells are desired, add coffee grounds or onion skins to water.

June Cohen

Bamyas
(Okra and Tomato Sauce)

1 #2 can tomato puree   ¼ cup brown sugar
1 clove garlic, minced   ¼ cup lemon juice
1 small onion, diced   2 packages frozen okra, thawed
1½ teaspoon salt

Cook all ingredients, except okra, for 1 hour until all flavors are absorbed. Add 2 packages of okra. Cook until okra is tender, about 10-15 minutes. You can serve this over fluffy cooked rice, noodles or spaghetti if you like. Serves 6-8. Note: May be cooked with stew meat or meatballs added.

June Cohen

Fijones (Beans)

1 pound white kidney beans or   4 cups water
  navy marrow beans   1½ teaspoons salt
1 medium onion, chopped   ⅛ teaspoon pepper
1 pound stew beef or short ribs ½ teaspoon paprika
1 8-ounce can tomato sauce   Oil

Before cooking, soak beans in water to cover for 2-3 hours. In a 4-quart Dutch oven, put in just enough oil to cover bottom of pot. Brown onion. Add meat and tomato sauce. Simmer covered about ¾ hour. Drain beans. add together with water, salt, pepper, and paprika to meat. Cover and cook for 3-4 hours over very low heat. Do not stir with a spoon; it will break up the beans. Just hold pot by the handles and shake if necessary. If mixture gets too dry, add water. Serves 6-8 as a side dish. Can be frozen; tastes better when frozen.

Sarah Calderon

Rice Pilaf

1 cup long grain rice, uncooked   2 tablespoons chicken fat (or
2¼ cups chicken soup (or beef   oil)
  broth)   Salt to taste
3 tablespoons tomato sauce

Toast rice in oven, carefully, so it will not burn. Rinse in cold water. Bring tomato sauce, chicken soup and chicken fat to a boil. Add rice slowly so boiling won't stop. Boil for 15 minutes, then cover and simmer gently for 8 minutes. Stir rice once and keep covered until all soup has been absorbed. Fluff up with a fork. Sauteed mushrooms and onions may be added when rice is served.

Dora Levy

Musaka
(Eggplant and Ground Beef Pie)

2 medium-sized eggplants	1 teaspoon salt
2 eggs, beaten	¾ teaspoon pepper
½ cup oil	2 tablespoons raw rice
1 onion, chopped	1 egg
2 tablespoons chopped parsley	½ cup water
1 pound ground beef	1 tablespoon pareve margarine

Peel eggplant and cut lengthwise into ½-inch slices. Dip slices into beaten eggs and fry in hot oil on both sides until browned. Set aside. Brown onion in same oil and add parsley. Remove. Combine meat, salt, pepper, rice and egg. Brown in same oil. Line baking dish with part of fried eggplant slices. Place meat mixture with onion and parsley added on layer of eggplant. Alternate fried eggplant and ground meat in layers. Add water and margarine and bake at 350° for 40 minutes. Serve hot.

Dora Levy

Leek Patties

1 pound ground meat	6 medium leeks
1 teaspoon salt	1 egg, beaten
⅛ teaspoon pepper	¼ cup flour or ¼ cup matzo
1/3 cup chopped parsley	meal
1 egg, beaten	

Clean leeks and cut into 1-inch pieces. Cook until very tender. Drain well and chop very fine. Add first 5 ingredients to leeks and form into 1½-inch patties. Dip first into flour, then into beaten egg and fry until golden brown. Serve hot, as a side dish. Note: Patties may be cooked with the juice of 1 lemon and a tablespoon of margarine or chicken fat. They may also be eaten cold. They are delicious this way. Serves 4.

Dora Levy

Spinach Patties

2 10-ounce packages frozen, chopped spinach	Salt and pepper to taste
	Oil
½ pound ground meat	1 cup condensed chicken soup
1 egg, beaten	1 cup water
1 tablespoon bread crumbs	

Thaw spinach; strain through colander, removing as much liquid as possible. In mixing bowl, add meat, egg, crumbs, salt and pepper to spinach. Mix thoroughly; let stand. Shape into small balls; flatten. Heat oil in frying pan; lightly fry patties, turn quickly and drain on toweling. Arrange 24 patties in baking dish; pour over chicken soup mixed with water. Cover with foil; punch holes in the top. Bake at 350° for 1 hour. Remove foil and allow to remain in oven until browned and liquid is mostly absorbed.

Marilyn Aroesty

Pastele

8 medium potatoes
1 pound ground meat
1 teaspoon salt
¼ teaspoon cinnamon
⅛ teaspoon pepper

1 onion, diced
½ cup water
½ cup flour
1 beaten egg

Mix ground meat with salt, cinnamon, pepper, onion, and water. Cook until all water evaporates. Boil potatoes in skins until tender. Peel and either grind or mash fine. Season with salt and pepper to taste. Take some of the mashed potatoes the size of a tennis ball, make a hole large enough to hold a soup spoon of ground meat mixture. Shape the mashed potato around the ground meat to form a round semi-flat knish. Do this until all the meat and potatoes are used up. Dip the Pastele (that is what you just made) in flour. Coat it on all sides. Dip it in beaten egg. Fry in oil until golden brown on both sides. Makes 10-12.

June Cohen

Stuffed Tomatoes, Peppers And Zucchini

6 fresh green peppers
6 tomatoes
3 medium zucchini
2 pounds ground chuck
2 slices challah, wet and
  squeezed dry
½ cup raw rice
1 onion, chopped fine

1½ teaspoon salt
Garlic powder, pepper, parsley
  flakes
2 medium onions, quartered
1 #2 can stewed tomatoes
1 teaspoon sugar
Salt and pepper

Parboil whole green peppers; allow them to steep in covered pot for a few minutes. Cut crown off tomatoes, scoop out middle and set aside. Peel zucchini and cut into thirds. Scoop out middle, making sure to leave one end closed. Remove stems and seeds from peppers, being very careful not to crack peppers. Set aside. Mix next 6 ingredients well. Stuff carefully into vegetables. Cover bottom of pan with all the scooped out insides of tomatoes and zucchini along with quartered onions. Place stuffed vegetables alternately in 8 x 11 pan. Pour can of stewed tomatoes over all vegetables. Sprinkle with sugar and a little salt and pepper. Bake covered at 300° for 1½ hours, uncovered at 350° for ½ hour until nicely browned. This can be frozen. Serves 4-6.

Evelyn Berlowitz

Yaprakes
(Stuffed Grape Leaves)

1 large jar grape leaves
2 onions, chopped
Oil
2 pounds ground meat

¼ cup raw rice
Salt and pepper to taste
Juice of 1 lemon

Separate leaves; break off one stem at a time and rinse. Saute onions in oil. Add ½ of onions to meat; add washed rice, salt and pepper; mix. Place a spoonful of meat mixture on shiny side of leaf and roll up as for cabbage. Spread remainder of sauted onions on bottom of roasting pan; place 2 layers of rolled meat over onions. Bake, covered, at 350° for 1½ hours. Towards end, pour on juice of 1 lemon, or more to taste. Makes 60 hors d'oeuvres.

Dora Nahmias

Arroz Con Pollo
(Spanish Chicken and Rice)

1 medium size chicken,
    cut in eighths
1 medium size jar of
    marinara sauce
1 or 2 onions
1 green pepper

1 can mushrooms
1 cup green olives
2 teaspoons oregano
1 teaspoon garlic salt or
    fresh garlic
1 cup white rice, raw

Place chicken in large baking pan. Pour marinara sauce over chicken. Cut up onions, green pepper, mushrooms and olives. Spread over chicken. Add seasoning. Cover and bake at 325° for about 1 hour. There will be a lot of gravy. Cook rice according to package directions. Pour gravy over rice and serve.

Maddy Rubens

Lemon-Egg Sauce

5 eggs, beaten
Juice of 1 lemon

1 tablespoon water
Salt to taste

Beat eggs well, add lemon juice, water and salt. Heat oil in pan; add egg mixture and cook over low heat, stirring constantly until thickened. Excellent over meat or fowl.

Marilyn Aroesty

Baklava

2 cups walnuts
1 cup almonds
3 slices toasted bread
1/3 cup sesame seeds

1 teaspoon cinnamon
¼ cup sugar
1 package Filo leaves
Oil

Grind nuts, toasted bread and sesame seeds together. Add cinnamon and sugar. Mix well. Take Filo leaves out of package and lay out on table. Cover with damp towel, so they will not dry out. Brush a 13 x 9 or 14 x 10 pan with oil. Lay 2 Filo sheets in pan, sprinkle with oil, lay another 2 Filo sheets, sprinkle again with oil. Sprinkle with some of the nut mixture. Continue in this manner until pan is filled within 4 sheets of the top. Take 2 of the last 4 sheets, lay them on top, sprinkle with oil, then lay the last 2 sheets and brush with oil. First cut lengthwise 1½ inches wide, then cut diagonally to make diamond-shaped pastry. Bake at 350° for 30 minutes or until golden brown. Pour hot syrup over baked pastry upon removing from oven. Allow to cool overnight.

Syrup

3 cups sugar
3 cups water

½ teaspoon lemon juice
½ cup honey

Combine sugar and water. Bring to boil and continue cooking for 15 minutes until slightly thick. Add honey and lemon juice while still boiling. Remove from heat and pour over Baklava.

Dora Levy

Taraleekoos
(Sesame Cookies)

3 eggs
1 cup sugar
½ cup oil
1 teaspoon vanilla

3 cups flour
1 teaspoon baking powder
½ teaspoon salt
Sesame seeds

Beat eggs, add sugar, oil, vanilla and mix well. Add flour, baking powder and salt; mix first with large spoon then with hands until workable. Roll out ⅛ of dough into strip to thickness of little finger; cut off pieces about 5 inches long, shape like donut and sprinkle with sesame seeds. Repeat for remainder of dough. Bake on greased cookie sheet at 350° for 15-20 minutes. Makes 50-60.

Sarah Cassorla

Kadayif
(Dessert)

40 large shredded wheat
1 cup chopped nuts
2 tablespoons sugar

1 teaspoon cinnamon
¼ cup margarine or butter
2 tablespoons water

Grease 9 x 13 pan and place 20 shredded wheat on bottom. Biscuits may overlap as they shrink a great deal. Combine nuts, sugar and cinnamon and sprinkle over first layer. Cover with remaining biscuits. Melt butter, add water and pour over biscuits. Bake 40-45 minutes at 350° until crisp.

Syrup
½ cup cold water
½ cup light corn syrup

½ cup sugar
1 teaspoon lemon juice

Boil together until soft ball forms when dropped in cold water. Cool and pour on biscuits. Serve cold. Whipped cream may be used for topping.

Veda Aroeste

Arroz con Letche
(Rice Pudding)

1 cup rice, raw
2 cups water
1½ quarts milk

¾ cup sugar, heaping
Cinnamon for topping

Wash, drain and steam rice in water, about 10 minutes. Add milk and sugar; continue cooking, stirring occasionally. After mixture comes to a boil, cook over medium heat 30-35 minutes, or until rice and milk blend to a soft consistency. Pour into bowl and sprinkle liberally with cinnamon, while still warm. Cool at room temperature, cover, then refrigerate. Serve chilled in sherbet glasses. Serves 6-8.

Marilyn Aroesty

Falafel

Falafel is the national "nash" of Israel, comparable to the American hot dog. It consists of a round flat bread (pita), which has been split open at one end and stuffed with fried chick pea balls (falafel), fresh, chopped vegetables and seasoned with a spicy salad dressing (tahina).

Pita (Israeli Flat Bread)

1 ounce fresh yeast or 2
    packages dry yeast
1 teaspoon sugar

1¼ cups lukewarm water
4 cups flour
1 teaspoon salt

Dissolve yeast and sugar in water. Sift flour and salt and add dissolved ingredients. Mix and knead. Divide dough into 20 balls; roll each one out very thin on a floured board. Cover with a towel and set in a warm place for ½ hour. Roll once more very thin and let rise for ½ hour. Bake in a 500° oven for a few minutes until puffed. Fill with falafel balls and salad makings. May be dipped into hommos and tahina as an appetizer.

Carol Goldberg

Falafel

1 pound dry nahit (raw chick
    peas)
¾ cup dry bread crumbs
1½ teaspoon salt

6 cloves fresh garlic
⅛ teaspoon black pepper
1 teaspoon ground Cumin

Soak dry nahit, overnight in cold water. Drain and grind in fine chopper together with the garlic. Add the rest of ingredients. Mix well and form into 1-inch balls. Fry in deep oil until golden brown.

This should be served with Pita (Israeli bread), but can be put in rolls instead. This should be served with Tahina of which a salad dressing is made. The Tahina can be purchased in an import store. The Falafel can be dipped into Tahina dressing and served as hors d'oeuvres.

June Cohen

Tahina Salad Dressing

¼ cup Tahina
¼ cup lemon juice
¼ cup water

1-1½ teaspoons salt
1 clove garlic, chopped fine
1 tablespoon chopped parsley

Mix together above ingredients well. If you find that it is too thick, continue to add extra lemon and water until it is the consistency of a very thick dressing.

June Cohen

Hommos (Israeli Dip)

1 1-pound can cooked nahit
    (Garbanzos)
¾ cup Tahina salad dressing

2 tablespoons chopped parsley
Paprika

Drain can of nahit and reserve the liquid to use if necessary. Mash nahit very well, then add Tahina salad dressing. Mix together. It should be the consistency of a dip. If more liquid is needed, use reserved liquid. Place it in a dish and decorate with chopped parsley and paprika. This can be eaten with Pita (Israeli bread), chips, and other kinds of "nash".

June Cohen

Israeli Vegetable Salad

½ head lettuce	1 cucumber
1 tomato	2 stalks of celery
1 fresh green pepper	

Break lettuce in ½-inch pieces. Dice tomatoes, peppers, and celery. Slice cucumber very thin, Pour dressing over all and toss. Serves 4.

Dressing

¼ cup lemon juice	¼ cup vegetable oil
½ cup water	1 teaspoon oregano
1½ teaspoons salt	1 clove garlic

Mash garlic very fine or put through garlic press. Blend all ingredients very well and pour over cut vegetables. This goes well with Falafel.

June Cohen

Passover Buenueloes (Matzo Fritters)

6 matzos	3 tablespoons matzo meal
6 eggs, beaten	Oil
1/3 cup sugar	Chopped nuts

Break matzos into small pieces and soak in cold water, drain very well. Add eggs, sugar and matzo meal. Blend well. Drop batter by tablespoonfuls into hot fat. Deep fry until golden brown. Drop into syrup, remove and roll in finely chopped nuts.

Syrup

2 cups sugar	Juice of ½ lemon
2 cups water	

Boil sugar and water until syrup spins thread, 212° on candy thermometer. Add lemon juice.

Dora Levy

Passover Pastele (Meat Pie)

1 pound ground beef	½ teaspoon pepper
8 large onions, chopped fine	3 matzos
2 eggs, slightly beaten	Chicken soup or chicken fat
1 teaspoon salt	

Simmer ground beef and onions slowly in uncovered pan until mixture loses its raw look. Cover pan and simmer slowly for about 2 hours. Mixture should be liquidy. Add water if necessary, but mixture should be slowly cooked together. Cool. Add eggs, salt and pepper. Mix well. Grease thoroughly an 8 x 8 pan. Warm pan in oven. Soak matzos in water until soft but not falling apart. Place ½ wet matzos on bottom of pan to fit, add meat mixture, top with matzos, dot top with chicken soup or chicken fat. Bake at 350° for 30 minutes. Serve with hard boiled eggs and lemon wedges. Serves 6-8 as an appetizer.

Janis Baker

Passover Peete de Lecha (Custard Casserole)

6 eggs, well beaten	¾ cup sugar
2 cups cold milk	1 matzo crushed

Mix thoroughly. Place in well-greased casserole. Drop crushed matzo on top of mixture. Sprinkle cinnamon over top if desired. Bake in moderate oven 350° until firm.

Evelyn Berlowitz

Turkish Coffee

3½ demitasse cups water   3 teaspoons pulverized coffee
3 teaspoons sugar   (Turkish type)

Bring 3 cups of water to a boil; remove from heat and add coffee and sugar. Bring this to a boil again and remove from heat. Add remaining ½ cup water and once again bring to a boil. Remove from heat. Heat serving cups with hot water and spoon some of the foam into each cup before filling.

Betty Hurvitz

Rose Petal Jelly

2 cups rose petals   2 tablespoons honey
2 cups water   Juice of 1 lemon
2 cups sugar

Wash petals in cold water. After shaking dry, cut into very small pieces. Cook in water until tender, about 10-15 minutes. Strain the liquid. Make a syrup of 1 cup rose petal liquid, sugar and honey. Cook to soft ball stage or 220° on candy thermometer. Add drained petals and cook over low heat approximately 15 minutes. Add lemon juice and cook 5 minutes longer. Pour into 2 sterile 4-ounce jars and seal. Note: Roses should be in full bloom of the deep red and velvety petal variety.

Betty Buckler

Candied Grapefruit Peel

1 large thick-skinned grapefruit   2 cups water
2 cups sugar

Peel fruit, keeping peel in large pieces. Wash peel and trim out most of the white from inside. Cut into strips. Cover with cold water and boil for 5 minutes. Drain. Repeat process several times until peel is tender. Combine sugar and water and add peel; simmer until peel is glazed, about 20 minutes. Drain. Roll in granulated sugar.

Susam (Sesame Seed Candy)

2 pounds sesame seeds   ¾ cup water
½ cup flour   1 teaspoon lemon juice
¾ cup sugar   2 cups sliced almonds, toasted
1 cup honey

Toast sesame seeds and flour in large skillet until golden brown. Boil sugar, honey, water and lemon juice 20-30 minutes, until thick. Add sesame seeds and nuts to syrup. Simmer about 10 minutes, stirring with a wooden spoon. Cool. Spread sesame mixture on a wet wooden board to about ½-inch thickness. Allow to cool until firm enough to cut into diamond shaped pieces. Yield: 96 pieces.

Sarah Cassorla

Soups

Soup Stock

1½ pounds meat
2 or 3 beef soup bones
1 large onion
3 or 4 carrots
2 or 3 leeks
4 or 5 pieces celery
1 small green pepper

Cut all vegetables fine. Put in gallon pot or steamer filled to within 2 inches of top with water. Cook about six hours over slow fire. When cold, strain and put in glass container. May be kept in refrigerator for several days.

Lucille Michel

Dairy Barley Soup

2½ quarts water
½ cup medium barley
1 carrot, diced
1 potato, diced
Salt and pepper, to taste
1 cup milk

Bring water to boil. Add barley and seasonings. Skim. Reduce heat and cook for 2 hours. Add diced carrots and potatoes. Continue cooking for another hour. More water and seasonings may be added during cooking time, if mixture is getting too thick. Ten minutes before serving, add the milk.

Helen Jassin

Beef and Barley Vegetable Soup

1½ pounds cut up stew meat
2 quarts water
1½ tablespoons salt
½ teaspoon lemon pepper (not regular pepper)
2 tablespoon minced parsley
½ cup barley
1 cup carrots, diced
½ cup diced onions
1 #2½-can tomatoes
1 10-ounce package frozen peas
1 10-ounce package frozen baby lima beans
5 parsnips, cut up

Cover tightly and cook over low heat for 4 to 5 hours. Add additional water as needed during cooking time. Can be divided and frozen. Do not omit parsnips. This ingredient gives the exceptional taste.

Nancy Hoffman

Beef Chowder

1 large onion
1 pound ground beef
2 carrots, diced
2 stalks celery, cut up
½ cup raw rice
2 teaspoons salt
Pepper to taste
Dash chili powder
1 can tomato soup
3 soup cans of water

Brown onion and ground beef. Add remaining ingredients. Simmer 1 hour.

Ruth Moser

Blender Borscht

1 cup sour cream
1 1-pound can diced beets, chilled and drained
½ slice lemon, peeled
½ small onion, sliced
½ teaspoon salt
½ teaspoon sugar
1 cup crushed ice

To blender, add ¾ cup sour cream, beets, lemon, onion, salt and sugar. Cover and blend at high speed about 15 seconds. Scrape down sides of container; add ice. Cover and blend about 10 seconds longer. Serve immediately, with dollops of remaining sour cream. Serves 5.

Millie Rosenbaum

Meat-Beet Borscht

1½ pounds flank
1 large onion, chopped
Salt
Pepper

Juice of 2 lemons
Sugar, to taste
4 large beets

Cook meat in boiling water to cover. Add the chopped onion, salt and pepper. Cook about two hours. Add the juice of two lemons, sugar to taste, beets which have been grated on largest grater. Simmer about 45 minutes or until meat is tender. Cook 15 or 20 minutes more, if desired.

Ruth Kominz

Real Russian Borscht

1 large bunch beets
Small head cabbage
2 marrow soup bones
Small piece flanken, 1 pound
2 or 3 pieces sour salt, or to taste

1 onion, whole
¼ cup sugar, or to taste
1 8-ounce can tomato sauce
3 cloves garlic, mashed
Salt, to taste

Shred beets on grater. Cut up cabbage, discarding core. Place in large soup pot with 3 quarts water. Add bones, flanken, onion and salt to taste. Let cook for 45 minutes. Add sour salt and sugar to taste. Let cook another 45 minutes. Add tomato sauce. Correct seasonings. Cook until cabbage is soft. Add garlic cloves. 4 potatoes cut in halves can be added with bones and flanken if desired. Serves 10 or more.

Hedy Bagatelle

Cabbage Soup

2 pounds cabbage
1 large onion
Salt to taste
2-3 pounds brisket of beef
2 quarts boiling water

1 carrot
½ cup vinegar or lemon juice
 (or citric acid crystals)
4 tablespoons brown sugar

Shred or chop the cabbage and onion. Salt lightly and let stand about 45 minutes, or until it "sweats." Squeeze out the moisture. Sear the meat in the pot in which soup is to be cooked. When brown on all sides, add the cabbage, and continue to sear meat and vegetables. When light brown, stir in the boiling water, add grated or diced carrot and the seasonings. Cook over a low heat about 1½ hours, or until meat is tender. A thickening may be made of 1 tablespoon browned flour and 1 tablespoon shortening, adding ½ cup soup, and stirring until smooth. Add this thickening 15 minutes before serving time. Serves 6. Variation: Add 1 cup stewed tomato or ½ cup tomato paste, or ½ cup seeded raisins, or 1 tart apple, diced or grated.

Ruth L. Kominz

Easy Cabbage Soup

Soup bones with meat (as many
 as desired)
.2 8-ounce cans tomato sauce

1 1-pound-11-ounce can sauerkraut
1 large onion, chopped

Put all ingredients in large soup pot, bring to boil, then simmer until meat is tender (several hours). Sweeten with sugar to taste.

Shirley Jacobson

Chicken Soup

4-5 pounds chicken, cut into
    eighths
1 large onion
3 large carrots
1 stalk celery

1 parsnip
4 sprigs parsley
⅛ teaspoon dill seed
1 package broth seasoning
½ teaspoon salt

Cover chicken with water, bring to a boil, drain and scrape skin clean. Rinse well in cool water. Place chicken in clean pot, cover with fresh water (about 2½ quarts) and bring to a boil. Skim. Add vegetables and seasoning, cover and simmer about 80 minutes or until chicken is tender. Taste for salt correction during cooking. When cool, drain soup from chicken and discard vegetables. Chicken may be used for dishes calling for cooked chicken. Serve soup with noodles which have been cooked and drained separately. Serves 8.

Adeline Evans

Fish Chowder

1½ pounds haddock fillets
2 large carrots, diced
1 large potato, diced
1 small onion
1 8-ounce can tomato sauce

Salt
Pepper
Butter
8 cups boiled water
Warm milk

Skin the fish and cut in small pieces. Add diced potato and carrots. Fry onion in a little butter, add to fish and vegetables. Add seasoning and boiling water. Skim after it comes to a second boil and add tomato sauce. Simmer for ½ hour. Add a little warm milk just before serving. Serves 4-6.

Mrs. Samuel Polakoff

Lox and Potato Soup

2 quarts water
1 large onion, diced
3 large potatoes, quartered
Pepper, to taste

½ pound lox
1 cup milk
1 tablespoon butter

Bring water to a boil in a 3-quart pot. Add onion, potato and pepper and boil gently for ½ hour. Add lox, milk and butter and simmer 15 minutes.

Louise Vigdor

Gazpacho

1 1-pound loaf French bread
2 cloves garlic
1 pound tomatoes, peeled and
    cut
1 large onion

1 cucumber, peeled
½ cup olive oil
½ cup wine vinegar
Salt and pepper, to taste

Cut up bread, soak in water and squeeze almost dry. Put in blender with next four ingredients. Thoroughly mix. With blender still turned on, remove feeder cap and add olive oil gradually. Pour into bowl and stir in the wine vinegar, salt and pepper. Chill. Serve in large, flat bowls. Pass garnishes: croutons, finely diced cucumber, tomato, onion, parsley and hard cooked egg, to be used in individual bowls. Serves 4-6.

Bea Hanft

Gazpacho

1 28-ounce can tomatoes
1 cup tomato juice
2 cloves garlic, minced
1½ teaspoon dried basil or ½ cup fresh basil
2 sprigs parsley
Few leaves celery
1½ teaspoons salt
Freshly ground black pepper, to taste
1 bunch green onions, cut
1 or 2 Italian onions, cubed

2 medium green peppers, seeded and cubed
3 large fresh tomatoes, peeled, seeded and cubed
2 cucumbers, peeled, seeded and cubed
4 stalks celery, cubed
2 tablespoons olive oil
1 tablespoon wine vinegar
¼ cup dry sherry
Croutons, diced cucumber, onion and green pepper, for garnish

Place first eight ingredients in large skillet. Cover and cook gently over low heat for about one hour, or until flavors are well mingled. Force through food mill or blender. Cool and store overnight. Put coarsely cubed vegetables in blender and chop. Chop in 2 or 3 lots. Combine chopped vegetables with strained tomato mixture, adding a little more tomato juice, if necessary. Mix with oil, vinegar and sherry and taste for seasoning. Chill. Serve very cold. Garnish with croutons and diced vegetables. Serves 12. Will keep in refrigerator several days or can be frozen.

Hannah Dankoff

Lentil Soup

1 pound soup meat
1 pound lentils
1 onion, whole
1 carrot, whole

1 stalk celery
Salt
Ketchup
6 hot dogs, sliced

Put soup meat in a 3-quart pot and fill with water to within 3 inches from top. Boil and skim. Add lentils, carrots, celery, onion and salt to taste. Simmer for two hours. An hour before soup is done add ketchup and sliced hot dogs.

Joyce Axelrod

Minestrone Soup

½ cup salad or olive oil
1 clove garlic, minced
2 cups chopped onion
1 cup chopped celery
4 tablespoons chopped parsley
2 carrots, thinly sliced
2 teaspoons salt
¼ teaspoon pepper
1 6-ounce can tomato paste

1 #303 can kidney beans
1 zucchini squash, thinly sliced (optional)
1 cup frozen green beans
1 cup cabbage, coarsely chopped
1 cup elbow macaroni
1 package brown flavor broth powder
10 cups cold water

Heat oil in large soup pot. Add garlic, onion, celery, and parsley. Cook until soft. Stir in tomato paste and all remaining ingredients except zucchini, green beans and macaroni. Lower heat, cover and simmer slowly one hour. Add the remaining three ingredients. Cook additional ½ hour. Makes 8 generous servings. Make this soup a day ahead of serving. Can be frozen well.

Louise Vigdor

Minute Minestrone

1 envelope tomato-vegetable
soup mix
3 cups boiling water
1 medium onion, chopped
1 1-pound can red kidney beans

1 #303 can whole kernel corn
1 8-ounce can tomato sauce
1 teaspoon salt
½ cup chopped parsley
Grated Parmesan cheese

Stir soup mix into boiling water in large saucepan, add onion, kidney beans, corn, tomato sauce, salt and pepper. Cover. Heat to boiling, cook 10 minutes or until onion is tender, stir in parsley. Serve in mugs or bowls with a generous sprinkling of Parmesan cheese.

Idaire Leichtner

French Onion Soup

5 medium onions
4 tablespoons pareve margarine
Little garlic
1½ quarts chicken or beef broth

½ cup white wine (optional)
2 tablespoons flour
Salt and pepper to taste

Brown onions in margarine. Add rest of ingredients. Simmer approximately 15 minutes. Serve with French bread. Serves 4.

Ruth Kominz

Triflach or Onion Soup a la Grama Eva

1 small onion, chopped
1 egg
1/3 cup matzo meal
1 tablespoon bread crumbs
(optional)

1 pinch salt
3 cups boiling water
½ teaspoon salt
Pinch of pepper
2 cups milk

Fry onions until golden brown. Pour over beaten egg and add salt and matzo meal. Mix well. Into boiling water, drop by ½ teaspoonfuls of mixture, first dipping spoon into hot water so the mixture will drop off. Let cook on medium flame for about 10 minutes. Add last 3 ingredients, cook about 10 minutes and serve.

Esther Solomon

Lickety Split Pea Soup

1 pound soup meat
1 onion, whole
1 carrot, whole
1 stalk celery
1 pound green split peas

Salt to taste
1 8-ounce can mushrooms, drained, or
¼ pound fresh mushrooms

Put meat in 3-quart pot and fill with water to 3 inches from top. Bring to boil and skim. Add split peas, celery, carrot, onion and salt to taste. Simmer for two hours. Add fresh or canned mushrooms an hour before done.

Joyce Axelrod

Norwegian Yellow Pea Soup

2 pounds short ribs of beef
1 large onion
2 bay leaves
Salt to taste

Peppercorns
½ to ¾ pound yellow peas
1 pound carrots, optional

Cover meat with water, add spices and peas. Bring to boil. Simmer until peas are tender and soup is done. Add carrots and cook until done.

Nancy Berger Hauger

Green Split Pea and Barley Soup

4 quarts water	1 teaspoon salt
2-pound slice of beef, cut in cubes	4 carrots, cut up
4 or 5 marrow bones	3 stalks celery
1-pound box green split peas	¼ cup barley

Boil water with meat and bones. Skim the top of water. Add rest of ingredients, except barley. Bring to a boil and simmer for 3 hours. Add barley and cook for 2 more hours.

Belle Kessler

Old Fashioned Tomato Soup

2 cups canned tomatoes, crushed	¼ teaspoon baking soda
1 cup milk	Salt and pepper, to taste
1 tablespoon butter	

Heat tomatoes to a boil. Add baking soda and stir. Add butter, stirring until melted. Add salt, pepper and milk, stirring continuously until hot, but do not boil. Serve immediately. Serves two.

Eulah Feier

Tomato Soup With Meat

1 pound soup meat	1 stalk celery
Sour salt, to taste	1 carrot
Brown sugar, to taste	46-ounce can tomato juice
1 whole onion	Water

Cook meat in water to cover, and skim. Add tomato juice, onion, celery, carrot, brown sugar and sour salt to taste. Simmer for 2 hours.

Joyce Axelrod

Tomato Rice Soup

2 quarts cold water	Juice of 1 lemon
1 8-ounce can tomato sauce	¼ cup sugar
1 large onion, diced	½ pound ground chuck meat, made into small balls
1 large meaty soup bone	
½ cup raw rice	

Cook the first five ingredients 1½ hours. Add lemon juice, sugar and the small meat balls. Simmer for 45 minutes longer.

Louise Vigdor

Dairy Vegetable Soup

6 cups water	1 20-ounce can tomatoes
2 cups carrots, cubed	Salt and pepper to taste
3 large stalks celery, cubed	1 #303 can whole kernel corn, drained
1 large or 2 medium onions, cubed	½ pound American cheese, cubed
1 large green pepper, cubed	
2 cups cabbage, bite-size	

Combine all ingredients except corn and cheese, in a 4-quart pot. Bring to boil and cook for 30 minutes over low heat. Add drained corn and cubed cheese, and cook until cheese is completely melted and mixes with the soup. Serves 10-12. Keeps or freezes well.

Pearl Felderstein

Beef Vegetable Soup

5 pounds soup meat and bones	½ cup vegetable shortening
2 quarts water	1½ cups finely cut celery
1 clove garlic, minced	1 cup carrots, diced
1 tablespoon salt	1 cup green beans, diced
1/3 cup barley	1 cup potatoes, diced
½ cup chopped celery tops	1 cup finely cut cabbage
2 cups onions, chopped	1 10-ounce package frozen peas
1 28-ounce can tomatoes	1 cup frozen spinach

Combine first 7 ingredients in large pot, cover and simmer about 3 hours or until meat is tender. Skim soup, remove meat and bones. Set meat aside. Add canned tomatoes to soup. In skillet, place next 6 ingredients. Cook for 7 minutes stirring often. Add to soup, cover and simmer for 20 minutes. Add frozen peas, spinach and meat (cut into pieces). Cover and simmer for 10 minutes. Season with salt and pepper. This makes 5 quarts of soup. If too thick, more water may be added. This soup can be frozen.

Hetty Jacobson

Esther's Vegetable Soup

2 pounds flank	¼ teaspoon pepper
3 large soup bones	¼ cup lima beans
1 medium onion	¼ cup green split peas
1 large carrot	¼ cup rice, raw
1 large potato	¼ cup yellow split peas
1 tomato (optional)	¼ cup barley
2 large stalks celery	Handful of fine noodles (optional)
1 tablespoon coarse salt	

Put first 9 ingredients in a large pot with 3 quarts of water. Cover and let stand for 5 minutes. Bring to a boil and cook on low flame for 2½-3 hours, until all vegetables are soft. Wash each of the next 5 ingredients separately, combine in a second pot and cover with water, about one quart. Cook until the lima beans are soft. When they are soft, it is done. Strain first mixture into the second pot, mashing the vegetables as you strain. Transfer meat into second pot. (If you wish, add a handful of noodles and cook for 5 minutes longer). This makes at least 2 quarts of vegetable soup. If you want thinner soup, add water to bones originally used, cook a few minutes, and strain into soup. The meat serves 3-4. The soup can be frozen for future use. You may add 1 tablespoon of ketchup to this soup, if desired.

Esther Solomon

Peasant Soup

2 tablespoons pareve margarine	¼ cup carrots, diced
2 tablespoons celery, finely chopped	½ cup thinly sliced frankfurter
	3 cups cold water
2 tablespoons onion, finely chopped	1 envelope green pea soup mix
	1 teaspoon lemon juice

In a saucepan, melt margarine and saute celery, onion and carrots for 5 minutes. Add frankfurter slices. Stir in water and soup mix. Simmer until vegetables are tender. Stir in lemon juice. Makes 4-5 servings.

Idaire Leichtner

Sour Cherry Soup

2 cups sour cherries	4 cups water
1 teaspoon salt	1 tablespoon flour
2 tablespoons sugar	1 cup sour cream

Combine cherries, salt, sugar and water. Boil 10 minutes if canned cherries are used, 20 minutes for fresh cherries. Make a paste of flour and a little cold water, gradually add to soup and boil 5 minutes longer. Remove from heat. Chill thoroughly. Stir in sour cream just before serving. Serves 6.

Helen Hecker

Plum Soup

1½ pounds plums	1 tablespoon flour
5 cups water	Sugar to taste

Slice plums and cook in water until fruit is soft, about 20 minutes. Press plums through a sieve. Thicken liquid with 1 tablespoon flour blended with a little cold water. Add sugar to taste and cook 5 minutes more. Chill. Serves 6.

Frosty Wine Soup

2 jars baby food, strained peaches or apricots with applesauce	or champagne Cinnamon Lemon juice or grated lemon
4 cups ice cold Sauterne wine	rind

Combine baby food and wine. Season to taste with cinnamon and lemon juice or grated lemon rind. Garnish with an ice cube and mint leaves. Serve this instead of fruit cocktail as a first course for a summer supper.

Ruth Baker

Egg Drop (Einlauf)

1 egg, beaten	3 tablespoons flour
Dash of salt	¼ cup cold water

Stir all ingredients together until smooth. Drop slowly from end of spoon into boiling soup. Cover and cook 5 minutes. Serve immediately. Variation: Pour well-beaten egg gradually into boiling soup, stirring with a fork, just before serving.

Meat Kreplach

Dough

1 large egg	2/3 cup flour
¼ teaspoon salt	

Beat egg and salt together. Add flour to make a stiff dough. Roll out thin and cut into squares.

Filling

1 pound ground cooked meat	1 egg
Salt and pepper to taste	3 teaspoons chicken fat

Mix all ingredients together. Place a spoonful in the center of square and fold into triangles. Add kreplach to boiling salted water. Boil for 12 minutes. Drain and fry until crisp.

Celia Mittleman

Kreplach

Dough

2¼ cups flour
3 eggs
4 tablespoons cold water

3 tablespoons oil
1 teaspoon salt

Mix all ingredients so firm ball is formed. Knead until smooth and elastic. Roll out with rolling pin fairly thin on floured linen cloth or on board. Cut into two-inch squares. Makes 8 dozen.

Filling

1 pound soft meat, such as
    flanken
½ pound lung

1 onion
1 egg

Stew meat with diced onion, in small amount of salted water until tender. (Any cooked meat can be used; lung gives a particularly nostalgic flavor.) Grind all meat through meat grinder. Mix with egg. Place ball of mixture about size of walnut in the middle of each square. Fold one corner to meet opposite corner and pinch edges to form closed puffed triangle. Two lower corners can be bent down to meet so that shape is like ring or cap. Drop kreplach one at a time into large pot of continuously boiling salted water, and allow to cook for 15 to 20 minutes. Before eating, brush kreplach with melted fat, spread on tin, and brown for ½ hour in moderate oven, 350°. They may be boiled or heated in soup, or added to soup at table.

Mrs. Aaron Karp

Liver Dumplings

½ pound liver
1 onion, small, diced
1 egg

2 slices bread
2 tablespoons flour
Salt and pepper to taste

Broil liver and grind. Break bread into small pieces. Mix all ingredients until pasty. Drop from teaspoon into boiling stock or soup. Cook 30 minutes. Serves 2.

Eve Mendelson

Matzo Balls or Kneidlach

See Passover, p. 21, p. 22

Vegetables

Artichokes

4 artichokes	3 cloves minced garlic
2 slices fresh lemon or 2 table- spoons bottled lemon juice	1 cup Parmesan cheese
4 tablespoons oil	6 ounces melted butter

Cut stalks from artichokes short enough to allow them to sit in small plate. Cut top of leaves straight across, approximately 1 inch from tip. Turn artichoke upside down and holding it in palm of hand, slam down hard on bread board or cutting board 2 or 3 times. Leaves will open and spread. Fill 4 or 5-quart pot ½ to ¾ full of water. Put in oil, lemon and garlic, and bring to a boil. Place artichokes in boiling water and when boiling starts again, sprinkle all the cheese evenly over all 4 artichokes. Cook at steady boil for about 30-45 minutes. Remove artichokes from pot, and drain upside down through slotted spoon. Serve with hot melted butter. Dip each leaf into butter before removing meat of leaf with teeth. Serves 4.

Ricky Sands

Asparagus Casserole

1 #303 can asparagus	mushroom soup
2 or 3 hard-cooked eggs, sliced	1/3 cup milk
1 can condensed cream of	Cheese crackers

Alternate layer of asparagus, eggs, and soup which has been mixed with milk. Top with layer of crushed cheese crackers. Bake about 30 minutes at 350° in 1½-quart uncovered casserole. Serves 6.

Florence Salitan

Baked Beans

1 pound large, dry lima beans	1 cup catsup
2 tablespoons chicken fat	1 cup brown sugar
½ teaspoon salt	

Soak beans overnight, covering generously with water. Next day, using the same water, cook over medium heat until tender, covered. Before thoroughly cooked, add 2 tablespoons chicken fat and salt. When tender, add catsup and brown sugar. Bake for 2-2½ hours covered at 350°. Serves 8-9.

Hannah Dankoff

Spicy Baked Beans

4 #303 cans butter-limas	1 teaspoon dry mustard
1 bottle ketchup	2 large onions, sliced
½ cup brown sugar	1 pound Beef Frye

Put all ingredients in baking pan 8 x 10, and put Beef Frye on top. Bake in 350° -375° oven for 35-45 minutes. Serves 8-10.

Elaine Hoffman

Dill Green Beans

2 9-ounce packages frozen green beans	1 teaspoon dill weed
¼ cup chopped pimento	¼ teaspoon salt
1/3 cup melted butter or margarine	½ cup coarse toasted bread crumbs
½ teaspoon dill seeds or	

Cook beans according to package directions and drain. Combine pimento, melted butter, dill and salt. Pour over green beans. Toss toasted bread crumbs with bean mixture. Serves 8-10.

Merle Markus

Dilled Green Bean Bundles

1 teaspoon dill seed
¾ cup warm water
2 medium lemons

2 tablespoons vinegar
2 teaspoons salt
1 16-ounce can whole green beans

Place dill seed in warm water for 1 hour. Drain green beans and place in bowl. Wash lemons and cut each in half. Extract juice, reserving ¼ cup. Slice lemon rind from each lemon half into 2 rings about ¼ inch wide. Place on top of beans. Combine dill seed, water, lemon juice and vinegar and salt in saucepan. Bring to boil. Pour this mixture over beans and rings and marinate overnight. Drain off marinade and arrange 10-12 beans in each lemon ring. Yield: 8 "Bundles".

Bea Hanft

Green Bean Casserole

½ cup sliced onions
1 tablespoon chopped parsley
2 tablespoons butter
2 tablespoons flour
1 teaspoon salt
¼ teaspoon pepper

½ teaspoon grated lemon peel
1 cup sour cream
5 cups cooked green beans
½ cup grated American cheese
½ cup dry bread crumbs

Saute onions and parsley in butter. Add flour, salt, pepper and lemon peel. Stir in sour cream and green beans. Pour into a greased 1½-quart casserole and top with grated cheese and bread crumbs. Bake at 350° for 30-45 minutes until bubbly.

Marcia Isner

Green Bean Casserole with Wine

2 packages frozen, French style
   green beans
1 can cream of mushroom soup

2 tablespoons dry sherry
2 ounces grated sharp cheese
1 ounce sliced almonds

Cook beans 5 minutes and drain well. Mix soup and sherry. Toss with green beans and put into 1-quart casserole. Sprinkle with cheese and almonds. Bake uncovered at 375° for 30 minutes. Serves 8.

Eulah Feier

Green Bean Melange

1 16-ounce can French style
   green beans, drained
1 16-ounce can bean sprouts,
   drained
1 4-ounce can sliced mushrooms,
   drained
¼ cup Parmesan cheese

3 tablespoons melted butter or
   margarine
1 8-ounce can tomato sauce
½ teaspoon salt
1 3½-ounce can French fried
   onions

Early in day, toss first five ingredients together and place in an 8 x 12 baking dish. Cover and refrigerate. About 50 minutes before serving, preheat oven to 350°. Combine tomato sauce and salt and pour over vegetable mixture in baking dish. Cover and bake 35 minutes. Uncover, sprinkle on French fried onions and bake 10 more minutes. Serves 6.

Rose Hurwitz

Party Green Beans

8 ounces fresh sliced mushrooms
   (or 3-ounce can, drained)
2 tablespoons butter
2 cups cooked green beans

½ cup sour cream
½ teaspoon salt
1 teaspoon grated onion (or
   ¼ teaspoon powdered onion)

In heavy skillet saute mushrooms in butter until they are tender. Add green beans and heat thoroughly. Heat sour cream and salt, but do not boil. Add onion, green beans and mushroom mixture. Toss until well mixed. Serves 4.

Rose Adelstein

Savory Green Bean Casserole

1 pound fresh green beans
1/3 cup finely chopped onion
1 medium green pepper, chopped
1 teaspoon basil

4 teaspoons butter or
   margarine
Salt and pepper
1 tablespoon water

Cut green beans into 1½-inch pieces. Lightly toss all ingredients together. Place in 1-quart casserole. Cover and bake 60-70 minutes at 350°. Serves 4.

Eleanor Goldsmith

Special Green Beans

2 cans water chestnuts, sliced
1 1-pound can bean sprouts
2 packages frozen French-style
   green beans
1 pound fresh mushrooms
1 small onion, diced

2-3 tablespoons butter or
   margarine
1 10-ounce can cream of mushroom soup, undiluted
1 3½-ounce can French-fried
   onions, slightly broken

Drain water chestnuts and bean sprouts, rinse with cold water, then place in ice water to crisp while preparing other ingredients. Partially cook green beans (approximately 4 minutes); drain well. Saute mushrooms and onion in butter or margarine. Lightly mix together green beans (reserving ½ cup for top of casserole), bean sprouts and water chestnuts (well-drained), sauteed mushrooms and soup. Place in 8x12 casserole, placing ½ cup green beans on top. Bake uncovered at 400° for 20 minutes. Then sprinkle French-fried onions on top and bake 10 minutes more. Serves 12-14.

Edith Perlman

Beets with Apricots

2 bunches beets
¼ cup butter or margarine
20 dried apricot halves, cut in
   half

½ cup boiling water
½ cup firmly packed light brown
   sugar
¼ teaspoon salt

Pare and quarter beets. Put 4 pieces beets in blender container; cover and run on low speed until chopped. Empty into large fry-pan; repeat process until all beets are chopped. Add butter to beets. Put remaining ingredients in blender until apricots are pureed, add to beets in pan; cover and cook over medium heat until beets are tender, about 30 minutes. Serves 6.

Sylvia Tepperman

Beets in Pineapple Sauce

1 1-pound can sliced beets	1 tablespoon lemon juice
3 tablespoons margarine	1 8½-ounce can crushed pineapple
3 tablespoons all-purpose flour	¼ teaspoon salt
2 tablespoons dark brown sugar	

Drain beets thoroughly and reserve 1 cup of liquid. If less than 1 cup, add water. Melt margarine in 1-quart saucepan over medium heat. Stir in flour, cook until mixture bubbles, remove from heat. Gradually stir in beet liquid. When flour and liquid are blended, return to heat, add brown sugar and lemon juice, and stir until sauce is smooth and thick. Add pineapple and salt. Pineapple should not be drained. This part of preparation may be completed slightly in advance and sauce kept covered until dinner. Just before serving, reheat, add beets and stir gently until very hot. Serves 5-6.

Priscilla Brown

Broccoli au Gratin

2 packages frozen broccoli spears	½ cup water
1 can cream of mushroom soup	Grated American cheese
1 pinch garlic salt	Bread crumbs

Cook broccoli as directed on package. Lift out of water and cool. Empty 1 can cream of mushroom soup into broccoli, add garlic salt and water. Mix. Place layer of broccoli in 8 x 8 x 2 casserole dish, spread layer of soup over broccoli, sprinkle with cheese. Repeat layers until all ingredients are used. Top with bread crumbs, dot with butter. Bake 350°, 1 hour or until brown. Can be prepared in advance. Serves 4 - 6.

Sara Charney

Broccoli Casserole

2 packages chopped broccoli	1 can French-fried onion rings
¼ pound margarine	1 cup broccoli liquid
1 cup stuffing mix	½ cup Parmesan cheese
1 can cream of mushroom soup	

Cook broccoli according to directions on box. Drain and save 1 cup liquid. Melt margarine and mix with stuffing. Grease 1½-quart casserole. Put in layers beginning with broccoli, then stuffing, soup, and onions. Pour broccoli liquid over last layer. Sprinkle on cheese. Bake 1 hour at 325°. If cheese begins to brown, cover dish.

Judy Schwartz

Broccoli Cheese Casserole

3 eggs	2 teaspoons salt
1 8-ounce carton cottage cheese	Dash pepper
1 4-ounce package shredded cheddar cheese	2 10-ounce packages frozen broccoli, thawed
3 tablespoons flour	

In large bowl, beat eggs slightly, beat in both cheeses, flour, salt and pepper. Drain broccoli well. Pat dry with paper towel. Stir into egg mixture and pour into greased 9x9 pan, spreading evenly with spoon. Bake until firm and pulls away from sides, at 350° for 35 minutes. Loosen with spatula. Cut and serve hot. Serves 6-8.

Lillian Karn

Sesame Broccoli

1 pound fresh broccoli	1 tablespoon sesame seed, toasted
4 teaspoons suger	1 tablespoon vinegar
1 tablespoon salad oil	1 tablespoon soy sauce

Cook broccoli in small amount of water about 15 minutes. In a small saucepan, combine oil, vinegar, soy sauce, sugar and sesame seed; heat to boiling. Pour sauce over hot broccoli, turning spears to coat. Serves 4 or 5.

Florence Salitan

Company Broccoli Souffle

1¾ cups cooked broccoli	¼ teaspoon nutmeg
1½ cups hot milk	⅛ cup soft butter or margarine
¾ teaspoon salt	3 tablespoons flour
¼ teaspoon pepper	6 eggs, separated

Preheat oven to 350°. Butter a 2-quart casserole or souffle dish. Put cooked broccoli in blender container; cover and run on high speed until smooth; empty into saucepan. Put milk, salt, pepper, nutmeg, butter, flour and egg yolks in blender; cover and run on low speed until smooth; add to broccoli; cook over low heat stirring constantly until thick. Cool slightly. Beat egg whites until stiff; fold carefully and slowly into broccoli mixture. Pour into casserole, bake 25 minutes or until browned and puffed. Serve immediately. Serves 6-8.

Sylvia Tepperman

Creamy Brussels Sprouts

2 packages frozen Brussels sprouts	⅛ teaspoon ground black pepper
	¼ teaspoon ground marjoram
2 tablespoons butter or margarine	¼ teaspoon ground thyme
2 tablespoons flour	1½ cups milk
½ teaspoon salt	Chopped parsley

Cook Brussels sprouts according to package directions. Meanwhile, melt butter in saucepan. Blend in flour and seasonings. Remove from heat and gradually add milk. Return to heat. Stirring constantly, cook until thickened. Drain cooked Brussels sprouts and pour seasoned white sauce over all. Garnish with chopped parsley just before serving. Serves 6-8.

Eleanor Goldsmith

Surkal (Norwegian Sauerkraut)

1 head of cabbage	2 cups water
4 tablespoons flour	2 tablespoons vinegar
2-3 tablespoons caraway seeds	2 tablespoons sugar

Cut cabbage into strips. Put in large kettle alternately with salt, pepper, flour and caraway seeds between layers. Cover bottom of pot with water. Bring to boil. Reduce heat and cook several hours until it begins to turn brown. Add vinegar and sugar until desired sweet and sour taste is achieved. Serve hot.

Nancy Berger Hauger

Cabbage Strudel

9 Filo pastry leaves
1 head green cabbage
¼ box golden raisins
1 large onion, sliced
4 apples, peeled and sliced
2 tablespoons sugar

Quarter and thinly cut cabbage. Saute cabbage and onion in butter until limp; mix occasionally. Add apples, raisins and sugar to cabbage, mix and cool. Butter each strudel leaf. Place generous 2-inch row of filling down leaf. Roll up as for jelly roll. Brush with melted butter. Bake on greased baking pan 400° for 30 minutes or until browned and crisp. Slice on diagonal into 2-inch pieces, 5 pieces per leaf. Serves 15. If this is to be frozen, cut baking time to 20 minutes, then re-heat when ready to serve.

Lois M. Kuh

Carrot Ring

12 large cooked carrots
1 cup sugar
2 cups flour
1½ teaspoons baking soda
Pinch salt
4 eggs
¼ pound soft butter or margarine

Mix together in mixmaster. Bake in buttered 10 or 11-inch mold at 375° for 45-60 minutes. Serves 10-12.

Florence Salitan

Carrot Ring

½ cup vegetable shortening
¾ cup brown sugar
3 eggs, separated
2 cups grated carrots
¼ teaspoon salt
1 cup flour
½ teaspoon baking powder
½ teaspoon baking soda
1 tablespoon lemon juice
1 tablespoon water
Bread crumbs

Cream shortening with brown sugar, add egg yolks, grated carrots and salt. Add sifted dry ingredients, lemon juice and water. Fold in beaten egg whites. Pour into a greased 9-inch ring mold, sprinkled with bread crumbs. Bake in 350° oven in a pan of hot water for 45 minutes. Serves 6-8.

Ethel Simon

Carrots in Savory Sauce

2 pounds carrots
1 cup boiling water
¼ teaspoon salt
½ cup water
¼ cup lemon juice
1 tablespoon cornstarch
2 tablespoons butter or
margarine
½ cup firmly packed brown sugar
½ tablespoon prepared mustard
2 tablespoons chopped dry
roasted peanuts

Wash and scrape carrots; cut diagonally into 1½-inch pieces. Place in saucepan and add salt and boiling water, bring to boil, reduce heat. Cook gently about 20 minutes or until tender. Drain well. In saucepan, mix ½ cup water and lemon juice into corn starch, butter, brown sugar and mustard. Stir constantly over low heat until thickened. Add cooked carrots, and heat thoroughly. Sprinkle peanuts on top and serve. Serves 4-6.

Eleanor Goldsmith

Carrot Souffle

½ pound carrots (5 medium)	½ teaspoon salt
3 tablespoons butter or	½ teaspoon pepper
margarine	¼ teaspoon nutmeg
2 tablespoons minced onion	1 cup milk
3 tablespoons flour	3 eggs, separated

Wash and scrape carrots. Cut into 1½-inch pieces. Cook covered in boiling salted water until very tender, about 20 minutes. Drain, then strain through food mill. It should give you ¾ cup strained carrot. Melt butter or margarine in sauce pan, add onion and cook gently, but not browned. Stir in flour, salt, pepper and nutmeg. Remove from heat and gradually stir in milk, keeping smooth. Return to moderately low heat and cook, stirring constantly until thickened. Stir in carrots. Cool. Beat egg yolks until thick and lemon colored. Beat egg whites until in stiff peaks. Stir beaten yolks into cooled carrot mixture. Fold in whites. Turn into an ungreased 1-quart baking dish. Bake for 35-40 minutes at 350° until golden brown and mixture in center doesn't shake. Serves 4-6.

Millie Rosenbaum

Carrot Tzimmes

4 pounds carrots	3 tablespoons flour
1 onion	¼ cup cold water
1 cup sugar	3 tablespoons honey
2 tablespoons salt	1 cup brown sugar
10-20 dry prunes (optional)	

Peel or scrape carrots, slice into thin rounds. Dice onion; add. Mix well with sugar and salt in large bowl. Let stand several hours or overnight. Liquid will form. Transfer to large heavy pot with tight-fitting cover and cook in water that has formed until carrot slices are tender. Add 10 to 20 dry prunes, if desired, and continue simmering one hour on top of stove. To make thickening, dissolve flour in cold water. Add honey and brown sugar, stirring well to remove all lumps. Add some hot liquid from pot to form smooth liquid. Pour over and mix well through pot of carrots. Cover pot and bake in moderate oven for 2 hours or more, until glaze forms and all liquid is absorbed. Some prefer to finish baking in uncovered pot so that carrot slices become crisply candied. Tzimmes may be eaten cold as well as warm, and tastes better after a few days.

Mrs. Aaron Karp

Tzimmes without a Tzimmes

1 pound prunes	drained
½ cup raisins	1 6-ounce can frozen orange
2 #303 cans yams, drained	juice, defrosted
2 #303 cans sliced carrots,	1 6-ounce can water

Stew prunes and raisins. Cool and drain. Cut yams into ½-inch squares. Put prune and raisin mixture, carrots and yams into 2½-quart baking dish. Pour orange juice and water over all. Let stand for at least 3 hours. Bake 1 hour at 300°. Serves 10-12.

Dora Morgenstern

Cauliflower Divan

3 cups cooked cauliflower
  rosettes
2 tablespoons butter
2 tablespoons flour
1¼ cups milk

1½ teaspoons salt
¾ cup grated sharp cheddar
  cheese
½ cup soft bread crumbs
1 tablespoon butter

Melt the 2 tablespoons butter in saucepan and blend in flour. Remove from heat and gradually stir in milk. Return to heat and cook to medium thickness, stirring constantly. Add ½ teaspoon salt and cheese. Arrange cauliflower in greased 1-quart casserole, sprinkling with remaining teaspoon salt. Pour cheese over all and top with bread crumbs. Dot with remaining butter. Bake uncovered in 350° oven, 45 minutes or until crumbs are brown. Serves 6.

Arlean Levinson

Company Cauliflower

1 medium head cauliflower
Salt and pepper to taste
½ cup sour cream

½ cup shredded sharp processed
  American cheese
Toasted sesame seeds*

Rinse cauliflower and break into flowerets. Cook, covered, in small amount of boiling salted water until tender, 10-15 minutes. Drain well. Place half of cauliflower in a 1-quart casserole. Season with salt and pepper. Spread with sour cream, cheese and sesame seeds. Repeat layers. Bake at 350° for 5-10 minutes. *To toast sesame seeds, place in shallow pan in 350° oven for 10 minutes, until brown, shaking pan occasionally.

Leah Mermelstein

Zippy Cheese Topped Cauliflower

1 large head cauliflower,
  trimmed and washed
¾ cup salad dressing

2 teaspoons prepared mustard
¼ pound cheddar cheese, grated

Cook cauliflower whole in large pan in boiling, lightly salted water for 20 to 30 minutes. Drain and place in baking dish. Mix salad dressing and mustard and spread over cauliflower. Sprinkle with cheese. Bake at 325° until cheese melts and is bubbly. Serves 6.

Eulah Feier

Ranchero Corn

2 tablespoons oil
1 4-ounce can sliced mushrooms
3 teaspoons finely chopped onion

2 12-ounce cans mexicorn,
  drained
½ cup Bacos

Saute mushrooms and onion in oil Add corn and Bacos. Heat thoroughly.

Terri Ross

Scalloped Corn

1 #303 can creamed corn
1 #303 can whole kernel corn
1 egg
2 tablespoons butter

Salt and pepper to taste
1 teaspoon sugar
¼ cup milk
10 crumbled saltine crackers

Mix all ingredients together. Bake in 1-quart casserole, uncovered, in 350° oven for about 1 hour. Serves 6.

Jan Cornelius

Eggplant Parmesan

1 eggplant (1½-2 pounds)	1 8-ounce package mozzarella cheese
Seasoned flour	1 quart meatless spaghetti sauce
Flavored bread crumbs	Garlic salt
1 egg, beaten	Garlic powder
Margarine	Parmesan cheese

Peel eggplant and slice in ¼-inch thick slices. Dip each slice in seasoned flour, then in beaten egg, then in flavored bread crumbs. Fry on low heat in margarine or oil until brown. Remove to large, deep baking dish. Cover each slice with mozzarella cheese and spaghetti sauce. Repeat, sprinkling each with garlic salt and garlic powder. Pour any remaining sauce over filled pan. Sprinkle with Parmesan cheese, heavily. Bake at 350° for 30 minutes. Serves 6-8.

Sue Kiner

Stewed Eggplant

1 medium eggplant, peeled and sliced	2 tablespoons oil
	½ can tomato paste
1 large green pepper, sliced	1 small can tomatoes
2 medium onions, chopped	1 tablespoon lemon juice
½ pound fresh mushrooms, sliced	Dash sugar and oregano
	Salt and pepper

Saute eggplant, green pepper, onions and mushrooms in oil. Add remaining ingredients. Simmer until vegetables are tender. Do not overcook. Zucchini squash may be substituted. Serves 6-8.

Ruth Kravetz

Stuffed Eggplant

1 small eggplant	2 tablespoons Bacos
2 tablespoons bread crumbs	¼ teaspoon oregano
1 egg, beaten	4 small pieces cheese

Boil whole, unpeeled eggplant about 10 minutes, until fork tender. Split lengthwise and scoop out pulp, leaving some around edges to keep shape of shell. Chop pulp, add beaten egg and other ingredients, except cheese. Mix well. Divide mixture in half and fill each shell. Top each with 2 pieces of cheese. Bake at 350° for ½ hour. (If shells are weak, place them in foil shaped like boats for extra strength.)

Judy Schwartz

Mushroom Souffle

3 tablespoons butter	¾ cup milk
2 small onions, chopped	¾ cup light cream
2 eggs	2 teaspoons salt
2/3 cup packaged dry bread-crumbs (or stuffing)	¼ teaspoon pepper
	1 pound fresh mushrooms, chopped

Melt butter and saute onions. In 1½-quart greased casserole, beat eggs, mix crumbs, milk, cream and seasonings. Let stand until crumbs absorb liquid. Blend in mushrooms and onions. Bake 60 to 70 minutes, uncovered, at 350°. Can be mixed together in advance and baked the next day. Bake just before serving. Serves 6.

Barbara Scheiner

Baked Onions

4 medium Bermuda or red
  Italian onions
½ cup pareve bouillon

Butter
Grated cheese
Salt and pepper to taste

Cut off ends of onions and peel off dry outer skin. Arrange in buttered casserole and add bouillon. Sprinkle lightly with salt and freshly ground pepper and dot liberally with butter. Cover and bake at 350° for 1 hour or until tender. Add more bouillon if necessary. Remove cover, sprinkle with grated cheese (Parmesan, Swiss or sharp). Place under broiler to melt cheese or return to oven until cheese melts. Serves 4.

Ruth Markin

Onion Pudding

2 cups onion, chopped
¼ cup butter
1 egg, beaten
1 tablespoon dried parsley
½ teaspoon salt
⅛ teaspoon pepper
2 cups flour
3 teaspoons baking powder

1 teaspoon salt
¼ cup butter
¾ cup milk
12 ounces sour cream
2 eggs, unbeaten
½ teaspoon salt
⅛ teaspoon pepper

Saute onion and butter in 9 x 9 pan. Stir in egg, parsley, salt and pepper. Spread over bottom of pan. Sift together flour and salt in mixing bowl. Cut in butter until particles are fine. Add milk. Stir until dough clings together. Knead on lightly floured surface 10-12 times. Pat out to 9-inch square and place over onion mixture. Combine sour cream, eggs, salt and pepper. Beat well. Pour over dough. Bake at 375° for 35-40 minutes, until golden brown. Serve hot. Serves 6.

Rachel Hyman

Peas Paprika

2 packages frozen peas
1 teaspoon sugar
½ teaspoon salt
¼ cup finely chopped onion
¼ cup butter
¼ cup flour

1 teaspoon salt
¼ teaspoon pepper
½ teaspoon paprika
¼ cup pea stock
½ cup milk
½ cup grated cheese

Cook peas with sugar and salt. Saute onion in melted butter until golden brown; add flour, salt, pepper, paprika, pea stock and milk. Cook five minutes, until sauce thickens. Then add cheese. Combine with drained peas. Place under broiler for a few minutes until golden brown. Serves 6-8.

Elaine Braverman

Baked Peppers and Cheese

4 large green peppers
4 cups firm bread cubes
4 eggs, slightly beaten
1 clove garlic, crushed
2 slices Swiss cheese, diced

⅛ teaspoon salt
⅛ teaspoon pepper
1 cup grated Parmesan cheese
2 small cans tomato sauce

Remove seeds and membrane from peppers and cut each pepper into 5 or 6 pieces. Cover with boiling water and drain. Soak bread cubes in water and squeeze as dry as possible. Add next 5 ingredients. In 2-quart casserole, alternate layers of peppers and bread mixture. Sprinkle with Parmesan cheese and bake at 350° for 45 minutes. Serve with tomato sauce. Serves 6.

Bea Hanft

Italian Style Green Peppers

4-5 large green peppers	2 teaspoons sugar
½ cup thinly sliced onion	1 teaspoon salt
2 cloves garlic, minced	Dash pepper
1 tablespoon olive or salad oil	½ teaspoon basil
2 cups stewed tomatoes, or	3 tablespoons olive or salad oil
1 1-pound can	

Cut green peppers into ¾-inch strips (about 4 cups). Cook onions and garlic in 1 tablespoon oil until tender, not brown. Add tomatoes and seasonings. Simmer until sauce is slightly thick, about 20 minutes. Cook pepper strips in 3 tablespoons oil, turning frequently, until tender but still crisp. Lift from oil to serving dish; sprinkle with salt and pepper. Pour tomato sauce over all. Serves 5-6.

Lee Breiman

Baked Potatoes with Onion Soup

6 medium potatoes	¼ pound butter or margarine
1 package dried onion soup mix	

Scrub potatoes and cut almost through the potato every 1-1½ inches. Mix onion soup and butter to a loose consistency. Place this mixture in cuts of potato. Wrap potatoes in foil and bake at 375° for 45 minutes or until tender.

Mrs. Donald Friedman

Baco'd Potatoes

6 potatoes for baking	Salt and pepper to taste
4 tablespoons margarine	Milk substitute as needed
½ cup Baco bits	

Bake potatoes at 425° for 1 hour. Scoop out inside, combine ingredients using enough milk substitute for nice texture to mash potatoes. Pile back into shells, sprinkle with paprika. Place back in oven at 350° for 10 minutes. Serves 6.

Bradleigh Kolko

Dutch Potatoes

1 medium onion, minced	2 cups hot moist mashed potatoes
½ cup diced celery	1 tablespoon minced parsley
3-4 tablespoons margarine	Salt to taste
2 cups croutons	Pepper to taste
2 eggs	Paprika

Saute onion and celery in margarine. Add croutons and brown slightly. Add eggs to mashed potatoes; also parsley, salt, pepper and crouton mixture. Spread into 1-quart buttered casserole. Sprinkle with paprika. Refrigerate one hour. Bake at 350° for 20-30 minutes or until brown. This may be frozen before heating.

Judy Kaplan

Potato Fluff

1 8-ounce package cream cheese, softened	1/3 cup finely chopped onion
	¼ cup chopped pimento
4 cups hot mashed potatoes	1 teaspoon salt
1 egg, beaten	Dash pepper

Blend cheese into hot mashed potatoes. Add rest of ingredients. Bake in 1-quart casserole at 350° for 1 hour. For best results, serve at once.

Lillian Karn

Gourmet Potatoes

6 medium potatoes
2 cups shredded cheddar cheese
¼ cup butter or margarine
1½ cups sour cream (room
temperature)

1/3 cup chopped onions
1 teaspoon salt
¼ teaspoon pepper
2 tablespoons butter

Cook potatoes in skins. Cool. Peel and shred coarsely. In saucepan over low heat, combine cheese and ¼ cup butter, stirring occasionally until almost melted. Remove from heat and blend in sour cream, onions, salt and pepper. Fold in potatoes and turn into greased 2-quart casserole. Dot with 2 tablespoons butter and bake at 400° for 25 minutes. Serves 8.

Lillian Karn

Instant Potato Knishes

8 cups sifted flour
2 cups shortening
1 tablespoon sugar
1 tablespoon salt
2 cups cold water
6 cups boiling water
4 envelopes French's Instant

Mashed Potato granules
1 teaspoon salt
Dash black pepper
2 onions, chopped
1/3 cup shortening
3 eggs

Combine flour, shortening, sugar, salt and cold water and mix thoroughly until firm. Refrigerate until chilled. Meanwhile, add instant mashed potatoes to boiling water with salt and pepper, mixing well. Allow to cool. Saute onions in shortening and add to potatoes with 1 beaten egg, mixing well. Remove dough from refrigerator and roll out very thin into strips 10 x 3-inches. Place potato filling on dough. Moisten edges of dough with beaten egg and roll by pulling up 10-inch length sides and overlapping them. Place strips on lightly greased baking pan; cut strips into 1-inch pieces. Brush tops with beaten egg and bake in 350° oven for 25 minutes. Makes about 20 servings.

Potato Kugel

3 eggs
3 cups grated, drained potatoes
1/3 cup potato flour
½ teaspoon baking powder
1½ teaspoons onion salt

Dash pepper
3 tablespoons grated onion
¼ cup grebenes
4 tablespoons melted chicken fat

Beat eggs. Add remaining ingredients. Put into 1½-quart greased baking dish and bake at 325° about 1 hour. Serves 8.

Irene Friedman

Potato Latkes

6 medium potatoes
1 small onion
2 tablespoons sour cream
1 teaspoon salt
2 eggs

½ teaspoon pepper
¼ cup flour
½ cup bread crumbs
Oil or shortening

Grate potatoes with onion, either by hand or blender. Drain excess water. Add sour cream quickly to keep the potatoes white. Add eggs, flour and crumbs, salt and pepper. Mix well. Fry in hot oil, turning when golden brown. Serve with applesauce, cinnamon, sugar or sour cream. Can be frozen and reheated in low oven for about 15-20 minutes. Note: Be sure to drain the latkes on paper toweling before serving or freezing.

Sarah Derman

Pareve Blender Potato Latkes

4 medium potatoes, peeled
  and cubed
Ice water
2 eggs
1 medium onion, cut up

1 teaspoon salt
⅛ teaspoon pepper
3 tablespoons flour
Oil for frying

Put half potato cubes in blender: add enough ice water to cover. Cover blender and whirl potatoes, just till grated. Drain grated potatoes and place in mixing bowl. Repeat with rest of potatoes. Put eggs and onion in blender; whirl to combine. Add to potatoes; add salt, pepper and flour to thicken batter slightly. Heat oil in large skillet, drop 1 tablespoon potato mixture for each pancake; fry crisp and golden brown on both sides.

Shirley Jacobson

Potato-Nick

4 pounds large Idaho potatoes
1 0.6-ounce cake of yeast or
1 package of dry yeast
⅛ cup lukewarm water

4 eggs
2 cups flour
¼ cup oil
Salt and pepper to taste

Peel and grate potatoes. Add yeast dissolved in lukewarm water, eggs and 1 cup flour. Mix these ingredients together and cover with cup of flour to prevent potatoes from turning black. Let it rise to double in size. Add oil, salt and pepper. Then mix in the flour from the top. Pour into well-greased (with oil only) 13 x 9 pan and let rise again. Bake in 400° oven for 1 hour. Remove from oven immediately and turn out of pan to permit air to escape.

Rachel Hyman

Potato Puff

¼ cup chopped green pepper
¼ cup chopped green onion
2 tablespoons margarine
1/3 cup milk
4 servings instant mashed

potato (as directed on label)
4 eggs, separated
½ teaspoon salt
⅛ teaspoon pepper
½ cup grated American cheese

Saute vegetables lightly in margarine. Add milk to potatoes, then beat in yolks, one at a time. Add vegetables, salt and pepper, and fold into stiffly beaten egg whites. Pour into shallow 1½-quart baking dish. Bake at 350° for 35 minutes, or until firm. Remove from oven and sprinkle with cheese.

Rachel Hyman

Mushroom-Scalloped Potatoes

1 can mushroom soup
½ cup grated processed
  American cheese
½ teaspoon salt
4 ounce can mushroom stems
  and pieces, drained

2/3 cup evaporated milk
4 cups thinly sliced raw
  potatoes
½ cup grated processed American cheese

Mix soup, cheese, salt and mushrooms. Add milk and potatoes gradually. Put into greased shallow 1½-quart baking dish. Top with ½ cup grated cheese. Bake at 350°, 1 hour until potatoes are tender. Serves 6.

Renee Rosenbaum

Scalloped Potatoes (Non-Dairy)

12 large potatoes
1 4-ounce can French fried
 onion rings
1 8-ounce can mushrooms,
 chopped
2 10-ounce cans chicken soup,
 undiluted

Salt and pepper to taste
1 cup bread crumbs
4 tablespoons margarine,
 melted

Peel potatoes and slice ¼-inch thick into a 2½-quart greased casserole. Alternate layers of potatoes, crushed French fried onion rings and chopped mushrooms. Pour chicken soup over potatoes. Add salt and pepper to taste. Toss bread crumbs with melted margarine; sprinkle on top and bake at 350° for 50-60 minutes, covered. Uncover and bake 30-40 minutes more until potatoes are cooked and top is golden brown. Serves 12.

T'Mahry Axelrod

Spinach Casserole

2 packages frozen chopped
 spinach
1 pint sour cream

½ package dry onion soup mix
1 5-ounce can water chestnuts,
 chopped

Cook and drain spinach. Combine with other ingredients. Bake at 350° in buttered, 1-quart casserole, for ½ hour. Serves 4-6.

Terri Ross

Spinach Rice Bake

1 cup chopped onion
2 tablespoons butter
3 cups cooked rice
1 package frozen chopped
 spinach, cooked

½ teaspoon garlic powder
½ teaspoon dry basil
½ teaspoon thyme
3 eggs
½ cup grated Parmesan cheese

Saute onion in butter until tender. Add rice, spinach, drained, and seasonings. Beat eggs and stir into rice mixture. Turn into 2-quart, greased casserole. Sprinkle with Parmesan cheese. Bake at 375° for 20 minutes, uncovered. Serves 6.

Jane Hanft

Spinach Ring

1¾ cups cooked chopped spinach
2 tablespoons flour
2 tablespoons butter

½ cup milk
3 eggs, separated
Salt and pepper

Heat butter in skillet, add flour, then milk. When smooth and thick, stir gradually into the well-beaten egg yolks. Add spinach and seasoning (grated onion if desired). Cool and add stiffly beaten egg whites. Place in well-greased 9-inch ring, set in pan half filled with boiling water. Bake at 350° for 30 minutes, or until well set. Chopped broccoli may be used instead of spinach. Serves 8-10.

Arlean Levinson

Sesame Spinach

2 packages frozen leaf spinach
¼ cup soy sauce
2 tablespoons cider vinegar
¼ teaspoon sugar

1 medium onion, cut into rings
2 tablespoons toasted sesame
  seeds

Cook spinach according to package directions. Don't overcook. Combine soy sauce, vinegar, and sugar. Drain spinach and add onion rings. Add soy mixture and toss. Chill for 1 hour tossing frequently. Serve in portions like a salad. Garnish with sesame seeds. Gently heat 1 box sesame seeds in skillet. Stir frequently, toast but don't burn. Press seeds, using bottom of water tumbler to extract oil and enhance flavor. Serves 6-8.

Millie Rosenbaum

Spinach with Walnuts

2 packages frozen, chopped
  spinach
½ cup walnuts, finely chopped

2 tablespoons melted margarine
2 tablespoons orange juice

Prepare spinach according to directions on package. Drain water, add walnuts, margarine and orange juice. Mix thoroughly and serve immediately. Serves 4-6.

Priscilla Brown

Caramel Butternut Squash

4 cups cooked squash
1 teaspoon salt
2 tablespoons cream
2 tablespoons melted butter

5 tablespoons brown sugar
¼ teaspoon cinnamon
Ground pecans or walnuts

Mash squash, add salt and cream and place in a greased 1½-quart casserole. Mix butter, brown sugar and cinnamon and cook for 3 minutes; pour over casserole. Sprinkle with ground nuts. Bake in 350° oven for 15 minutes.

Bertha Cravets

Baked Summer Squash or Zucchini
with Grapefruit

Summer squash
Grapefruit, sectioned
Orange, sectioned
¼ cup coconut

¼ cup pecans, chopped
½ cup brown sugar
2 tablespoons melted butter

Cut squash in half lengthwise and parboil. Hollow out and place in shallow baking dish. Fill with grapefruit and orange sections. Cover with coconut and pecans. Drizzle brown sugar and melted butter over pieces and bake until heated through, 350° for 20-30 minutes.

Frumel Ureles

Squash Supreme

2 packages frozen squash
1 small jar applesauce

Marshmallows

Completely defrost squash. Spread on bottom of greased 1-quart casserole. Cover with applesauce, then marshmallows. Bake 350° for 1 hour uncovered. Serves 6-8.

Terri Ross

Harvest Baked Squash

3 large acorn squash
1 cup water
1 13½-ounce can pineapple
  tidbits
1½ cups diced apple, unpeeled
1 cup chopped celery

½ cup chopped walnuts
½ teaspoon cinnamon
½ cup butter
½ cup brown sugar, packed
¼ teaspoon salt

Cut squash into halves. Scoop out seeds. Place cut side down in large glass baking dish. Add water and bake at 350° for 45 minutes. Meanwhile, combine drained pineapple, apples, celery and walnuts. Melt butter, blend in sugar, cinnamon and salt. Pour over pineapple mixture, tossing lightly to combine. Remove squash from oven; drain off water and turn cup side up. Spoon pineapple mixture into squash, return to oven and bake 15-20 minutes longer until tender. Serves 6.

Eleanor Goldsmith

Gourmet Sweet Potato

4 medium sweet potatoes (or
  1-pound 2-ounce can)
½ cup brown sugar
1 tablespoon corn starch
¼ teaspoon salt
1 cup orange juice

¼ cup raisins
¼ cup butter or margarine
3 tablespoons sherry
2 tablespoons chopped walnuts
½ teaspoon grated orange peel

Cook potatoes in boiling salted water until tender. Drain, peel and halve lengthwise. Arrange in shallow baking dish or pan. Sprinkle lightly with salt. Mix brown sugar, corn starch and salt. Blend in orange juice, add raisins and stir while bringing quickly to a boil. Add remaining ingredients and pour over potatoes. Bake uncovered in 350° oven about 20 minutes or until potatoes are well glazed. Makes 4 servings.

Martha Lovenheim

Quick Glazed Sweet Potatoes

1 18-ounce can sweet potatoes
1/3 cup water
¼ cup brown sugar

1 tablespoon orange flavored
  drink powder
3 tablespoons butter

Place drained sweet potatoes in 9 x 9 baking dish. Add water. Combine brown sugar and orange flavored drink powder; sprinkle over potatoes and dot with butter. Bake at 350° for 20-25 minutes or until glazed, basting often with syrup in dish. Serves 4.

Eleanor Harris

Sweet Potato Apricot Surprise

6 sweet potatoes
1½ cups brown sugar
1½ tablespoons corn starch
1 teaspoon grated orange rind
⅛ teaspoon cinnamon

1 cup apricot juice
1 cup apricots, drained
2 tablespoons butter or margarine
½ cup chopped pecans

Boil potatoes in jackets until tender, about 30 minutes. Then peel, cut in halves and arrange in buttered 7 x 12 casserole dish. Combine sugar, corn starch, orange rind, cinnamon, apricot juice in a saucepan. Cook until thick, stir constantly. Stir in apricots, butter and pecans. Pour over potatoes and bake at 375° for 25 minutes.

Min Shapiro

Sweet Potato Orange Casserole

2 17-ounce cans sweet potatoes
1/3 cup brown sugar
¼ cup melted margarine
2 teaspoons salt
1 teaspoon nutmeg
4 medium oranges, sectioned

In large bowl, beat potatoes with electric mixer at medium speed until well blended with sugar, margarine, salt and nutmeg. Fold ½ of the orange sections into potato mixture. Pile into 2 quart casserole.

Topping

¼ cup pecans
1 tablespoon brown sugar
2 tablespoons melted margarine

Combine above ingredients. Sprinkle over potato mixture. Arrange remaining orange sections in a circle on top. Bake covered at 350° for 1 hour.

Lillian Karn

Sweet Potato with Pineapple

4 boiled sweet potatoes
1 cup brown sugar
½ cup pineapple juice
4 pineapple rings
1 tablespoon margarine

Peel potatoes and cut into ½-inch slices. Arrange in 1-quart greased baking dish. Combine sugar and juice and stir over low heat until sugar is dissolved. Pour syrup over potatoes and cover with halved pineapple rings. Dot with margarine and bake in moderately hot oven (425°) for 30 minutes until syrup thickens slightly. Serves 6.

Priscilla Brown

Sweet Potato and Prune Casserole

6 medium sweet potatoes
   (3 pounds)
1-pound jar stewed prunes
¾ cup honey
¾ teaspoon cinnamon
1 teaspoon salt
2 tablespoons prune juice
2 tablespoons lemon juice
¼ cup melted margarine or
   chicken fat

Cook potatoes until tender. Skin and cut into ¼-inch slices. Cut prunes in half. Make mixture of remaining ingredients. In a 2-quart casserole, arrange alternate layers of sweet potatoes and prunes, pouring the honey mixture over each layer. Bake uncovered, basting occasionally, for 45 minutes at 350°. Serves 4.

Pearl Albert

Pineapple Yam Balls

1 2-pound can yams, drained
1½ cups crushed pineapple, drained
¼ cup soft butter or margarine,
   melted
½ cup brown sugar
¼ teaspoon cinnamon
¼ teaspoon nutmeg
1¼ cups chopped nuts, optional

Mash yams, and combine with pineapple, brown sugar, butter and spices. Scoop into balls. You may roll them in the nuts, if you wish. Place on greased baking sheet and bake in preheated oven, at 350° for 20 minutes. Makes about 16 balls.

Jill Musicus

Pineapple Yam Puff

4 large yams, 2 pounds
¼ cup butter or margarine
¼ cup dark brown sugar, firmly
  packed
1 9-ounce can crushed pineapple,
  undrained

1 tablespoon orange rind, grated
1 teaspoon salt
¼ teaspoon nutmeg
2 eggs
Toasted pecan halves for garnish

Pare, cut and cook yams in boiling water for 30 minutes until tender. Drain and mash in foodmill or mixer. In small skillet, melt butter, add brown sugar and heat, stirring until bubbly. Stir into mashed yams, adding undrained pineapple, orange rind, salt and nutmeg. In small bowl, beat eggs until thick and ivory colored. Fold into yam mixture. Turn into ungreased deep casserole or 1½-quart souffle dish. Bake at 350° about 1 hour until top is slightly crusted. Add pecans if desired. May be prepared ahead, covered and refrigerated until time to bake. Serves 6-8.

Rose Bresloff

Tomato and Onion Pie

8 medium onions, sliced
5 cups bread cubes
8 medium tomatoes, peeled and
  sliced

½ teaspoon salt
1 tablespoon sugar
⅛ teaspoon pepper
2 tablespoons butter

Boil onions in salted water until they are almost tender. Line bottom of a well-greased, 2-quart baking dish with bread cubes. Cover them with a layer of onions and tomatoes, which have been placed in alternate rows. Sprinkle salt, sugar, pepper and remaining bread cubes over the vegetables. Dot with butter. Bake at 350° for about 30 minutes. Serves 8-10.

Ricky Sands

Scalloped Chili Tomatoes and Cheese

1 28-ounce can whole peeled
  plum tomatoes
2 tablespoons chopped onions
1 teaspoon salt
2 teaspoons chili powder

2 tablespoons sugar
¼ teaspoon pepper
1 cup soft bread crumbs
2 tablespoons melted butter
1 cup shredded cheddar cheese

Combine first 6 ingredients in shallow 1½-quart baking dish. Top with bread crumbs, tossed with butter. Sprinkle with cheese. Bake at 400° for 25 minutes or until browned. Serves 4.

Bea Hanft

Jiffy Tomato Stack-ups with Broccoli

3 large tomatoes
Salt
4 ounces processed Swiss
  cheese (1 cup shredded)

1 10-ounce package frozen broccoli,
  cooked and drained
¼ cup chopped onions

Cut tomatoes into ¾-inch slices. Sprinkle each lightly with salt. Set aside 2 tablespoons shredded cheese. Combine remaining cheese, broccoli and onions. Place tomato slices on baking sheet, spoon broccoli mixture on tomatoes, sprinkle with reserved cheese. Broil 7-8 inches from heat for 10-12 minutes, or until cheese bubbles and tomato slices are hot. Serves 6.

Linda Rubens

Baked Stuffed Tomatoes

6 medium tomatoes	Dash oregano
4 tablespoons finely chopped green pepper	Salt and pepper
2 tablespoons finely chopped onion	4 tablespoons melted butter or margarine
¼ teaspoon sugar	¾ cup fine dry bread crumbs

Cut off tops of tomatoes, scoop out centers. Chop pulp; mix with green pepper, onion, sugar, oregano, salt, pepper, and ¼ cup bread crumbs which you have combined with butter. Spoon into tomato shells. Spoon remaining bread crumbs and butter mixture (½ cup) over tops of stuffed tomatoes. Bake uncovered at 375° for 25 minutes or until tomatoes are tender and crumbs are lightly brown and crisp. Serves 6.

Eleanor Goldsmith

Zucchini Parmesan

2 medium-sized zucchini squash	8 ounces sliced mozzarella
Salt to taste	8 ounces tomato sauce
1 7½-ounce jar roasted peppers	Parmesan cheese, grated

Slice squash lengthwise into quarters and brown lightly in heavy skillet. Salt. Place in baking dish. Cover squash with slices of pepper, add cheese slices and tomato sauce. Top with grated Parmesan cheese. Bake at 350° for 20 minutes. Serves 4-6.

Hannah Dankoff

Puffed-up Zucchini

4 cups chopped zucchini	¼ teaspoon pepper
1 cup chopped onion	1 tablespoon grated horseradish
¼ cup water	1 egg, slightly beaten
2 tablespoons margarine	1 cup coarse cracker crumbs
½ teaspoon salt	3 tablespoons margarine

Combine zucchini and onion in saucepan and add water. Cover and cook until tender, about 15 minutes. Drain well. Mash zucchini and onion, add margarine, salt, pepper, and horseradish. Cool, add egg and mix thoroughly. Pour into greased 1-quart baking dish. Top with crumbs which have been browned in extra margarine. Bake at 350° for 30 minutes, uncovered. Serves 4-6.

Hattie Lipsky

Ratatouille Nicoise

1/3 cup butter	removed
2 cloves garlic, peeled and chopped	3 tablespoons flour
1 large onion, sliced	2 green peppers, seeded and cut into strips
2 zucchini squash, well-scrubbed	5 ripe tomatoes, peeled and sliced
1 small eggplant, stem	Salt and fresh ground pepper

Heat butter in large skillet; add garlic and onion and saute until transparent. Meanwhile, slice zucchini; peel and cube eggplant. Flour pieces of both slightly. Add squash, eggplant, and green pepper to the skillet. Cover and cook slowly for about ½ hour. Add tomatoes and simmer uncovered until mixture is thick. Season with salt and pepper to taste. Serve hot or cold. Serves 5-6.

Norma Erdle

The spelling of traditional Hebrew and Yiddish terms may vary according to the different backgrounds of our contributors. —*Ed.*

ROASTING

MEAT	Set Temperature		Time in Minutes Per Pound	Time in Minutes per Lb. Started Cooking from Frozen State
BEEF				
Standing Rib 6-8 lb.	300	Rare	18-20	43
		Medium	22-25	47
		Well Done	27-30	55
Less than 6 pounds	300	Rare	33	55
		Medium	45	60
		Well Done	50	65
Rolled Ribs	300	Rare	32	53
		Medium	38	57
		Well Done	48	65
LAMB				
Rolled Shoulder	300		40-45	40-45
Shoulder (bone in)	300		30-35	40-45
VEAL				
Shoulder	300		25	40-45
Boned and Rolled	300		40-45	40-45
POULTRY				
CHICKEN				
Stuffed 3-4 lb.	350		40-45	
Stuffed 4-5 lb.	350		35-40	
Stuffed over 5 lb.	325		30-35	
TURKEY				
8-10 lb.	325		20-25	
10-14 lb.	325		18-20	
14-18 lb.	300		15-18	
18-20 lb.	300		13-15	
GOOSE				
10-12 lb.	325		25-30	
DUCK				
5-6 lb.	350		30-35	